Sex as Crime?

Sex as Crime?

Edited by

Gayle Letherby, Kate Williams,
Philip Birch and Maureen Cain

WILLAN
PUBLISHING

Published by

Willan Publishing
Culmcott House
Mill Street, Uffculme
Cullompton, Devon
EX15 3AT, UK
Tel: +44(0)1884 840337
Fax: +44(0)1884 840251
e-mail: info@willanpublishing.co.uk
website: www.willanpublishing.co.uk

Published simultaneously in the USA and Canada by

Willan Publishing
c/o ISBS, 920 NE 58th Ave, Suite 300,
Portland, Oregon 97213-3786, USA
Tel: +001(0)503 287 3093
Fax: +001(0)503 280 8832
e-mail: info@isbs.com
website: www.isbs.com

First published 2008

ISBN   978-1-84392-267-4 paperback
       978-1-84392-268-1 hardback

British Library Cataloguing-in-Publication Data

A catalogue record for this book is available from the British Library.

Project managed by Deer Park Productions, Tavistock, Devon
Typeset by GCS, Leighton Buzzard, Bedfordshire
Printed and bound by T.J. International Ltd, Padstow, Cornwall

Contents

Part 2   Sex as Violence

Acknowledgements

Gayle, Kate, Phil and Maureen would like to extend their sincere thanks to a number of people without whom this text would not have been possible. The idea for this collection – and the majority of the chapters in the book – originated from a most successful and enjoyable conference organised by the Editors on joint behalf of the British Society of Criminology (BSC) and the British Sociological Association (BSA), held at the University of Central England (now Birmingham City University) in April 2006. We would therefore like to thank these organisations for their support, and in particular Paul Kiff and Emma Hodgkinson at the BSC for their administrative assistance. Further thanks must also be given to our speakers and participants for their hard work and fruitful contributions. A number of chapters were sought to supplement the collection, and our thanks are conveyed to those authors as well. For their patience, assistance and editorial advice, we would like to express our thanks to Brian Willan and his colleagues at Willan Publishing, and we are also grateful to Alison Wagstaff for her invaluable work in preparing the papers for publication.

Notes on contributors

Flavia Agnes is a women's rights advocate, activist and researcher. A pioneer of the women's movement, she has worked consistently on issues of gender and law reform. As co-founder of Majlis, a legal and cultural resource centre, her primary engagement has been to provide quality legal services to women and children. Flavia has played an important role in bringing women's rights to the forefront within the legal system in India and in contextualising issues of gender and identity. A prolific writer, she has provided incisive analysis of many social trends and legal reforms including domestic violence, minority law reforms, secularism and human rights. Significant among her many publications is her autobiographical book *My Story Our Story ... of Rebuilding Broken Lives* which has been translated into several languages. Her other publications include *Law and Gender Inequality – The Politics of Personal Laws in India* (Oxford University Press 1999). She has an MPhil degree from the prestigious National Law School, Bangalore. One of her recent engagements has involved challenging the trend of sexual morality in the context of the bar dancers of Mumbai. After the state government implemented a ban, her organisation, Majlis, successfully helped the bar dancers to challenge the ban through a Writ Petition in the Bombay High Court.

Christien van den Anker (BA/MA Amsterdam 1990; PhD Essex 1996) is Reader in Politics at the University of the West of England, Bristol. Before coming to Bristol, she was Deputy Director of the Centre for the Study of Global Ethics, University of Birmingham (2001–6) and Lecturer in International Relations at Sussex University

(1996–2001). Her most recent publications in the area of contemporary slavery are: 'Contemporary slavery and global ethics', in *Global Social Policy*, Spring 2007; 'Trafficking and women's rights: beyond the sex industry to "other industries"', in A. Guichon and R. Shah (eds) *Women's Rights in Europe: Special Issue of Journal of Global Ethics*, 3(1), December 2006: 161–80; with J. Doomernik (eds) *Trafficking and Women's Rights* (Palgrave 2006); with A. Guichon and I. Novikova (eds) *Women's Social Rights and Entitlements* (Palgrave 2006); C. van den Anker (ed.) *The Political Economy of New Slavery* (Palgrave 2004). Christien is also lead editor of the *Journal of Global Ethics*. Her current research interests are cosmopolitanism, human rights, contemporary forms of slavery, healing from war and minority rights. She currently leads a European Social Fund project on 'Trafficking for Forced Labour in Europe'.

Philip Birch (BSocSci (Hons), PGCert (SSRM), PGDip (SocSci), MSc) is a Senior Lecturer in the Division of Criminal and Community Justice and a University Associate in the Applied Criminology Centre at the University of Huddersfield where his research interests include sex offenders, domestic violence, sex work and rape and sexual assault. Philip has also worked as a practitioner in the field of criminology; for the past five years he has held a number of posts in the Crime and Disorder Reduction Partnerships in Kirklees, Bolton and Oldham Metropolitan Councils. Within these roles Philip has managed a number of projects and initiatives around sex work, domestic violence and hate crimes, as well as taking a lead on programme evaluation and other strategic developments relating to the field. Prior to entering local government Philip spent three and a half years within the Prison Service where he worked in both a high-security adult male establishment and a young and juvenile male establishment. Over the last few years Philip has presented a number of conference papers on the issues of sex offenders, domestic violence and sex work. He is currently an elected member of the Executive Committee of the British Society of Criminology. Philip is also a member of the Social Policy Association and NOTA (National Organisation for the Treatment of Abusers).

Maureen Cain studied sociology at the LSE in the 1950s and was awarded a PhD in 1969. Her major posts have been at Brunel University, at the University of the West Indies, St Augustine, Trinidad where she held the Chair of Sociology, and at the University of Birmingham. She edited the *International Journal for the Sociology* *of Law* from 1978 to 1987, and has published on policing, on the sociology of law, on Caribbean criminology and on transgressive and feminist methodologies. Her recent papers and edited works include: *For a Caribbean Criminology* (ed.), special double issue of *Caribbean Quarterly* (University of the West Indies Press 1996); 'Orientalism, occidentalism, and the sociology of crime', *British Journal of Criminology* (2000); 'Globality, glocalization, and private policing: a Caribbean case study', in C. Sumner (ed.) *The Blackwell Companion to Criminology* (Blackwell 2004); *Ageing, Crime, and Society* (with A. Wahidin, eds) (Willan 2006); and (with A. Howe, eds) *Women, Crime and Social Harm: Towards a Criminology for the Global Age* (Hart 2008). From 2003 to 2006 she was President of the British Society of Criminology and Chair of the Committee to develop a QAA Benchmarking Statement for the discipline. Maureen is now retired but continues to publish Caribbean materials.

Rosie Campbell was a founder member of the UK Network of Sex Work Projects (UK NSWP) and as chair of this organisation works with sex work projects throughout the UK. Rosie is currently Project Co-ordinator for Armistead Street and Portside, sex work outreach and support projects in Merseyside, within the Armistead Centre, Liverpool Primary Care Trust. She has carried out applied policy research and consultation on sex work since 1995. She was part of the research team at Loughborough, Staffordshire and Strathclyde Universities, which carried out the Joseph Rowntree Foundation-funded, multi-site study *From Conflict to Coexistence: Living and Working in Areas of Street Sex Work* (Polity Press 2006). She has been involved in the development of good practice guidance for service interventions for sex workers and the provision of policy advice to authorities developing policies related to sex work at local, regional and national levels. Rosie has published widely on sex work and has presented her work at a wide range of national and international conferences. With Maggie O'Neill she is co-editor of *Sex Work Now* (Willan 2006). Rosie is a sociologist and has over 16 years' experience of applied social research.

Kris Christmann joined the Applied Criminology Centre at Huddersfield University in 2000 after completing a BSc in Psychology at Oxford Brookes University, an MA in Philosophy and Social Theory at Warwick and an MA in Criminology at Keele. He has been involved in research projects on a wide range of topics. His specific research interests lie in policing and police accountability, as these configure with theories of political obligation. He is completing his PhD at Keele University.

Julia Davidson is Principal Lecturer in Criminology and Research Methods and is Director of the Criminology Research Cluster at the University of Westminster. She has undertaken research with young victims, serious violent and sexual offenders, criminal justice practitioners and sentencers. Recent work includes: a study funded by the Metropolitan Police Authority and Crimestoppers, which sought to explore child safety on the internet and the role of the police in raising awareness among children about sexual abuse (2005); an evaluation and overview of approaches to risk assessment and management of internet sex offenders funded by the Risk Management Authority (Scotland) (2007); and an exploration of young victims' experiences and perceptions of the investigative process undertaken on behalf of the Metropolitan Police Child Abuse Investigation Command (2007 ongoing). Julia is a reviewer (from December 2006) for the Department of Health and National Institute for Mental Health *Victims of Violence and Abuse Prevention Programme* (*VVAPP*). She also provides regular expert advice on child protection and abuse issues to the media, having worked extensively with ITV Evening News, the ITV News Channel, BBC 24 News Channel, BBC Radio Four Woman's Hour and BBC Five Live Radio.

Sarah Earle is Lecturer in Health and Social Care at the Open University. She is interested in the sociology of human reproduction, sexuality and sexual health. She is co-editor of *Gender, Identity and Reproduction: Social Perspectives* (Palgrave 2003); *Sociology for Nurses* (Polity 2005); *A Reader in Promoting Public Health: Challenge and Controversy* (Sage/Open University 2007); *Theory and Research in Promoting Public Health* (Sage/Open University 2007); and *Policy and Practice in Promoting Public Health* (Sage/Open University 2007). She is co-author with Keith Sharp of *Sex in Cyberspace: Men Who Pay for Sex* (Ashgate 2007) and has published numerous articles, chapters and other works.

Lyvinia Rogers Elleschild has taught youth policy, sexuality studies and feminist studies for many years. She was a Senior Lecturer at Leeds Metropolitan University throughout the 1990s and is currently an Associate Lecturer at the University of Plymouth. Her PhD analyses contemporary policy formulation on youth prostitution and she is currently researching the socio-economic and moral regulation of young people.

Glenn P. Harvey (BCom) is a Research Assistant in the Faculty of Education, Health and Professional Studies at the University of New England. He has worked on a number of projects on male sex workers with Professor Victor Minichiello.

Bill Hebenton graduated in psychology from the University of Glasgow (MA), specialised in criminology at Aston University (MSc) and gained his PhD from Manchester in 2002. He is a faculty member of the Centre for Criminology and Socio-Legal Studies at the School of Law, University of Manchester. He worked with the Home Office and ACPO on the policing of sexual offenders in the community in the late 1990s, and completed an evaluation for the Home Office of the pilot areas for Multi-Agency Public Protection Panels in England and Wales (2004). As well as numerous academic journal articles and book chapters, he is co-author of several books and monographs. These include: *Criminal Records: State, Citizen and the Politics of Protection* (Avebury 1993); *Policing Europe* (Macmillan 1995), *Keeping Track: Observations on Sex Offender Registers in England and Wales and the USA* (Home Office 1998), *Law Enforcement and International Assistance: A Case Study of Estonia* (United Nations 2001), *Introducing Lay Members into Multi-Agency Public Protection Arrangements in England and Wales* (Home Office 2004). Current research interests continue to lie in comparative cross-national criminological research in general and in particular crime and punishment in Taiwan and the People's Republic of China (PRC). He is also working on the Shanghai Municipal Police archives (1916–45) at the Bodleian Library, Oxford and was a Visiting Scholar at St John's College, Oxford (2005). He is a member of the editorial board of *Crime and Criminal Justice International*. His new book, *Comparative Research in Crime and Punishment*, will be published in 2008 by Palgrave Macmillan.

Adrian Howe has recently returned to Australia from the UK where she held the Chair of Criminology and Criminal Justice at the University of Central Lancashire. She now teaches social policy in the School of Global Studies, Social Science and Planning at the Royal Melbourne Institute of Technology. She wrote *Punish and Critique: Towards a Feminist Theory of Penality* (Routledge 1994); *Sexed Crime in the News* (Federation Press 1998) and *Lindy Chamberlain Revisited:*

A 25th Anniversary Retrospective (Lhrpress 2005). She is currently completing *Sex, Violence and Crime in a Postmodern Frame* (Routledge-Cavendish) and an edited text (with Maureen Cain) titled *Women, Crime and Globalisation* to be published by Hart. She has written extensively on feminist legal theory, on violence against women and on the deployment of provocation defences in femicide and so-called 'homosexual advance' cases.

Liz Kelly is Roddick Chair of Violence Against Women at London Metropolitan University, where she is also Director of the Child and Woman Abuse Studies Unit (CWASU). She is the author of *Surviving Sexual Violence* (University of Minnesota Press 1989), which established the concept of a 'continuum of violence' and for the last decade has been exploring the question of attrition in reported rape cases. As an engaged academic, Liz is a Commissioner for the Women's National Commission and the Fawcett Society's Commission on Women and the Criminal Justice System, and chairs the End Violence Against Women Coalition. CWASU has a national and international reputation for its policy-relevant research, training and consultancy. The Unit has completed 60 research projects and is known for making connections between forms of gender violence, and between violence against women and child abuse. This has recently been institutionalised through the first MA in Women and Child Abuse. A complete list of projects and publications can be found at http://www.cwasu.org.

Jenny Kitzinger is Professor of Media and Communications Research at Cardiff University. She originally graduated in Social Anthropology from Cambridge and worked there in the Department of Social and Political Science before moving to the Glasgow Media Group and then on to Cardiff. Jenny has written extensively both about sexual violence and about the media coverage of health and scientific issues. Her books include *Framing Abuse: Media Influence and Public Understanding of Sexual Violence Against Children* (Pluto Press 2004); *Developing Focus Group Research* (Sage 1999); *The Mass Media and Power in Modern Britain* (Oxford University Press 1997); *The Circuit of Mass Communication in the AIDS Crisis* (Sage 1999); and *Human Cloning in the Media* (Routledge 2007).

Gayle Letherby (BA (Hons), PhD Ac SS) is Professor of Sociology at the University of Plymouth. Before joining Plymouth in October 2005 she was Reader in the Sociology of Gender and Deputy Director of the Centre for Social Justice at Coventry University. Writing and research interests include reproductive and non/parental identities, working and learning in higher education, crime and deviance, and travel and transport. Gayle is fascinated by issues of method, methodology and epistemology and stimulated by the political potential of the social sciences. Key publications include: *Feminist Research in Theory and Practice* (Open University Press 2003); *Extending Social Research: Application, Implementation and Publication* with P. Bywaters (Open University Press 2007); and *Introduction to Gender: Social Science Perspectives* with J. Marchbank (Pearson 2007). Throughout her career Gayle has always enjoyed working on collaborative projects, this book being one more example of this. Gayle was Chair of the British Sociological Association Council from 2006 to 2008.

Jen Marchbank (BA (Hons), MA, PhD, FHEA) is Director of Explorations in Arts and Social Sciences at Simon Fraser University, Canada. Jen has taught for eight universities in the UK, USA and Canada for more years than she cares to count. Her publications include *Introduction to Gender: Social Science Perspectives* with Gayle Letherby (Pearson 2007); *Women, Power and Policy: Comparative Studies of Childcare* (Routledge 2000); and *States of Conflict: Gender, Violence and Resistance* with Susie Jacobs and Ruth Jacobson (Zed Books 2001). Outside of work Jen is occupied driving the children hither and thither.

Rodrigo Mariño (PhD) is a Senior Research Fellow and public health researcher in the Faculty of Medicine, Dentistry and Health Sciences at the University of Melbourne. Rodrigo has conducted a number of studies on the public health implications of sex work and sex workers in Argentina and Australia. These have been widely published in journals such as *AIDS Care*, the *International Journal of Sexually Transmitted Diseases and AIDS*, the *Journal of Homosexuality*, the *Archive of Sexual Behaviour* and the *Journal of Sex Research*.

Elena Martellozzo is a Lecturer in Criminology and Research Methods at the University of Westminster. Elena is currently conducting PhD fieldwork at New Scotland Yard analysing case studies of online grooming and the distribution of indecent images of children, and studying police practice. Elena's primary research interests lie at the intersection between cybercrime, child abuse and policing and she has presented her research findings at a range of international venues. She has recently worked on a project funded by the Metropolitan Police Authority and Crimestoppers, which sought to explore child safety on the Internet and the role of the police in raising awareness among children about sexual abuse (2005). She is now exploring young victims' experiences and perceptions of the investigative process, undertaken on behalf of the Metropolitan Police Child Abuse Investigation Command (2007 ongoing). Publications include: *Policing the Internet and Protecting Children from Sex Offenders on Line: When Strangers Become Virtual Friends* (article describing findings from research funded by the Metropolitan Police and Crimestoppers) with J. Davidson (2005); *Women With and Against the Mafia: A Case Study of Sicily* (Zeitshrift für Polizeiwissenshaft und Polizeiliche Praxis. B.M.I. Republik Österreich Bundesministerium für Inneres 2005); *Educating Children About Sexual Abuse and Evaluating the Metropolitan Police Safer Surfing Programme* with J. Davidson (Project Report for the Metropolitan Police 2004).

Amanda Matravers is Associate Professor in the Department of Justice, Law and Society at the American University, Washington, DC. She was formerly a Lecturer in Criminology and Director of the Master's Programme in Applied Criminology and Police Management at the University of Cambridge Institute of Criminology (UK) and a Lecturer in the Department of Criminology at Keele University (UK). She holds a PhD in Criminology from the University of Cambridge, where she carried out the first UK study of women convicted of sex offences. Her research interests include sex offenders, policing, prisons and psychosocial criminology. She has published an edited book, *Sex Offenders in the Community: Managing and Reducing the Risks* (Willan 2005).

Victor Minichiello (PhD) is Professor in Health in the School of Health at the University of New England in Armidale, Australia. Dr Minichiello has published over 140 articles including those on the topic of sex work in international medical and social science journals. He is currently completing a study of male sex workers in Argentina using the research protocol developed for one of the largest studies on male sex workers, and also another study that explores the client's perspective of commercial sex.

Maggie O'Neill is a Senior Lecturer in Criminology and Social Policy in the Department of Social Sciences at Loughborough University. She has previously worked at Nottingham Trent and Staffordshire Universities. She co-edited *Sociology* (with Tony Spybey) from 1999 to 2002, and is a member of various professional associations including the Visual and Sensory Studies Research Group at Loughborough University, the Midlands Centre for Criminology and Criminal Justice, the National Network of Sex Work Projects, the British Sociological Association and the British Society of Criminology. She is also a member of the Board and Academic Advisor to the Human Dignity and Humiliation Studies Global Network founded by Professor Evelin Lindner. Maggie is an expert in participatory action research, ethnography (especially visual ethnography), the sex industry and forced migration. She has published extensively in these areas as well as on critical theory, feminisms and creative consultation. Her research and consultancy have been funded by the British Council, the Arts and Humanities Research Council, the Joseph Rowntree Foundation, the Home Office and the Government Office East Midlands. Her books include *Adorno, Culture and Feminism* (Sage 1999); *Prostitution and Feminism: Towards a Politics of Feeling* (Polity 2000); *Prostitution: A Reader*, with Roger Matthews (Ashgate 2002); *Gender and the Public Sector*, with Jim Barry and Mike Dent (Routledge 2003); and *Sex Work Now,* with Rosie Campbell (Willan 2006).

Jo Phoenix gained her PhD from the University of Bath in 1997 and is now Reader in Criminology at the School of Applied Social Sciences, Durham University. Her work focuses on the links between formal criminal justice and social justice. An expert in discourse analysis and qualitative research, she has published extensively in the following areas: women's involvement in prostitution, young people and prostitution and prostitution policy reform; sexual violence and the formal regulation of sex in the UK; and youth justice and punishment. Research has been funded by the Economic and Social Research Council and the Nuffield Foundation. Her latest research project, 'Doing Youth Justice', was funded by the ESRC. Her key books include: *Making Sense of Prostitution* (Palgrave 2001) and *Illicit and Illegal: Sex, Regulation and Social Control*, with Sarah Oerton (Willan 2005).

Teela Sanders is a Senior Lecturer in the School of Sociology and Social Policy at the University of Leeds and, sitting on the borders of criminology and sociology, specialises in the sociology of crime and deviance. Her main research interests have been in the UK sex industry examining the social organisation of sex work, regulation regimes and men who buy sex. She has published in a wide range of journals such as *Sociology*, *Urban Studies*, *Sociology of Health and Illness*, *Gender, Work and Organization* and the *British Journal of Sociology.* Her book on the indoor sex markets, *Sex Work: A Risky Business* (Willan 2005), was shortlisted for the Philip Abrahams prize. Her most recent work is *Paying for Pleasure: Men Who Buy Sex* (Willan 2007). Teela has recently completed a project 'Pathways Out of Prostitution: Becoming an Ex-Sex Worker' (funded by the British Academy), published as 'Becoming an ex-sex worker: making transitions out of a deviant career', *Feminist Criminology*. Current interests focus on the regulation of sexuality and illegal and informal economies across Europe. Teela is an Associate Member of the UK Network of Sex Work Projects, and has been the Chair of the outreach charity, Genesis, in Leeds for the last two years.

Keith Sharp is Dean of the Faculty of Education, Humanities and Sciences at the University of Gloucestershire. He has research interests in social theory and the role of the internet in the formation and management of identities. He is co-author with Sarah Earle of *Sex in Cyberspace: Men who Pay for Sex* (Ashgate 2007), and has published widely in areas such as qualitative methodology, the nature of professional knowledge and assessment in higher education.

Aidan Wilcox joined the Applied Criminology Centre at Huddersfield University full time in December 2005 to work with Professor Alex Hirschfield on the policy and crime prevention implications of social contexts of pathways into crime (SCoPiC). Following completion of an MPhil at the Institute of Criminology, University of Cambridge in 1998 Aidan worked as a research officer at the Centre for Criminology at the University of Oxford. While there he conducted a number of research projects including an evaluation of restorative justice for young people, a reconviction study of sex offenders and a study of the parole decision-making process as well as research investigating variation in the grant of legal aid in magistrates' courts. His research interests include reconviction data analysis, evidence-based policy-making and the assessment of the validity of empirical research. In 2005 he was awarded a PhD from the University of Oxford for his thesis entitled 'The Validity of Reconviction Studies'. In addition to SCoPiC, he has recently worked on a study of male sex workers and a survey of residents' views of speed cameras.

Kate Williams was awarded a PhD from Keele University in 2006. Currently she is a Senior Lecturer in Criminology at the University of Wolverhampton and was previously a Research Fellow at the Centre for Criminal Justice Policy and Research at Birmingham

City University. Her research interests focus on voluntary citizen involvement in policing, vigilantism and sex work using ethnographic methodologies. She is Secretary of the British Society of Criminology Executive, chairs the Postgraduate Committee and is a member of several other Committees. Her publications include '"Caught between a rock and a hard place": police experiences with the legitimacy of Street Watch Partnerships', *Howard Journal* (2005), 44 (5): 527–37.

Problematising sex: introducing sex as crime

Gayle Letherby, Kate Williams, Philip Birch and Maureen Cain

Introduction and motivation

This edited collection represents a multi-disciplinary consideration of sex as crime. The majority of the chapters build on pieces presented at a joint British Society of Criminology/British Sociological Association Conference (April 2006). The motivation for the conference 'Sex as Crime' was the recognition of how crimes such as sex work, domestic violence, rape and sexual assault have risen up the government agenda in recent years, for example the 'Paying the Price' consultation exercise on sex work in 2004 and the subsequent *Coordinated Prostitution Strategy* (2006), and other recent legislation around sex crimes including the Sex Offences Act 2003. We were also motivated by the need to question relationships between sex, crime and violence more generally given that this area of research within the criminological domain is often overshadowed by issues such as policing and community safety. The conference was attended by academic researchers, researchers outside of academia, policy-makers, practitioners and sex workers.

As noted this book takes forward many of the key issues considered at the 'Sex as Crime' conference and is a social scientific, pro-feminist, gender-sensitive collection, drawing on practice, empirical research, documentary analysis and overviews of research in the areas of sex work and sexual violence. The purpose of this introduction is not to introduce specific papers (we do this in the two part introductions: 'Part 1: Sex for Sale' and 'Part 2: Sex as Violence') but rather to set the context for the collection and to highlight the originality of our approach.

There are several themes/values underpinning our (both editors and book chapter authors) work. Thus:

- *humanist* – because sex workers, sex offenders and victims of sexual offences need to be treated with respect and allowed to tell their own stories their own way; failure to listen leads to a lack of fit between good intentions and intended outcomes, and to ostensible good intentions being experienced as either patronage or active harm;

- *minimalist* – in that we believe that the harms of intervention can sometimes outweigh any purported risk, and that when offenders' views are not taken seriously – which means both more particularity in our understanding and avoiding a rush to either blame or over-generalise theory – then society's efforts to change people's behaviour will fail;

- *tolerant* – in that we take the view that legal (if from some perspectives deviant) clients of sexual service providers also need to be heard respectfully: what is wrong with looking for a mime of love or passion if the real thing is hard to come by? Or even if it isn't?

- *responsible* – for we consider that the same rules apply to purveyors of sexual or deviant services as to purveyors of all other services: that just as toymakers should not poison the children of their customers with lead in the paint on their toys, so vendors of sexual services should not infect their customers with venereal or other diseases: caveat emptor does not apply;

- *pro-feminist* – in that we attempt to apply the above criteria even-handedly to the academic and social treatment of both women and men.

Not all of the chapters address each of these themes/values, and each of the 18 chapters which comprise the two parts ('Sex for Sale' and 'Sex as Violence') can be read discretely. Yet the identification of the broader, overriding and certainly problematic link constituting sex as crime, as dangerous to good order, as something to be forced into a dyad between the conventional and the deviant, is the paramount theme that spans this book.

In this collection we have supplemented the original conference papers with new work where we identified gaps which could lead to inadequate theorisation. Thus we have added chapters on male sex workers, which enable a contrast to be drawn between male sex workers' experiences of the sex trade and those of female sex workers, and points to the gendered nature of societal responses to the selling of sex. Other commissioned chapters address how the limited discursive construction of 'the child' in policy documents leaves the needs of adolescents unaddressed and thus enhances their vulnerability; and also supplement our growing understanding of the fact that men are the audience for male sexual exploits, not least within war.

Overall, the discussion spans the impact of new regulations on sex workers and of street sex work on community residents; the use of the internet by men who pay for sex, by men who sell it and by those who are trying to protect children from cyber predators; sex-based violence and its impact on choice and identity whether in war zones or in the home, whether by the state or by a sexual partner. Chapter authors also consider the power of written images of child sex victims and of men who have abused children, reasons for offending behaviour and how best to work with women who wish to leave prostitution. Finally, the problems of women trafficked for sex or other work – the trafficking itself being the crime – are seen as being in the same plight as all trafficked workers, regardless of country of origin and destination, and cosmopolitan rather than national solutions to their difficulties are recommended.

This book is original not simply because of its scope, but also because of the theoretical underpinning which unifies these diverse issues; that is, despite the range of contexts in which these gendered relationships are played out, men emerge not only as the audience for but also as the judges of women's behaviour. Indeed, there is only one context here in which women judge men: a group of feminist lawyers seeking to protect female bar dancers in Mumbai. This and other chapters highlight the way that women – and women sex workers in particular – only have a voice when politically organised. Attention to women's voices should be central to any discussion of sex as crime and we have attempted to pay attention to these, but barely managed it, which highlights the importance of further research and writing in this area. In sum then, this collection represents an original approach in terms of:

- the gendered analysis which draws attention to women and men as sex workers, perpetrators and victims of sexual violence;
- the consideration of the advantages and disadvantages of new legislation and regimes of order and control in the areas of sex work and sexual violence;

- the identification of sex workers and victims of sexual violence as (actual or potential) active agents rather than inevitably passive;
- the connections that are made between sex for sale and sex as violence within and between each section of the book; and
- the focus on the relationship between national and international concerns.

Traditionally, criminology has at best marginalised and at worst ignored gender. Consider the *Oxford Handbook of Criminology* (edited by Mike Maguire, Rod Morgan and Robert Reiner). In the introduction to their first edition (1994) the editors accepted that women have had a particular and significant influence on criminology especially in the areas of gender and crime, sexual and domestic violence, victimisation and the fear of crime which were previously neglected by male criminologists. Given this, they ask should gender (and 'race') be addressed in every chapter? Or should they be assigned to chapters for 'specialist coverage'? Their decision is to go for the 'specialist coverage' option and with reference to gender the result is a chapter entitled 'Gender and Crime' (by Frances Heidensohn). The consequence of course is that the rest of the book is sexless: a book about men without a gendered identity. Men remain the proper subject of criminology but the gendered nature of their crimes and experiences is not considered. In the fourth edition of the *Oxford Handbook* (published 2007) the chapter devoted to gender is produced by Frances Heidensohn and Loraine Gelsthorpe, who write:

> The history of the relationship between feminism and criminology is now rich with critical explorations of the contours of each discipline, epistemology, methods, politics, policy and praxis. Scholars within this field have set out to question some of the gender-blind assumptions within criminology and not only to create a space for women's voices and experiences, but at a theoretical level to examine constructions of gender. (Heidensohn and Gelsthorpe 2007: 381)

Indeed, although we would argue that a truly gendered analysis of sex as crime specifically and of the gendered nature of crime more generally is still lacking. In the past it may have been possible to forgive or at least justify the fact that much more academic attention is given to men and crime than women and crime, as it is overwhelmingly men who commit crime. But such an approach belies our knowledge that (a) crime is a social act (usually) involving at least two people;

(b) that all social activity is gendered because identities, however constructed, are always gendered; and (c) acting subjects too are intrinsically gendered – we gender ourselves. Therefore we need also to address such questions as why is women's crime seen as 'doubly deviant' in that they have broken not only the law but the norms of femininity? Why is it that men's crime is often seen as a 'natural' extension of so-called 'normal' masculinity? Why are the victims of (sex) crime – women, children and men – often seen as at fault rather than those who perpetrate the crime? With these questions in mind we agree with Loraine Gelsthorpe and Allison Morris that:

> Gender blindness is not a trivial oversight: it carries social and political significance. Moreover, theories which do not address gender are not merely incomplete; they are misleading. (Gelsthorpe and Morris 1988: 98)

It remains the case that 'sex crime' (defined in its broadest sense to include issues such as soliciting, violence against sex workers, rape in war, internet grooming) is often considered to be less important, both legally and academically, than issues such as policing, community safety, white-collar crime and imprisonment. It is also fair to say that, given the current backlash against feminism and women's studies and the misconception that only women are victims of sexual violence and only women do sex work, these issues are even further marginalised. Critical study in this area challenges both the workings of the criminal justice system and definitions of 'traditional' criminology.

Our pro-feminist, gender-sensitive approach highlights the problems with the stereotypical definitions of genderless 'sex crime'. Like Anne Campbell (1999, cited by Heidensohn 2000: 13) we would argue that 'contemporary [pro-]feminism is not a moral manifesto, it is a space in which to take sex and power seriously as a problem of politics'.

The only other book that we can find that takes a similarly broad focus is from the United States – *Sex Crimes: Perpetrators, Predators, Prostitutes and Victims* (second edition) – written by R. Barri Flowers (2006). Flowers considers, among other things, sex-related homicides, rape (including marital, same sex and date), incestuous crime, child molestation, pornography and sex crime, sex trafficking, male and female prostitution. He argues:

> Though statistics and surveys suggest that crime in general is on the decline in the United States, sex crimes appear to

be on the rise and are one of the more common and frequent crimes. Each year, millions of people are victims of sexual homicides, rape, incest, child molestation, child pornography, sexual slavery, paraphilic acts, and sexual perversions such as voyeurism, exhibitionism, and sadism. Anywhere from hundreds of thousands to, some believe, well into the millions of adults and children are willing or forced participants in prostitution and pornography. These include a growing number of victims of human traffickers who are forced into sexual servitude and exploitation in this country. Most sex crimes go unreported or underreported, making it the most hidden group of crimes and thereby the most difficult to detect, assess, treat, and control. (Flowers 2006: v)

The authors within this book consider similar and also different issues, some with reference to specific countries including the UK and Australia, while others take a more comparative or global perspective. Our broad inclusive approach, in terms of behaviour, experience, method, theory, place and perspective, has led us in the editing of this book to begin to question our original title. A recurrent theme in the following chapters is that of ambiguity, which raises a number of questions, including: who defines sex crime? do these definitions change with reference to time and place? are all of those involved in sex crime likely to hold the same definitions? Although there are some behaviours and actions that are easy (or at least easier) to define as criminal, many of the chapters in this book are concerned with behaviour and activities more difficult to define, in the margins between legal and illegal activity. With this in mind we have decided to include a question mark at the end of our book title, acknowledging that in considering the connections between sex for sale and sex as violence and in examining these issues in detail, we have highlighted inherent tensions and ambiguities.

In the remainder of this introductory chapter we consider further some of the background substantive issues to the concerns considered by our chapter authors. In 'Sex and sexuality, crime and deviance: definitions and concepts', we focus more generally on the meanings of sex and sexuality in contemporary society. In 'Sex for sale and/or sex as violence' we briefly introduce the two substantive areas of the book. Finally, in 'Reflections on studying sex as crime' we consider some issues of method, methodology and epistemology. In addition to an overview of the methods and methodological approaches taken by individual chapter authors, we reflect here on the implications of our (the editors) epistemological assumptions and discoveries during the production of this book.

Sex and sexuality, crime and deviance: definitions and concepts

Increasingly it seems that we live in a world obsessed by sex and sexuality. Although our sexual identity and sexual experience are on the one hand a very private and personal thing, it is something that we are encouraged to assess and reaffirm, justify and/or exploit according to norms and values that are formally (i.e. in law) and informally (e.g. through the media) sanctioned. Yet, some aspects of sex and sexuality are still considered to be taboo: heterosexuality and heterosexual relationships are still sanctioned in law and social policy in a way that homosexuality and homosexual relationships are not and this is supported by media and lay understandings of heterosexuality as *normal* and *natural*. In addition heterosexuality is also sometimes subject to sanction and censure. For example the gendered double standard – which among other things supports the view that boys and men have stronger, sometimes uncontrollable sexual urges that need to be fulfilled and that girls and women should be responsive to those needs but at the same time sexually passive and undemanding – encourages, even promotes, the appropriation of women's bodies by men (Jackson and Scott 1996; Abbott *et al.* 2005; Marchbank and Letherby 2007). All of this suggests that our socialisation affects both our sexual identity and our sexual experience (Plummer 1975, 1995; Hirst 2004).

In recognition of all this, many social scientists have argued that sex is a political phenomenon characterised by power relations. An early challenge to the eighteenth and nineteenth centuries' medical and psychiatric identification of some sexual behaviours and identities as perverse and abnormal was offered by Michel Foucault (1981), who considered how our sexual values and beliefs are constructed. He argued that sexuality is not a biological entity governed by natural laws but an idea specific to certain cultures and historical periods. More recently, Jeffrey Weeks (1986, 2000), like Foucault, stresses that sexual identities are historically and socially shaped. Weeks (1986: 15) insists that it is simplistic to reduce a complex pattern of sexual relations and identities to biological factors and stresses that it is important to study the history of sexuality in order to understand the range of possible identities, based on class, ethnicity, gender and sexual preference. A historical perspective also helps us to understand the interrelationship between gender and other differences. Stuart Hall (1997), for example, considers how the hegemony of the white race was reinforced against a backdrop of sexualised racist metaphors for Asian and African people with 'black' bodies defined as corruptive, promiscuous and animalistic. One legacy of this is the perpetuation of views of 'black men as dangerous to white women, of black women as sources of illicit sex for white men, and of sexual relationships that cross racial boundaries as degrading and unacceptable' (Hirst 2004: 69).

The view that human sexuality is rooted in biology, and that a 'normal' sex drive is a heterosexual drive, supports the view that the only point of sexual activity is the perpetuation of the species. So sexual activity that is not intended for procreation – which includes prostitution as well as homosexual activity – is defined as deviant, unnatural and perverse (e.g. Jackson and Scott 1996; Weeks 2000; Bell and Binnie 2000). Furthermore, many argue that the social construction of sex and sexuality and the way in which sexual relations have been institutionalised through heterosexuality result in the oppression and exploitation of all women and some men (e.g. Rich 1980; Jeffreys 1990; Jackson and Scott 1996).

One aspect of the sexual exploitation of women is the objectification of women's bodies through the 'male gaze' (the way in which men are encouraged to gaze at women's bodies from a male point of view) (Mulvey 1975; Bartky 1990). According to Laura Mulvey (1975) the male gaze can be characterised by voyeurism, fetishism and sadism. One extreme version of this objectification is pornography. Many pro-feminists argue that pornography is the foundation of male dominance, as its objectifying and dehumanising portrayal of some women shapes how men see all women by reinforcing and sexualising women's subordinate status (McKinnon 1987; Dworkin 1988; Itzin 1992; Russell 1993; Jensen 2004). Some go so far as to claim that there is a direct causal link between pornography and sexual violence, whereas others focus on pornography as an aspect of sexual abuse and misogyny more generally.

The justification for men's use of pornography relates to the sexual double standard that suggests that men have a stronger sex drive than women and a 'natural' need for regular sexual gratification while 'normal' women are more passive sexually. Thus the reputation of girls and women depends on sexual modesty and the reputation and identity of boys and men rely on sexual prowess. Women who openly display an interest in sex are seen as unnatural, aggressive and 'loose' (Moore and Rosenthal 1993; Lees 1993; Holloway 1994). This provides yet another example of how heterosexuality is 'risky' for women, not least because the objectification of women as objects of pleasure for men leads to the justification of male violence towards women. On the other hand, these views also lead to the violence of women towards men being seen as a slur on the masculine identity of the man involved (Stolenberg 1990).

Alongside a critical consideration of definitions and meaning of sex and sexuality, it is also necessary to interrogate definitions and meanings of crime and deviance. Deviance refers to any behaviour that differs from that considered to be the norm in society and behaving deviantly means breaking these (sometimes unwritten) norms or 'laws'. Crime on the other hand is any act that breaks the criminal law which is likely to lead to criminal proceedings and formal punishment. Although deviance is not necessarily criminal, crime is always (at least legally) deviant. Both deviant and criminal behaviour are relative to both time and place and even within one society different groups may have their own (different) norms.

From the late 1960s, feminists began to challenge traditional criminology for its lack of attention to gender and crime, both in relation to female victims and perpetrators and male victims and perpetrators. Carol Smart (1977) argued that most discussions on crime from the nineteenth century onwards virtually ignored women and when women are present they are grouped alongside the mentally ill and juvenile delinquents. Thus the assumption was that women need not be considered as the male experience was extrapolatable to women. More recently Claire Valier (2002) agrees that huge numbers of studies have ignored the presence of women offenders and have assumed that the male experience included and explained the female. At the same time the gendered nature of men's crime has been rarely explored as male crime is seen as a 'natural' aspect of masculinity (Messerschmidt 1993; Walklate 2003).

Feminist criminologists have aimed to raise the visibility of women within criminological knowledge and to address women's relationships with crime not only as offenders but also as victims, and have attempted to understand crime as a male-dominated activity produced not as a result of physiological differences but as a product of gender differences (see, for example, Smart 1977; Leonard 1982; Heidensohn 1985; Morris 1987 for some early work). Feminist criminologists argue that to understand the gendered aspects of crime requires a paradigm shift and a consideration of how gender interplays with class and ethnicity, in addition to how gendered expectations affect girls' and women's and boys' and men's behaviour. Thus, whereas boys and men construct masculinities with reference to their position in social structures and (sometimes) express their masculinity through crime when other opportunities and resources are unavailable to them (Messerschmidt 1993; Valier 2002), girls and women similarly define their feminine identity with reference to dominant perceptions of them as the natural nurturers within society (Lloyd 1995; Abbott *et al.* 2005). The implication of this is that when men commit crime (or behave deviantly) this is considered to be normal, but when women engage in deviant and/ or criminal behaviour they are seen to be behaving abnormally in breaking the norms and values of femininity as well as the norms and values of society. Female criminals are therefore viewed, by the criminal justice system and by society in general, as 'doubly deviant' (Lloyd 1995).

Already the tension and ambiguity inherent in any consideration of sex as crime must be clear. Given the complicated definitions and meanings surrounding sex and sexuality and crime and deviance and the further complications added through undertaking a gendered analysis of these issues, we are not able to offer definitive practical or theoretical solutions to the problematic attitudes, behaviours and experiences raised here. Like others before us though we, and the other authors in this book, attempt to challenge the various double standards that surround issues of sex and sexuality and sex as crime. Critical analysis in these areas necessarily treats the (extent of) presence or absence of men in these areas as worthwhile empirical questions, and similarly treats the manner of these male presences and absences and their structural similarities and differences from those of women as crucial observations, for example as to the relative extent of choice about entry or departure, the relative distribution of locations within sex work, relationships with clients, subjective meanings for sex workers, and so on. This collection as a whole, then, considers how gender plays out in society, and our aim is not merely to 'level things up' but to highlight and interrogate the ambiguities and ambivalences surrounding the gendered aspects of sex as crime.

Sex for sale and/or sex as violence

The concept of sex for sale is arguably part of our everyday lives, becoming more accessible – and some would argue, more acceptable and normalised – whether through the opening of local massage parlours, lap dancing venues in city centres, television programmes or internet and magazine advertisements. It is a growing business that is worth millions of pounds per year in the UK alone.

Sex for sale has also recently received more attention than usual from the media, government and the public due to two main reasons. Primarily, this is due to the government's first major overhaul of the sex laws in over 50 years, resulting in the *Coordinated Prostitution Strategy* (2006) following the 'Paying the Price' consultation (2004). Although it may be too soon to ascertain the overall impact of the Strategy, it has met with a mixed response. It is somewhat ironic that the Strategy has been criticised for its focus on attempting to reduce street prostitution, thereby targeting sex workers on the street to a greater degree, for it is the working conditions of these women that form the focus of another reason for the recent spotlight on sex for sale. The murder of five women sex workers in Suffolk (UK) during November and December 2006 brought into sharp view the stark reality of the types of situations that street sex workers may find themselves in, their vulnerability and lack of protection against (sometimes fatal) attack. Although it is debatable whether the huge volume of the resulting media coverage was due to the speed of the murders of the five women or the glamorised notion of a 'serial killer' – in this case the 'Ipswich Ripper' – at work, it should nonetheless be recognised that the victims were portrayed as such: they were described as women with lives and families and not merely 'prostitutes'. It can be hoped that the murders in Suffolk may serve as a reminder to the government of the crucial importance of the need for policy change in order to bring about the most useful methods to assist and protect street sex workers.

The Suffolk murders highlight the complex relationship between sex for sale and sex as crime and highlight the 'otherhood' of the sex worker and the need to pay attention to their clients and the regulatory controls surrounding prostitution. As Belinda Brooks-Gordon (2006) notes, to focus only on the sex worker means that two sides of the commercial and regulatory triangle remain unexplored and untheorised.

It is not only sex for sale that is of interest to the media, for as Cynthia Carter and C. Kay Weaver (2003) note, representations of sexual violence are endemic to western culture and reports of such violence has long been a feature within the British press. In this type of reporting there is no ambiguity: 'undeserving' victims are 'virginal' and 'innocent', attacked by 'monsters' and 'fiends', whereas those women and children attacked by 'ordinary' men, by husbands and fathers, are likely to blame themselves (Carter and Weaver 2003: 37).

Violence in general and more specifically sex as violence is a gendered concern for, as R.W. Connell (2001) argues, violence is deeply connected to the gender order as it is overwhelmingly the dominant gender who hold and use the means of violence. Violence though is not just directed at the less dominant gender, for in addition to the use of violence by dominant groups to maintain their privilege – everything from wolf-whistling to rape and murder – violence is also part of gender politics among men and most major violent acts occur between men. Thus violence is a way of exerting masculinity, illustrated by homophobic attacks on gay men as well as sexual violence towards women. Another way of defining sex as violence then is as a 'hate crime' which, as Sara Ahmed (2004) argues, is crime committed because of an individual's group identity – in terms of race, religion or sexuality.

One response to sex as violence could be increased attention to highlighting danger. But in the past we know that this has not necessarily helped either in terms of general understanding of sex as violence or in terms of the experience of those at risk. So a focus on external dangers – 'stranger danger' – has kept women in the home and has ignored the violence of significant others (Ahmed 2004; Marchbank and Letherby 2007). As Ahmed (2004) argues, fear of violence is a response to the threat of violence shaped by dominant perceptions of what is and is not threatening and who are and who are not to be feared. Furthermore, despite the relative success of Zero Tolerance and other campaigns (Marchbank and Letherby 2007), a recent Economic and Social Research Council survey of 1,300 children found that 75 per cent of teenage boys thought that women are hit if they make men angry and a Zero Tolerance Trust national survey found that 1:2 boys and 1:3 girls thought that there were some circumstances when it could be acceptable to hit a woman or force her to have sex.

Carolyn Hayle and Lucia Zedner (2007) chart the grass-roots developments that influenced academic understandings of sex as violence in the UK. In summary these were: the growing awareness of 'vulnerable' victims (e.g. in 1972 Erin Pizzey founded the first home for victims of domestic violence); the development of Victim Support – in 1974, the first Victim Support Group was founded in Bristol, which eventually was replicated around the country to become what we have today, a national charity; the establishment of the first Rape Crisis Centres (London 1976) which was also replicated around the country. From the mid-1990s and the rise of the New Labour government there has been a focus on the way offending behaviour is addressed and victims of crime are treated. Since the election of New Labour, the criminal justice system and related fields such as local government have been bombarded with new legislation with sex crimes being a focus. Key legislation includes the Code of Victims Practice, the Sexual Offences Act 1997, the Rape Action Plan 2002, the Sexual Offences Act 2003 and the Victims of Crime and Domestic Violence Act 2004. In the updated National Community Safety Plan 2006–2009 which links the national policing plan to a partnership approach in tackling crime and disorder, domestic violence is clearly identified as a priority whereby a more 'coordinated response' is a key concern. The aim is to develop specialist support services as well as to ensure a more effective response from the CJS in the sentencing and managing of offenders. The approach is victim led and the National Community Safety Plan aims to improve the reporting and attrition rates linked to such crimes.

Just as there is ambiguity surrounding the identity – as victim or not, as in danger or not – of those that experience or might experience sex as violence, there is also ambiguity surrounding the identity of the sex worker. In addition to raising questions about the social construction of male and female sexuality, sex for sale also raises general questions about the exploitation of certain groups (of women and men) within the labour market. Yet, as Keith Sharp and Sarah Earle (2003: 41) note, 'empirical studies of women sex workers portray images of both power *and* powerlessness, and of choice *and* control, as well as exclusion *and* exploitation' (original emphasis). Similarly, Laura Agustín (2007) challenges one-dimensional views of migrants who sell sex, and argues that the label 'trafficked' does not accurately describe the lives of migrants who make rational choices to travel and work in the sex industry. Thus sex work is not inevitably undertaken by individuals who can be classified as victims with no agency.

Reflections on studying sex as crime

Traditionally the academy was a male space and it was not until the second half of the twentieth century that women began to enter higher education in any great numbers. It is perhaps not surprising then that historically, the focus of academic endeavour was on men and male experience. However, historically, the problem was not only that men were the primary focus of research but that the so-called 'scientific' method was unquestioned as the best way to study both the natural and the social world. From this perspective, the research process is seen as linear and orderly and all the researcher has to do is put all biases aside and follow the rules in order to discover the 'truth' (Stanley and Wise 1993; Kelly *et al.* 1994; Letherby 2003).

Feminist researchers were critical of this approach and argued for the need to do things differently. Attention to the literature suggests that feminist researchers (and others who aim for anti-sexist research approaches) should:

- give continuous and reflexive attention to the significance of gender as an aspect of all social life and within research, and consider further the significance of other differences between women and (some argue) the relevance of men's lives to a feminist understanding of the world;

- provide a challenge to the norm of 'objectivity' and the assumption that knowledge can be collected in a pure, uncontaminated way;

- value the personal and the private as worthy of study;

- develop non-exploitative relationships within research;

- value reflexivity and emotion as a source of insight as well as an essential part of the research process (Marchbank and Letherby 2007: 24–5).

Diane Millen (1997: 6.3) pulls this together in a way which mirrors our own gendered approach to the study of sex as crime:

Any research may be considered 'feminist' which incorporates two main aims: a sensitivity to the role of gender within society and the differential experiences of males and females and a critical approach to the tools of research on society, the structures of methodology and epistemology within which 'knowledge' is placed within the public domain.

As you read the chapters within this book, you will see that all of the authors attempt to highlight ambivalence and challenge ambiguity, but often do so in a way that raises further questions and concerns. One interesting issue to consider is the motivation of those (and of course we include ourselves as editors here) that study (which includes researchers, policy-makers and students) sex as crime. In addition to our serious (often political) concerns to detail injustice and inappropriate behaviour in some and to defend and protect others, is there an element of voyeurism in our interest? In this twenty-first century where social science has become influenced by 'soundbite' 'special-effects' media and university courses have to become 'sexy' to attract enough students to survive, are we also guilty of academic 'ambulance chasing', of focusing on topics that might both horrify and titillate (Letherby 2006)?

References

Abbott, P., Wallace, C. and Tyler, M. (2005) *An Introduction to Sociology: Feminist Perspectives* (3rd edn). London: Routledge.

Agustín, L.M. (2007) *Sex at the Margins: Migration, Labour Markets and the Rescue Industry*. London: Zed Books.

Ahmed, S. (2004) *The Cultural Politics of Emotion*. Edinburgh: Edinburgh University Press.

Bartky, S.L. (1990) *Femininity and Domination*. London: Routledge.

Bell, D. and Binnie, J. (2000) *The Sexual Citizen: Queer Politics and Beyond*. Cambridge: Polity.

Brooks-Gordon, B. (2006) *The Price of Sex: Prostitution, Policy and Society*. Cullompton: Willan.

Carter, C. and Weaver, K.C. (2003) *Violence and the Media*. Buckingham: Open University Press.

Connell, R.W. (2001) 'The social organization of masculinity', in S.M. Whitehead and F. J. Barrett (eds) *The Masculinities Reader*. Cambridge: Polity.

Dworkin, A. (1988) *Letters from a War Zone*. London: Secker & Warburg.

Flowers, R. Barri (2006) *Sex Crimes: Perpetrators, Predators, Prostitutes and Victims* (2nd edn). Springfield IL: Charles C. Thomas.

Foucault, M. (1981 [1976]) *The History of Sexuality Vol. 1: An Introduction*. Harmondsworth: Penguin.

Gelsthorpe, L. and Morris, A. (1998) 'Feminism and criminology in Britain', *British Journal of Criminology*, 28: 93–110.

Hall, S. (1997) 'The spectacle of the "Other"', in S. Hall (ed.) *Representation: Cultural Representations and Signifying Practices*. London: Sage.

Hayle, C. and Zedner, L. (2007) 'Victims, victimisation and criminal justice', in M. Maguire, R. Morgan and R. Reiner (eds) *The Oxford Handbook of Criminology* (4th edn). Oxford: Oxford University Press, pp. 461–95.

Heidensohn, F. (1985) *Women and Crime*. London: Macmillan.

Heidensohn, F. (2000) *Sexual Politics and Social Control*. Buckingham: Open University.

Heidensohn, F. and Gelsthorpe, L. (2007) 'Gender and crime', in M. Maguire, R. Morgan and R. Reiner (eds) *The Oxford Handbook of Criminology* (1st edn). Oxford: Clarendon Press, pp. 381–420.

15

Hirst, J. (2004) 'Sexuality', in G. Taylor and S. Spencer (eds) *Social Identities: Multidisciplinary Approaches*. London: Routledge.

Holloway, W. (1994) 'Women's power in heterosexual sex', *Women's Studies International Forum* 7 (1): 63–8.

Itzin, C. (1992) *Pornography: Women, Violence and Civil Liberties*. Oxford: Oxford University Press.

Jackson, S. and Scott, S. (eds) (1996) *Feminism and Sexuality: A Reader*. Edinburgh: Edinburgh University Press.

Jeffreys, S. (1990) *Anticlimax: A Feminist Perspective on the Sexual Revolution*. London: Women's Press.

Jensen, R. (2004) 'Knowing pornography', in C. Carter and L. Steiner (eds) *Critical Readings in the Media*. Maidenhead: Open University Press.

Kelly, L., Burton, S. and Regan, L. (1994) 'Researching women's lives or studying women's oppression? Reflections on what constitutes feminist research', in M. Maynard and J. Purvis (eds) *Researching Women's Lives From a Feminist Perspective*. London: Taylor & Francis.

Lees, S. (1993) *Sugar and Spice: Sexuality and Adolescent Girls*. Harmondsworth: Penguin.

Leonard, E. (1982) *A Critique of Criminology Theory: Women, Crime and Society*. London: Longman.

Letherby, G. (2003) *Feminist Research in Theory and Practice*. Buckingham: Open University Press.

Letherby, G. (2006) 'Between the devil and the deep blue sea: developing professional and academic skills and building an inclusive research culture in a climate of defensive evaluation', in D. Jary and R. Jones (eds) *Widening Participation in Higher Education – Issues, Research and Resources for the Social Sciences and Beyond*. Birmingham: C-SAP.

Lloyd, A. (1995) *Doubly Deviant, Doubly Damned: Society's Treatment of Violent Women*. London: Penguin.

MacKinnon, C. (1987) *Feminism Unmodified: Discourses on Life and Law*. Cambridge MA: Harvard University Press.

Maguire, M., Morgan, R. and Reiner, R. (eds) (1994) *The Oxford Handbook of Criminology* (1st edn). Oxford: Clarendon Press.

Maguire, M., Morgan, R. and Reiner, R. (eds) (2007) *The Oxford Handbook of Criminology* (4th edn). Oxford: Clarendon Press.

Marchbank, J. and Letherby, G. (2007) *Introduction to Gender: Social Science Perspectives*. Essex: Pearson.

Messerschmidt, J.W. (1993) *Masculinities and Crime: Critique and Reconceptualization of Theory*. Washington, DC: Rowan & Littlefield.

Millen, D. (1997) 'Some methodological and epistemological issues raised by doing feminist research on non-feminist women', *Sociological Research Online*, 2 (3), at www.socresonline.org.uk/socresonline/2/3/3.html.

Moore, S. and Rosenthal, D. (1993) *Sexuality in Adolescence*. London: Routledge.

Morris, A. (1987) *Women, Crime and Criminal Justice*. Oxford: Basil Blackwell.

Mulvey, L. (1975) 'Visual pleasure and narrative cinema', *Screen*, 16 (3): 6–18.

Plummer, K. (1975) *Sexual Stigma: An Interactionist Account*. London: Routledge & Kegan Paul.

Plummer, K. (1995) *Telling Sexual Stories: Power, Change and Social Worlds*. London: Routledge.

Rich, A. (1980) 'Compulsory heterosexuality and lesbian existence', in A. Rich (ed.) *Blood, Bread and Poetry*. London: Virago.

Russell, D.E.H. (1993) *Making Violence Sexy: Feminist Views on Pornography*. New York: Teachers College Press.

Sharp, K. and Earle, S. (1993) 'Cyberpunters and cyberwhores: prostitution on the internet', in Y. Jewkes (ed.) *Dot.cons: Crime, Deviance and Identity on the Internet*. Cullompton: Willan.

Smart, C. (1977) *Women, Crime and Criminology*. London: Routledge & Kegan Paul.

Stanley, L. and Wise, S. (1993) *Breaking Out Again: Feminist Ontology and Epistemology*. London: Routledge & Kegan Paul.

Stolenberg, J. (1990) *Refusing to Be a Man*. London: Fontana.

Valier, C. (2002) *Theories of Crime and Punishment*. Essex: Pearson Education.

Walklate, S. (2003) *Understanding Criminology: Current Theoretical Debates* (2nd edn). Buckingham: Open University Press.

Weeks, J. (1986) *Sexuality*. London: Tavistock.

Weeks, J. (2000) *Making Sexual History*. Cambridge: Polity.

Part I

Sex for Sale

*Kate Williams, Maureen Cain, Philip Birch
and Gayle Letherby*

In the first part of this book we bring together nine papers, some research based and some purely theoretical, on the theme of sex for sale. Together they underpin a critical stance on both theory and practice debates. While the subject matter of the chapters is purposely wide ranging and each contribution stands alone on its own merits, there are a number of themes which emerge and link the chapters together. These links, which can only be identified within the context of a collection, offer the potential for a greater depth and breadth of critical analysis. These linking themes which give rise to new understandings are:

- differences in the practice of, and policy for, indoor and outdoor sex work;
- transnational perspectives on sex work;
- methods of researching sex for sale;
- engendering sex work;
- ambiguity and ambivalence in public policy and popular attitudes.

Indoor/'outdoor' sex work

Four chapters in particular reveal how the site of sex work shapes both the public response and the sex worker's experience. The first of these is by Jo Phoenix, who argues in Chapter 1 – 'Re-inventing the wheel: contemporary contours of prostitution regulation' – that the government's *Coordinated Prostitution Strategy* (CPS) is leading to an increasingly tight system of regulation for those women selling sex from the streets. Phoenix provides an overview of the recent history of prostitution policy in the UK, and brings us right up to date with a critical analysis of the new Strategy.

In contrast, Teela Sanders and Rosie Campbell concentrate on the perspective of the indoor sex worker, to ask, in Chapter 2, 'What's criminal about female indoor sex work?' Again with reference to the CPS, Sanders and Campbell argue the need in policy-making for a discourse which recognises sex as work. Only if selling sex is recognised as work will it be possible to insist on safe working conditions for women who choose to sell sex for a living. Only then will the risks currently inherent in the job be minimised. It is not enough simply to decriminalise this way of making a livelihood. It is also necessary to avoid implied censure, and so criminalisation by the 'back door'.

In Chapter 5 – 'The bar dancer and the trafficked migrant: globalisation and subaltern existence' – Flavia Agnes offers a perspective from a different culture, telling a story which reveals that in the end 'indoor' sex workers may be as vulnerable as those who work from the streets. The bar dancers of Mumbai are paid both for their performance and for partnering clients; some of them acquire long-term protectors/partners and become courtesans. Agnes first discusses a legal crackdown on bar dancing and the legal efforts of feminist NGOs to help. However, in a reflexive conclusion she ponders the evidence that the campaign by feminist well-wishers made life more difficult for the dancers, most notably for the immigrant women from Bangladesh. She argues that migration itself should be the point of intervention at which to assist impoverished women, not the particular form of work the migrant chooses on reaching her destination.

Kate Williams, in Chapter 9, 'From the oblivious to the vigilante: the views, experiences and responses of residents in areas of street sex work' – provides a different perspective on outdoor sex work. Her focus is on the responses of other residents in the areas where sex workers work. In a finely balanced discussion based on interviews with both residents and sex workers, as well as observations of encounters between them, Williams explores both the difficulties experienced by residents and the range of actions in response to the sex workers and their clients that the residents take.

International and 'cosmopolitan' perspectives

In this part of the book we, the editors, have also attempted a broadening of research and debate. Several chapters in particular make this possible.

Victor Minichiello, P.G. Harvey and Rodrigo Mariño present the results of an international web-based study of 'The sexual intentions of male sex workers: an international study of escorts who advertise on the web' (Chapter 8). Using data from 14 cities across the world, they explore the practice of safe sex in the light of rising numbers of AIDS carriers. In particular they focus on unprotected anal sex ('barebacking') in homosexual transactions. For methodological sceptics, this study shows the important contribution that can be made to the sociological studies of social problems by quantitative work. They conclude with a call for wider public education on sexual health problems.

As has been discussed, Agnes considers the plight after the ban of those former bar dancers in Mumbai who were in-migrants to the city from bordering countries such as Bangladesh. Even campaigns driven by local, city-based, politics take place in, and impact upon, a global context. The need of the migrants was to keep a low profile and find alternative work, albeit on the margin of the host society. The publicity surrounding the ban on the bar dancers drew unwelcome attention to them such that at least one woman begged the activists to stop their campaign. One methodological message is that there is no longer any possibility for a parochial social science. Another methodological connection is with the pioneering work of Maggie O'Neill, discussed below, which raises the question of what it means to 'represent' the dispossessed. The substantive question never to be dodged by sociological researchers is 'who are we for?' Not all contributors to this section would answer that question the same way. Probably not all the editors would either, but it supplies a submerged theme running throughout the collection.

There is no doubt, however, as to whom Christien van den Anker (Chapter 7) is for. Drawing on research from the UK, Ireland, Portugal and the Czech Republic, van den Anker develops this theme of 'Cosmopolitanism and trafficking in human beings for forced labour'. Importantly, she extends our lens towards forced labour in other industries, most notably agricultural and construction work. In these fields, as in sex work, not all labour is forced, and the assistance of the trafficker may help in getting work. So the global problems are the immiseration and inequality which lead to migration, and the question of force, which can always be deemed to be present in the case of children and is present or absent in variable degrees in the case of adults. For these reasons van den Anker argues that trafficking is most usefully approached from the cosmopolitan perspective of global justice, which focuses on an understanding of what is practical and of root causes, and which also goes deeper than the individualist conception of rights, although rights remain an integral part of the solution. This perspective has implications for the assessment of current policies on combating trafficking, which must look towards a victim-centred human rights approach.

Researching sex for sale

The majority of the chapters in this section of the book are based on direct experience or empirical research. They therefore provide a fascinating and important insight into the often difficult task of researching the topic of sex for sale.

As noted above the themes of whom the research is for and of how to ensure that it meets the needs of those on whose behalf it speaks is central to the work of Maggie O'Neill, who discusses identifying a method for giving voice to street sex workers in her reflexive chapter 'Sex, violence and work: transgressing binaries and the vital role of services to sex workers in public policy reform' (Chapter 4). She argues that in constructing an alternative and transgressive approach it is necessary to find ways in which women can express themselves through the medium of the researcher. She uses pictorial as well as literal methods to achieve this, emphasising the need for participatory action research if policy development is to be relevant to the lives of the women who are ostensibly to be helped. This again resonates with Agnes' sad discovery that even from a feminist perspective goodwill is not enough.

Using the internet in researching sex for sale is a technique adopted by two of our authors in relation to gathering data on the behaviour of men. Sarah Earle and Keith Sharp's discussion of 'Intimacy, pleasure and the men who pay for sex' in Chapter 3 explores the users of the services of indoor female sex workers by means of an analysis of their reviews, posted on a website, of their experiences with women. This path-breaking study reveals, among other findings, how masculinity is constructed in terms of giving pleasure to women. One point that piqued the interest of the editors is that the audience for these reports of prowess was apparently other men. As with all rich and detailed research reports, there is much to provoke thought here, in this case about both intra-gender relationships and also relationships with the 'opposite' gender.

As discussed earlier, Minichiello *et al.* also used the internet to identify their sample of men who sell sex. But that conventional methodology remains equally powerful in this area is demonstrated by Aidan Wilcox and Kris Christmann's semi structured interview-based study with a small sample of men who sell sex in the English town of Huddersfield – '"Getting paid for sex is my kick": a qualitative study of male sex workers' (Chapter 6). All the men were 'escorts', contactable at home, although their sexual transactions occurred in diverse locations. Some of these men were married; others had long-term partners. None wanted to change jobs, though some considered retiring. The authors focus, in their theoretical conclusion, on the question of choice of occupation. Their data suggest that the choice was a relatively open and rational one, no more constrained than other choices made by people from their social background. While the authors seem reluctant to take this finding at face value, we as editors have no problem with that. But it *is* what the men said – on that all can agree. Perhaps we – and our readers – can also agree that this and other insights revealed in these pages must give pause to those who are concerned, by covert force under the guise of helping, to force a change of career choice upon those who sell sex.

A gendered analysis

By now it should be clear that this section of the book is intended to provide a gendered analysis. We do this in part by highlighting the ways the differences between the sexes are constructed within the remit of sex for sale. This methodological perspective, we hope, enables both male and female engendering to appear in our text, and to appear as permanently in process; it enables, and is constituted by, new insights into the behaviour of those involved, in whatever capacity, and therefore a fuller – if still a patchwork – understanding of the social interactions constituting sex-as-work and sex-for-sale. What is particularly unusual is the inclusion of the perspective of the punters, made possible, as discussed, by the pathbreaking work of Earle and Sharp. We know now – if not before – that fantasy is crucial to the sex-for-purchase punter, that the skill of the vendor in creating a complete 'girlfriend' experience is appreciated, that emotion knowingly pretended on both sides is integral to the physical pleasure of the purchaser. So what is deviant about this encounter? Nothing, maybe, for it would not be so widely advertised on the net if it were also widely censured.

Yet in this collected research on sex for sale we have reached the view that sex work involves an exchange that guarantees the social marginalisation of sex work and the sex worker. Arguably, the legal, social and moral ambiguities surrounding sex work and its regulation provide a more effective form of social control than any other, for they create a permanent state of uncertainty and displacement among the female street sex workers in particular. This is a thread running through Part 1 of our collection. In particular, Phoenix highlights the ambiguity of regulation in relation to prostitution, while Sanders and Campbell present the (ambiguous) regulatory framework surrounding client behaviour. Even in the most recent government proposals, ambiguity remains as to what exactly constitutes legal behaviour within sex work. In India, as Agnes reveals, while the bar dancers do not regard themselves as sex workers, that appears to be the way they are viewed by the state. Van den Anker calls for 'illegal' trafficked migrants not to be criminalised but viewed in the same way as other migrant workers, and insists that all such workers should be accorded full human rights. For most such workers, neither criminalisation nor human rights is their lot, but maintenance in a state of constant uncertainty and tension, facing at best ambivalence from the host community and ambiguity from its laws. More locally Williams's research reveals a diversity of opinions and widespread ambivalence in the population at large about the differing activities of sex workers, while Earle and Sharp's respondents too reveal ambivalent attitudes to sex workers themselves and to the regulation of the 'Punternet' site. Others argue that the site and its contents are neither illegal nor deviant. Who then is regulation *for* – the provider of sexual services, the user or the simultaneously prurient and unwilling audience? Moreover, why, sociologically speaking, is sex work itself stratified by the way it is managed by the state?

In sum, in the first half of the book we offer a critical debate on a wide range of issues surrounding the so often hidden and only partially researched world of sex for sale. The questions this raises can be partially answered if we spend more time listening to the workers and their clients, also to all those directly affected by sex work, and in developing even more, even better, creative and imaginative research methods in order to do so – all the while, of course, holding on firmly to what is best within feminist and other social-justice-orientated methodological approaches. What these papers also collectively show is that the ambivalence may be integral: for some vendors sex work is an obvious choice, offering flexibility and a good lifestyle and pay which ranges from adequate to very good; for others the income from sex work is a millstone which enables them to pursue an untamed and unsocial drug habit. Sex work is no more one job than management is one job, and just as much. Ambiguity and ambivalence may stem in part from ignorance about or denial of these real differences, while nonetheless sensing their presence. But because ambiguity and ambivalence, the ever presence of mixed messages, characterise the scene, we invite our readers at least to listen to the voices of the sex workers in these pages, to decide where they stand and to support any clear and caring policy which has included the voices of the workers and their clients in its formulative stages.

Chapter 1

Reinventing the wheel: contemporary contours of prostitution regulation

Jo Phoenix

Introduction

More than a decade ago (1997) the newly elected New Labour government in the UK promised to review all sexual offences and to this end an independent Sexual Offence Review Committee was set up in 1999. Its terms of reference were clear. In the place of the preceding 50 years of piecemeal reform, the Review would suggest a legal framework, that would be coherent, that would protect individuals from sexual abuse and exploitation, that would facilitate the 'proper' punishment of abusers, and that would be fair and non-discriminatory. The findings of the Sexual Offences Review (published as *Setting the Boundaries Parts I & II*) formed the basis of a White Paper (*Protecting the Public*) and were subsequently adopted in the Sexual Offences Act 2003. The Sexual Offences Review was drawn as widely as possible. It covered everything from rape, sexual assault and abuse of trust to the age of consent for homosexuality and sex with corpses or animals.

Yet prostitution and prostitution-related offences were excluded from the consultation and reform process. This was despite nearly four decades of campaigning about the discriminatory and stigmatising nature of the legal framework. Instead, on publication of *Protecting the Public* (2003), the then Home Secretary David Blunkett announced the government's intention to investigate the possibility of piecemeal reform of prostitution-related offences. The intention was only to 'examine the scope for a review of the issues surrounding prostitution and the exploitation, organised criminality, and class A drug abuse associated with it' (Home Office 2002: 31). Subsequently, the resulting consultation document, *Paying the Price* (Home Office 2004) sought input in regard only to three areas: (a) preventing young people's coercion into or exploitation in prostitution; (b) protecting and supporting those adults already involved, and in ways which would help them leave; and (c) providing justice for families and communities 'blighted' by prostitution while also ensuring 'justice' was done with regard to pimps, traffickers and exploiters. In January 2006, the New Labour government announced the outcome in a document entitled *A Coordinated Prostitution Strategy and a Summary of Responses to Paying the Price.* This drew together descriptions of existing provisions and made recommendations as to how statutory and voluntary organisations should respond to the issues raised by prostitution. It made no suggestion for radical reform although it did signal the intention of government to introduce primary legislation to address the gendered nature of some prostitution-related offences as well as to change the legal definition of a brothel to facilitate safer working environments for indoor sex workers.

This chapter reviews developments in the regulation of prostitution and identifies some of the emerging trends in its governance. My argument is that the contemporary governance of prostitution comprises a contradictory set of regulations that, while offering support to many, also extends the reach of formal control (and punishment) to a smaller group of women in prostitution – those working from the streets. Particular attention is paid to the lines of demarcation drawn between the needy and victimised and the threatening and criminal. Such lines of demarcation constitute particular populations as appropriate subjects for state-sponsored paternalistic interventions backed by the full force of criminal justice, and others as appropriate subjects of harsher and harsher criminal justice control. The importance of tracing these differing systems of regulation (i.e. child protection, harm minimisation, criminal justice vs. welfare provision) is not to note their existence but rather to note that these systems exist simultaneously. Together, they form a system of interlocking definitions that facilitates an expansion of the sites of governance of prostitution at the same time as a growing emphasis on the criminal justice response.

The final section of this chapter examines the recommendations for reform contained in *A Coordinated Prostitution Strategy and a Summary of Responses to Paying the Price* in order to trace the shift in state governance of prostitution over the last five years towards an abolitionist response. It will be argued that one emerging trend is that criminal justice mechanisms are used not just to manage the visibility of prostitution, but to reduce it and compel women to leave sex work. It is argued that while this shift is justified by government as 'helping' women in prostitution, its effect is to regulate not just the prostituting activities of a particular group of women (i.e. street-working women), but also their wider social relationships, in ever-tightening systems of control.

Empirical realities of prostitution: changes and continuities

Two centuries of research demonstrate that despite social changes in regard to the family, birth control, employment and education, the empirical realities of engagement in prostitution have remained relatively constant. Prostituting is above all an economic activity and, as such, there can be little or no understanding of how and why women get involved (especially in relation to street-working women) which does not take account of women's socio-economic status more generally. As Eileen McLeod (1982) argues, women's decisions to enter prostitution are shaped by broader economic push and pull factors not limited to whether and how much money women can earn through paid employment. Support for childcare, unequal distribution of familial resources, access to social security benefits, access to housing, all impact on women's decisions to sell sex. Importantly, other empirical research provides evidence of the continuing reality that for many women access to financial security, social security benefits, pension and so on are still mediated by and through their relationships with men (Bellamy, Bennett and Millar 2006). Combined with this, other research indicates that economic dependency on men and the struggle to break free of it contain a hidden risk of violence (Phoenix 2001; Walby and Allen 2004). Regardless of years of campaigning and successive policy reform, domestic violence remains all too common. An examination of ten domestic violence prevalence studies across Europe demonstrates that one in four women will experience domestic violence over their lifetime and between 6 and 10 per cent of women suffer domestic violence in the course of a given year (Council of Europe 2002). While domestic violence happens across all classes, the significance of its persistence for working-class women is simple: many women find themselves locked into violent relationships because of economic dependency. Leaving these relationships further compounds their already existing experiences and risks of poverty.

In terms of the experience of being a sex worker, empirical studies of the last two centuries also tell remarkably similar tales. Women sex workers, particularly those working from the streets, have backgrounds marked by the shattering effects of poverty, homelessness, social insecurity, economic dependency on men, violence and histories of family abuse, or growing up in local authority care (Pearce 2006). The women in these studies are like many other working-class women in that they face the risks of poverty (and violence) and make choices in their struggle to survive (Agustín 2006). Some of the choices are commonplace, such as claiming benefits, whereas others are more extraordinary, such as engaging in prostitution (Phoenix 2001; O'Neill 2001; Sanders 2005). Contemporary detailed ethnographic studies of prostitution have provided descriptions not just of women's poverty, but of the numerous other economic and social problems encountered that often drive their decisions to sell sex. So, as Margaret Melrose *et al.* (1999) and I (Phoenix 2001) have described, involvement in prostitution is not simply a response to economic necessity – it may also be a response to violence within the family or from other men and a means of creating a better life, of being independent. Quite simply, for many researchers the 'bottom line' is that involvement in prostitution is a response to economic and social need (Carlen 1996; Melrose *et al.* 1999; O'Neill 2001; Phoenix 2001). Adult women in prostitution regularly cite inadequate income or benefits, drug and alcohol problems, homelessness and housing difficulties as some of the primary reasons for getting into prostitution.

Continuities aside, there have also been changes to the empirical realities of prostitution in the last few decades. The wholesale reduction of social security benefits for the young has meant that younger women are turning to sex work for much the same reasons as older women – rather than as a result of exploitation and coercion. There are now few or no social benefits that the young can claim: entrance into the legitimate labour force and the provision of social security benefits are all age-restricted (Hill and Tisdall 1997). The practice of informal school exclusions has meant that many young women effectively leave school long before the official leaving age. In this context, it should come as no surprise, therefore, that adult and young women report that selling sex provides them with a means to get money to buy things that they cannot otherwise afford (such as consumables), to fund drug and alcohol problems (both their own and their partner's) and as a means of supporting themselves and any dependents they may have while avoiding begging or other criminogenic activities which attract (up to now) much harsher and higher levels of punishment.

Empirical research on sex work also tells another tale. Violence, intimidation and extortion are commonplace – especially for street-working women (Barnardo's 1998; Phoenix 2001). Ethnographic research demonstrates the regularity with which street-working women experience physical attacks, sexual assaults, rapes, broken bones, bruises and burns, kidnapping and harassment from neighbours, community groups and police, and of having most if not all of the money earned taken by boyfriends, partners, pimps and a host of other men (Phoenix 2001; O'Connell Davidson 1998; Kinnell 2006). In this respect, while street prostitution might well provide women with a strategy to survive the shattering effects of poverty and social problems, it also exposes them to risks that further entrap them in that poverty and exacerbate the social difficulties that they experience. So, for instance, recent qualitative research has described the way in which working in prostitution leads to even greater levels of dependency on men, through economic exploitation, greater levels of poverty, homelessness and violence (Phoenix 2001; Kinnell 2006). The impact of these problems is so severe as to adversely affect women's longer-term physical, sexual and mental health (Phoenix 2001; Ward, Day and Weber 1999) as well as directly to increase their risks of drug and alcohol problems (May, Edmunds and Hough 1999; May and Hunter 2006).

In summary, empirical research on women's involvement in prostitution demonstrates that prostitution is a gendered survival strategy often used by poor women trying to create a better future for themselves and their dependents. However, such security and independence are often illusory because involvement in prostitution is also a form of gendered victimisation as those self-same women are exposed to the regularity of sexual violence, even greater levels of poverty, economic dependency on men who exploit them, and further degradation of their financial and social well-being and security through and because of their involvement in prostitution.[1] The rest of this chapter examines the different ways that (street-based) prostitution is regulated and controlled.

Existing forms of governance: regulating nuisance

For most of the twentieth century, prostitution has been governed through a system of partial criminalisation in which criminal justice sanctions have been used to 'manage' sex work by criminalising only those activities deemed to be 'injurious' or 'offensive' to the ordinary citizenry. Within this framework, sex workers in the UK find themselves in an ambiguous legal position: while the sale of sex is not illegal, many of the activities connected with it are. In practice, the only way that a woman can sell sex without committing an offence is in private and only when there is just one woman in the premises. The range of restrictions on where, when and how women can sell sex is so wide that it is often said that sex workers in the UK are only criminalised when they attempt to work.

This approach was adopted following the Wolfenden Report (Home Office 1957). In its preamble, the Wolfenden Committee asserted that the purpose of the criminal law is:

> ... to preserve public order and decency, to protect the citizen from what is offensive or injurious and to provide sufficient safeguards against exploitation and corruption of others, particularly those who are specially vulnerable because they are young, weak in body or mind, inexperienced, or in a state of special physical, official, or economic dependence. (Home Office 1957: 9–10)

The committee then continued:

> It is not in our view the function of the law to intervene in the private lives of citizens, or to seek to enforce any particular pattern of behaviour, further than is necessary to carry out the purposes we have outlined. (Home Office 1957: 10)

In this way, the Wolfenden Report drew a line of distinction between criminal justice interventions and matters of private morality, i.e. sex, and in so doing defined prostitution as both a form of sex and a matter of private morality. The only exceptions were activities and behaviour that caused an affront to public decency or a public nuisance. The Wolfenden Committee was clear:

> ... ordinary citizens who live in these areas [i.e. those in which street prostitution takes place] cannot, in going about their daily business, avoid the sight of a state of affairs which seems to them to be an affront to public order and decency. (Home Office 1957: 82)

The Wolfenden Committee asserted that the law should focus not just on street prostitution per se, but specifically on the activities of women working from the street rather than women working from indoor locations or the clients because, by virtue of their visibility, street prostitutes cause offence.

The result of the Wolfenden Report has been a system of regulation which makes it illegal to loiter or solicit in a public place for the purposes of prostitution and uses 'prostitutes' cautions' in which women (and only women) suspected of loitering or soliciting for prostitution are given two cautions before being charged as a common prostitute. The Wolfenden Committee also recommended that the punishment of prostitution-related offences should start with a fine and become progressively more severe and culminate with imprisonment for up to three months.[2] Such partial criminalisation in which the criminal justice system is used to regulate the visibility of sex-working women has remained unchanged in the intervening 50 years, with two exceptions. In 1982, sentencing guidance was introduced which altered the punishment of soliciting or loitering to fines only. In 1985, kerb-crawling was criminalised although police were not given powers of arrest until 2001.

Managing prostitution through the criminalisation of its visible aspects – or more particularly the visibility of working women – means that the burden of governance has fallen disproportionately on street-working women and in ways which are discriminatory. By so clearly defining the problem of prostitution as a problem of the visibility of prostitute women, the Wolfenden Committee effectively created a special and unique category of offenders ('common prostitutes') who, unlike less visible sex workers, are deemed fit to be punished.

The approach adopted in Wolfenden has led to the comparative under-enforcement of provisions designed to protect women sex workers (Matthews 1986; Edwards 1997; Phoenix 2001; Sanders 2005). Take, for example, the provision in the Sexual Offences Act 1956 against 'living off the earnings of prostitution', i.e. pimping, and 'exercising control over a prostitute', i.e. brothel-keeping. The focus of criminal justice attention on the visible aspects of prostitution has enabled the less visible activities to go virtually unregulated (Matthews 1986). In 2003, 30 convictions and four cautions were secured for living off earnings of prostitution or exercising control over a prostitute. The same year saw 2,627 convictions and 902 cautions for soliciting or loitering in a public place for the purposes of prostitution (Office for Criminal Justice Reform Group, Home Office 2005[3]). Susan Edwards (1997) is direct and argues that the failure to regulate proscriptions against exploitation is an example of the discriminatory treatment given to women who work as prostitutes. Current practice requires that the victims of exploitation and violence give evidence against the very individuals who threaten and abuse them – a situation which inhibits many of the victims from coming forward (Phoenix and Oerton 2005). And yet there is also an irony. When such proscriptions are enforced, the provisions fail to differentiate between those individuals who extort, exploit, control and/or intimidate women in prostitution and those who simply share money and resources (Smart 1995; Phoenix 2001). The intimate and personal relationships of sex workers can also become the object of criminal justice interventions.

A final problem of the Wolfenden framework is the way in which fining women for prostitution-related offences creates a revolving door and exacerbates the poverty many women experience. In order to pay their fines, the women often return to prostitution, or in many cases merely let their fines accrue and then face prison sentences for fine defaulting (see Matthews 1986; Phoenix 2001). Again, the burden of regulation and punishment falls disproportionately on the one group least able to afford it – street working poor women.

The rise of sexual health programmes and the decline of criminal justice

Throughout the 1980s and 1990s and in response to the concern about an HIV/AIDS pandemic, fears grew about the impact of prostitution (and, more specifically, prostitutes' *bodies* (Spongberg 1997)) on the sexual health of the 'innocent' and 'moral' general populace. Such concerns were not new. The Contagious Diseases Acts of 1864, 1866 and 1869 and the Defence of the Realm Act 1914 were all justified by differentiating sex workers from the general populace on the grounds that they posed a threat to the sexual health of the nation and/or to the army. With the arrival of the HIV/AIDS pandemic in the 1980s, popular media and public discussion drew on these same lines of differentiation to construct sex workers as little more than drug-addicted reservoirs of sexual disease. At the time, various calls were made to restrict their freedom of movement or to segregate them. Although the tone of public discussions was comparatively vituperative, such concerns opened the space for a new system of regulating prostitution that had a direct and arguably positive impact on the lives of street working women. Specifically, during the 1990s attention was drawn away from sex workers per se to the specific behaviour and the lifestyles of all women in prostitution – not just street-working women. As a result, a plethora of new services developed with the aim of minimising the potential risks to the health of sex workers (Phoenix 2001). The methods pioneered were non-judgmental and educative. The new sexual health agenda had as its ultimate aim reducing the harm from prostitution (i.e. the spread of sexually transmitted infections) both to the individual woman and to the general populace. Throughout the early 1990s, considerable resources were made available to genito-urinary clinics and sexual health outreach projects to work with women in prostitution. The types of interventions that sexual health outreach projects, in particular, offered sought to educate women about 'high-risk' behaviour and in particular to provide advice, services and help for women in order that they could do sex work in a healthy way. The underpinning philosophy of most of these projects was one that drew no line of distinction between sex workers and other workers and constituted the interventions as little more than health and safety provisions in the workplace. In order to do this, most sexual health outreach projects adopted a multi-agency approach in which everything from general and sexual health concerns, drug and alcohol abuse and misuse, housing and homelessness, and domestic violence were addressed. Women were brought into the service either by referral from another agency or through personal contact. Involvement with sexual health outreach projects was voluntary and anonymous.

Outreach projects also liaised with the local police about community issues regarding prostitution and the arrest and prosecution of violent 'punters' (clients) and local men who were exploiting women. For example, during the 1990s, the SAFE Project in Birmingham provided not only sexual health education, but gave women condoms, took them to the genito-urinary clinic and helped them access other multi-agency projects and services. In addition, SAFE workers went with the women to court and pioneered the 'Ugly Mugs Scheme' in which they would pass identifying information about violent and dangerous punters from woman to woman and communicate with police about the violent punters, as well as helping the police deal with community issues caused by a vociferous vigilante movement (the Streetwatch and Care Association; see also Williams, this volume). By the mid-1990s most major cities in the UK had sexual health outreach projects.

The refusal to distinguish sex workers from other workers produced direct and positive effects for street-working women and began to change the way prostitution was governed (see also Matthews 2005). By 1999, the police scaled down their direct regulation across the country and instead worked in conjunction with the outreach projects to help produce a more 'manageable' street trade without resort to hard-line policing, arrest and conviction. The result was a remarkable decrease in the number of women being arrested and convicted for loitering or soliciting in public for the purposes of prostitution. In 1989, there were over 15,739 women cautioned or convicted for soliciting. By 2002, this number had fallen to 4,102. By 2003, the number had fallen still further to just under 3,000 (Criminal Justice Reform Group, Home Office 2005[4]).

To summarise then, concerns about how prostitution might threaten public sexual health have resulted in the growth and establishment of sexual health outreach projects. While these projects are not part of the formal system of regulating prostitution, they nevertheless play an important role. Policing and punishment have dramatically reduced as formal criminal justice interventions give way to a health agenda. That said, the welfare services offered by sexual health outreach projects, while still focused on women's prostituting activities, have not *replaced* criminal justice mechanisms for regulating prostitution. Traditional methods of arrest, charge and punishment coexist (albeit in a reduced capacity) with the harm minimisation approaches of sexual health outreach. The deference given by the police to these outreach projects has effectively expanded the sites through which prostitution is governed, although arguably in ways that have benefited most sex workers and particularly street-working women. Not only has it meant a reduction in prosecution and punishment, outreach projects are often the only sites for healthcare and welfare professionals who will provide advice and, more importantly, practical help for street-working women.

A question of age: child protection and prostitution

By the late 1990s, concern about young people's involvement in prostitution created the impetus for some of the first formal reforms to the regulation and governance of prostitution since the Wolfenden Report. The major UK children's charities ran campaigns calling for a change in the way in which girls in prostitution were treated. They claimed that not only was the practice of charging and convicting girls under the age of sexual consent for prostitution-related offences a legal anomaly (Lee and O'Brien 1995), but that most girls in prostitution were the victims of exploitation and child abuse (Van Meeuwan *et al.* 1998). Pressure culminated and eventually the Department of

Health and the Home Office jointly issued a guidance document in May 2000, entitled *Safeguarding Children in Prostitution*. This guidance directed all individuals working with young people in prostitution to treat them as victims rather than potential (prostitution-related) offenders. The claim was that no child (legally defined as anyone under the age of 18 years old) could consent to being involved in prostitution, that most young people are coerced into it and that at any rate the men who entrap them in prostitution or buy sex from them are child sexual abusers and should be prosecuted.

> The Government recognises that the vast majority of children do not voluntarily enter prostitution. They are coerced, enticed or utterly desperate. We need to ensure that local agencies act quickly and sensitively in the best interests of the children concerned … They should treat such children as children in need, who may be suffering, or may be likely to suffer significant harm. (Department of Health/Home Office 2000: 3)

The introduction of these changes was based on a line of demarcation being drawn between young victims in prostitution, adult sex workers and criminal, abusive men. Quite simply, *Safeguarding Children Involved in Prostitution* rested on an age-based distinction between different categories of sex worker and then ascribed characteristics, motivations and entire social circumstances to those individuals who were younger than 18 years old. Unlike their adult counterparts, children in prostitution were deemed to be victims who should not be punished for their involvement in prostitution.

This line of demarcation expanded further the sites through which prostitution is governed and paradoxically strengthened the criminal justice response. Sexual health outreach programmes continue to work with adult women and provide general welfare and health services, but have reported difficulties in sustaining their work with anyone under the age of 18 years as the involvement in prostitution of such people is now defined as a child protection issue which has the potential to contravene the strict confidentiality ethos of many sexual health outreach projects (see Phoenix 2002 for a fuller explanation). Instead, a plethora of multi-agency teams now exists to meet the needs of these young people. These multi-agency teams frequently are little more than constellations of local police, existing statutory social services and voluntary children's services and are oriented around more traditional child protection methods of work and intervention.

Using existing social services, voluntary organisations and the police to regulate young people's involvement in prostitution is not without difficulty. Voluntary organisations and social services now have a legal obligation to get young people out of prostitution often without extra funding. A broader workplace culture of legal liability has created a great deal of anxiety on the part of professionals about being blamed if any specific girl does not leave prostitution or gets severely hurt while in prostitution. Perhaps more importantly though, the complex needs of young people are not easily accommodated by child protection methods of working (see also Elleschild, this volume). Many agencies report that they can offer little more than 'working where the young person is at' through self-esteem work, counselling and advocacy. In the five years since the introduction of this guidance, many young women in prostitution have ended up incarcerated in secure units, not as a punishment for their involvement in prostitution but as a means of limiting the liability of the organisation and the individual professional when girls continue to sell sex.

Earlier in this chapter, I claimed that one of the emerging trends in the governance of prostitution has been the simultaneous expansion of the sites of regulation and the tightening of controls in relation to street-based workers. Many young people in prostitution find themselves working from the streets, if only because young people tend to be less socially organised, more chaotic in the way in which they undertake sex work and more fearful or reluctant about self-identifying as sex workers (Pearce *et al.* 2002). Government guidance to treat young people in prostitution as victims of child abuse has extended the types of control in which these young women find themselves enmeshed. Empirical research conducted at the point of implementation of these reforms indicated that adopting child protection strategies for dealing with young women's involvement in prostitution focuses attention and intervention not simply on a girl's prostituting activities but on her wider relationships and deeper psychological states of being. Such a focus is generated by the requirement that organisations assess both the girl's status as a victim (of specific men) and her motivation to change. For official policy recommends that where a girl is not a victim and continues to sell sex, the full use of criminal justice sanctions is appropriate. Therefore any particular girl's motivation and victim status is all important.

However, it would be wrong to say that a boy or girl under 18 *never* freely chooses to continue to solicit, loiter or importune ...

and does not knowingly break the law ... The criminal justice process should only be considered if the child persistently and voluntarily continues to solicit, loiter or importune for the purposes of prostitution. (Department of Health/Home Office 2000: 27–8, emphasis in the original)

Young people in prostitution are thereby caught within three interlocking systems of regulation: (a) social welfare-based services for abused children which frequently offer these young people more of the same social service interventions that they have already experienced and often rejected; (b) harm minimisation, re-educative programmes of sexual health outreach (where such programmes choose to continue to work with young people); and (c) criminal justice sanctions when nothing else works.

New forms of governance: regulating victimisation and vulnerability

One of the emerging trends in the governance of prostitution has been a shift away from 'managing' the visibility of prostitution towards abolishing it. Recent reforms to prostitution-related legislation have implicitly collapsed the line of demarcation drawn in the Wolfenden Report of 1957 between law and morality by claiming the purpose of reform is to 'challenge the view that prostitution is inevitable and here to stay [and] achieve an overall reduction in street prostitution' (Home Office 2006: 1). Put simply, current proposals for policy change are not geared towards regulating the public nuisance of prostitution but towards disrupting sex work – and in particular street-based sex work – altogether. The justification for such a policy change is recognition of women's victimisation in prostitution. Contained within the most recent governmental recommendations is a line of demarcation between the 'needy' and 'victimised' women in prostitution for whom responsible local authorities should provide services geared to helping them leave prostitution, and the threatening and criminal adults in prostitution for whom greater and harsher levels of criminal justice sanctions are advocated. Or rather, recent reforms are constituted by and within the distinction between victimised women not voluntarily engaged in prostitution and those who voluntarily choose sex work. Such a conceptualisation discursively creates an imperative for action and the action that is recommended is a greater use of welfarist-based interventions, not as an alternative to criminal justice sanctions, but backed by the full range of criminal justice sanctions. In this way, the 'unwitting' victims of prostitution are compelled to seek help and the voluntarily engaged are given the choice to have help to leave or face harsher punishments. What is demonstrated in what follows is that the burden of regulation falls, yet again, on the more vulnerable sex workers – street-working women. It will also be demonstrated that the emerging trend in the governance of prostitution is the regulation not just of street-working women's prostituting activities but also of the entirety of their social lives, of the choices that they make in relation to intimate relationships and leisure activities and of how they spend their money.

Paying the Price and *A Coordinated Prostitution Strategy* regularly repeat that the 'problems' that need tackling are (a) the exploitation of women and children, (b) the trafficking of individuals for commercial sexual exploitation, (c) the ways in which debt and drug addiction trap individuals into prostitution and (d) the links between drugs markets, serious and organised crime and prostitution. Throughout both documents there are constant references to 'pimps', 'traffickers', 'dealers', 'sexual abusers', 'coercers' and a host of other hypermasculine criminal men. Both documents draw on the explanation of involvement in prostitution that was put forward in relation to young people where poverty, the constrained social and economic difficulties that women experience and the ways in which women make choices to be involved in prostitution are rendered less important than the presence of coercive or exploitative individuals. To be clear, the problem of prostitution is now defined almost entirely in relation to the misdeeds of criminal men. And it is these criminal men's presence that contributes to the understanding of prostitution as causing an even wider community problem – that is the very destruction of local communities.

Contemporary official policy draws on the stereotype of a prostitute-victim. In policy documents, doubt is cast about any expression of choice on the part of the women.

> Debt and drug addiction play a major part in driving people into prostitution as a survival activity … Those involved in prostitution can be particularly difficult to reach, claiming that prostitution is their choice and that they don't want to leave – through a combination of fear, the process of normalisation, or in an effort to maintain their dignity. (Home Office 2004: 55)

Such conceptions create the very conditions for increasing the levels of regulation and, indeed, criminalisation of women in prostitution. This occurs for two reasons: (a) the stereotype of the prostitute-victim is treated as though it is an adequate explanation; and (b) by using an enforcement plus support approach to regulation, the current reforms relocate the centrality of criminal justice responses to women who do not leave prostitution voluntarily. I will explain each of these in turn.

In *Safeguarding Children in Prostitution*, *Paying the Price* and *A Coordinated Strategy*, individuals in prostitution are constituted as victims because they do not voluntarily consent to sell sex. They are victims because something or someone else has forced or compelled them. Put another way, policy defines consent and voluntarism as the capacity to make a different choice from being involved in prostitution: the only free choice which is discursively possible is not to work in prostitution. The key problem that policy now addresses is therefore how to create a situation in which women make their own choice to leave prostitution.

Such a simple and naive understanding of the conditions in which women get involved in prostitution belies the economic and social realities discussed at the beginning of this chapter. This formulation also contradicts the ethnographic research which argues that women and young people do make choices, albeit not in conditions of their own choosing (Phoenix 2001; Sanders 2005). The experiences of the women who speak through more careful ethnographic work plainly do not fit the model of explanation which frames current policy directions. So, the better evidence is that while many street working women do suffer some form of victimisation and exploitation, they are not all victims waiting to be saved by the police or other agencies! Many are just poor women struggling to survive.

The enforcement plus support approach that has now been adopted reinforces the centrality of criminal justice sanctions in the regulation of prostitution. This is a result of the very demarcation between victims and offenders that is at the heart of current policy. On this point, *Paying the Price* is clear. The criminal law can and should be used to 'rigourously clamp down on unacceptable behaviour [i.e. voluntarily engaging in prostitution] and criminality'. This is an approach in which, unless there is the presence of a 'pimp' or other such controlling man, the responsibility for involvement in prostitution is attributed solely to poor choices made by the individual – a formulation in which the questions of need or necessity never appear. Here, the full force of criminal justice is used to compel women to leave *without* any attention being paid to the socio-economic circumstances that created the impetus for prostitution. In other words, this new layer of regulation generates greater and greater levels of intervention and control in women's lives while at the same time making them responsible (as in blameworthy) for their own poverty and their attempts to survive it.

> The current offence of loitering or soliciting is a very low-level offence and, as such, the court will usually only consider imposing a fine. This is said to have very little deterrent effect and does not address the underlying causes of the offending behaviour. (Home Office 2006: 37)

In practice this means a variety of interventions which include: voluntary self-referrals to outreach programmes; the use of civil Anti-Social Behaviour Orders and Intervention Orders by the police and local authorities, compelling women into drug treatment or other treatment programmes (breach of either of which constitutes the possible grounds for a prison sentence of up to five years); pre-charge diversion in which individuals are referred to drug intervention programmes; conditional discharge; mandatory drug testing and compulsory attendance at drug intervention programmes following charge; and also the full range of ordinary criminal justice sanctions following repeated conviction. The aim is clear:

> Under this staged approach those women (and men) who respond to informal referrals and seek help from support services to leave prostitution, and those who engage with the CJIT (Criminal Justice Integrated Team) workers to receive treatment and other support, may avoid further criminalisation. However, for those individuals who, for whatever reason, continue to be involved in street prostitution, the criminal justice system will respond with rehabilitative intervention to reduce re-offending and to protect local communities. (Home Office 2006: 39)

Under this new 'coordinated' regulation system, it is not merely and only the individual's prostituting activities that become the focus of intervention and sanction. Instead it is the totality of their lives and relationships. Their patterns of drug use, the appropriateness of their housing, their personal relationships with the men in their lives, their mental health, their educational and work status and so on all become the target of regulation.

It is this very net-widening in terms of both the interventions and the objects of intervention which creates the conditions in which women who engage in prostitution will have their lives more intensely governed and regulated than they have hitherto experienced. And, when their wider behaviour, actions, relationships and choices are judged and found wanting, they become, by definition, appropriate subjects of even harsher criminal justice punishments. For, as stated before, the question of economic necessity has been excluded from policy both as an explanation for women's engagement in prostitution and as an issue that should be addressed.

Conclusion

One of the key changes that has occurred in the governance of prostitution in the last 50 years has been the expansion of sites of regulation. Whereas in the 1950s, criminal justice responses were the key site through which the policing and regulation of prostitution was achieved, now voluntary organisations, sexual health outreach programmes, children's services and criminal justice agencies are all involved in the governance of prostitution. This expansion of the sites of governance produces contradictory effects – personal, welfare, and health support is offered to many of those involved in prostitution, most particularly those working from the streets, at the same time that formal control and punishment have also been extended. In addition, whereas traditional criminal justice responses have tended in the past to focus on the law-breaking activities of street-based sex workers, newer systems of regulation also target the totality of sex workers' lives in ways that leave them vulnerable to state-sponsored and sanctioned assessment and intervention. In this way, new trends in the governance of prostitution are directed at a small group of poor women, their relationships and their choices in the struggle to survive their own poverty. What remains unaddressed in policy and practice is that it is precisely those women who are most vulnerable to victimisation and poverty who continue to bear the brunt of regulation and punishment, i.e. women working from the streets.

More than this, however, the shift from the management of 'nuisance' and harm minimisation approaches to enforcement plus support has the potential to undermine what support is currently offered to the more vulnerable working women. Put simply, current support services could find themselves caught between continuing to support women in prostitution and being forced to reorient their work towards getting women to leave prostitution. And of course, when these support services fail, new reforms ensure that the women face greater and harsher punishments.

Notes

1 It is important to acknowledge that not all prostitution is the same. Some women are more able to control their working environments than others (Sanders 2005). Specifically, the experiences of poverty, social welfare and health problems and violence are more typical of those women working from the streets and not necessarily shared by those who work indoors in saunas and brothels or who work within escort agencies. So, for example, women working in saunas talk about the way in which simply working with other women helps to protect them from the threat of predatory violence (Sanders 2005). In comparison, street-working women regularly report the difficulties that they have of protecting themselves from potentially abusive punters with each 'purge' or clamp-down on punters (Church et al. 2001). As Sanders (2005) and Phoenix (2001) have argued, the experience and social organisation of prostitution is shaped not just by the marketability of sex, i.e. the commodification process, but through the various ways in which prostitution is regulated and policed through formal criminal justice and social policies.

2 The Wolfenden Report was implemented through the Street Offences Act 1959. However, the Sexual Offences Act 1956 also consolidated some prostitution-related offences and made it illegal to control the activities of, live on the immoral earnings of or procure a prostitute. As will be seen later in the chapter, these provisions protecting women in prostitution are not policed at the same rate or level.

3 These statistics were provided in a personal e-mail communication between myself and the Criminal Justice Reform Group division within the Home Office Research and Statistics Directorate.

4 See note 3.

References

Agustín, L. (2006) 'The conundrum of women's agency: migration and the sex industry', in R. Campbell and M. O'Neill (eds) Sex Work Now. Cullompton: Willan.

Barnardo's (1998) Whose Daughter Next? Children Abused Through Prostitution. Ilford: Barnardo's.

Bellamy, K., Bennett, F. and Millar, J. (2006) Who Benefits? A Gender Analysis of the UK Benefits and Tax Credits System. London: Fawcett Society.

Carlen, P. (1996) *Jigsaw: A Political Criminology of Youth Homelessness*. Milton Keynes: Open University Press.

Church, S., Henderson, M., Barnard, M. and Hart, G. (2001) 'Violence by clients towards female prostitutes in different work settings: questionnaire survey', *British Medical Journal*, 332: 524–5.

Council of Europe (2002) *Recommendation Rec(2002)5 of the Committee of Ministers to Member States on the Protection of Women Against Violence adopted on 30 April 2002 and Explanatory Memorandum*. Council of Europe: Strasbourg, France.

Department of Health/Home Office (2000) *Safeguarding Children in Prostitution*. London: HMSO.

ECP (1997) 'Campaigning for Legal Change', in G. Scambler and A. Scambler (eds) *Rethinking Prostitution*. London: Routledge, pp. 83–103.

Edwards, S. (1997) *Sex, Gender and the Legal Process*. London: Blackstone Press Limited.

Equal Opportunities Commission (2003) *Women and Men in Britain: Pay and Income*. London: Equal Opportunities Commission.

Hill, M. and Tisdall, K. (1997) *Children and Society*. London: Longman.

Home Office (1957) *The Wolfenden Committee's Report on Homosexual Offences and Prostitution*. London: HMSO.

Home Office (2002) *Protecting the Public*. London: HMSO.

Home Office (2004) *Paying the Price: A Consultation Document*. London: HMSO.

Home Office (2006) *A Coordinated Prostitution Strategy and a Summary of Responses to Paying the Price*. London: HMSO.

Kinnell, H. (2006) 'Murder made easy: the final solution to prostitution?', in R. Campbell and M. O'Neill (eds) *Sex Work Now*. Cullompton: Willan.

Lee, M. and O'Brien, R. (1995) *The Game's Up: Redefining Child Prostitution*. London: Children's Society.

McLeod, E. (1982) *Women Working: Prostitution Now*. London: Croom Helm.

Matthews, R. (1986) 'Beyond Wolfenden: prostitution, politics and the law', in R. Matthews and J. Young (eds) *Confronting Crime*. London: Sage, pp. 188–210.

Matthews, R. (2005) 'Policing prostitution: ten years on', *British Journal of Criminology*, 45: 877–95.

May, T. and Hunter, G. (2006) 'Sex work and problem drug use in the UK: the links, problems and possible solutions', in R. Campbell and M. O'Neill (eds) *Sex Work Now*. Cullompton: Willan.

May, T., Edmunds, M. and Hough, M. (1999) *Street Business: The Links Between Sex and Drug Markets*, Police Research Series, Paper 118. London: Home Office.

Melrose, M., Barrett, D. and Brodie, I. (1999) *One Way Street? Retrospectives on Childhood Prostitution*. London: Children's Society.

O'Connell Davidson, J. (1998) *Prostitution, Power and Freedom*. London: Polity Press.

O'Neill, M. (2001) *Prostitution and Feminism*. London: Polity Press.

Pearce, J. (2006) 'Finding the "I" in sexual exploitation: young people's voices within policy and practice', in R. Campbell and M. O'Neill (eds) *Sex Work Now*. Cullompton: Willan.

Pearce, J. with Williams, M. and Galvin, C. (2002) *It's Someone Taking a Part of You*. London: National Children's Bureau.

Phoenix, J. (2001) *Making Sense of Prostitution*. London: Palgrave.

Phoenix, J. (2002) 'Youth prostitution policy reforms: new discourse, same old story', in P. Carlen (ed.) *Women and Punishment: A Struggle for Justice*. Cullompton: Willan.

Phoenix, J. and Oerton, S. (2005) *Illicit and Illegal: Sex, Regulation and Social Control*. Cullompton: Willan.

Roberts, N. (1992) *Whores in History*. London: Harper Collins.

Sanders, T. (2005) *Sex Work: A Risky Business*. Cullompton: Willan.

Self, H. (2003) *Prostitution, Women and the Misuse of Law*. London: Frank Cass.

Smart, C. (1995) *Law, Crime and Sexuality: Essays in Feminism*. London: Sage.

Spongberg, M. (1997) *Feminising Veneral Disease*. London: Macmillan Press.

Van Meeuwen, A., Swann, S., McNeish, D. and Edwards, S. (1998) *Whose Daughter Next? Children Abused Through Prostitution*. Ilford: Barnardo's.

Walby, S. and Allen, J. (2004) *Domestic Violence, Sexual Assault and Stalking: Findings from the British Crime Survey*. London: Home Office.

Ward, S., Day, S. and Weber, J. (1999) 'Risky business: health and safety in the sex industry over a nine-year period', *Sexually Transmitted Infections*, 75 (5): 340–43.

Chapter 2

What's criminal about female indoor sex work?

Teela Sanders and Rosie Campbell

Introduction

This chapter focuses on the indoor sex markets in the UK, the current legal framework in which sex work operates and the implications of the *Coordinated Prostitution Strategy* (Home Office 2006) for those working in and managing indoor sex-work venues. Taking a realistic approach to the everyday working settings of massage parlours and women working in flats, we draw on the established literature and research on indoor sex work. Both authors have extensively researched many aspects of the sex industry in the UK and, at the time of writing, are actively involved in managing sex-work outreach projects.

Located at the heart of the current policy debates, this chapter draws attention to the differences between assumed perceptions of risk and the reality of risk for indoor sex workers. In addition, we highlight the complexities surrounding sex work, safety and a policy environment that seeks to criminalise rather than regulate. We focus on finding a balance between the need to provide safe working conditions, enabling policing agencies to investigate exploitation and abusive environments and coercers, while providing a safe system that allows opportunities for both sex workers and men who buy sex to make decisions about private consensual sexual interactions. Our arguments lead us to conclude that in the absence of any acknowledgment of the labour rights of women who voluntarily sell sex or any legitimacy given to the actuality of sexual services as work, sex-work policy in the UK cannot protect women or provide adequate long-term solutions to managing the sex industry. Finally we state that the actions and philosophy promoted in the *Coordinated Prostitution Strategy* will allow serious exploitation to thrive, increase violence in a sector that has traditionally been a safer working environment compared with the street and permit poor working conditions and irresponsible management.

Challenging assumed risks

Assumptions of 'risk' are plenty when considering the sex industry. Whether considering the street or the massage parlour, it is generally assumed that any involvement in the sex industry will mean women are putting themselves at risk. 'Risk' is assumed to be connected to physical, mental and sexual health because the nature of the work involves multiple sexual partnerships, dangerous working environments, risky activities (such as drug use and unsafe sex) and risky relationships such as coercive 'pimps' and boyfriends. There are stereotypes about the women who are involved in selling sex, namely that they were abused as children, runaways or coerced into the industry by unsavoury people. These generalisations and misinformed assumptions are not confined only to the thinking of the layperson or the salacious journalist but are widespread among some academics who claim that prostitution is violence against *all* women and deny that some women, under certain circumstances, can make choices to voluntarily sell sexual services (for instance, Farley 2004). These sweeping assumptions that *all* sex workers are at risk because of the intrinsic nature of sex work ignore the realities of the diversity and difference of experience among sex workers.

We want to set out our own position on the sex industry at this point. While we recognise that exploitation is prevalent in some aspects of the sex industry where there is obvious criminality such as children and vulnerable adults groomed, coerced and tricked into sex work, we want to promote that this is not the general or overwhelming case. We argue from a perspective that values diversity in analysing the sex industry and promotes the realities that women can and do choose to sell sex rather than earn money through other mainstream activities. In no way are we trying to undermine the realities of violence on the street, or the intricate dependency between the drug and street sex markets already established (see May, Edmunds and Hough 1999). We do not want to detract from the more recent issues around women being brought to the UK to be forced into sex work without their consent. Like Laura Agustín (2006), we want to make the distinction between women who voluntarily migrate to the UK to work in the sex industry and another category of vulnerable women who are victims of human trafficking (Ruggiero 1997). These distinctions highlight the complexity of the sex industry and those who work in and manage sex work and therefore require a complex policy and policing response rather than a 'one size fits all' approach. We believe that the sex markets are increasingly disparate and that the characteristics, working conditions and nature of different markets are vastly diverse. This section draws on empirical evidence to outline the reality of risks for indoor female sex workers, how risks manifest themselves and where environment and policy can enhance rather than reduce 'risky' sex work.

The occupational culture

The indoor sex work markets are varied in Britain, reflecting the fact that the actual act of selling or buying sex between two consenting adults is legal. Julia O'Connell Davidson (1998) reports on a familiar scenario of an entrepreneurial sex worker, Desiree, who worked independently from her own premises with a receptionist. Deborah Whittaker and Graham Hart (1996) describe the 'walk-up' flats of Soho, while massage parlours in the UK flourish in rural towns and cities. The impact of the internet has been significant on the expansion of sex work businesses with entrepreneurial sex workers using websites and e-mail to manage and negotiate business (Sanders 2005: 18).

The reality of many indoor sex work premises, particularly massage parlours and women who work alone or in small groups, is that the 'everyday' nature of the business mimics similar systems, rules and organisational features of mainstream business. For instance, Tiggey May, Alex Harocopos and Michael Hough (2000: 26) report that parlour owners operate through a set of house rules including 'Never employ juveniles, no anal sex, condoms always to be used, no partners allowed in the workplace, no overcharging, no rudeness or unpunctuality, no drunkenness and no clients under the age of 18'. In our own studies in Birmingham and Merseyside, we found these rules also existed (Sanders and Campbell 2007). The use of drugs among sex workers and clients was a rarity in the massage parlours and independent flats. These rules, along with others such as organised shift rotas, using a set of screening strategies to assess clients and employing a receptionist to manage the day-today activities, characterise the massage parlour setting as an ordered workplace with a distinct occupational culture.

Safer sexual services

Returning to the classic assumptions of risk, traditionally, women who sell sex have been labelled 'carriers' of disease and have been scapegoats for public health concerns (Sprongberg 1997; Walkowitz 1980). With the moral panic that surrounded HIV/AIDS in the last two decades (Weeks 2003) there was a rekindling of blame targeted towards women involved in sex work. The recent Home Office (2004: 67) review *Paying the Price: A Consultation on Prostitution* perpetuated this stereotypical view that continues to associate prostitution with disease and decay, ignoring up-to-date medical evidence of low levels of infection rates among sex workers (Ward *et al.* 2004) and high rates of condom use unless in coerced or violent situations (Sanders 2004). The everyday safe sex practices of sex workers at work explains why the rates of sexually transmitted infections are decreasing compared with the general population where sexual health risks are at an all time high. Helen Ward and colleagues (1999) analysed the health risks of 402 women who sold sex in Britain over a nine-year period and found condom use in commercial sex had increased significantly during the period 1986–94, with the majority of transactions upholding safe sex practices. However, the insistence on using condoms at work meant that there were ambiguous feelings about using condoms in their personal sexual relationships. Tim Rhodes and Linda Cusick (2000) note that in these situations, where love and intimacy are concerned, health risks can prevail. These discourses can lead to prolific non-condom use among sex workers in their intimate relationships (as opposed to commercial) (see Warr and Pyett 1999 and Cusick 1998).

Violence at work: safety indoors

Reflecting trends from across the globe, it is an established fact that in the UK the sex industry can be a dangerous and volatile working environment. As a Home Office report on homicide states (Brookman and Maguire 2003), the risks faced by street sex workers can be fatal, leaving this group of women highly vulnerable to murder. The murders of five women involved in street sex work in Ipswich in 2006 is a sad reminder of the continued vulnerability of street sex workers in the UK, and the lack of safety policy that directly addresses the dangers sex workers face. Hilary Kinnell (2006) reports that over the past decade 90 sex workers have been murdered, confirming that street sex workers in the UK are twelve times more likely to die from violence at work than women of their own age (Ward *et al.* 1999). If street sex workers did not have to go to isolated locations where there are few or no other people aware of their presence in order for them and their clients to avoid the police, they would be much less likely to be subject to violence and murder. Such an approach requires some degree of decriminalisation in relation to street sex work.

Despite these incredible levels of violence for street sex workers, any complete analysis of the literature across the world suggests that the trends in violence against sex workers are not generic across sex markets. There has been much evidence to suggest that the indoor markets, in particular massage parlours and women working collectively from independent flats, are safer than on the street (see Raphael and Shapiro 2004). In the UK, Stephanie Church *et al.* (2001) investigated violence among a sample of 125 indoor sex workers in Leeds and Edinburgh and found that there was a low incidence of violence amongst women who worked in parlours, although women reported poor working conditions with no recourse against exploitative managers or practices. Whittaker and Hart (1996) reported a low incidence of violence from women who worked in flats in London, although there was the risk of robbery and a climate of fear because of potential violence. Violence against sex workers is rare where regimes are strictly regulated, such as in Las Vegas, Nevada. Barbara Brents and Kate Hausbeck (2005: 270) interviewed sex workers, brothel owners and policy-makers in the legalised brothels of Nevada to examine the relationship between violence, prostitution policy and safety, concluding that 'the legalization of prostitution brings a level of public scrutiny, official regulation and bureaucratization to brothels that decreases violence'.

Without wanting to detract from the grave reality of the vulnerability to violence, we have argued from our own research (Sanders and Campbell 2007) that there are different levels of the risk of violence in different sex markets. This is mainly due to the safer nature of indoor sex work based on physicality, locality, reduced vulnerability, safety in numbers and general safer working conditions. A recent survey of 47 mainly indoor sex workers carried out by Brighton and Hove City Council found that 77 per cent felt safe or very safe in their working environment and 79 per cent said they were satisfied or very satisfied with the working conditions (Campbell and Farley 2006). However, the issue of calculating the risk of violence depends on the definition of violence and what behaviours are considered under this general category. For instance, Rosie Campbell and Melissa Farley (2006) note that the three most common experiences of 'violence' were 'unagreed touching', 'abusive or offensive language' and 'being threatened with physical violence'. This suggests that the current working conditions that are without legitimacy and exist outside normal channels of workplace protection allow these mistreatments to happen.

Although the rate of violence is lower indoors, premises and women are exposed to robbery, which could be accompanied by violence. Whittaker and Hart (1996) note that although the actual experience of violence was low in the walk-up flats of Soho, there was a climate of fear around robbery and many women had experienced this form of crime. Indoor sex work premises are targeted by both opportunist robbers and organised criminal gangs that assume there are large amounts of cash left on the premises and that only women will be present. Although many establishments have CCTV and other security systems installed, sometimes including male security on the door, the lack of legitimacy of the venue as a place of work leaves the workers exposed as a vulnerable target (Summers 2006).

Where lies the criminality?

Up until recently, the prostitution laws in the UK have been more concerned with public nuisance and 'decency' according to the influential Wolfenden Report in 1957. The Street Offences Act 1959 that resulted from this inquiry set out the laws against street prostitution, establishing laws such as soliciting and loitering as crimes against public decency. However, the Wolfenden Report staunchly believed that there was a point where the law had no place in private morality and therefore did not seek to make the buying or selling of consensual sexual services illegal. Instead, a loophole was left open whereby it was, and still is, legal for a woman to work on her own in her own premises without charges of brothel keeping. Yet this legality sits uncomfortably with other historical and more recent legislation that has been written directly and indirectly to control the sex industry. Most notably the Sexual Offences Act 1956 makes it illegal to procure (encourage) a woman into prostitution, live off immoral earnings or keep a brothel, essentially placing those who manage, own and organise massage parlours at risk of prosecution. These laws can also be applied to sex workers who are working together in small numbers as the charge of 'procurement' could be brought against those who are more experienced or introduce women into the industry.

New offences under the Sexual Offences Act 2003 strengthened laws against managing, controlling or recruiting women into prostitution involving a custodial sentence of up to seven years. The International Criminal Courts Act 2001 also includes crimes of 'enforced prostitution' as well as sexual slavery and rape, all of which can be tried in an international court and carry sentences of up to 30 years' imprisonment. In a UK context, anti-trafficking laws have been established under the Sexual Offences Act 2003 that make 'recruiting', 'harbouring' or 'facilitating' the movement of people for sexual exploitation into the UK, within the UK or out of the UK serious offences that hold heavy sentences. The introduction of specific prostitution-related human trafficking laws is most welcome to target organised criminal gangs.

Other pieces of legislation make the running of a legitimate sex work business difficult. The Criminal Justice and Police Act 2001 makes advertising prostitution-related services an offence (Brooks Gordon 2006: 32) which can lead to six months' imprisonment or a fine. This law mainly targeted the card advertisements placed in telephone booths in London (Hubbard 2002). The Proceeds of Crime Act 2002 which established the Assets Recovery Agency has given police the powers to seize and freeze the assets of brothel owners, with reports of £3.6 million pounds 'recovered' between 2004 and mid-2006 (Brooks Gordon 2006: 37). Although not directly relevant to men who buy sex from indoor sex markets, there has been a refocus, through legislation and policing crackdowns, on kerb-crawlers and a leaning towards rehabilitation programmes. It is clear from the stepping up of the law against the organisation of sex work, sexual exploitation and trafficking that the sex industry has been drawn onto a range of political agendas in the UK and that despite consensual commercial services between adults remaining legal, they occur in a fragile and hostile legal climate.

Local regimes

Despite the law, there are different localised regimes that enable the sex industry to exist, up until recently, relatively free from police interference unless there is reasonable cause to intervene. Some local authorities in the UK operate a system of licensed massage parlours under the Licensing Act 2003 where business owners are required to apply to the local magistrate court for an entertainment licence for the purpose of massage only. Checks are carried out by environmental health agencies to ensure the premises have the facilities (such as fire precautions) fit for access by the public. This system has traditionally been a cover for facilitating the sale of commercial sex, and is generally free from police interference. In our studies (Sanders and Campbell 2007) only two owners reported being charged with brothel keeping over a long-term career. The parlours tended to have a functionary relationship with the law enforcement agencies and in several cases the police would inform the parlours if there was to be a crackdown (see Sanders 2005). However, since 2004 there have been a series of raids on parlours from immigration services, and women who were illegally in the UK have been deported to their home country (BBC News, 18 April 2004). The policy shift to sexual exploitation and trafficking in actuality means that all establishments are under suspicion even if they are mindful of 'good' management and the rights of the sex workers.

Disrupting indoor sex markets

The *Coordinated Prostitution Strategy* (Home Office 2006), like the *Paying the Price* (Home Office 2004) consultation document that led up to it, paid little attention to the realities of the indoor markets. There was no real account of the existing literature in either of the documents (Soothill and Sanders 2004), and there was little evidence that those directly involved in managing, owning or working in the indoor sectors were consulted. Indeed, at the time of the consultation, parlour owners and managers in Manchester had formally organised with the assistance of the police and health agencies to form the Manchester Sauna Owners Forum (see Sanders 2005: 175). This group aimed to work towards good practice in the management of saunas and set up guidelines on safety, hygiene and good working conditions for sex workers. Such efforts to promote good management in parlours were rebuffed by the government. Instead, the outcome of the consultation has been the aim of disrupting not only the street market but also the indoor sex work markets that are operating without cause for concern.

There is a degree of ambiguity in the language used in the *Coordinated Prostitution Strategy* regarding indoor sex markets. Section 5 of the Strategy (2006: 60–4) notes the diversity of indoor markets: 'from high earning entrepreneurs to small brothels in residential areas and premises licensed as massage parlours and saunas in residential areas', yet makes the statement that:

> It is also clear that working off street can be as dangerous and exploitative as working on the street. While some respondents to *Paying the Price* find this to be a sensationalist view of off street prostitution, the government must address sexual exploitation wherever it exists, and particularly when it involves the most vulnerable members of our communities – including children and women trafficked from abroad for the purposes of prostitution.

We have seen that there are indeed 'risks' and 'exploitation' within indoor sex work, but to focus only on these ignores the relatively safer working conditions experienced by many off-street sex workers. But what is this government statement meant to translate to at local policy level? Is the Home Office directing responsible authorities to focus specifically on detecting and acting against the abuse of children in indoor settings and trafficking? Or is the Home Office suggesting all indoor sex work is 'sexual exploitation'? This is, we argue, an important distinction and something that was not made clear. The UK Network of Sex Work Projects pointed to this lack of clarity in *Paying the Price*:

> ... whilst some people feel harmed by their involvement in sex work, others do not. There is a literature, not included in *Paying the Price*, which reflects the views of those who do not experience sex work *per se* as harmful, although this does not mean they do not encounter some difficulties and problems in their work. For balanced and appropriate policies and interventions, UKNSWP feels it is important that changes in legislation and policy acknowledge the distinction between coerced and non-coerced prostitution. Any changes to legislation should work from a starting point of making a clear distinction between definitions of 'prostitution/sex work' and 'exploitation, coercion and abuse'. (UKNSWP 2004: 8)

The overwhelming need to concentrate policy on sexual exploitation detracts from the reality that the majority of the indoor sex markets are *not* exploitative but are in fact practising 'good' management. The Strategy fails to deliver adequate consideration or policy responses to what is the majority of indoor sex work practices but has a skewed perception that all sex work is harmful to individuals and communities and therefore needs disrupting rather than regulating.

Rejection of a licensing regime

When discussing the feedback from the consultation phase, the Home Office wrote: 'The aim of the Strategy is to minimise the opportunities for exploitation' (2006: 61). This is used to justify the rejection of a licensing system (decriminalisation) or a registration system (legalisation), yet takes no responsibility for allowing a large and growing industry to persist without any system that checks or monitors the standards of working conditions. The Strategy (ibid.) states some benefits of regulation: 'licensing ... offered the prospect of imposing certain standards of health and safety, and regularising the nature of the business to remove the current stigma associated with it'. The rejection of this sensible option was based on concerns that a hierarchy would exist between parlours capable of working to standards and those which were not, as well as sending wider messages that sex work was acceptable which, the Home Office suggests, would lead to all markets increasing.

The reasons presented by the Home Office for rejecting a licensing system are weak on two accounts. First, even in a climate where there are substantial laws (as outlined above) to prevent indoor sex markets escalating and exploitation, the industry seems to have grown at a heightened speed, particularly since both the mobile phone and the internet revolutionised communication in the industry. Helen Ward *et al.* (2005) note that there has been an increase in the number of men buying sex over the last two decades. We would suggest this is related to a wider acceptance of a sexualised culture in the night-time economy. Secondly, rejecting a proposal to license indoor premises on the basis that it would forge a hierarchy between good and bad premises shows no understanding of the current massage parlour scene. At present there is already a hierarchy between parlours that practise good management and those that are more concerned with profits than the rights and conditions of work for sex workers. This hierarchy has been established across the country in cities such as Birmingham, Liverpool, Manchester and more recently Brighton. Sex workers suggested some of the characteristics of poor management included: 'a view that sex work was easy money, limited knowledge of the sex industry, no vetting of clients, a lack of security measures, permitting drug use, employing under 18s, expectation of free sexual services to the male management, unfair cut of earnings taken by manager' (Campbell and Farley 2006: 57). These established expectations of good and bad working practices highlight how there is already a hierarchy of establishments and that a regulatory regime could only reduce this disparity and limit the unfair treatment of some sex workers.

One positive proposal in the Strategy that has the safety of women at the forefront of policy is the suggestion that an amendment is made to the law to alter the definition of a brothel to enable 'two (or three) individuals to work together from the same premises' (Home Office 2006: 61). The current status of the law, that only makes it legal for one woman to work alone, is recognised by the government as contrary to safety guidelines. However, there has been no further direction on this proposal a year after the Strategy, with no timetabling in Parliament for this change to be taken forward. Instead, across the country there have been more raids and arrests on women who are working together. Rather than taking this opportunity to explore a regulatory regime that could check, monitor and license establishments, the Strategy has focused heavily on 'trafficking' and the victims of sexual exploitation.

Policing of massage parlours

The Strategy as it is being implemented currently in relation to off-street markets suggests that there is no clear distinction between indoor establishments which employ and exploit trafficked people and those who manage sex work in a more 'benign' or 'responsible' manner. Some force areas are no doubt adopting a more selective intelligence-led approach, focusing on establishments where they have evidence of trafficking, other forms of exploitation and links to organised crime. In some areas, intelligence and investigative expertise had been built up through Operation Reflex and officers involved continued their work under Pentameter. Some others appear to be adopting a more blanket approach, i.e. targeting and raiding establishments not necessarily based on prior evidence of trafficking and other forms of exploitation. Indeed, calls for local forces to disrupt indoor sex markets may legitimate such a blanket approach.

The *Coordinated Prostitution Strategy* did not propose an approach which encouraged the regulation of indoor establishments and did not encourage owners and managers to work within certain specified criteria to avoid prosecution. It did suggest a change in legislation, making it legal for two or three women to work together to improve safety. However, this did not address the position of owners/managers whom the Home Office Strategy approaches as a homogenous group without any distinction between them, in terms of the working conditions they provide and their practices with regard to forms of exploitation and organised and international crime. The government seems to approach all sex work establishment managers and owners as exploiters and criminals.

Not addressing these differences but instead adopting a repressive policy approach to brothels may be a disincentive to responsible management. Why should owners and managers invest in their premises, creating secure and safer working environments in a climate of uncertainty regarding whether their business will be raided? Why should brothel owners and managers who have been mindful of the circumstances of non-UK nationals and have attempted to assess whether they are working voluntarily and independently be lumped together with those who are involved in serious offences should as trafficking or the exploitation of children? For example, one parlour in the North West which employed predominantly local women born in the North West and two Polish women was raided in early July 2006. These premises were run as a gentleman's club with a membership system, the premises were modern and in a good state of repair and an improved CCTV system had been recently installed. At the time of writing three women were released on bail, awaiting possible charges of running or assisting in the management of a brothel and/or controlling for gain. The assets of at least one of these women had been frozen. The establishment had reopened under new management arrangements the week following the raids but without the CCTV and computer system which had been taken by the police.

Concluding thoughts: the need for selectivity in policing

Our argument about what the focus should be for both policy and policing is based around a sharp division between what is to be considered exploitation and what is to be considered voluntary engagement in sex work. The focus on criminal investigation should be on those crimes where sexual exploitation and poor working conditions exist, which leaves sex workers with little choice or options to control their work or environment. The focus of criminalisation and policing investigations should *not* be on receptionists, owners, managers or others involved in the periphery of the establishment where good practice is evident. Policing 'ordinary' and non-problematic establishments that are causing no exploitation, harm or nuisance to individuals or the local communities are in fact detrimental to sex workers and puts them at risk. Diminishing the confidence that sex workers and parlour managers have in the police can have a significant effect on the reporting of crimes. Given that robbery and the incidence of fatal violence in parlours is on the increase (Dodds 2006), relationships between police and the indoor sex industry do not need to be thwarted with concerns of arrest and prosecution when increasingly sex workers are victims of crime.

The balance between which indoor sex work venues are targeted by policy and policing can only be reached if the brothel keeping legislation is abandoned in place of some other form of regulatory system. There is evidence that good management exists already and that owners have organised themselves to promote this. The need for responsible management could be at the heart of policy and policing. Under a regulated system there is scope for supporting good management as is evident in the licensed systems of Nevada, New Zealand and some states in Australia, and also the legalised system in Germany (Laskowski 2002). Under the current system – that has also demonised men who buy sex (see Kinnell 2006) – there is no recognition that there can be a responsible sex work industry, or that those involved in managing and owning sex work venues are not all exploiters. Just as buying sex can be respectful, safe and based on a formal contract between seller and buyer, the relationship between sex worker and owner is not necessarily exploitative. There is need for strong communication between all parties in order to work together to prevent exploiters setting up businesses and mistreating vulnerable women in the sex industry. At the same time the police need to be educated about the complexity of the indoor working scene as there are assumptions at work, in particular about those who own or manage sex work businesses.

While we are not disputing that 'trafficking' and other forms of serious sexual exploitation need to be a priority for policy and policing, we suggest that if this prioritisation brings the majority of normalised indoor sex work establishments under suspicion, this Strategy can only work against the safety of sex workers. With a worrying trend of the criminalisation of street sex workers trickling into the indoor markets as receptionists, sex workers and managers are arrested under the existing laws such as 'procurement' and 'managing a brothel', the possibilities of a system that protects sex workers in the UK seems a long way off. We would hope for a system that prioritises setting strict standards of hygiene, safety and procedure for male clients to follow, and which would allow women to work in safe and appropriate working conditions. Acknowledging and working alongside advocacy groups such as the International Union of Sex Workers (Lopes 2006) that promote the labour rights of those involved in sex work would enable a practical policy that encompassed employment rights. This would leave policing free to target those establishments that do not meet the standards but are involved in running exploitative, criminal and risky businesses.

References

Agustín, L.M. (2006) 'The disappearing of a migration category: migrants who sell sex', *Journal of Ethnic and Migration Studies*, 32 (1): 29–47.

Brents, B. and Hausbeck, K. (2005) 'Violence and legalized brothel prostitution in Nevada: examining safety, risk and prostitution policy', *Journal of Interpersonal Violence*, 20 (3): 270–95.

Brookman, F. and Maguire, M. (2003) *Reducing Homicide*. London: Home Office.

Brooks Gordon, B.M (2006) *The Price of Sex. Prostitution, Policy and Society*. Cullompton: Willan.

Campbell, R. and Farley, M. (2006) *Towards a Strategy on Sex Work for Brighton and Hove: Service Monitoring and Sex Worker Views and Experiences*. Brighton and Hove City Council, Sex Work Strategy Group.

Church, S., Henderson, M., Barnard, M. and Hart, G. (2001) 'Violence by clients towards female prostitutes in different work settings: questionnaire survey', *British Medical Journal*, 322: 524–25.

Cusick, L. (1998) 'Non-use of condoms by prostitute women', *Occupational Health and Industrial Medicine*, 35 (1): 1–11.

Dodds, V. (2006) 'Two found dead with "significant" head injuries', *The Guardian*, 3 July.

Farley, M. (2004) '"Bad for the body, bad for the heart": prostitution harms women even if legalized or decriminalized', *Violence Against Women*, 10 (10): 1087–125.

Home Office (2004) *Paying the Price: A Consultation Paper on Prostitution*. London: HMSO.

Home Office (2006) *A Coordinated Prostitution Strategy*. London: HMSO.

Hubbard, P. (2002) 'Maintaining family values? Cleansing the streets of sex advertising', *Area*, 34 (4): 353–60.

Kinnell, H. (2006) 'Demonizing clients: how not to promote sex workers' Safety', in R. Campbell and M. O'Neill (eds) *Sex Work Now*. Cullompton: Willan.

Laskowski, S. R. (2002) 'The new German prostitution act – an important step to a more rational view of prostitution as an *ordinary* profession in accordance with European Community Law', *International Journal of Comparative Labour Law and Industrial Relations*, 18 (4): 479–91.

Lopes, A. (2006) 'Sex workers and the Labour Movement in the UK', in R. Campbell and M. O'Neill (eds) *Sex Work Now*. Cullompton: Willan.

May, T., Edmunds, M. and Hough, M. (1999) *Street Business: The Links Between Sex and Drug Markets*. London: Home Office Policing and Reducing Crime Unit.

May, T., Harocopos, A. and Hough, M. (2000) *For Love or Money: Pimps and the Management of Sex Work*. London: Home Office Policing and Reducing Crime Unit.

O'Connell Davidson, J. (1998) *Prostitution, Power and Freedom*. London: Polity.

Raphael, J. and Shapiro, D. (2004) 'Violence in indoor and outdoor prostitution venues', *Violence Against Women*, 10 (12): 126–39.

Rhodes, T. and Cusick, L. (2000) 'Love and intimacy in relationship risk management: HIV positive people and their sexual partners', *Sociology of Health and Illness*, 22 (1): 1–26.

Ruggiero, V. (1997) 'Trafficking in human beings: slaves in contemporary Europe', *International Journal of the Sociology of Law*, 25 (3): 231–44.

Sanders, T. (2004) 'The risks of street prostitution: punters, police and protesters', *Urban Studies*, 41 (8): 1703–17.

Sanders, T. (2005) *Sex Work. A Risky Business*. Cullompton: Willan.

Sanders, T. and Campbell, R. (2007) 'Designing out violence, building in respect: violence, safety and sex work policy', *British Journal of Sociology*, 59 (1): 1–19.

Soothill, K. and Sanders, T. (2004) 'Calling the tune? Some observations on Paying the Price: A Consultation on Prostitution', *Journal of Forensic Psychiatry and Psychology*, 15 (4): 642–59.

Sprongberg, M. (1997) *Feminizing Veneral Disease: The Body of the Prostitute in Nineteenth Century Medical Discourse*. Basingstoke: Macmillan.

Summers, C. (2006) 'Dangers of being a sex worker', *BBC News*, 5 July.

United Kingdom Network of Sex Work Projects (2004) *United Kingdom Network of Sex Work Projects Response to Paying the Price*, at http://www.uknswp.org/.

Walkowitz, J. (1980) *Prostitution and Victorian Society: Women, Class, and the State*. Cambridge: Cambridge University Press.

Ward, H., Day, S. and Weber, J. (1999) 'Risky business: health and safety in the sex industry over a 9-year period', *Sexually Transmitted Infections*, 75 (5): 340–43.

Ward, H., Day, S., Green, K. and Weber, J. (2004) 'Declining prevalence of STI in the London sex industry 1985–2002', *Sexually Transmitted Infections*, 80 (3): 374–76.

Ward, H., Mercer, C.H., Wellings, K., Fenton, K., Erens, B., Copas, A. and Johnson, A.M. (2005) 'Who pays for sex? An analysis of the increasing prevalence of female commercial sex contacts among men in Britain', *Sexually Transmitted Infections*, 81 (3): 467–71.

Warr, D. and Pyett, P. (1999) 'Difficult relations: sex work, love and intimacy', *Sociology of Health and Illness*, 21 (3): 290–309.

Weeks, J. (2003) *Sexuality*. London: Routledge.

Whittaker, D. and Hart, G. (1996) 'Research note: managing risks: the social organisation of indoor sex work', *Sociology of Health and Illness*, 18 (3): 399–413.

Chapter 3

Intimacy, pleasure and the men who pay for sex

Sarah Earle and Keith Sharp

Introduction

It is widely accepted that the performance of sex work involves both emotion work and emotional labour – the shaping of feelings, as well as their public management (for example, Chapkis 1997; Sanders 2004). However, while much is known about the feelings and experiences of female sex workers, very little is known about the experiences of their clients – the men who pay for sex. This chapter seeks to make men's voices heard by drawing on a study exploring men's cyber-accounts of paid-for sex posted on the British internet site http://www.punternet.com and focuses, specifically, on men's accounts of intimacy and pleasure.

Firstly, the chapter explores men's accounts of intimacy and romance within paid-for-sex showing how patterns of ritualised courtship in commercial sex often echo those found in non-commercial sexual encounters. However, while emotional labour plays an important role in sex work, the commodification of pleasure is also important. Secondly, this chapter moves on to examine men's accounts of pleasure in paid-for sex, showing that just as non-commercial consensual heterosex is based on the normative assumption of sexual reciprocity, men's accounts of commercial sex also follow these normative expectations.

Researching men who pay for sex

There is a large and increasing body of literature exploring the feelings and experiences of both male and, particularly, female sex workers (for example, see Walkowitz 1980; Chapkis 1997; McKeganey and Barnard 1996; Sanders 2005). However, there is comparatively little research on the clients of sex workers. Roberta Perkins (1991) estimates that less than 1 per cent of research on sex work focuses on the men who pay for sex, and in the UK, the situation is particularly dismal. The reasons for this are fairly straightforward.

Methodologically, researchers have found it much easier to access sex workers – they can be found on the streets and in parlours and walk-ups, and many sex workers advertise in newspapers, contact magazines, via calling-cards and, most recently, on the internet. Some sex workers may also access outreach or similar services and can be approached there. It could be argued, then, that there is a reasonably accessible pool of sex workers from which to sample. The same cannot be said for their clients, for whom the act of paying for sex is likely to be a deeply discrediting activity and one with which they would prefer not to be publicly and openly associated. Indeed, many other researchers have documented their difficulties in trying to include male clients within their research. For example, in their study of street sex work in Glasgow, Neil McKeganey and Marina Barnard (1996) note that men often lied about why they were parked within the red-light district, claiming that they had just stopped to 'catch up on some paperwork'. They argue: 'The response was almost always the same, a more or less polite "get lost"' (p. 14). Historically, female sex workers have also been perceived as 'the problem', not their clients. As such, it is women who have been subject to intense medical intervention, surveillance and regulation (O'Neill 2001). This has led the female sex worker to become increasingly visible within lay and professional discourses on sex work (Weitzer 2000) and, thus, also the most researched.

However, there is now a growing body of literature on what Rosie Campbell (1998) calls the 'invisible men', or what Elroy Sullivan and William Simon (1998) describe as the 'unseen patrons of prostitution'. The study on which this chapter is based forms part of this growing body of literature which focuses on men's accounts of paying for sex. The data are drawn from the British website www.punternet.com: 'The Online Community for Patrons and Providers of Adult Personal Services in the UK'. The website has existed since January 1999 and is dedicated primarily to the publication of men's field reports (or reviews) of encounters with female sex workers. However, the site contains other sections, including a message board facility as well as links to women's own websites. The website predominantly reviews indoor rather than outdoor – or street – sex work and, as far is it is possible to determine, reviews relate to consensual adult commercial heterosex.

At the time of data analysis, which was carried out between 1999 and 2000, www.punternet.com contained 5,067 field reports on 2,661 different sex workers written by 2,554 separate authors. While the majority of authors post just one field report, many publish several, the highest number for any one individual being 46. Similarly, while the majority of women are reviewed only once, many are reviewed several times, the highest number being 32. We chose to sample the reviews by author and, at random, selected a 10 per cent sample (n = 255). Since several of these authors had published more than one field report, one of their reports was randomly selected to be included in the sample. However, at the time of writing (in October 2006), there were 41,952 online field reports written by 40,097 authors. The highest number of posts by any author was 134 and the highest number of posts for an individual woman was 173. According to www.punternet.com this represents a total spend of nearly £5 million and an average cost, per visit, of £124 (www.punternet.com, 2006, online).

The field reports are highly structured in that when men post a report they are required to complete an online pro forma. This pro forma asks for the name of the sex worker, her location, telephone number and/or website address, the price paid and the length of time spent in her company. Comments are then organised under three headings: 'her place', 'description' and 'comments'. Finally, reviewers are asked to indicate whether they would recommend her to others and whether they would visit her again themselves.

The data were analysed iteratively, both manually and with the assistance of qualitative data analysis software, the latter being used primarily for preliminary searching and coding (for a further discussion of this see Earle and Sharp 2007). Emergent categories and themes were developed and the data were interrogated further using these themes; some of these themes form the basis of the remainder of this chapter. Generally, the data have been reported verbatim, and include original spelling, grammatical or typographical errors. Men's original user names, as included in www.punternet.com, have also been used here.

Why do men pay for sex?

Our research did not set out to answer the question: why do men pay for sex? So, it may seem rather odd to focus on this at all. However, Martin Monto (2000) suggests that academics, policy-makers, researchers and others presume that they already know why men pay for sex, arguing that 'people tend to assume that the motives of johns are obvious, not worthy of serious exploration' (p. 76). However, of the little research that has focused on men, much of it has been motivated by the desire to find out and report the reasons why men pay for sex. The Glasgow study carried out by McKeganey and Barnard (2000), for example, reports men's desire for specific sex acts and the lewd or illicit nature of paid-for sex. Monto's (2000) US study of men also reports that men often make requests for specific sex acts, particularly fellatio. A telephone survey of Australian men (Louie *et al.* 1998) found that 'good sex' and convenience also motivated men to pay for sex. Another survey carried out in Australia found that men reported how paying for sex offered them sexual relief (Pitts *et al.* 2004). However, commercial sex is not just about the exchange of sex for money. Other researchers have noted that the majority of men are probably motivated to pay for sex by a range of factors (Chapkis 1997; Campbell 1998). The research reported here would support this; explanations are likely to be wide-ranging and there is unlikely to be one clear motive to explain why men pay for sex that applies universally across place and time, and across men of different ages and cultural and ethnic backgrounds. The data suggest that commercial sex involves emotional exchange between client and sex worker as well as the development of relationships based on notions of love, intimacy and romance. The data also suggest that sexual satisfaction is important but that, for many men, this is often framed within the context of both giving and receiving pleasure.

Intimacy, romance and ritualised courtship

Men, intimacy and emotional labour

The concept of 'intimacy' has considerable contemporary currency (Giddens 1992). Intimacy can refer to knowing, loving and closeness between people, emotional, rather than physical, intimacy. Although 'intimacy' can be used euphemistically in place of sexual intercourse (Jordan 2004), Lynn Jamieson (1998) argues that intimacy can be analysed at different levels. Firstly, intimacy can refer to the acquisition of familiarity. Secondly, it can refer to the possession of detailed personal knowledge. Thirdly, intimacy refers to notions of trust between individuals. Lastly, intimacy can refer to feelings of loving, caring and sharing.

It is now well established that the performance of erotic labour involves the commodification of intimacy and emotion. Drawing on her study of flight attendants, Arlie Hochschild (1983) develops the concepts of emotion work and emotional labour. The concept of emotion work presupposes that individuals are capable of reflecting on and shaping their innermost feelings. Hochschild describes emotion work as the 'act of trying to change in degree or quality an emotion or feeling … Note that "emotion work" refers to the effort – the act of trying – and not to the outcome, which may or may not be successful' (1979: 561). She describes emotional labour as 'the management of feeling to create a publicly observable facial and bodily display; emotional labour is sold for a wage and therefore has exchange value' (Hochschild 1983: 7). In the context of sex work, Maggie O'Neill argues that:

> Emotional labour is a central aspect of the working women's relationship with their clients. Emotional energy is directed at minimizing their own feeling worlds at work, and emotional energy is used in and around their interactions with and for clients … women have to be good at 'gentling' men, at flattering, counselling and consoling the male ego while at the same time providing his ideal fantasy woman, even though he may make her 'feel sick'. (O'Neill 2001: 142–3)

The literature is widely supportive of the idea that sex workers engage in emotional labour. Teela Sanders' (2005a) study of sex workers in Birmingham, UK, for example, highlights how the management of emotion poses a significant and persistent problem for sex workers. Men's reviews of paid-for encounters on www.punternet.com illustrate the successful outcomes of women's emotional labour:

> Angie is very chatty and will trust you with info most working girls would not which makes you feel special, family life etc. [Legman]

> Afterwards we chatted for a while – nothing contrived. [Daveinascot]

The data indicate that some of the men reviewing for www.punternet. com form long-term relationships with sex workers. For example, 'Beardyone' describes a twelve-year relationship with sex worker Alexandra:

> I've been seeing Alexandra for about twelve years (we worked it out the other day) and I have a wonderful time every time I see her. She meets me at the door, usually dressed in a housecoat and nothing else, undone down the front. We have a kiss, then a chat, then into her bedroom with its big double bed. She gives an excellent massage, lovely oral and sex in every position you want. An absolute delight ... [Beardyone]

Other reviews posted on the www.punternet.com site indicate that relationships between sex workers and their clients can range from months to years:

> I've been seeing this lady for about 2 years and keep going back. [Lw]

> I've been to see Lindsey many times over the years and so this report is an amalgam of all my visits. [Tommo]

Although not all men seem to have, or want, continued ongoing relationships with a sex worker, in spite of this, importance is often placed on a sense of knowing and familiarity. These feelings, Jamieson (1998) would argue, are implicit to the development of intimacy between two individuals. One client, 'Eddie', writes:

> Jacqui is very friendly and makes you feel very relaxed. We chatted for ages and it felt like I had known her for years. [Eddie]

Ritualised courtship and romance

Ken Plummer (1975) suggests that the organisation of sexual life is constructed through categories of sexual meaning. There is a range of categories, he argues, ranging from the utilitarian, the erotic, the romantic and the symbolic. Sexuality can, thus, manifest in symbolic form to provoke feelings of sexiness, highlight gender differences or demonstrate notions of love. Arguably, the romantic symbols of modern ritualised courtship are infused with these symbolic forms.

Writing about non-commercial heterosexual scripts, David Wyatt Seal and Anke Ehrhardt (2003) argue that courtship 'may be defined as the process or set of behaviours that precedes and elicits sexual behaviour' (p. 295). The typical symbols of non-commercial heterosex in modern western cultures might include candlelight, soft music, good food and champagne, all of these helping to create the setting for romantic courtship. Some of men's reviews on www.punternet.com would be difficult to distinguish from such imagery, for example 'Entranced' writes:

> We met, we ate a lovely lasagne (Charise loves Italian food!), we drank wine. We talked. We played some music. We took our time.

According to Wyatt Seal and Ehrhardt (2003), the 'courtship game' also commonly includes small talk. Men's reviews illustrate the way in which commercial sex often follows a courtship script similar to that of non-commercial heterosex:

> Anyway, we had some wine and a lengthy chat and then strawberries and cream … [Rumblingtum]

Men also commonly report being offered a drink of some sort on arrival, sometimes wine or beer, or a cold soft drink, and sometimes tea or coffee. Having a drink is an expected preamble and part of a ritualised system of courtship. As with any exchange, commercial or otherwise, a drink can be used as a form of relaxation, serving to put an individual at their ease and is an activity typical of real dates (Lever and Dolnick 2000), as 'Okydoky' describes:

> We chatted over a few drinks for a while then we went up to her bedroom … [Okydoky]

Other reviews on www.punternet.com refer to the use of other romantic props, such as the use of candles or soft music, as 'Adrian' and 'Alan' both note:

> Very friendly and made every attempt to make you feel relaxed from the start. Comfortable bedroom, clean, candles, and soft music. [Adrian]

There was candlelight and soft music was playing. [Alan]

Previous research highlights that indoor sex workers often report receiving gifts. These gifts can include items such as perfume, flowers or champagne which, as Janet Lever and Deanne Dolnick rightly note, are 'the type of gifts a man might give to a girlfriend or wife' (2000: 94). These symbols of romantic courtship can also be found in men's reviews on www.punternet.com, for example:

> ... if you really want to get the best from Peaches a few suggestions. Firstly take some champagne with you when you visit – she drinks little else and it makes her very randy. [Valentine]

However, the use of such romantic symbols is not dissimilar to non-commercial sex in which the 'bottom line dynamic' is often one of romantic negotiation in the pursuit and exchange for sex.

Girlfriend sex

While intimacy and romance play an important role in paid-for sex, some of the reviews posted on www.punternet.com stand out from the rest. As already discussed elsewhere (Sharp and Earle 2003; Earle and Sharp 2007), some of the reviews refer to the phenomenon of 'girlfriend sex'. Girlfriend sex is about 'making love' rather than 'having sex'. As Julia O'Connell Davidson (1995, 1996) points out, sex workers and their clients exist within a normative moral order where particular meanings are ascribed to human sexual interactions. These meanings dictate that 'legitimate' sex is that which occurs between men and women who are 'in love'. Indeed Wyatt Seal and Ehrhardt (2003) highlight how, within narratives of emotional intimacy, men often contrast 'having sex' with 'making love'. As 'Entranced!' writes:

> I suppose the best I can say is that it was more like making love than having sex ... the nicest – in every sense – girl I've met for absolutely ages.

Many of the other reviews echo this phenomenon and, in contrast to some of the previously published literature on female sex work (for example, Brewis and Linstead 2000), men describe experiences of cuddling, kissing and feelings of being loved and cared for within paid-for sex:

I was after a 'girlfriend' experience and Barbie plays this part to perfection, giving lots and lots of love, and attention, and forever asking if you are ok (YES!!) This young lady has it all, looks, personality, brains and a terrific sense of humour an absolute joy to be with. [David Murphy]

There are lots of cuddles and she actually appears to enjoy the sex … The well used term 'girlfriend sex' seems to be totally appropriate here. Without being crude, Tiff feels superb while 'inside'. I'll be back as soon as possible. I came away feeling great and had to phone her back and tell her. [Visitor]

All the way through we had been kissing so this was a real girlfriend experience. I can't wait to see her again what a jewel she is. [SharpShooter]

Girlfriend sex also invokes feelings of exclusivity, or the reluctance to share a sex worker with other clients. For example, 'Nealmort' and 'Fboc' write:

The only sadness is that after this review I may have to share her with more of you. [Nealmort]

Great girlfriend like sex. We finished up in a heap of very sweaty tangled bodies. She is one sexy lass. Hands off. [Fboc]

It is only in the last 20 years or so that sociologists have paid attention to the concept of 'love'. Love is part of public culture, and it is socially and culturally constructed rather than personal and private. Stevi Jackson (1993) makes the distinction between 'falling in love' and 'being in love', and, drawing on Shere Hite's (1988) study, notes that while people in long-term relationships may not be 'in love', they do say that they 'love' their partners. In his work on intimacy, Anthony Giddens (1992) also draws a distinction between passionate love and romantic love, the former evoking fervour and danger and the latter being something that is normatively desirable. In men's reviews of paid-for sex both are evident. Of course, not all men are concerned with developing emotional intimacy when paying for sex, nor do they all regularly visit the same sex worker. Many do not describe their paid-for encounters within the context of emotion or romance, nor do they refer to the phenomenon of girlfriend sex.

Pleasure is also an important emergent theme within men's reviews of paying for sex and this is explored below.

Men, pleasure and normative heterosex

The quick fuck

Some men do want just a 'quick fuck' or 'a good hard shag', as two of the men on www.punternet.com write:

> Leonne is a good choice if you want a quick fuck with a nice looking girl. Don't expect intimacy, GFE [girlfriend experience] or a long stay, just a good hard shag. [Nobbin the Nob]

> This woman is dynamite! I visited her once at Liasons and was as good if not better this time round. This is not gentle, this is not girlfriend sex, it is frenzied raw physical pleasure. If sex was on at the Olympics, this girl would take home gold for the emerald isle ... I left knackered, bow-legged but very very satisfied! [Dv]

On www.punternet.com the vast majority – over 90 per cent – of sexual encounters are reviewed positively and men tell stories that centre on their own physical pleasure. Not surprisingly, then, men's sexual pleasure is central to the experience of paying for sex. Men's accounts often focus on a woman's willingness to please. The phrase 'she is keen to please' can often be found in men's reviews, for example:

> she was keen to please and did all that I wanted, even performing again after a rest ... [Robbie]

> I watched both girls together for a while then I had Anya while Lara sat on her face so that I could kiss those lovely tits of hers ... both ladies are a pleasure to be with and keen to please. [Nig2259]

However, although the data suggest that most paid-for encounters are reviewed positively, for others, a negative sexual experience is usually blamed on the sex worker, as the following extract shows:

Her technique is appalling, spend more time wanking than sucking, won't suck to completion, and struggled to please me at all. [Blowman]

The data suggest that, although intimacy and romance can be important to some men, for others paying for sex is a purely commercial transaction – nothing more – but honesty and good service are vital. The view expressed above also allows men to place their own sexual desires at the fore in a way that may not be possible within consensual non-commercial heterosex. As Neil McKeganey (1994: 295) states: 'By paying for sex the males felt able to place their own sexual desires at centre stage ...'.

Reciprocal heterosex

While men's own sexual pleasure features strongly within men's reviews, contemporary discourses on normative consensual heterosex often centre on sexual reciprocity in that definitions of sex 'are focused on the notion of reciprocity, where sex involves giving (and receiving) pleasure' (McPhillips, Braun and Gavey 2001: 235). What is unusual, given the previously published literature on sex work, is that the data suggest that such discourses apply equally to commercial, as well as non-commercial, sex. Of course, this is unlikely to be universally true across the whole sex industry and is more likely to apply to indoor rather than outdoor sex work (Lever and Dolnick 2000).

Accounts of non-commercial heterosex indicate that heterosexual behaviour is highly patterned. Drawing on script theories, some authors suggest a prescribed sequence of events. William Gagnon and John Simon describe this as:

Kissing, tongue kissing, manual and oral caressing of the body, particularly the female breasts, manual and oral contacts with both the female and male genitalia, usually in this sequence, followed by intercourse in a number of positions. (Gagnon and Simon 1987: 2)

Men's reviews of paid-for sex on www.punternet.com show striking similarities with the sexual script outlined above. As 'Alan's' review indicates:

During the session Racquel kisses (with tongues) and cuddles, she also appears to enjoy receiving oral. Her oral (with) is exceptional and very gentle, she kissed and nibbled my balls then licked and sucked my cock taking it deep into her mouth. The sex to completion (her on top) was also excellent.

Men's reviews highlight that giving pleasure to female sex workers – usually in the form of cunnilingus or masturbation – is important. This could be interpreted either as highly altruistic behaviour, or as an action which maintains and constructs masculine heterosexual identity; the latter view is endorsed here. Indeed, some men purport to be so good that they believe the sex worker should pay them:

> … she starts licking my balls and all along my very stiff cock licking the end like a lollipop finally sucking down on me hard she seems to love sucking cock … now I'm ready to have that wet pussy and is she wet, her legs hook around my neck and do I ram her hard, she is really thrusting me hard now pleading for more maybe she should pay me for the pleasure I am giving her. [Bigjohnuk]

Carol Vance (1984) suggests that men's concern with reciprocity may demarcate a more egalitarian type of sexual standards. However, it is more likely that such gifting is gendered and unequal, as Jackie Gilfoyle et al. note:

> … women are seen as the object who is both 'given away' and 'given to'; while men, on the other hand, are seen as the subject, maintaining their dominance by both being the recipient of the woman and conferring on the object (woman) the gift of pleasure or orgasm. (Gilfoyle, Wilson and Brown 1992: 218)

There is very limited evidence within the previously published literature on sex work which suggests that women enjoy sex work. Joanna Brewis and Stephen Linstead, for example, refer to the term 'heaven trade' to describe 'clients whom the worker finds irresistibly attractive' (2000: 220). In contrast, other researchers such as Roberta Perkins and Garry Bennett (1985) and Susan Edwards (1993) argue that sex workers have little job satisfaction and rarely experience any sexual excitement. Men's reviews of paid-for sex would beg to differ.

Oooh! Pleasure and the female orgasm

The majority of positive reviews on www.punternet.com highlight the way in which men believe that they give pleasure to sex workers. 'DelBoy' and 'Fireblade' describe their experiences of this:

> More kissing was followed by me going down on her which she seemed to enjoy … [DelBoy]

> Not wishing to disclose too many personal details – but suffice to say Paula's speciality is her 'A' level, where I believe she passed with honours, and as I've already said I'm a 'bum' man, and so this was a great experience. An added bonus was that Paula seemed to really enjoy that part too. [Fireblade]

André Béjin (1986) has written about the 'orgasmic imperative', arguing that it is a pervasive feature of modern heterosex. That is, orgasm is now seen as the 'normal' and 'natural' outcome of sexual experience. According to Paula Nicholson (1993), this imperative has come to symbolise sexual competence, and has been (re)produced in sexological, therapeutic and feminist discourses. The orgasmic imperative is also evident in everyday talk, for example as Tavella argues, 'Men have become very concerned about this lately, always asking "Did you? Did you come?"' (Tavella 1992: 2). However, as Celia Roberts *et al.* argue, central to this is not women's pleasure per se but that: 'Giving women an orgasm is a demonstration of the man's sexual capacities and skill' (1995: 526).

In www.punternet.com men's accounts of giving pleasure in paid-for sex are dominated by discussion of the female orgasm, as the following extract indicates:

> Her pussy tasted sweet, and I could tell she was enjoying herself, as I licked her her hand came down to spread her lips and tease her clit, her moans got louder and she tensed up, I tasted her juices as she reached her climax, her fingers had gone White while gripping the bed as she came. [Slappy]

In fact, men spend proportionately more time writing about women's pleasure than they do writing about their own experiences of orgasm, which is often just described as 'the inevitable' and left at that.

Men's reviews of sexual pleasure are generally consistent with what is known about this within a non-commercial context; that is, while women frequently report faking orgasm, the majority of men do not believe that the women they have sex with do (Holland *et al.* 1998; Roberts *et al.* 1995). However, considerable attention is given within men's reviews to establishing the genuineness of women's orgasm. This issue is often discussed in detail with men providing a full account of how and why they believe a genuine orgasm has taken place. According to the data, seemingly verifiable signs include plentiful lubrication and pleasure noises. For example:

> ... she started to ride my (covered) cock she just went wild. I am sure she came from the noises she was making. [Sj]

> I must have spent a good 10 mins down there. She made all the right noises and I think she definitely orgasmed. [Bob]

Of course, one only has to recall the now famous scene in the film *When Harry Met Sally* in which, in a busy Manhattan diner, Sally loudly proves her point that men cannot tell when women are faking an orgasm! Indeed, previous research highlights that sex workers commonly fake orgasm for their clients' benefit. For example, Charlotte, a London sex worker, states; 'The men really want to believe that you fancy them. They love it when you make a lot of noise. They really kid themselves that you're enjoying it' (in Salvadori 1997: 120).

Faking orgasm generates anxiety for both men and women (Roberts *et al.* 1995) in that commercial sex is not only about men's pleasure but about men giving pleasure to women. However, just as non-commercial heterosex centres on notions of reciprocity so, too, does commercial sex. When men pay for sex they are also paying for a sexual performance – real or otherwise – in which their sexual prowess is affirmed through the sex worker's own pleasure. As Paula Nicolson and Jennifer Burr note, the orgasmic imperative ensures that women are responsible for ensuring that men experience themselves as good lovers and 'if the woman fails to enjoy sex, then she is somehow to blame, because if she were not, it would suggest male sexual inadequacy' (2003: 1737).

Bringing men in: concluding thoughts

The internet has offered men who pay for sex an opportunity to create a social world in which paying for sex is no longer the activity of the lone, deviant male, but part of a collective, normative social and moral order. Websites such as www.punternet.com also offer men the opportunity to communicate, exchange ideas and engage with one another, and with sex workers. Such websites also provide academics, researchers and other interested parties a window into the world of men who pay for sex – a window which has only ever partially been opened.

Excluding men from research on sex work has served to perpetuate the myth that the 'problems' of the sex industry can, yet again, be blamed on women, serving to (re)focus attention on female sex workers as the subjects of discussion, regulation and surveillance. Excluding men also buys into the illusion that the men who pay for sex are either bad, mad or sad, and perpetuates the idea that 'we' know what 'they' want and, therefore, should not bother to find out. Although raising many challenges (for example, see Earle and Sharp 2007), using the internet to research paid-for sex has presented researchers with an exciting opportunity to bring men into analyses of sex work.

References

Béjin, A. (1986) 'The influence of the sexologists and sexual democracy', in P. Ariès and A. Béjin (eds) *Western Sexuality: Practice and Precept in Past and Present Times*. Oxford: Basil Blackwell.

Brewis, J. and Linstead, S. (2000) *Sex, Work and Sex Work: Eroticizing Organization*. London: Routledge.

Campbell, R. (1998) 'Invisible men: making visible male clients of female prostitution', in J.E. Elias, V.L. Bullough, V. Elias and G. Brewer (eds) *Prostitution: On Whores, Hustlers, and Johns*. New York: Prometheus Books, pp. 155–71.

Chapkis, W. (1997) *Live Sex Acts: Women Performing Erotic Labour*. London: Cassell.

Earle, S. and Sharp, K. (2007) *Sex in Cyberspace: Men Who Pay for Sex*. London: Ashgate.

Edwards, S.S.M. (1993) 'Selling the body, keeping the soul: sexuality, power, the theories and realities of prostitution', in S. Scott and D. Morgan (eds) *Body Matters*. London: Falmer Press, pp. 89–104.

Gagnon, J.H. and Simon, W. (1987) 'The sexual scripting of oral genital contacts', *Archives of Sexual Behavior*, 16: 1–25.

Giddens, A. (1992) *The Transformation of Intimacy: Sexuality, Love and Eroticism in Modern Societies*. Cambridge: Polity.

Gilfoyle, J., Wilson, J. and Brown, B. (1992) 'Sex, organs and audiotape: a discourse analytic approach to talking about heterosexual sex and relationships', *Feminism and Psychology*, 2 (2): 209–30.

Hite, S. (1988) *Women and Love: A Cultural Revolution in Progress*. London: Viking.

Hochschild, A.R. (1979) 'Emotion work, feeling rules and social structure', *American Journal of Sociology*, 85 (3): 551–75.

Hochschild, A.R. (1983) *The Managed Heart: The Commercialisation of Human Feelings*. London: University of California Press.

Holland, J., Ramazanoglu, C., Sharpe, S. and Thomson, R. (1998) *The Male in the Head: Young People, Heterosexuality and Power*. London: Tufnell Press.

Jackson, S. (1993) 'Even sociologists fall in love: an exploration in the sociology of emotions', *Sociology*, 27: 201–20.

Jamieson, L. (1998) *Intimacy: Personal Relationships in Modern Societies*. Cambridge: Polity.

Jordan, B. (2004) *Sex, Money and Power: The Transformation of Collective Life*. Cambridge: Polity.

Lever, J. and Dolnick, D. (2000) 'Clients and call girls: seeking sex and intimacy', in R. Weitzer (ed.) *Sex for Sale: Prostitution, Pornography, and the Sex Industry*. London: Routledge.

Louie, R. Crofts, N. Pyett, P. and Snow, J. (1998) 'Project Client Call: Men who Pay for Sex in Victoria', McFarlane Burnet Centre for Medical Research, unpublished report.

McKeganey, N. (1994) 'Why do men buy sex and what are their assessments of the HIV-related risks when they do?', *AIDS Care*, 6 (3): 289–302.

McKeganey, N. and Barnard, M. (1996) *Sex Work on the Streets: Prostitutes and their Clients*. Buckingham: Open University Press.

McPhillips, K., Braun, V. and Gavey, N. (2001) 'Defining (hetero)sex: how imperative is the "coital imperative"?', *Women's Studies International Forum*, 24 (2): 229–40.

Monto, M.A. (2000) 'Why men seek out prostitutes', in R. Weitzer (ed.) *Sex for Sale: Prostitution, Pornography, and the Sex Industry*. London: Routledge.

Nicholson, P. (1993) 'Public value and private beliefs: why do women refer themselves for sex therapy?', in J.M. Ussher and C.D. Baker (eds) *Psychological Perspectives on Sexual Problems: New Directions in Theory and Practice*. London: Routledge.

Nicolson, P. and Burr, J. (2003) 'What is "normal" about women's (hetero)sexual desire and orgasm? A report of an in-depth interview study', *Social Science and Medicine*, 57 (9): 1735–45.

O'Connell Davidson, J. (1995) 'The anatomy of "free choice" prostitution', *Gender, Work and Organization*, 2 (1): 1–10.

O'Connell Davidson J. (1996) 'Prostitution and the contours of control', in J. Weeks and J. Holland (eds) *Sexual Cultures: Communities, Values and Intimacy*. New York: St Martin's Press, pp. 180–98.

O'Neill, M. (2001) *Prostitution and Feminism: Towards a Politics of Feeling*. Oxford: Polity.

Perkins, R. (1991) *Working Girls: Prostitutes, Their Life and Social Control*. Canberra: Australian Institute of Criminology.

Perkins, R. and Bennett, G. (1985) *Being a Prostitute: Prostitute Women and Prostitute Men*. London: Allen & Unwin.

Pitts, M.K., Smith, A.M.A., Grierson, J., O'Brien, M. and Misson, S. (2004) 'Who pays for sex and why? An analysis of social and motivational factors associated with male clients of sex workers', *Archives of Sexual Behaviour*, 33 (4): 353–58.

Plummer, K. (1975) *Sexual Stigma: an Interactionist Account*. London: Routledge.

Punternet (2006) website, at www.punternet.com [last accessed 2 October 2006].

Roberts, C., Kippax, S., Waldby, C. and Crawford, J. (1995) 'Faking it. The story of "ohhh!"', *Women's Studies International Forum*, 18 (5/6): 523–32.

Salvadori, H. (1997) 'UK report: my life in a London brothel', *Marie Claire*, October: 116–22.

Sanders, T. (2004) 'A continuum of risk/ The management of health, physical and emotional risks by female sex workers', *Sociology of Health and Illness*, 26 (5): 557–74.

Sanders, T. (2005) *Sex Work: A Risky Business*. Cullompton: Willan.

Sharp, K. and Earle, S. (2003) 'Cyber-punters and cyber-whores: prostitution on the internet', in Y. Jewkes (ed.) *Dot.cons: The Construction of Criminal and Deviant Identities on the Internet*. Cullompton: Willan.

Sullivan, E. and Simon, W. (1998) 'The client: a social, psychological, and behavioural look at the unseen patron of prostitution', J.E. Elias, V.L. Bullough, V. Elias and G. Brewer (eds) *Prostitution: On Whores, Hustlers, and Johns*. New York: Prometheus Books, pp. 134–54.

Tavella, P. (1992) 'Long climb to the peak', *Connexions*, 38: 2–3.

Vance, C.S. (1984) 'Pleasure and danger: towards a politics of sexuality', in C.S. Vance (ed.) *Pleasure and Danger: Exploring Female Sexuality*. London: Routledge, pp. 1–27.

Walkowitz, J. (1980) *Prostitution and Victorian Society*. Cambridge: Cambridge University Press.

Weitzer, R. (2000) *Sex for Sale*. London: Routledge.

Wyatt Seal, D. and Ehrhardt, A.A. (2003) 'Masculinity and urban men: perceived scripts for courtship, romantic, and sexual interactions with women', *Culture, Health and Sexuality*, 5 (4): 295–319.

Chapter 4

Sex, violence and work: transgressing binaries and the vital role of services to sex workers in public policy reform

Maggie O'Neill

Introduction

In this chapter I develop a feminist analysis of the relationship between sex, work and violence in order to challenge binary thinking (sex as work or sex as violence) in relation to sex work, and argue for analysis that disrupts binaries and fosters collaborations with women working in the sex industry using principles of participatory action research (PAR). I argue that in collaborating, in sharing our differences and similarities, we can work together to develop knowledge that is interpretive, interventionist and action oriented, and that creates change and makes interventions in policy and practice. Within the current socio-political context of sex work in the UK I examine: safety and violence as the basis for collaborative work across binaries; the vital importance of services to sex workers as part of this process; and the impact/importance of governance that engages and works with complexity and promotes social justice in contrast to that which re-creates binaries/liminality and the illusion of justice (however well intentioned). The chapter is illustrated with art forms created by sex workers as part of a research project commissioned by Walsall South Health Action Zone and undertaken by the author and Rosie Campbell.

Context and background

Feminist sociological and criminological research on sex work offers a wealth of rich phenomenological and epistemological data about women and young people's lived experiences, social exclusion, the endemic nature of male violence, structural, cultural and psycho-social alienation, as well as documenting and actioning resistance to these sexual and social inequalities in the form of advocacy, justice for women, networking, the development of support services to women and, recently, unionisation (McKintosh 1978; McLeod 1982; Edwards 1993; Campbell *et al.* 1995; O'Connell-Davidson 1998; Melrose *et al.* 1999; Phoenix 1999; Matthews and O'Neill 2003; Hester and Westmarland 2004; Agustín 2005; Cusik and Berney 2005; Sanders 2005). Many of us since 1982 have argued that the social organisation of prostitution is linked to poverty.

> One of the most significant aspects of contemporary heterosexual prostitution is that prostitutes, women, are grappling with their disadvantaged social position in the context of a capitalist society. Recruitment to the ranks of prostitute is not appropriately characterised as only concerning a small group of highly deviant women. It is secured by women's relative poverty still being such that for large numbers sex is their most saleable commodity. (McLeod 1982: 1)

Poverty and economic need are the bottom line for entry into street-based sex work, linked also to drug cultures and the intersection with sex markets (May *et al.* 1999; Hunter and May 2004). The socio-economic disadvantages experienced by this diverse group (sex workers) foster processes of social exclusion (O'Connell Davidson 1998; Campbell and Kinnell 2001; Pearce *et al.* 2002; Scoular 2004). Social exclusion is not just defined as poverty and economic need but also as cultural, emotional and associational exclusion – including both psychic and social alienation (O'Neill 2001).

At around the same time as McLeod was working and writing, Maureen Cain (1990) was developing a theory that made important interventions in feminist criminology. 'Transgressive criminology', constituted by reflexivity, deconstruction and reconstruction towards creative political change, sought to go beyond the traditional limits of feminist criminology, presented by Cain (1990) as a three-pronged focus on: unequal treatment; the nature of female criminality; and women as victims. In the prostitution literature we find reference to all three modes of understanding women's involvement, routes into and sustained involvement in selling sex, as well as more transgressive models.

The nature of female involvement in selling sex has been treated in an essentialist way in both policy and the academic literature, involving the construction of fixed notions of male and female sexuality and/or the nature of female criminality. Susan Edwards (1993) documents accounts of immutable male/female sexuality and how these impact upon law and the operation of justice. Yet there is a wealth of research that focuses upon women's involvement in selling sex due to being victims of sexual exploitation, poverty and male violence. Safety and violence are another key theme that I would like to highlight in this chapter and indeed I argue are a focus for potential collaborative work that transgresses the current binaries operating with respect to feminist research on prostitution. The complexities of understanding sex markets and women's involvement have led to a bifurcation in feminist responses between feminists who argue that prostitution is violence and abuse and those who argue that selling sex is 'work' – sex work – for those who choose, albeit pragmatically, to sell sex, and that they should have the protection of labour law as well as criminal law.

One camp argue that women selling sex are exploited by those who manage and organise the commercial sex industry, notably men, and that this serves to underpin and reinforce prostitution as a patriarchal institution just as patriarchy is implicated in all women's lives and gendered relations. The unequal exchange of sex and access to a woman's body in exchange for payment – albeit a bed, money, a meal – prioritises the capitalist exchange value of women's bodies and undermines the feminist project which includes challenging sexual and social inequalities and the endemic nature of male violence against women. On the other hand, prostitution is embedded in patriarchy and capitalism and underpinned by sex worker rights, and thus selling sex is defined by the second camp as work, often within the context of severely limited options for women and the fact that sex work is a 'constituent part of national economies and transnational industries within the global capitalist economy' (Kempadoo and Doezema 1999: 8). Sexual labour is a primary source of profit and the commercial sex industry operating beyond street sex markets makes a huge revenue (see Sanders 2005: 13–20, who divides the sex economy in Britain into six distinct markets[1]). Moreover, in recent years, within this context of globalisation, changing patterns of consumption and the growth of the commercial sex industry, if women selling sex were able to do so freely, with the attendant rights enjoyed by other workers and citizens, then violence would be drastically reduced and women would not be suffering such endemic levels of violence and losing their lives. Kinnell documents the murder of 84 sex workers in the UK since 1990 (Kinnell 2006). To this figure we must add the murders of five women in Ipswich over a period of ten days in December 2006. The illegal nature, particularly of street-based sex work, leaves women extremely vulnerable to violence, abuse and homicide and, as Teela Sanders makes clear, 'relying on the rhetoric of a moral order and public nuisance that frames women *either* as nefarious outcasts that need containing or as innocent victims that need protection and relocation is a dated and unrealistic reflection of the majority of women who sell sex in Britain' (2006: 111).

I argue here, as in earlier work (O'Neill 2001), that it is essential that we explore ways of transgressing these binaries. Social stigma, taboo and prejudice are embedded in social structures, processes, law and the public imagination and serve to reduce and set limits to citizenship rights and social justice for women who sell sex. This is reinforced by the current Home Office *Coordinated Strategy on Prostitution*, especially for women working on the street (Phoenix, this volume). My own position (O'Neill 2001) is a combination of the two positions outlined above in that I am committed to challenging sexual and social inequalities and the abuse and exploitation of women, young people and children, and I am committed to opening up the intellectual and practical spaces for women working in the sex industry to speak for themselves, from multiple standpoints, as critical feminist praxis. While I would like to imagine a time when women do not have to exchange access to their bodies for money, a roof, a meal or because of the pressure from boyfriends, pimps, traffickers and significant others (and remain vehemently opposed to the abuse of women and children through forced entry into prostitution), I do respect the choices that women make, especially within the context of limited options, advanced capitalism and globalisation that include the opening up of transnational markets (see Kempadoo and Doezema 1999; Agustín 2007). I am vehemently opposed to women having no choice in these matters as a result of trafficking or exploitation and remain committed to the inclusion of women in the development of policy and reform.

The influence of western Marxism, competing feminisms, ethnography and the postmodern turn in ethnographic research have led me to explore alternative ways and forms of re-presenting women's lived experience. Through ethnography and participatory action research I seek to work with the stereotyped subjects of research, to include women in the research process without reducing them to versions of ourselves. In this I have been influenced by cultural criminology and cultural sociology and also informed by equality feminism, difference feminism and postmodern feminisms (Buikema 1992). This combined approach produces strategies and a theoretical position that transgress the binaries between the two positions of 'prostitution as violence' and prostitution as 'sex work' and also negotiates a centre ground. Ethnographic and participatory research grounded in the multiple standpoints of the co-creators (women) of the research and rooted in critical theory is my chosen method. This method privileges women's voices and triangulates these voices with cultural texts, such as the photographs in the next section, that can provide a feminist perspective and analysis through 'feeling forms' that can impact on our 'understanding' of prostitution and feed into policy-making as well as feminist politics and practice.

The works of Maureen Cain (1990) and Eileen Mcleod (1982) chime well with my own feminist project. I have been researching prostitution since 1990 from the perspective of feminist critical cultural theory, and more recently have identified this work (especially the creative, visual methodologies I use) as situated within the field of cultural criminology (O'Neill 2004). Much of my research has involved combining ethnographic approaches with visual methodologies and action oriented research praxis. I am personally committed to feminist, participatory, multi-agency approaches and finding ways of working with women, young people, communities, support projects and agencies to inform and create change, and remain firmly committed to participatory action research approaches, not just methodologically, but as a philosophical, moral stance. By this I mean that I am constantly aware, personally and politically, that the relationship between knowledge, power and justice (especially when taking participatory approaches) is vital in order to produce purposeful knowledge – praxis – that challenges and seeks to transform sexual and social inequalities.

Returning to Cain's (1990) 'transgressive criminology', method-ologically participatory action research (PAR) is a very useful method/ methodology for developing a politics of inclusion and grasping the complexity of current debates on prostitution as well as for offering a critical reading of the current highly contradictory approach to prostitution policy reform documented in the Home Office National Coordinated Strategy (January 2006). Reflexivity, deconstruction and reconstruction are key ingredients of PAR as outlined below. In the Home Office strategy, involvement in selling sex appears to be incompatible with dominant meanings of citizenship (see Scoular and O'Neill 2007a), in that the strategy takes the stance of zero tolerance to street-based sex work with a focus upon compelling women to exit from prostitution. Jane Scoular and I have argued that premising social inclusion on forcing those who continue to sell sex on street to exit may fall foul of the norms of citizenship and inclusion apparent in the strategy and make social outcasts of those who refuse to accept victim status, rehabilitation and forced exit. We also argue that the strategy fails to engage with either the complexity of women's lives or an ethics of inclusion (Scoular and O'Neill 2007a). As such it is an example of the operation of the moral forces of authoritarianism (Phoenix and Oerton 2005, and see Phoenix, this volume). A major concern is that the very support services which currently offer non-judgmental, holistic services to sex workers may be compelled to focus instead primarily on exit strategies, tied to strategy-specific funding streams. PAR is an approach which can feed into more varied and user-friendly policy reforms.

The potential of participatory action research (PAR)

William F. Whyte (1989) and Orlando Fals Borda (1988), two major proponents of PAR, suggest that PAR can advance sociological knowledge in ways which would be unlikely to emerge from more orthodox sociological research. For Whyte, the element of creative surprise (that can come, for example, from working with practitioners, sex workers and residents in areas affected by street sex markets as co-researchers) is a central aspect to conducting participatory action research and advancing social-scientific knowledge. For Fals Borda the sum of knowledge from both participants and academics/researchers allows us to acquire a much more accurate picture of the reality we want to transform, and may give us a new paradigm. Fals Borda defines PAR as anticipating postmodernism, for it drew on a range of conceptual frameworks to guide fieldwork: western Marxism, phenomenology and classic theories of participation including action, and yet went beyond them (Fals Borda 1999: 1).

In my usage PAR combines critical theory, lived experience and praxis and involves creative visual methodologies as illustrated below. Maria Mies (1991) talks about the integration of research into the emancipatory process and how, in her fieldwork, women sharing the reality of their lives with other women raised questions for the women and their value systems, in such a way that a deconstructive process of 'un-learning' or critical testing took place in relation to that which women previously experienced as 'natural', 'normal' or 'universal' as a result of their socialisation. Each group of women brought their 'affectedness' (subjectivity and concern) into the research process and this led to sharpening and extending perceptions and prompted new questions (reconstruction). For Mies (1991), all this was possible because the research situation did not represent a power relationship (see also Hanmer and Saunders 1984).

What is PAR?

Participatory action research (PAR) is a methodology which encompasses social research, action or intervention, and the production and exchange of knowledge from a grass-roots perspective. Typically it enables the participation of the very people who might be the subjects or even objects of traditional research methods. PAR seeks to develop knowledge leading to social change by valuing the knowledge and experience of community members. PAR can give voice to marginalised people (without reducing them to versions of ourselves); enlighten and inform; raise awareness; make visible people's experiences and ideas for change (for example, the visual artistic can say so much more than words alone and reach a wider audience); and feed into social policy. PAR is interpretive, action oriented and interventionist and is constituted by:

- Inclusion – the stereotypical subjects of research can be included as co-researchers
- Participation – achieved through authentic participation/ collaboration not tokenism.
- Valuing All Local Voices – it involves people in theorising their practices as a learning process and it establishes 'self-critical communities' and critical analyses.[2]
- Community Driven Sustainable Outcomes – it is a political process and develops shared responses that emerge from inclusion, dialogue, learning and differences.

Reflexivity is a key component. Reflexivity is understood as 'the capacity of researchers to reflect upon their actions and values during research, whether producing data or writing accounts' (Seale 1998: 3). 'Our everyday practical accounts are not only reflexive and self referring, but also constitutive of the situations to which they refer' (Jary and Jary 2001: 550). In conducting PAR with women and young people selling sex (and refugees and asylum seekers), my aim is to recover and retell narratives of lived relations, experiences, meanings, practices and actions through immersion in their narratives. This process involves a high degree of reflexivity through immersion, dialogue, discussion and data collection followed by (not necessarily in a linear fashion) the critical distancing and reflexivity involved in interpretation, commentary and criticism. The aim throughout is the production of purposeful knowledge-praxis with the stereotypical 'subjects' of research. Social exclusion fosters a culture of silence and when researching sensitive issues PAR can provide safe spaces for dialogue. Moreover, it is inter-subjective, interpretive and action oriented.

PAR including creative and visual methodologies highlights the need for us to focus upon social justice which is distributive, cultural and associational (see Fraser 1997, 2000) and also upon cultural citizenship (Pakulski 1977). Cultural citizenship includes the right to presence and visibility rather than marginalisation, the right to dignifying representation rather than stigmatisation, and the right to identity and maintenance of lifestyle rather than assimilation to the dominant culture as the bases on which to build a radical democratic approach to prostitution reform in the UK (O'Neill 2007; Scoular and O'Neill 2007a).

In PAR research commissioned by Walsall South Health Action Zone in 1999 (and running from 2000 to 2002), Rosie Campbell and I aimed to involve communities themselves in the research process and produce research that informed policy development in order to improve the quality of life of communities. We interpret 'communities' as including sex workers. The research included partnership working across a number of agencies, the training of community co-researchers (residents) and the undertaking of creative consultation through arts-based workshops (a combination of PAR and participatory arts – PA) alongside qualitative interviews, focus groups, observation and a sex worker questionnaire. Outcomes so far include a report 'Working Together to Create Change', an art exhibition 'Safety Soapbox' and a pamphlet 'What You Told Us About Prostitution' published by members of the community who were dissatisfied with the responsible authorities, responses to the research recommendations and who wanted to produce something in order to keep the issue and dialogue on the local agenda (all available on http://www.safetysoapbox.co.uk). The collaboration was also written up in a book chapter with the community co-researchers 'Red Lights and Safety Zones' (Saleem 2003). PAR and PA offer the opportunity through reflexive practices for deconstructing and reconstructing the problem of street-based sex work in Walsall through: providing the opportunity for reflection, dialogue and creating arts work that makes visible the participants' concerns, ideas and hopes. A key finding was the focus on safety by all three groups with whom we conducted creative consultation: young people in looked after accommodation; residents living in areas of street sex work; and women selling sex. The images[3] shown in Figures 4.1–4.4 illustrate at a feeling level the issues that women selling sex are experiencing and help us to develop a better understanding of concerns around safety.

The suggestion here (but see also O'Neill 2001; Campbell and O'Neill 2006) is that, contextualised within the pioneering work of McLeod (1982), Cain (1990), Hanmer and Saunders (1984) and Mies (1991), in collaborating, in sharing our differences and similarities, we can together develop work that is interpretive, interventionist and action oriented, that creates change and makes interventions in policy and practice and that can transgress binaries. Within this context I want now to say something about safety and violence as the basis for collaborative work across binaries, the vital importance of services

Figure 4.1 Tools of the trade: 'Condoms are so important. I wouldn't go to work without them – it's a matter of life and death.'
With kind permission of Kate Green, Walsall Youth Arts.

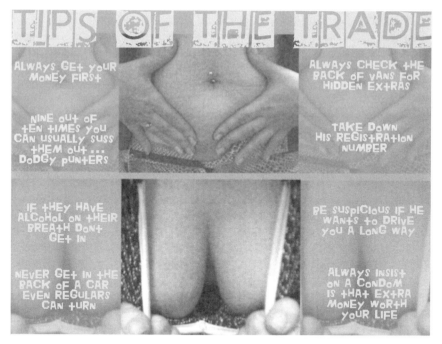

Figure 4.2 Tips of the trade: a woman who has experienced many violent attacks documents her safety tips and at the same time we see the desire of the male gaze – 'punters' in the fragments of her body on display here. 'Women working on the streets need to be aware of safety issues to protect themselves and save their lives.'
With kind permission of Kate Green, Walsall Youth Arts.

to sex workers as part of this process and the impact/importance of governance that engages and works with complexity and promotes social justice in contrast to that which re-creates binaries/liminality and the illusion of justice (however well intentioned).

Safety versus violence as the basis for collaborative work

Violence against women selling sex is endemic. Low levels of reporting and the marginal status of women who sell sex contribute to their vulnerability to sexual violence. Stigma, taboo, prejudice and moral regulation that deem street sex workers to be in need of rehabilitation serve to remove agency, disempower women and lead to a process of Othering (O'Neill *et al.* 2008). Thus women are marked as marginal, as liminal, as beyond citizenship and inclusion,

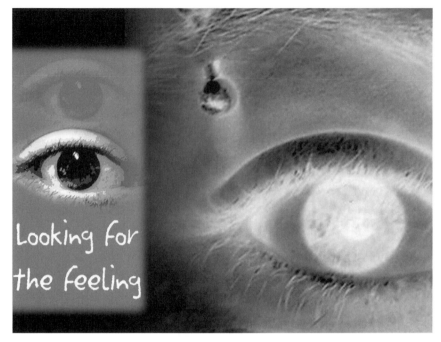

Figure 4.3 Looking for the feeling: a young woman produces a piece that reflects her feelings and could be interpreted at a number of levels – looking for emotional warmth, a feeling relationship, a connection with a potential client that indicates if he is 'safe' or not. 'When a car pulls up I look into the driver's eyes to help me decide if my life is safe or not. It is down to instinct.'
With kind permission of Kate Green, Walsall Youth Arts.

and this ultimately helps to support what Lowman calls 'discourses of disposal' (Lowman 2000).

I am not alone in arguing that even legal commercial sex is bedevilled by law enforcement strategies that 'prevent neither violence, nor exploitation, nor even public nuisance' (Kinnell 2006: 164). There is also a growing chorus of voices arguing that the 'discourse of disposal' of sex workers elaborated by residents, the media, the police and the law enhances the vulnerability of the sex worker to crimes of violence, stigma and legal bias while making exit more difficult (Bridgett and Robinson 1999; Lowman 2000).

The current national coordinated strategy on prostitution helps to frame street-based prostitution as a nuisance to communities and as a crime against moral order and public decency, and off-street prostitution as tolerable within certain limits. Within a discourse of

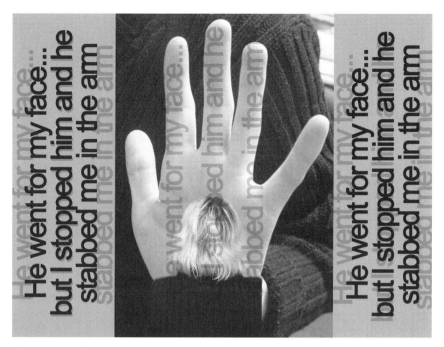

Figure 4.4 He went for my face, but I stopped and he stabbed me in the arm. 'Working on the street can lead to violent situations – our lives are at risk.'
With kind permission of Kate Green, Walsall Youth Arts.

moral and political marginalisation the addition of a discourse of zero tolerance plays a major role in the marginalisation of women who sell sex and also 'creates a social milieu in which violence can flourish' (Lowman 2000: 1009). In mapping out the contours of the discourse of disposal Lowman (2000) maintains that:

1 legal structures promote victimisation;
2 prostitution takes place in illicit markets;
3 there is convergence with other illegal markets;
4 together this alienates prostitutes from protective sources/forces.

This takes place within the context of global capitalism, consumerism, the growth of a broader sex industry that makes huge revenues and the feminisation of poverty.

What this means effectively is greater levels of alienation from cultural citizenship and from social justice for women selling sex, especially on the street. And what is most disturbing is that in the interests of safety and challenging violence, zero tolerance approaches actually offer little in the way of preventing violence against women, because any attempts to create the conditions for holistic social justice and cultural citizenship are seen as condoning sex work. Zero tolerance is antithetical to social justice for street sex workers.

Thus we desperately need to build bridges across the divisions between sex as work and sex as violence. We can and should disrupt the binaries in our collaborative work through renewing methodologies and developing participatory approaches that lead to policy-oriented praxis, and focus our collaborations on safety and violence, social justice, citizenship and governance.

In a publication in 2000 Rosemary Barberet and I argued that in part intervention strategies that were free from value judgments and which targeted women's needs offered the most effective approach to addressing violence – as part of a multi-stranded approach that includes law reform (O'Neill and Barberet 2000: 135–7). The role of support projects is vital to a multi-stranded approach. Promoting safety and challenging violence can be one of the bases upon which we foster collaborations that transgress binaries – especially with regard to feminist discourses and public policy. Support services emerged in the late 1980s funded by resources that were created to address what was called the AIDS epidemic.

Services to sex workers

Support services emerged in the late 1980s funded by resources that were created to stem what was called the AIDS pandemic. HIV prevention monies were targeted at prostitutes who were seen to be possible vectors of transmission to the general population. I had the privilege to be part of the development of POW!, a pioneering project in Nottingham, and also a witness to the work of Karen Hughes (Health Authority) who ran an outreach service for Nottingham's sex workers and went on to develop and manage the Health Shop – a drop-in service for all users offering non-judgmental, open access to all comers in addition to excellent services. I was also inspired by the work of SAFE and Hilary Kinnell whom I met in 1990 in the process of the Nottingham-based work that ran from 1990 to 1994, and undertook collaborative work with the then sex worker project (now the Women's Project) in Stoke-on-Trent.

Drawing upon work by Jane Pitcher (2006: 236) support services currently respond to a multiplicity of needs by providing:

- sexual health support and advice to marginalised groups;
- general health, welfare and legal advice;
- drug and alcohol treatment and prevention services;
- violence and safety support and advice;
- housing and homelessness support;
- arrest referral and court diversion schemes (in Manchester and Coventry);
- prison visits (undertaken in some projects);
- mediation with local communities; and
- exiting support.

These services reflect the needs of women as documented in a range of research that highlights low self-esteem, violence, drug and alcohol abuse, homelessness, harassment from police and communities, a revolving door experience with the criminal justice system, difficulties accessing statutory services and sexual health needs. Pitcher (2006) recommends that where projects can link with criminal justice agencies there is the possibility for integrated service provision but, more importantly, in the transition to exiting or temporary exiting different stages emerge for women depending upon their complex and unique personal experiences, relating to life stages, the need for seasonal work or short-term needs for additional resources.

My concern is that current public policy reform will impact upon service provision and the effectiveness and principles of good practice currently in operation in support services by compelling a shift in service provision to meet funding criteria tied to government targets. The UKNSWP[4] suggests the following good practice principles – user focused, user led/involvement, safe space, outreach services, holistic, partnership working, information sharing and harm minimisation – as being central to the work of projects. These are the backbone of quality services offering support to street-based sex workers.

There are clear difficulties in delivering good practice in a climate of criminalisation, zero tolerance and discourses of responsibilisation, rehabilitation and disposal, with exiting as the sole route to inclusion and citizenship. Projects may inevitably steer their work to exit in relation to funding streams and targets and a change in culture may emerge that will serve only to reinforce a discourse of disposal (for those who do not or cannot choose to exit) and put women at greater risk of violence and abuse. Currently, resources and funding are major barriers to projects providing holistic services and insufficient funding can lead to limited services and closure.

It is clearly important that we acknowledge the impact of public policy reform as it currently stands, and ask ourselves whose knowledge counts in contributing to reform. My suggestion is that researchers, academics and policy-makers focus upon working with women, projects, agencies, residents and communities through PAR methods in order to develop radical democratic change and collaboration across binaries. This will make it possible to challenge, address and change sexual and social inequalities. As Scoular and O'Neill (2007a: 764) write, in terms of services to sex workers there is no one size fits all and 'more nuanced understandings are necessary in order to develop public policy reform and social awareness that reflects this very complex social issue'.

The impact of governance and 'social justice'

Governance and the shaping of public policy reform on prostitution focus upon partnerships and the co-ordination of welfare and policing to enforce the law and to divert, deter and rehabilitate women who sell sex on street. We need an analysis of progressive governance in this area, and although this is outside the remit of this chapter, it is vital that this takes place. I suggest here, and elsewhere,[5] that a renewed research agenda that uses social justice and cultural citizenship as the leverage on which to base a radical democratic approach to prostitution reform is necessary. Thus, from the standpoints of feminist and critical criminology (that values phenomenological research as well as action research utilising PAR methodologies) we might engage with the theories and practices of governance and seek transformative change through dialogue and by imagining a radical democratic politics of prostitution reform with the very women who are the current subject-objects of reform.

In this chapter I have argued that concerns about the safety issues and the endemic nature of violence experienced by women selling sex should be at the centre of attempts to develop a transgressive feminist analysis of the relationship between sex work and violence using participatory methodologies. Feminists in this area working together across the binary thinking (sex as work or sex as violence) to develop knowledge that intervenes in policy and practice is crucial to the development of more women-centred policies and reform. Zero tolerance of street-based sex work is not the answer, as it leads to the increase of risks to sex workers who do not or cannot 'responsibly exit'. Instead we could advocate a shift to holistic support in the vital role of sex worker support projects. To fully understand and seek to transform prostitution policy and reform practices, we need to engage with broader governance on this issue to promote social justice for all women by working together across the divide between sex as violence and sex as work. We can create change by working with women, intervening in issues of governance and valuing the excellent work undertaken by sex worker projects which are providing support services to meet the complex needs of this highly marginalised, stigmatised and vulnerable group: street-based sex workers.

Notes

1 These are: licensed saunas, brothels, working premises, escorts, working from home and street markets.
2 'This critical analysis will help the participatory action researcher to act politically by (a) involving others collaboratively in the research process and inviting them to explore their practices, and (b) by working in the wider institutional context towards more rational understandings, more just processes of decision-making, and more fulfilling forms of work for all involved' (Taggart 1989).
3 All images can be found following the 'Gallery' link at http://www.safetysoapbox.co.uk.
4 The UK Network of Sex Work projects facilitates networking, mutual support and information for sex worker projects as well as providing a voice and common reference point. It offers a web-based resource and archive, and good practice guidelines, and runs a working group on 'Safety, Violence and Policing' as well as conferences.
5 Scoular and O'Neill (2007b).

References

Agustín, L (2005) 'Migrants in the mistress's house: other voices in the "trafficking" debate', *Social Politics*, 12 (1: 96–117.
Agustín, L. (2007) *Sex at the Margins: Migration, Labour Markets and the Rescue Industry*. London: Zed Books.
Bindell, J. (2004) 'Streets Apart', at http://www.guardian.co.uk/weekend/story/0,,1215900,00.html.
Bindman, J. and Doezema, J. (1997) *Redefining Prostitution as Sex Work on the International Agenda*, at http://www.walnet.org/csis/papers/redefining.html#1

Bridgett, M. and Robinson, J. (1999) *Sex Workers and Sexual Assault: The Hidden Crime*. Paper presented at the Restoration for Victims of Crime Conference convened by the Australian Institute of Criminology in conjunction with Victims Referral and Assistance Service and held in Melbourne, September.

Buikema, R. (1992) *Women's Studies and Culture*. London: Zed Books.

Cain, M. (ed.) (1988) *Growing Up Good: Policing the Behaviour of Girls in Europe*. London: Sage.

Cain, M. (1990) 'Towards transgression: new directions in feminist criminology', *International Journal of the Sociology of Law*, 18 (1): 1–18.

Campbell, R. and Kinnell, H. (2001) 'We shouldn't have to put up with this: street sex work and violence', *Criminal Justice Matters*, 42 (Winter): 12.

Campbell, R. and Storr, M. (2001) 'Challenging the kerb crawler rehabilitation programme', *Feminist Review*, 67 (1): 94–108.

Campbell, R. and O'Neill, M. (2004) *Evaluation of Sex, Lies and Love*. Coventry: NACRO.

Campbell, R. and O'Neill, M. (eds) (2006) *Sex Work Now*. Cullompton: Willan.

Campbell, R., Coleman, S. and Torkington, P. (1995) *Street Prostitution in Inner City Liverpool*. Liverpool: Liverpool City Council/Liverpool Hope.

Cusik, L. and Berney, L. (2005) 'Prioritizing punitive responses over public health: commentary on the Home Office consultation document "Paying the Price"', *Critical Social Policy*, 25 (4): 596–606.

Edwards, S. (1993) 'Selling the body, keeping the soul: sexuality, power and the theories and realities of prostitution', in S. Scott and D. Morgan (eds) *Body Matters: Essays on the Sociology of the Body*. London: Falmer Press.

Fals Borda, O. (1988) *Knowledge and People's Power: Lessons with Peasants in Nicaragua, Mexico and Columbia*. New York: Horizon Press.

Fals Borda, O. (1999) *The Origins and Challenges of Participatory Action Research*. Amherst, MA: Center for International Education, School of Education, University of Massachusetts at Amherst.

Fraser, N. (1997) *Justice Interruptus: Critical Reflections on the 'Postsocialist' Condition*. New York: Routledge.

Fraser, N. (2000) 'Rethinking recognition', *New Left Review*, May/June, pp. 107–20.

Hanmer, J. and Saunders, S. (1984) *Well Founded Fear: A Community Study of Violence to Women*. London: Hutchinson.

Hester, M. and Westmarland, N. (2004) *Tackling Street Prostitution: Towards a Holistic Approach*, Home Office Research Study 279. London: HMSO.

Hester, M., Radford, J. and Kelly, L. (eds) (1995) *Women, Violence and Male Power: Feminist Activism, Research and Practice*. London: Routledge.

Home Office (2006) *A Coordinated Prostitution Strategy: A summary of responses to Paying the Price*. London: The Home Office.

Hunter, G. and May, T. (2004) *Solutions and Strategies: Drug Problems and Street Sex Markets: Guidance for Partnerships and Providers*. London: Home Office.

Jary, D. and Jary, J. (eds) (2001) *The Collins Dictionary of Sociology* (3rd edn). Glasgow: Harper Collins.

Kelly, L. and Regan, L. (2000) *Stopping Traffic: Exploring the Extent of, and Responses to, Trafficking in Women for Sexual Exploitation in the UK*, Police Research Series Paper 125. London: HMSO.

Kempadoo, K. and Doezema, J. (eds) (1998) *Global Sex Workers: Rights, Resistance, and Redefinition*. London: Routledge.

Kinnell, H. (2006) 'Murder made easy: the final solution to prostitution?', in R. Campbell and M. O'Neill (eds) *Sex Work Now*. Cullompton: Willan.

Lowman, J. (2000) 'Violence and the outlaw status of (street) prostitution', *Violence Against Women*, 6 (9): 987–1011.

McKintosh, M. (1978) 'Who needs prostitutes? The ideology of male sexual needs', in C. Smart and B. Smart (eds) *Women, Sexuality and Social Control*. London: Routledge & Kegan Paul.

McLeod, E. (1982) *Working Women: Prostitution Now*. London: Croom Helm.

Matthews, R. (1996) 'Beyond Wolfenden, prostitution, politics and the law', in R. Matthews and J. Young (eds) *Confronting Crime*. London: Sage, pp. 188–215.

Matthews, R. (2005) 'Policing prostitution ten years on', *British Journal of Criminology*, 45, pp. 1–20.

Matthews, R. and O'Neill, M. (2003) *Prostitution* (Aldershot: Ashgate).

May, T., Edmunds, M. and Hough, M. (1999) *Street Business: The Links between Sex and Drug Markets*, Police Research Series Paper 118. London: Home Office, PRCU.

Melrose, M. and Barrett, D. (1999) *One Way Street: Retrospectives on Child Prostitution*. London: Children's Society.

Mies, M. (1991) *Patriarchy and Accumulation on a World Scale*. London: Zed Books.

O'Connell Davidson, J. (1998) *Prostitution, Power and Freedom*. Cambridge: Polity Press.

O'Neill, M. (1995) 'Researching prostitution and violence: towards a feminist praxis', in M. Hester, J. Radford and L. Kelly (eds) *Women, Violence and Male Power: Feminist Activism, Research and Practice*. London: Routledge.

O'Neill, M. (1997) 'Prostitute women now', in G. Scambler and A. Scambler (eds) *Rethinking Prostitution: Purchasing Sex in the 1990s*. London: Routledge.

O'Neill, M. (2001) *Prostitution and Feminism: Towards a Politics of Feeling*. Cambridge: Polity Press.

O'Neill, M. (2004) 'Crime, culture and visual methodologies: ethno-mimesis as performative praxis', in J. Ferrell, K. Hayward, W. Morrison and M. Presdee (eds) *Cultural Criminology Unleashed*. London: Glasshouse Press.

O'Neill, M. (2007) 'Community safety, rights and recognition: towards a cooordinated prostitution strategy?', *Community Safety Journal*, 6 (1): 45–52.

O'Neill, M. and Barberet, R. (2000) 'Victimization and the social organisation of prostitution in England and Spain', in R. Weitzer (ed.) *Sex for Sale*. New York and London: Routledge.

O'Neill, M. and Campbell, R. (2001) *Working Together to Create Change: Walsall Prostitution Consultation Research*. Walsall: Staffordshire University/Liverpool Hope University/Walsall Health authority, at http://www.safetysoapbox.co.uk.

O'Neill, M., Campbell, R., Hubbard, P., Pitcher, J. and Scoular, J. (2008) 'Living with the Other: street sex work, contingent communities and degress of tolerance', *Crime Media Culture*, 4 (1): 73–93.

O'Neill, M., Campbell, R., James, A., Webster, M., Green, K., Patel, J., Akhtar, N. and Saleem, W. (2003) 'Red lights and safety zones', in D. Bell and M. Jayne (eds) *City of Quarters*. Aldershot: Ashgate.

Pakulski, J. (1977) 'Cultural citizenship', *Citizenship Studies*, 1: 73–86.

Pearce, J. with Williams, M. and Galvin, C. (2002) *'It's Someone Taking a Part of You': A Study of Young Women and Sexual Exploitation*. London: National Children's Bureau for Joseph Rowntree Foundation.

Pitcher, J. (2006) 'Support services for women working in the sex industry', in R. Campbell and M. O'Neill (eds) *Sex Work Now*. Cullompton: Willan.

Pitcher, J., Campbell, R., Hubbard, P., O'Neill, M. and Scoular, J. (2006) *Living and Working in Areas of Street Sex Work: from Conflict to Co-existence*. Bristol: Policy Press.

Phoenix, J. (1999) *Making Sense of Prostitution*. London: Macmillan.

Phoenix, J. and Oerton, S. (2005) *Illicit and Illegal: Sex, Regulation and Social Control*. Cullompton: Willan.

Sanders, T. (2005) *Sex Work: A Risky Business*. Cullompton: Willan.

Sanders, T. (2006) 'Behind the personal ads: the indoor sex markets in Britain', in R. Campbell and M. O'Neill (eds) *Sex Work Now*. Cullompton: Willan.

Seale, C. (1998) *Researching Culture and Society*. London: Sage.

Scoular, J. (2004) 'The "subject" of prostitution: interpreting the discursive, symbolic and material position of sex/work in feminist theory', *Feminist Theory*, 5 (3): 343–55.

Scoular, J. and O'Neill, M. (2007a) 'Regulating prostitution: social inclusion, responsibilisation and the politics of prostitution reform', *British Journal of Criminology*, 47 (5): 764–78.

Scoular, J. and O'Neill, M. (2007b) 'Inclusion/exclusion and the politics of prostitution reform', *British Journal of Criminology*, 47 (5): 764–78.

Taggart, R. (1989) '16 tenets of PAR', at http://caledonia.org.uk/par.htm#1.

Whyte, W.F. (1989) 'Advancing scientific knowledge through participatory action research', *Sociological Forum*, 4 (3): 367–85.

Chapter 5

The bar dancer and the trafficked migrant: globalisation and subaltern existence

Flavia Agnes

Bar dancers and differing perceptions

An important feature of a rally organised by bar owners against police raids in Mumbai on 20 August 2004 was the emergence of the bar dancer into the public arena. A large number of girls with their faces covered were at the forefront of the rally holding up placards with blown-up pictures of semi-clad Bollywood[1] stars. It was a statement questioning the hypocritical morality of the state and civil society. This image became the motif for the media for the following year when the controversy around the bar dancers was raging. The media reported that there are around 75,000 bar dancers in the city of Mumbai and its suburbs and they have organised themselves into a union to resist police raids.

The mushrooming of an entire industry called the 'dance bars' had escaped the notice of the women's movement in the city. Everyone in Mumbai was aware that there are some exclusive 'ladies' bars'. But women, especially those unaccompanied by men, are usually stopped at the entrance. So, many of us did not have any inside information regarding the bar dancers. Except for those within the closed doors during the late hours of the night, they led an invisible life. But the rally on 20 August changed all that.

Soon after the rally, the President of the recently formed Bharatiya Bar Girls Union, Ms Varsha Kale, approached us (the legal centre of Majlis) to represent them through an 'intervenor application' in a writ petition filed by the bar owners against police harassment. During the discussion with the bar dancers it emerged that, while for the bar owners it was a question of business losses, for the bar girls it was an issue of human dignity and the right to a livelihood. When the bars are raided, the owners usually are let off lightly and it is the girls who are detained overnight in police custody. During the raids the police molest them, tear their clothes and abuse them with filthy language. When they are detained in police custody they are subjected to further indignities. But in the writ petition filed by the bar owners, the concerns were confined to the public image of the bars which gets tarnished during the raids, and the plummeting profit margins of the bar owners. Hence it was essential that the bar dancers themselves be heard and that they become part of the negotiations with the state regarding the code of conduct to be followed during the raids.

As far as the abuse of power by the police was concerned, we were clear. But what about the 'vulgar and obscene display of the female body' for the pleasure of drunken male customers, promoted by the bar owners with the sole intention of jacking up their profits? It is here that there was a lack of clarity. I had been part of the women's movement that has protested against fashion parades and beauty contests and the semi-nude depiction of women in Hindi films. But the younger lawyers within Majlis had come to terms with such fashion parades, female sexuality and erotica.

Finally, after much discussion, we decided to take on the challenge and represent the bar girls' union in the litigation. In order to understand the issue we spoke to many bar dancers and also visited dance bars. Though I was uncomfortable in an environment of palpable erotica, I realised that there is a substantial difference between a bar and a brothel. An NGO (a non-government organization), Prerana, which works on anti-trafficking issues, had filed an intervenor application alleging the contrary – that bars are in fact brothels and that they are dens of prostitution where minors are trafficked. While the police had raided the bars on the ground of obscenity, the Prerana intervention added a new twist to the litigation because they submitted that regular police raids are essential for controlling trafficking and for rescuing minors. The fact that the police had not abided by the strict guidelines in anti-trafficking laws and had molested the women did not seem to matter to them. At times, after the court proceedings, we ended up being extremely confrontational and emotionally charged, with Prerana representatives accusing us of legitimising trafficking by bar owners and us retaliating by accusing them of acting at the behest of the police.

Out of the closet – into the public domain

Sometime in March 2005, when the arguments were going on in
the High Court, the first announcement on the closure of the dance
bars was made by the Deputy Chief Minister (DCM) Shri R.R. Patil.
The announcement was followed by unprecedented media glare and
we found ourselves, as lawyers representing the bar girls' union, in
the centre of a controversy with all the right ingredients – titillating
sexuality, a hint of the underworld and polarised positions among
social activists. Ironically the controversy and the media glare made
the dance bars more transparent and accessible to women activists.
Some women's groups came out openly in support of the dancers. But
an equal or even greater number of non-governmental organisations
(NGOs) and social activists issued statements supporting the ban.
Among them were child-rights and anti-trafficking groups led by
Prerana. The women members of the National Congress Party (NCP),
to which Shri R.R. Patil belongs, came out in protest, brandishing
the banner of depraved morality. Paid advertisements appeared in
newspapers and signature campaigns were held at railway stations.
'Sweety and Savrithi – who will you choose?' goaded the leaflets
distributed door to door, along with the morning newspaper. The
term Savrithi denoted the traditional *pativrata*,[2] an ideal for Indian
womanhood, while Sweety denoted the woman of easy virtue, the
wrecker of middle-class homes.

Suddenly the dancer from the shadowy existence of the city's
sleazy bars had spilled over into the public domain. Her photographs
were splashed across the tabloids and television screens. She had
become the topic of conversation at street corners and marketplaces,
in ladies' compartments of local trains and at dinner tables in middle-
class homes. Every one had an opinion, and a strong one at that:
in her favour, or more likely against her: was she 'saint' or 'sinner'
… 'worker' or 'whore' … spinner of easy money and wrecker of
homes or victim of patriarchal structures and market economics?
The debate on sexual morality and the debasement of metropolitan
Mumbai seemed to be revolving around her existence (or non-
existence). The anti-trafficking groups who had been working in the
red light districts had no impact on the child trafficking brothels that
continue to thrive. But in this controversy, brothel prostitution and
the trafficking of minors were relegated to the sidelines. The brothel
prostitute was viewed with more compassion than the bar dancer
who might or might not resort to sex work.

The bar dancer was made out to be the cause of all social evils and depravity. Even the blame for the Telgi scam[3] was laid at her door: the news story that Telgi spent Rs 9,300,000 on a bar dancer in one night was cited as an example of their pernicious influence. The criminal means through which Telgi amassed his wealth faded into oblivion in the fury of the controversy.

Hypocritical morality

Was it her earning capacity, the legitimacy hitherto awarded to her profession or the higher status she enjoyed in comparison to a sex worker that invited fury from the middle-class Maharashtrian moralists?

While the proposed ban adversely impacted on the bar owners and bar dancers from the lower economic rungs, the state proposed an exemption for hotels which hold three or more 'stars', clubs and gymkhanas. Those of us who opposed the ban raised some uncomfortable questions. Could the state impose arbitrary and varying standards of vulgarity, indecency and obscenity for different sections of society or classes of people? If a number in a Hindi film can be screened in public theatres, then how can an imitation of the same be termed vulgar? The bar dancers imitate what they see in Indian films, television serials, fashion shows and advertisements. All these industries use women's bodies for commercial gain. There is sexual exploitation of women in these and many other industries. But no one has ever suggested that you close down an entire industry because there is sexual exploitation of women! Bars employ women as waitresses and the proposed ban would not affect this category. Waitresses mingle with the customers more than the dancers who are confined to the dance floor. If the anti-trafficking laws had not succeeded in preventing trafficking how could the ban on bar dancing prevent trafficking? And if certain bars were functioning as brothels why were the licences issued to them not revoked?

Since the efforts of the Deputy Chief Minister to get an ordinance signed by the Governor failed, the government drafted a bill and presented it to the State Assembly. It amended the Bombay Police Act 1951, by inserting certain additional sections. On 21 July 2005 the bill was passed at the end of a 'marathon debate'. Since the demand for the ban was shrouded with the mantle of sexual morality, it was passed unanimously. The debate was a marathon. There was little opposition, but every legislator wanted to prove his moral credentials.

No legislator would risk sticking his neck out to defend a lowly bar dancer and tarnish his own image. In the visitors' gallery we were far outnumbered by the pro-ban lobby, the 'Dance Bar Virodhi Manch', which had submitted 150,000 signatures to the Maharashtra state assembly insisting on the closure of dance bars.

It was a sad day for some of us, a paltry group of women activists, who had supported the bar dancers and opposed the ban. We were sad, not because we were outnumbered, not even because the Bill was passed unanimously, but because of the manner in which an important issue relating to women's livelihoods, which would render thousands of women destitute, was discussed. We were shocked at the derogatory comments that were passed on the floor of the House, by our elected representatives, who are under the constitutional mandate to protect the dignity of women! Not just the bar dancers but even those who spoke out in their defence became the butt of ridicule during the Assembly discussions. The comments by the legislators while debating the bill protecting the dignity of women were frivolous at best and downright bawdy and vulgar at their degenerate worst.

One member stated: 'We are not Taliban but somewhere we have to put a stop. The moral policing we do, it is a good thing, but it is not enough … we need to do even more of this moral policing.' Suddenly the term 'moral policing' had been turned into a hallowed phrase!

These comments were not from the ruling party members who had tabled the bill but were from the opposition. Their traditional role is to criticise a bill, to puncture holes in it, to counter the argument, to present a counter viewpoint. But on that day the house was united across party lines and all were playing to the gallery with their moral one-upmanship. No one wanted to be left out. Not even the Shiv Sena, whose party high command is linked to a couple of dance bars in the city, supported the ban on 'moral' grounds. The Marxists were also one with the Shiv Sainiks. The speech by the Community Party of India (Marxist) (CPI(M)) members was even more scathing than the rest.

It was a moral victory for Shri R.R. Patil. In his first announcement in the last week of March 2005 he said that only bars outside Mumbai would be banned. A week later came the announcement that the state shall not discriminate! All bars, including those in Mumbai, would be banned. What had transpired in the intervening period is unknown. But what was deemed as moral, legal and legitimate suddenly, a week later, came to be regarded as immoral, vulgar and obscene.

The demand for the ban was grounded on two premises which were contradictory. The first was that the bar dancers are evil and immoral – they corrupt the youth and wreck middle-class homes, hankering after easy money and amassing a fortune each night by goading innocent young men into sex and sleaze. The second was that the bars in fact are brothels and bar owners are traffickers who sexually exploit the girls for commercial gains. This premise refused to grant an agency to the women dancers. Rather unfortunately, both these populist premises appealed to the parochial, middle-class Maharashtrian sense of morality. What was even worse, the demand for a ban was framed within the language of 'women's liberation' and the economic disempowerment of this vulnerable class of women came to be projected as a plank which would liberate them from sexual bondage.

On 14 August 2005, at midnight, as the music blared in bars packed to capacity in and around the city of Mumbai, the disco lights were turned off and the dancers took their final bow and faded into oblivion. As the state celebrated Independence Day, an estimated 75,000 girls, mainly from the lower economic strata, lost their means of livelihood.

Some left the city in search of options. Some became homeless. Some let their ailing parents die. Some pulled their children out of school. Some were battered and bruised by drunken husbands as they could not bring in the money to make ends meet. Some put their pre-teen daughters out for sale in the flesh market. And some committed suicide … just names in police diaries – Meena Raju … Bilquis Shahu … Kajol … In the intervening months there were more to follow. A few hung on and begged for work as waitresses in the same bars.

The exit of the dancer brought the dance bar industry to a grinding halt. Devoid of glamour and fanfare, profit margins plummeted and many bars closed down. A few others braved the storm and worked around the ban by transforming themselves into 'silent bars' or 'pick-up points' – slang used for the sex industry. Left with few options, women accepted the paltry sums thrown at them by customers to make ends meet. Groups working for the prevention of HIV/AIDS rang a warning bell at the increasing number of girls turning up for STD check-ups.

Constructing the sexual subject

Soon after, petitions were filed in the Mumbai High Court challenging the constitutionality of the Act by three different segments – the bar owners' associations, the bar girls' union and social organisations.

After months of legal battle finally the High Court struck down the ban as unconstitutional. The judgment was pronounced on 12 April 2006 to a packed court room by a Division Bench comprising Justices F.I. Rebello and Mrs Roshan Dalvi. It made national headlines. The ban was struck down on the following two grounds:

- The exemption (given to certain categories of hotels as well as clubs, etc.) has no reasonable nexus to the aims and objects which the statute is supposed to achieve and hence it is arbitrary and violative of Article 14 of the Constitution of India (the clause of equality and non-discrimination).

- It violates the fundamental freedom of the bar owners and the bar dancers to practise an occupation or profession and is violative of Article 19(1)(g) of the Constitution.

The second ground is a significant development and nearly half of the extensive 257-page judgment deals with this concern. 'Are our fundamental rights so fickle that a citizen has to dance to the State's tune?' was the caustic comment.[4] Further, the court held:

> The State does not find it offensive to the morals or dignity of women and/or their presence in the place of public entertainment being derogatory, as long as they do not dance. The State's case for prohibiting dance in dance bars is that it is dancing which arouses physical lust amongst the customers present. There is no arousing of lust when women serve the customers liquor or beer in the eating house, but that happens only when the women start dancing … The right to dance has been recognised by the Apex Court as part of the fundamental right of speech and expression. If that be so, it will be open to a citizen to commercially benefit from the exercise of the fundamental right. This could be by a bar owner having dance performance or by bar dancers themselves using their creative talent to carry on an occupation or profession. In other words, using their skills to make a living …[5]

A glaring discrepancy in the arguments advanced by the state was in the realm of the agency of this sexual woman. At one level the state and the pro-ban lobby advanced an argument that the dancers are evil women who come to the bars to earn 'easy money' and corrupt the morals of society by luring and enticing young and gullible men. This argument granted an agency to women dancers. But after the ban, the government tried to justify the ban on the ground of trafficking and argued that these women lack an agency and need state intervention to free them from this world of sexual depravity in which they are trapped. Refuting the argument of trafficking, the court commented:

> No material has been brought on record from those cases that the women working in the bars were forced or lured into working in the bars. The Statement of Objects and Reasons does not so indicate this ... To support the charge of trafficking in order to prohibit or restrict the exercise of a fundamental right, the State had to place reliable material which was available when the amending Act was enacted or even thereafter to justify it. A Constitutional Court in considering an act directly affecting the fundamental rights of citizens has to look beyond narrow confines to ensure protection of those rights. In answer to the call attention Motion, an admission was made by the Home Minister and it is also stated in the Statement of Objects and Reasons that young girls were going to the dance bars because of the easy money they earned and that resulted also in immoral activities. There was no mention of trafficking.[6]

Rather ironically the anti-ban lobby also framed its arguments within this accepted 'victim' mould: single mothers, traditional dancers with no other options. Further, it was important for the anti-ban lobby to make a clear distinction between the dancer/entertainer and the street walker, and to base the arguments squarely upon the fundamental right to dance. The sexual eroticism inherent in dancing had to be carefully crafted and squarely located within 'Indian traditions' and the accepted norm of 'Bollywood gyrations' and not slip beyond into sexual advances. The emphasis had to be for a right to livelihood only through dancing and not beyond.

During the entire campaign, the world of the bar dancer beyond these confines lay hidden from the feminist activists who were campaigning for their cause and was carefully guarded by the bar dancer. Only now and then would it spill over more as a defiant statement. So while we were exposed to one aspect of their lives which had all the problems – of parenting, poverty, pain and police harassment – we must admit that this was only a partial projection, an incomplete picture. We could not enter the other world in which they are constantly negotiating their sexuality, the dizzy heights they scale while they dance draped in gorgeous chiffons studded with sequins, oozing female eroticism and enticing their patrons to part with a generous tip.

The trafficked woman

Prior to the ban, the state administration initiated some discussion about the possible rehabilitation of the bar dancers. However, when they realised the enormity of the proposition, they hastily modified their stand. According to the Deputy Chief Minister, Shri R.R. Patil, it was neither feasible nor desirable to rehabilitate the dancers. Showing little or no consideration towards the 'cause and effect' of its policies and actions, the Maharashtra government absolved itself of its responsibility, citing statistics of the larger proportion of women who come to Mumbai from 'outside' as an excuse for its indifference.

Finally, by the time the ban was implemented, the rehabilitation proposal had been abandoned altogether. This was justified by the baseless allegation that the dancers were earning easy money and that they had amassed huge amounts of unaccounted wealth. This assertion was completely untrue for the overwhelming majority of the dancers. Based on this myth, the government contended that there was no need for any rehabilitation measure.

Faced with negligible employment options and the destitution of their families, some dancers negotiated with the bar owners and via the media a solution was reached to employ the former dancers as waitresses in ladies' service bars. Given the fact that the majority were illiterate, this was the best option for them to 'rehabilitate' themselves at a lower rung within the familiar environment of the bars, where there is no stigma attached to the former bar girls.

Waitressing is a perfectly valid option with regard to all the existing legislation, including the latest Amendment to the Bombay Police Act. However, women employed as waitresses continued to face harassment. The police continued to hound these women and harass them on various pretexts. They were abused and taunted to and from work and the police continued to demand their haftas (bribes) from the women, now earning negligible amounts barely sufficient to meet their basic needs.

The state continued to hound the women in other ways too. In fact, no avenues were left out in the witch-hunt that followed and still continues to this day. The DCM went to the extent of announcing to the press that the witch-hunt could now be public – a licence and an invitation. The news that one or two bar dancers (e.g. Taranum) had been discovered to have large amounts of unaccounted wealth was blown out of proportion to suggest that all bar girls have such wealth. The DCM went to the extent of making a public announcement that people could now go out and hound the bar dancers. Whoever was successful would be rewarded with 20 per cent of the moolah (takings). This was not a general announcement, but one specifically targeted at bar dancers.

In the midst of this increasing public vilification of bar girls, on 26 August 2005 around 85 bar dancers who were working as waitresses were arrested. While the bar owners, managers and male staff who were arrested were released on bail the very next day, the women, driven to penury, could not pay the huge amount of Rs 15,000 and languished in prison cells. Along with students from the Tata Institute of Social Work who visit women's cells as part of their field work, we met these women. Later we intervened with the bar owners' association and after months of negotiations finally the girls were released on bail.

It was during our prison visits that we came across yet another layer of bar dancers. These were recent migrants and were the poorest of the poor and they were still in custody as they lacked even a basic support structure in the city. They had no friends or relatives in Mumbai. They also did not have any identification such as a ration card or voter card, and it was obvious that they were recent migrants. Most girls spoke Bengali and some admitted to being Bangladeshis, while others denied this. In a study conducted by SNDT University[7] along with women's groups, where 500 girls were interviewed, there were a significant number of Bengali girls, but they all hailed from Kolkota and most had Hindu names. (It is not uncommon for bar dancers to change their names when they come to the bars and the names they take on are usually of famous stars from Bollywood or television serials. When we asked them their names they would respond, 'Which name should I give – the family name or the bar name?' We would be taken aback by this response. For these girls the usual markers like name and address were not the markers of their existence in the city. So their lives had been truly invisible prior to the public bar girls controversy.)

Through our interviews we were able to detect a migration pattern and also to probe into issues of trafficking. The girls claimed that they came to Mumbai through networks. Initially they were brought to work as domestic maids but later they were introduced to bars where they worked as waitresses or dancers. There was no coercion or force in getting the women to work at the bar.

Though the women did not come to Mumbai intending to work in the bars, most now say that this work is the best option for them in their present circumstances since they are earning far more than they would as domestic workers and they enjoy a certain degree of economic freedom. During our interviews, when asked whether they would go back to the bars after their release, initially they denied this and stated vehemently that they would never work in a bar again because the work was undignified and humiliating. There was also the fear that they might get arrested. But on further probing they admitted that it was their best option and that if the ban was lifted then they would go back to working at the bar.

One could surmise that the women were 'duped' as they did not know that they were coming to Mumbai to work in bars. They came to seek better employment opportunities as domestic workers. But it is also possible that the so-called 'friend' who brought them to Mumbai did so with the intention of introducing them to the bars and one can surmise that there are certain chains through which women migrate to metro cities, which can be termed as trafficking. However, while there may be some sort of cheating/deception on the part of the friend, there do not appear to be any organised trafficking links operating to bring these girls and lure them into sex work.

There was no compulsion, other than their own economic compulsion, that made them become bar dancers. The women arrive at some sort of arrangement with the friend who had got them the bar work. Most paid the friend a daily amount, generally Rs 100/- for food and lodgings. The women were not in any manner controlled by the bar owners. They lived separately, were paid daily and travelled to and from their rooms.

As regards the accommodation, the system of daily rent of Rs 100/- is the norm. We had not come across it earlier as we generally dealt with a slightly more prosperous level of bar dancers. These women were from poorer strata than most dancers we had interacted with so far. Initially, in our minds we linked their living arrangements to prostitution, but later we realised that at this level it is common to have shared accommodation on daily rental basis with an average of about four to six girls sharing a room. If the girl changed her bar she would also change her accommodation. It was very simple. Thus our initial suspicion that the daily room rent was an indication of prostitution was not true.

String operation and the backlash

Just when we had surmounted the hurdle of getting these girls released on bail through negotiations with the bar owners, there was yet another incident, this time far more lethal and its implications far more grave. In October 2005, while the bar dancer issue still had a lot of news value and the High Court case was still pending, this incident made news headlines and shattered the lives of many former bar dancers. A television channel splashed a sensational story: the rape of a former bar dancer in the satellite town of Nerul in Navi Mumbai. The case as it unfolded had all the ingredients of a cheap thriller – the string operation carried out by a reporter of a television channel and her 'source', then the filing of the case and the media hype that followed, the detention of the victim in police custody for two days, followed by the news of her retraction before a magistrate and the questioning by the police of the journalist which ended in a dramatic suicide bid by the alleged 'source' who named the police and the reporter in his suicide note. In these murky events, it became extremely difficult to gauge who was the victim and who the culprit. The situation kept changing each day, and finally the cop emerged as the gullible victim of this sordid story.

Entangled amid the twists and turns of this high-profile sexual thriller were two powerful players – the state and the media. Whose career was intended to be boosted up through the string operation and whose tarnished image had to be salvaged through the retraction are questions which have easy and straightforward answers. The starkness of the plight of the former bar dancer, estranged from her husband and the butt of the state's moral purging, strikes you in the face and blinds you.

But what has not been so easily discernible is the vicious retaliation by the state on the entire local community of bar dancers in Nerul and surrounding areas. The day the retraction was reported, the papers also carried reports of a police crackdown, in what were termed as flushing out operations. They arrested around 91 people, of whom 65 were former bar dancers – impoverished and illiterate, mostly Muslim, predominantly Bengali speaking. Damned as illegal immigrants, they will be languishing in prison cells until they are able to produce papers to prove their claim to Indian citizenship.

Meeting the family members of these ill-fated women was a harrowing experience. That was when we confronted the naked strength of the state in a peacetime 'operation'. Forlorn teenaged boys sobbed while asking for news about their detainee mothers. Elderly women came with infants in arms asking what they ought to be doing with these motherless toddlers. Young girls reported that, fearing the midnight knock on the door, they are spending nights in deserted and dilapidated buildings in the outskirts of the township. Others confided that they lock their houses from the outside and huddle together in a corner the whole night, so that they are rendered invisible. Several girls, Bengali and non-Bengali, Hindu and Muslim, complained about daily police harassment and extortion. The raids are no longer carried out in the bars, now they are on the streets, in the marketplace, in their homes – there were no safe spaces left.

There was just one unspoken question in everyone's eyes: what had gone wrong? Nothing much really. Just that a lowly bar dancer living on the edge of life had been goaded, under a false sense of security, to dare to pose a challenge to the might of the state. The rape of a former bar dancer, which would otherwise have gone unnoticed, was pushed to the limit by the media and could have had grave implications for the state in the case pending before the High Court. So the entire community had to pay the price. This time the state machinery was wiser. The girls were not arrested under the newly amended Bombay Police Act but under the Foreigners' Act with no avenues open for bail or release. The only option ahead was deportation. The situation had become even worse due to certain extraneous political and legal incidents. One was the series of bomb blasts that occurred in Delhi markets on 27 October 2005. The newspapers reported that terrorists had entered the country not from Pakistan but through the porous borders between India and Bangladesh. The second was the Supreme Court decision regarding the Assam Foreign National Act where deportation could occur even without due process of law. The seal was secured firmly on the former bar dancers: they were guilty and could be held captive and later deported unless they could place before the court the necessary documents to prove their identity as Indian nationals. The requirements for proving nationality were far beyond this motley group of poverty-stricken women who had come to Mumbai to seek bare survival.

As one undernourished teenager who admitted that she was a Bangladeshi mentioned to us poignantly:

Didi, I had not eaten for a week, there was no milk in my breast and my three-month-old child was starving. If we had not crossed the border, we would have all died. After coming into India, I have left my baby with my mother in a village in West Bengal and have come here six months ago so I can earn some money to keep myself, my mother and my child alive. You may do anything, but I can never return to my country. If I do I will die.

How does one respond to this desperate pleading for mere survival, particularly when countered on the other side with grave questions like terrorism and national security?

It is not that there weren't such 'push back' operations in the past. But that was years ago, during the BJP-Shiv Sena rule. In those days, the 'illegal migrant labour' was predominantly male. And the voices of the secular forces protesting against them were loud and clear, and high-pitched. Several citizens' reports had condemned the inhuman manner in which the deportations were carried out. The left-wing government in West Bengal had protested against the treatment of Bengali Muslims and raised a voice against the deportations.

But times have changed. Now it is the secular and Left-supported Congress government at the centre and a Congress-NCP alliance in the state. Those who are arrested are not male migrant labourers but morally debased former bar dancers. Hence the voices of protest are weak and feeble, just a motley group of women activists. And no one else really cared.

You might wonder how the entire incident ended. We talked to lawyers, human rights activists and members of national and West Bengal Women's Commission groups in Bangladesh. We had the option of 'exposing' the story to the media, filing a writ petition in the High Court and gaining even greater visibility and thus a name for ourselves and our organisations. But as we were thinking and planning the desperate voices of the women and girls kept haunting us, 'Didi please leave us alone. Let us get deported rather than languishing in these prison cells. Let them take us to the border and we will find our way back.' It is this plea that paralysed us into inaction and gradually, as the High Court case regarding the ban progressed, we heeded their advice and retreated. In fact I can safely surmise that this was the first time I had retracted from a challenging situation. But I think our strength lay in not taking on the challenge but in quietly withdrawing, accepting our own limitations and their vulnerability. It was then that I began to question the entire issue of visibility and invisibility. Were all the girls managing their lives better before the media glare came upon them? Did all of us do-gooders, the good Samaritans, including the people who formed associations or the bar owners who brought them out of the closet for the 20 August rally, do more disservice to them than help their cause? They had only one concern: that they should be allowed to live and earn in the city. And it is this very concern that was eventually jeopardised despite all the gains for every other segment that was involved.

For the media there were stories every day of erotic dancing and scenes of money being thrown which the audience loved. So no matter what the issue, more than half the screen would be filled with these erotic images which served to arouse the middle-class Maharashtrian moral sense. For the bar owners, their money-making motive could be couched in human rights concerns. For those in the dance bar union there was the constant media publicity which made them leaders overnight. For women's rights activists, it provided a new cause and newer insights and prompted a feminist awakening regarding the bar girls and their concerns. At the end of the entire episode I wonder what exactly the bar girls gained from this. And more importantly, where have they all vanished? How and where are they living and how are they making ends meet? We do not know and frankly many of the segments do not even care. While the case remains pending in the Supreme Court (probably for years on end), we have all gone back to our other concerns. Perhaps this invisible existence is far better suited to the girls' own ends than the high level of publicity all of us collectively gave them.

Gender, migration and trafficking

I come now to the final section of the chapter in which I will attempt to situate this entire experience within a theoretical framework of female migration and concerns about trafficking in the sex trade.

The combination of the lack of data on the moral cultural panic and a general confusion in conceptual approaches to migration and trafficking has led not only to questionable responses from states but also to harmful interventions by NGOs and human rights and social justice groups at both the national and international level.

The need is to examine critically the intersections of migration trafficking, labour, exploitation, security and terrorism, women's rights, sexuality and human rights. Any analysis of the complexities of the transnational female migrant must extend beyond the confining parameters of the current conceptual and operational work on cross-border movements. To this end, diverse conceptual frameworks must be explored to understand and redress the vulnerabilities of the migrant woman in the causes, process and end conditions of her migration in order to evolve alternative approaches to migration and trafficking.

While both male and female migration is driven by economic reasons, female migration is impacted upon much more by value-driven policies, that is those policies that contain gender-biased and other assumptions about the proper role of women. There is also a difference in the kind of work available to male and female migrants in destination countries. Males expect to work as labourers whereas women find work in the entertainment industry or the domestic work sector. Women are also in demand for professional work of specific kinds such as nursing.

We need to accept that migration does not only take place between the developed First World and the under-developed Third World and that there is greater cross-border migration within regions than from the global South to North. This is particularly true with respect to the Asian region. For example, there is considerable migration from Bangladesh to India with numbers varying from 13 to 20 million.

The cross-border movement of the transnational migrant female subject is inadequately addressed in law and policy. This inadequacy results from two conflations: the tendency to address women's cross-border movements primarily within the framework of trafficking, and the conflation of trafficking with prostitution. In order to make migration policies (both international and national) conducive to women's rights, we need to consider the nuances in the relationship between trafficking and migration and de-link trafficking from prostitution.

In every region consideration of these conceptual distinctions has been an objective. And yet either due to ideological baggage and the positions of the various stakeholders or due to the vested interest of states, trafficking is often used as a facade to deter the entry of certain categories of migrants or to clean up establishments within the sex industry.

In view of these stated or unstated agendas and positions, a human rights approach to trafficking cannot merely be confined to achieving conceptual clarity. It must develop specific and contextualised strategies and arguments to extricate the genuine concerns related to the trafficking of persons from the unstated or moralistic concerns with migration, prostitution or national security.

Migration is not trafficking, irregular migration is not trafficking, and even smuggling is not trafficking.[8] And yet, there is an overwhelming tendency to address cross-border movements of women primarily through the framework of trafficking. Trafficking is the harm that may occur in the process of migration. The singular attention on trafficking turns attention away from the larger context of migration and distorts the broader picture of women's movements. It also enables governments to focus their attention on the protection of an increasingly limited few who are deemed to be 'trafficked victims'. States and other stakeholders seem prepared to leave the sex industry alone but are instead willing to press charges against their traffickers. In this way the trafficking framework is used in an exclusionary manner to deny assistance to all those trafficked persons who manage to escape a trafficking situation through their own means, and who do not comply with the conditions for securing assistance and support.

To some extent anti-trafficking NGOs need to accept responsibility for the propagation of this image of the trafficked person as a victim. When faced with the problem of trying to attract government attention to anti-trafficking initiatives, NGOs may have resorted to this simplistic image to garner support for their activities. This victim-image does not capture the complexities of women's own migratory experiences and agendas and the image of the trafficked person needs to be conceptually reworked. For example, one conceptual move may be to shift away from the notion of a vulnerable subject to that of the risk-taking subject.

It needs to be recognised that migrants and trafficked persons, including those in prostitution, exercise agency and demonstrate decision-making abilities which seek to maximise their own survival as well as that of their families. For example, many women negotiate the terms of their own movement and utilise technological networks to plan their migration and keep in contact with those in their country of origin. Women's perceptions of themselves and of their 'exploiters' provide a further challenge to the traditional and stereotypical images of victim and perpetrator. For example, while the dominant image of women in the sex industry is that of subjugated, dominated, objectified and abused persons who are preyed upon by conniving men, studies of women in the sex tourism industry in various countries reveal that women view it as an arena of negotiations to improve their own economic situation.

In tandem with the promulgation of female 'victimhood', the trafficking agenda has come to be increasingly influenced by a conservative sexual morality that has gripped some nation states. Women have been cast in terms of modesty, chastity and innocence. Women are also seen as the hallmark of the cultural and social fabric of society such that challenges to 'traditional' gender constructions are seen as posing a dual threat – to women and to the security of society. The first threat forms the basis for a protectionist approach towards women. Within the protectionist agenda, no distinction is drawn between consensual and coerced movement, resulting in the treatment of all movement of women as coerced and reinforcing assumptions of Third World women as victims, as infantile and as incapable of decision-making.

The combination of sexual conservatism and the construction of a woman as the symbol of national and cultural authenticity are seen to lead to the stigmatism and ostracism of the migrant woman who is portrayed as an aberrant female.

If the dominant anti-trafficking approach has blurred the portrayal of the female migrant, then one way to counteract this is to view migration within the broader context of the global reality of the transnational female migrant. Migration must take its rightful place within the context of globalisation. If the flow of capital and goods encounters no borders, why should the human participants of globalisation be treated any differently? If a juridical person can be granted a transnational/multinational identity which enables borders to be crossed largely unimpeded, why is it that a natural person is being denied her identity as a global citizen? These questions must be brought to the forefront of the debate and thoroughly examined.

Notes

1 A slang term used for the Mumbai film industry.
2 The term used for mythological women who worshipped their husbands as gods, an ideal now held out for all Indian women by the Hindu orthodox and conservative segments.
3 The name of the scam unearthed which concerned the printing of a large number of official stamp papers with the active involvement of government officials and the swindling of a large amount of government resources. Mr Telgi has subsequently been convicted.
4 Para. 61 at p. 163.
5 Para. 68 at p. 183.
6 Para. 86 at p. 235.

7 Shrimathi Nathibhai Dhamodhar Thakersay College: most commonly known by its acronym.
8 For this section I am relying upon the report organised by the Centre for Feminist Legal Research (2004).

References

Centre for Feminist Legal Research (2004) *International Seminar on Cross Border Movements and Human Rights*. India: New Delhi, 9–10 January.

Chapter 6

'Getting paid for sex is my kick': a qualitative study of male sex workers[1]

Aidan Wilcox and Kris Christmann

Introduction

As with its female counterpart, male sex work (MSW) has generally been regarded as deeply problematic, either because of negative societal attitudes to the selling of sex or the prevalence of psychosocial and economic problems among those attracted to MSW and the attendant health risks and dangers it presents. While the phenomenon of female sex work has received a great deal of scrutiny by social scientists, there has been comparatively less attention paid to male sex workers (MSWs). The current research aims to further our understanding of the motivations of MSWs, the risks they face, their engagement with support agencies and intentions for the future.

Aetiology of sex work

Sociologists, psychologists and psychiatrists have taken different approaches to identifying the 'causes' of men's involvement in sex work. Early contributions tended to view male sex work as 'pathological' (Coombs 1974) and identified predisposing psychological factors, including: low intelligence, learning difficulties, emotional disturbance, sex role confusion and oedipal fixation.

More recently attention has shifted from this individual pathology approach towards those social and situational factors believed to underlie the motivation to sell sex. These studies emphasise that MSWs tend to have multiple problems including: a disrupted family life, experience of abuse and neglect by parents (Boyer 1989), poor parental role models (including approval of sex work), deprived socio-economic backgrounds, delinquent peers, poor school attendance (Coombs 1974), alienation and problematic alcohol and drug use (Morse *et al.* 1992). Any decision to sell sex also involves what Ian Shaw and colleagues (1996) refer to as 'a mix of coercion and comfort' factors such as: developing an independent personality, the desire to gain adult attention and acceptance and the experience of negative labelling.

Sex work continues to be regarded as more problematic than legal work. John Scott and colleagues (2005) note that the stereotypical image of a MSW remains one of a coerced psychopathological misfit who has been sexually abused as a child and is desperate for money. Their research has increasingly come to challenge such a view, arguing that the dominant discourses of epidemiology and sociopathology have tended to overemphasise 'problematic male sex populations' (street prostitutes) at the expense of other relatively unproblematic male sex populations (independent escort). Victor Minichiello *et al.* (1999) report that non-street workers tend to be better educated, are likelier to see sex work as a long-term occupation, are more prone to engage in safer sex and feel more comfortable with sex work than do male street workers.

Characteristics of MSWs

According to research by Peter Aggleton (1999) and Donald West and Buz de Villiers (1993) not all MSWs can be characterised as psychologically unstable, desperate or destitute. While this is not to discount the experiences of those MSWs who have suffered child abuse or whose addiction problems drive their sex work, it is to accept that the profile of MSWs is diverse and that contextual factors need to be taken into account when explaining involvement. Minichiello *et al.* (1998) argue that the visibility and ease of research access has in the past tended to skew the categories of MSW used for research, the effect of which has been to exclude the context of sex work as an organised economic activity (although the same authors caution against romanticised narratives which suggest a less exploitative relationship in male sex work than female sex work).

What these studies show is that the intrinsic nature of sex work is not necessarily oppressive and that there are different kinds of worker and client experiences which encapsulate varying degrees of victimisation, exploitation, agency and choice (Minichiello *et al.* 1998), a theme explored later in this chapter.

Research aims, methodology and limitations of the research

The research on which this chapter reports explored the experiences of MSWs in Kirklees (West Yorkshire) and neighbouring areas. Specifically, it aimed, through interviews with MSWs, to investigate their socio-economic backgrounds, motivations for entering sex work and attitudes towards it, sexuality and the risks they faced.

The male sex industry is largely hidden which makes it difficult to estimate the size and boundaries of the population. It is also characterised by differentiation between those who primarily work indoors (at home or in a sauna) and those who work on the streets. It is important, therefore, to consider the extent to which the current sample is representative of the wider population of sex workers.

Not knowing any MSWs personally, we were somewhat at a loss where to start. Serendipitously, an article appeared on the BBC website[2] describing the murder of a MSW, which named two magazines carrying adverts for male escorts. Having located a number of interviewees through these publications, we then asked our first interviewees where else they advertised and we then searched those publications. We were also directed to a number of internet sites where escorts advertised. In total, we identified a potential sample of 43 MSWs. Of the 28 MSWs we were able to contact,[3] nine were willing to participate in the research within the timescale of the fieldwork (August–September 2006).

Conducting the research in a sensitive and ethical manner was a prime concern, and all participants were informed about the purposes of the research both verbally and in writing, and it was made clear that they could withdraw at any time.

The small size of this exploratory study of MSWs means that generalisations to the (unknown size of the) wider population of MSWs cannot reliably be made. Furthermore, the way in which participants were recruited (through advertisements for escorts/massages) meant that all those interviewed were 'indoor' sex workers. Our research cannot, therefore, shed any light on the experiences of 'outdoor' sex workers (or 'rent boys'), which other studies suggest is likely to be very different (e.g. Connell and Hart 2003). However, we believe that our sample is broadly representative of the indoor male sex industry in the region. Unlike Judith Connell and Graham Hart's (2003) study of MSWs in Edinburgh, for example, our sample included those who worked mainly with couples and females as well as those who worked only with males, and also included a transvestite sex worker.

Male sex worker profiles

The nine MSWs who participated in this study ranged in age from 19 to 45, with an average age of 34 (see Table 6.1 below). All were white and in terms of sexuality six described themselves as homosexual, two as heterosexual and one as bisexual. One of the homosexual interviewees worked as a transvestite.

All but one of the MSWs had held some form of paid employment prior to entering sex work. For some, their employment history had been sporadic or irregular, in part due to difficulties in adjusting to employment on leaving total institutions (armed services, church and prison). Others had white-collar, professional or business occupations and one had a university degree. The common factor was dissatisfaction with 'regular' work, which was instrumental in leading them into sex work.

A sharply contrasting picture emerges when examining the differing childhood and family relations among the MSWs. The majority of MSWs reported either having broadly unexceptional or happy childhoods, as one remarked:[4]

> **Eddie**: Just a loving, caring normal happy family, believe it or not. No problems. There was nothing that kind of stood out. You'd go home, there'd always be food on the table, we'd always be clean, we were always in school, we always went to Mass, we did all the normal things, there was no hidden secrets ... It was just a good time.

However, there were some exceptions to this. Two respondents reported regular physical abuse perpetrated by their parents, one of which included severe neglect and violence:

> **Chris**: I was shoplifting to feed myself because I had to ... I mean days and days without food. Lost my front teeth when I were seven because my dad just hit me in the face when I took chocolate out the fridge, I had to put my two front teeth in my

Table 6.1 Male sex worker characteristics

Name	Age	Sexuality	Physical abuse	Sexual abuse	Ever in care	Housing	Criminal convictions	Age at involvement	Length of involvement
Andy	45	Homosexual	No	No	No	Owner occupier	No	36	9 years
Britney	36	Homosexual (transvestite)	No	No	Yes	Owner occupier	Yes	24	12 years
Chris	43	Bisexual	Yes	Yes	Yes	Unknown	Yes	10 & 40	2 years
Dave	26	Homosexual	No	No	No	Private rented	Yes	19	7 years
Eddie	42	Homosexual	No	No	No	Owner occupier	No	24	18 years
Frank	32	Heterosexual	No	No	No	Private rented	Yes	29	3 years
Graham	26	Heterosexual	No	No	No	Private rented	No	25	6 months
Harry	19	Homosexual	Yes	No	No	With partner	No	15	4 years
Ian	38	Homosexual	No	No	No	Owner occupier	Yes	19	19 years*

*With a nine-year break from age 24–31.

gum and by the time I woke up in the morning they had been bent right back, … I'd had a red hot poker shoved on me but this is all before I was ten.

As result of the neglect and violence he went into local authority care, an experience which he found to be enjoyable (saying 'I'd recommend it to anyone'). Three MSWs reported fractured family relationships, primarily due to their families not being able to accept their sexuality. Family rejection accompanied by death of family members meant that the three had no further contact with their immediate family. While the other MSWs were not estranged from their families, none had told their family members of their involvement in MSW. None of the MSWs reported any instances of sexual abuse.

Although five of the men had criminal convictions, in most cases these were not recent, and none had been received as a result of their involvement in sex work. In Table 6.1, some of the characteristics of sex workers are summarised.

In the next section we explore the reasons why these men became involved in sex work, the nature of that work, their commitment to sex work and plans for the future.

Male sex work – motivations, involvement and leaving

Motivations

Reasons for involvement in female sex work have been explored by many researchers, and factors include coercion, poverty, prior physical or sexual abuse and drug use (e.g. Bagley and Young 1987; Edwards 1991). However, there is no reason to suspect that motivations for MSWs are similar: indeed the evidence from our interviews is that they become involved for very different reasons.

It is notable that none of the MSWs cited coercion of any form as a reason for involvement. Neither did any of the MSWs have pimps. Although Chris, Harry and Ian had current partners, it did not appear that the partner played a coercive role in the decision to become a sex worker. Frank had once had a relationship with a female escort, but again there was no coercion in his decision to enter sex work: instead it merely confirmed him in a choice he had already made.

Britney, the transvestite sex worker, had been brought up by his mother until the age of eight (when she died) and he found out in his mid-teens that she had been a prostitute. He decided to follow her into the profession, and it was apparent that there was an element of competitiveness in his motivation for sex work:

> **Britney**: I don't want to sound like I'm blowing my own trumpet
> – but I was really, really good at what I did, but not because I
> was interested in the money, does that make sense? ... I got a
> kick out of proving I was better than or as good as the girls.

While money was a motivation for some of the MSWs in our study, for only one was it the main one. For the rest, money was a secondary motivation, behind other factors such as the freedom offered by the lifestyle and the chance to escape from the perceived humdrum of 'normal' jobs:

> **Andy**: It was mainly boredom, oh bloody hell, how long am
> I going to have to keep doing this. When I was working in
> London, travelling up and down on the train was the pits ...
> I used to see the other people on the train and think I can't
> do this for the rest of my life ... I was just like 'arghh, not for
> me!'

There was no evidence that drugs were instrumental in any of the MSWs' decision to enter sex work. Only Harry said he was currently using drugs and his drug use did not appear to be the reason for his involvement, although he did admit that drugs were a way of dealing with the stresses of the job.

None of the men in our study said that they had been sexually abused as children (Chris did not consider his sexual experiences at the age of ten as abuse), although two had experienced some form of physical abuse (which in Chris's case was severe).

For three of the MSWs, a high sex drive was given as the main reason for their involvement. For example, Frank, a heterosexual ex-services male, used escorting as a means of satisfying his sexual needs:

> **Frank**: Main motivation is me sex, I'm very, very sexually
> minded. I've been to sexaholics anonymous, I've a very high sex
> drive, I masturbate a lot ... I'm like, say some woman walks in
> there now, the first thing that comes into my head is I wonder
> whether she'd be a good fuck, that is the first instinct I have,
> and it's bad in a way ...

Not everyone found it easy to identify exactly what had decided them to turn to sex work. Eddie, who had spent several years in the church, found it hard to pin down what was the turning point for him, as the following exchange demonstrates:

> **Interviewer:** Can I just ask, sometimes I sit at home bored of an evening. How do you make that kind of leap from, oh I'm fed up, life's not great, to I know I'm going to put an advert in the paper, where does that come from?
>
> **Eddie:** I don't know. I think because I needed a new challenge, I think that was probably what it was, it was getting a bit stale. I don't know. I was looking at that question and I thought I won't be able to answer that. I don't know where it came from.
>
> **Interviewer:** So you hadn't thought about it before that evening?
>
> **Eddie:** No. And it wasn't even the fact that the electricity bill was in and I needed 50 quid, because I was working full time, I had enough money, then I thought to myself, was it just pure loneliness, well no, because I've never really felt that I've been alone … I really don't know, I just thought, let's just do it, see what happens.

Each of the interviewees had different experiences and motivations for their involvement in sex work. Certainly their motivations differ from those typically associated with female prostitution, and what stands out is that they described their decisions as being freely made. Even when money was an influence, sex work was seen as an enjoyable uncoerced activity. We discuss the notion of agency in more detail later in the chapter. Before that, we turn to the business of sex work: how MSWs meet their clients, what they do and the dangers they face.

Involvement in sex work

For most of the sex workers, involvement in sex work began either in the late teens (two of nine) or mid-twenties (four of nine). Andy, who was the oldest of the participants (46), was 35 when he started. However, for two of the sex workers, involvement began at an early age. Chris (42) said that he had first been given money for sex at the age of ten while living in a care home:

> It happened before then like, when I were ten at ... which was another kind of allocated centre place, my first night in, there were three kids, 13, 14, and 15 I think they were, well a lot older than me, and they got me to suck their dicks ... somebody give me 10 bob, which were a lot of money.

After leaving the home, he stopped sex work, and only took it up again two years ago, with the knowledge and support of his wife. The only other example of child sexual prostitution was Harry who started escorting at the age of 15.

The length of our participants' involvement in sex work ranged from six months to 19 years, and most (six) had been involved for at least six years. All worked as escorts either from their own homes or visited clients; none of the MSWs we interviewed worked in premises such as brothels or saunas. In fact, in our search of print and internet advertisements, we found very few such places, and if the advertisements we saw are representative of the indoor sex market, the majority of MSWs are 'sole traders'.

We asked the MSWs how they met their clients and why they chose this method. All of those interviewed used advertisements in the print media, while a few additionally used internet sites. There was general agreement that the internet was less likely to generate business, or that those who did get in touch this way were less likely to be genuine clients. Somewhat surprisingly, two of the escorts said that they sometimes received new clients by 'word of mouth' from existing clients. Unlike the outdoor sex industry, the MSWs in our sample were entirely reactive, dependent on clients contacting them either through their adverts or recommendations.

The sexuality of MSWs determined what types of clients they would take. Two of the MSWs were heterosexual and so would not see single male clients. In fact most of their clients were couples, but they refused to have any direct sexual contact with the males (they would, however, participate in a 'threesome' or let the man watch). Of the rest, six described themselves as gay (including the transvestite), and their clients were almost exclusively male, although one or two entertained couples occasionally. Chris described his sexuality as 'universal', escorting males, females and couples, and providing the widest range of sexual services.[5] Although the adverts we saw are carefully worded so as not to suggest that sex is involved (they are in fact typically very briefly worded, for example 'mature male, M62, offers massage'), by definition, all the MSWs offered full sex:

Dave: It makes me laugh sometimes, some of them come along and say they just want a massage and they try to beat the price down because it's only a massage, but they never only want a massage!

When asked about the sexuality of their clients, they were described as 'all shades of the spectrum'. The gay MSWs thought that some of their clients were either bisexual or gay, and a surprising number were said to be married or with female partners. Britney, the transvestite, said that many of his clients claimed not to be gay, a claim he dismissed:

Britney: If I had a pound for every time someone said 'well I'm not gay really', oh fuck-off, no of course you're not love! What because I've got a fucking skirt or something on, you think that means that I'm a woman?

The amount of income generated through sex work varied considerably. Andy, who was the eldest MSW, charged £60 per session (which might last up to three hours) and saw perhaps five clients a week, generating around £300 per week. Most of the other MSWs earned more than this. Chris, for example, charged £85 for an hour and £350 for an 'overnighter', and typically earned more than £400 a week, while Frank and Graham, who both charged around £70 per hour for a minimum of two hours, and several hundred for an overnighter, said they made in excess of £600 a week. Harry and Ian were the most successful, claiming to make over £1,000 per week each. None of the men worked for an agency or pimp and thus kept all of the money they earned.

Five of the MSWs interviewed had paid jobs other than sex work. Andy, for example, was in the process of retraining as a plasterer, to prepare for the day when his declining sexual stamina would affect his sex work. Frank, who described the sex industry as cyclical, worked as a lorry driver during the 'lean times' such as during the summer holidays or after Christmas. Both Harry and Ian ran a successful pet products business, while Chris had a sideline as a gardener. The motivations for these secondary careers differed. In Andy's case, it can be seen as a way of preparing for an eventual exit from sex work, while in Frank's case, for example, it was a means of smoothing out income over the year.

We next asked MSWs about their future plans, and whether they wished to leave sex work.

Leaving sex work

None of the MSWs said that they currently wished to leave the profession. Even Andy, who was retraining as a plasterer, thought he would be doing this for years to come:

> **Andy**: I think it will probably continue, and even if I pull the ad in the [magazine] I think I'd get people ringing me up with 'are you still working?' and I'd say 'oh yes'.

Britney, who described his involvement as 'treading water', said that he would be involved, either as an active sex worker or as a 'manager', for the foreseeable future:

> **Britney**: One way or another probably forever to be honest ... recently, I've been mingling a bit, taking a day off and helping others set themselves up ... I think I'll be in it forever, until I drop dead.

All of the others similarly expressed their desire to remain in the profession, and when asked why, stressed the positive factors of the job such as the 'lavish lifestyle' (Harry), 'being my own boss ... and obviously the money' (Graham) and the flexibility of the job: 'you can choose to work two/three hours a week and take it easy, put your feet up' (Ian).

In order to explore more fully their commitment to sex work, we asked the MSWs specifically what their plans were for the future and what they thought they would be doing in five to ten years. Harry, Andy, Ian, Britney and Eddie all re-emphasised that they expected still to be in sex work. Andy, who was ambivalent about his involvement, and Britney, who was less so, thought they would still be in sex work in five to ten years' time due to its addictive nature, as Britney noted:

> It's a drug, it's addictive more than anything else because once you get into it it's so hard because even if you stop, and life is hard for everybody, and if you get a big bill for £200 it's like oh god, you know you can get back into it.

Both Graham and Chris said that they did not think five to ten years ahead or have any specific plans for the future:

Chris: Don't have none [plans]. Take each day as it comes. We used to plan things, but we don't plan nothing no more, there's too many people we know who's died ... every second of every day, people are just dying, why waste fucking time planning things, just get on with it.

Graham: Five years time is a hell of a long way away for someone who takes life day to day. It's not sort of something that I think about, the future, to be truthful. Sort of next week, the week after that, is as far as I am concerned.

Only Dave and Frank said that they would hope not to be in sex work in five to ten years. Dave said he would like to pursue property development, or a career in the creative industries, which would also offer the freedom he desired. For Frank (a heterosexual MSW) the desire to settle down and have children was creating a tension with his enjoyment of sex work:

I'm at a crossroads now, just short of 33, where if I want a family and settle down, I've got to look at the next few years. If I have a kid at 40, I feel that's too old for me, so I've only got a few years left, or in a few years time I could still want to carry on doing it, who knows?

When prompted to state who or what would help them to leave sex work, both Dave and Eddie said they would also consider leaving if they met the right person. In summary, none of the men was actively trying to exit sex work and they were generally content with their current involvement. For the minority who would consider giving it up in the future, only an external event, such as a new relationship, would cause them to reconsider.

Risks and precautions

Due to the hidden nature of MSW, sexual encounters invariably take place in locations, such as hotel rooms, or clients' or MSWs' houses, where there are no 'capable guardians', to use Larry Cohen and Marcus Felson's (1979) term. The potential for violence against MSWs therefore exists. The limited research that exists suggests that the risks are considerably lower than for female sex workers, for whom it has been argued that 'sexual and other physical violence is the normative experience' (Farley *et al.* 1998: 3). Violence from clients among 'indoor' MSWs is rare. Although outdoor workers face a higher level of violence, this tends to be related to their drug or alcohol use, or homelessness, rather than to the selling of sex per se (Connell and Hart 2003).

In order to determine the risks faced by our interviewees, we began by asking whether they had ever been sexually or physically assaulted or robbed while working. Only Ian said he had been assaulted (twice); none of the other MSWs had had any experience of physical or sexual assault or robbery, although Andy and Britney felt that they had had some 'near misses'. Even though personal experience of assault was rare, most of those interviewed believed that the profession was potentially dangerous, especially where first-time clients were concerned. Despite this, the MSWs we interviewed believed that they were able successfully to manage the risks and most took precautions. For example, when visiting a client these included letting a friend know where they would be, never turning their back on the client, scouting out the area for extra cars which might indicate there was more than one person in the house, or checking the rooms of the house on the pretext of going to the toilet. For 'incalls' MSWs would try to arrange for a friend to be in the house at the same time, or ensure access to an easy escape route. Ian and Harry, who were partners and worked together, took the most elaborate precautions, as Ian explained:

> **Ian**: I do a tag on him – he is dropped off, the phone is on all the time ... The minute his [Harry] phone goes off mine will make an alarm sound.
>
> ... For me there is a panic button in the massage area ... I have literally to open one door and 14 dogs would come through and it is not a thought you would want to cherish and people are very aware of the fact – and they're not small dogs ... We swap stories and learn who messed you about and who did this, who did that.

Only Eddie, who entertains in his own home, claimed to take no special precautions, apart from being nice to clients:

> **Eddie**: I've never had an incident where I've had violence or raised voices. I know it sounds hard to believe, but I think it's down to the way you conduct yourself and the way you conduct your business. If you are argumentative or short, or you don't

make people feel like it's their hour… that's when you're going to get problems.

Certainly by comparison with female sex work (Farley *et al.* 1998), or the outdoor male sex market (Connell and Hart 2003), the risks faced by the MSWs in our sample were very low, and generally they were taking steps to reduce the risks to a level which they found acceptable.

We return now to explore a central theme in the sex work literature, which is the extent to which one can consider MSWs victims of circumstance in need of help, or rational businessmen pursuing a fulfilling career.

Victims or businessmen?

It is common when explaining involvement in crime to talk about criminogenic risk factors, that is to say attributes of a person's character or environment which increase the likelihood of onset, frequency or persistence of offending (Farrington 1997). Common risk factors include impulsivity, parental supervision style, socio-economic deprivation and school factors (ibid.). It is argued by some that the existence of such factors *causes* involvement in crime.[6] Much of the literature on female sex work also stresses risk factors, and views involvement in sex work not as a rational choice but rather as an almost inevitable response to perceived negative influences, such as economic deprivation.

To a certain extent, the same can be said of much research into MSWs, at least those studies which concentrate on the 'rent boy' market. Connell and Hart's (2003) study on the experiences of rent boys explains involvement in sex work partly in terms of coercion or the negative influence of friends. The participants in our study, who represent the 'sole trader' indoor male sex market, present very different issues. It is true that some of the MSWs in our sample had experienced very difficult childhoods. Chris, for example, had been in care from the age of ten, and from his first night in care was selling sex. Looking at his case from the outside, this would seem to represent a clear case of victimisation and an obvious 'risk factor'. However, Chris's own views on the subject were very different. When asked if his early sexual experiences while in care were voluntary, he claimed that they were:

No, no, no, if I were forced into something I didn't want to do, I'd had got them, don't matter how many there was. And like, that weren't the first sexual experience obviously but it was in these kind of circumstances, and like the next day, the eldest of them all said he wanted to shag me arse that night and I'm only 10, so he says get a bar of soap, so I got a bar of soap, and he bent me over the bed, and he bottled it. If I knew now what I knew then, I'd have given him some fucking stick for bottling it, but he bottled it. And I never got a sore arse! [laughs]

Thus factors which normally would be seen as harmful – under-age paid sex and being brought up in care – were not viewed as such by Chris, and not the cause of his involvement in sex work, which he put down to his high sex drive. Chris was happily married and was escorting with his wife's knowledge and support. Some of the other MSWs experienced other 'risk factors' including being thrown out of home (Dave) and being made redundant (Frank and Eddie). In none of these cases, however, did these factors seem to precipitate the decision to enter sex work, and certainly none of them saw themselves as victims. Perhaps the exception to this pattern was Harry, who had started sex work at 15, and was the only one of the group to be a regular user of drugs. In his case, the decision to enter sex work could be seen as more influenced by circumstances. However, he was also in a stable relationship (with Ian), was financially secure and content with his involvement in sex work.

For the men in our study, the 'risk factor' model appears to lack explanatory power; indeed it is arguable whether the involvement in sex work of the men in our sample should be viewed as a problem in need of a solution. It was striking from our interviews how positive most MSWs felt about sex work. When asked directly what they thought about sex work, all were happy with their involvement:

Chris: I'd do it all day mate! At the end of the day, it's like me getting paid for sex is my kick ... Live and let live, I swear to God, if you're not hurting anyone what's the problem, and it won't be hurting me if I got paid!

Given such apparent enthusiasm, it sometimes felt redundant to ask questions about whether they wanted to leave sex work or what would help them to leave. Given that it was seen as a rational career choice by many, it was akin to asking successful plumbers what help they needed to leave their profession. There is some support in the literature for this view of MSW as a non-problematic commercial activity. In Sari Van der Poel's (1992) ethnographic research into MSWs in Amsterdam, the occupation was analysed as a commercial service-oriented business with economic and social characteristics typical of other small businesses.

That the MSWs believed themselves to be in charge of their own destiny is reinforced in their responses to our question about the differences between male and female sex work. Key to this was the physiological differences between males and females, in that for males to perform, they had to want to do it, as Frank explained:

> A man, some sort of thought has to go to his penis, there has to be a link between the head and the penis, the woman doesn't have to have any link between her head and her vagina.

It was believed that the physical passivity of female sex workers made them more vulnerable to exploitation or violence. For the MSWs in our sample, sex work was seen as a choice freely made. If, however, one considers the life stories of the men in our sample, with one or two exceptions, there was something in their backgrounds which served to limit the choices open to them – educational failure or personality characteristics meant that their 'choice' to participate in other, more legitimate, employment opportunities was limited. Chris is perhaps the clearest-cut example of a 'constrained' choice, in that his lack of any formal education ruled out many professions. It might also be the case that his early sexual experiences, even though perceived as enjoyable, may have caused his high libido, which in turn led him to enter sex work. The question remains, therefore, whether Chris (and the others) would have made the same decision had circumstances been different. This was not a question we were able confidently to answer. While we do not believe that certain aspects of their backgrounds propelled these men inevitably into sex work, as may be the experience of certain female or younger MSWs, neither was the choice entirely free.

In trying to understand the nature of their decision-making, it is useful to borrow from the criminological version of rational choice theory, as refined by Ronald Clarke (1987). Although sex work is not a criminal activity, the model of decision-making has wider applicability. In this, it is held that the decision to commit crime (or, as in this case, to enter sex work) is a more or less rational response to attempts to maximise self-interest. It is recognised, however, that dispositional factors and situational factors serve to constrain decision-making by closing off certain options or opening others (Bennett 1986). In terms of sex work, then, dispositional factors such as sex drive and situational ones such as level of income or the availability of alternative employment options might be expected to influence decision-making. From what the men in our sample have told us, we cannot describe them either as purely victims or calculating businessmen. It would be more accurate to locate them somewhere in between according to a 'constrained' rational choice model of decision-making.

Conclusions

This exploratory study has shed new light on this largely hidden population. The experiences and motivations of the men in our study contrasted sharply with those both of female sex workers and 'rent boys'. The indoor sex market, represented by our respondents, is relatively stable, self-contained and unproblematic. MSWs were unconcerned about their involvement in sex work, did not experience violence (with one exception) and practised safe sex. The decision to participate in sex work was seen by all to be freely made, and motivations for involvement were not primarily financial. Sex work was seen as a career like any other, but with the advantages of flexibility and variety. While some could imagine situations (for example meeting the right person) in which they would wish to leave the profession, most expected to remain in the profession for some years to come.

It is important to recognise that our sample of nine indoor MSWs is not representative of the male sex industry as a whole. However, the study does provide new insights into the experiences of the majority of MSWs – men who work on their own and for themselves. However, we have more to learn about the characteristics and motivations of these men and, in particular, the degree to which their choices are constrained by background and personal characteristics. Equally, we know very little about the motivations and experiences of the clients of these men. What is it about their backgrounds, for example, which leads them to pay for sex with male escorts? It is hoped that this study will prompt further research into this area. In particular there is a need for a larger study exploring the experiences of indoor and outdoor MSWs in order to compare these two groups both with each other and with the more thoroughly researched female sex industry.

Notes

1 This research was kindly supported by a grant from Kirklees Community Safety Service. In particular we are grateful to Phil Birch for his support and assistance.
2 See: http://news.bbc.co.uk/1/hi/uk/4939502.stm.
3 Almost all the numbers given in the adverts were of mobile phones, and some of these appeared to be permanently switched off.
4 Names have been changed to preserve anonymity.
5 Chris, for example, said he would be willing to hurt people for money: 'If they wanted me to chop their hands off or anything like that, I know it sounds callous ... but I don't see a problem with it, if both parties are happy about it, then fine'.
6 There are, of course, other theories of crime which place less weight on causes such as socio-economic deprivation and which stress the interaction of decision-making, opportunity and capable guardianship (e.g. Cohen and Felson 1979).

References

Aggleton, P. (1999) *Men Who Sell Sex* (London: UCL Press).

Bagley, C. and Young, L. (1987) 'Juvenile prostitution and child sexual abuse: a controlled study', *Canadian Journal of Community Mental Health*, 6: 5–26.

Bennett, T.B. (1986) 'Situational crime prevention from the offenders' perspective', in K. Heal and G. Laycock (eds) *Situational Crime Prevention: From Theory into Practice*. London: HMSO.

Boyer, D. (1989) 'Male prostitution and homosexual identity', *Journal of Homosexuality*, 17 (1/2): 151–84.

Clarke, R.V.G. (1987) 'Rational choice theory and prison psychology', in B.J. McGurk and R.E. McGurk (eds) *Applying Psychology to Imprisonment: Theory and Practice*. London: HMSO.

Cohen, L. and Felson, M. (1979) 'Social change and crime rate trends', *American Sociological Review*, 44: 588–608.

Connell, J. and Hart, G. (2003) *An Overview of Male Sex Work in Edinburgh and Glasgow: The Male Sex Worker Perspective*, Medical Research Council Social and Public Health Sciences Unit Occasional Paper No. 8. Glasgow: MRC, University of Glasgow, available online at: http://www.msoc-mrc.gla.ac.uk/Publications/pub/PDFs/Occasional-Papers/OP008.pdf).

Coombs, N. (1974) 'Male prostitution: a psychosocial view of behaviour', *American Journal of Orthopsychiatry*, 44 (5): 782–89.

Edwards, S. (1991) *Prostitution – Whose Problem?* Wolverhampton: Wolverhampton Safer Cities.

Farley, M., Baral, I., Kiremire, M. and Sezgin, U. (1998) 'Prostitution in five countries: violence and post-traumatic stress disorder', *Feminism and*

Psychology, 8 (4): 405–26.

Farrington, D.P. (1997) 'Human development and criminal careers', in M. Maguire, R. Morgan and R. Reiner (eds) *The Oxford Handbook of Criminology* (2nd edn). Oxford: Oxford University Press.

Minichiello, V., Mariño, R., Browne, J. and Jamieson, M. (1998) 'A review of male to male commercial sex encounters', *Venereology*, 11 (4): 32–41.

Minichiello, V., Mariño, R., Browne, J., Jamieson, M., Peterson, K. and Reuter, B. (1999) 'A profile of the clients of male sex workers in three Australian cities', *Australian and New Zealand Journal of Public Health*, 23 (5): 511–18.

Morse, E.V., Simon, P.M., Balson, P. and Osofsky, H. (1992) 'Sexual behavior patterns of customers of male street prostitutes', *Archives of Sexual Behavior*, 21 (3): 347–57.

Scott, J., Minichiello, V., Marino, R., Harvey, G., Jamieson, M. and Browne, J. (2005) 'Understanding the new context of the male sex work industry', *Journal of Interpersonal Violence*, 20 (3) 320–42.

Shaw I., Butler, I., Crowley, A. and Patel, G. (1996) *Paying the Price? Young People and Prostitution*. Cardiff: Cardiff University, School of Social and Administrative Studies.

Van der Poel, S. (1992) 'Professional male prostitution: a neglected phenomenon', *Crime, Law and Social Change*, 18 (3): 259–75.

West, D. and de Villiers, B. (1993) *Male Prostitution*. New York: Harrington Park Press.

Chapter 7

Cosmopolitanism and trafficking of human beings for forced labour

Christien van den Anker

Introduction

The theme of this chapter, trafficking in human beings, initially seems to fit extremely well with the title of the book: *Sex as Crime?*. However, on second thoughts both parts of the title need to be reflected on thoughtfully in order to see the wider context of this type of trafficking. First, the sex angle. It has been shown that trafficking in human beings occurs not only into the sex industry but also into a long list of 'other industries' (ILO 2005; Anderson and Rogaly 2004; van Ellemeet and Smit 2006; van den Anker 2006a). The most recent international law therefore refers to both the sex industry and other industries and places a duty on governments to harmonise their laws in the area with the Palermo Protocol.[1] Some of the industries in Europe in which cases of trafficking were found recently include construction, shipping, agriculture, food packaging, hospitality, domestic work and care, prostitution and criminal activities such as forced begging.[2] The attention for trafficked persons in other industries is well below the level of attention paid to trafficking for sexual exploitation. This is probably due to a set of factors, including the construction of women trafficked into the sex industry as 'deserving victims', separating them from sex workers who 'freely' opted for this type of work as well as from 'cunning deceivers' who come into the country illegally to work without permit in all kinds of other industries. As we will see later, 'illegality' is not always part of the story and should not be the focus of attention in cases of trafficking anyway, as the human rights violations that people experience should rather be the basis for the response of services. The separation of sex workers into categories is also unhelpful and does not reflect the complexity of personal experiences that lead to ending up in this type of work. The debate on trafficking for sexual exploitation was for a long time polarised into abolitionists and liberals; the question of how to support all trafficked persons needs to address why people's options to enter and leave a job are restricted and not whether or not it is moral for them to do the work they do.

Secondly then: the crime angle. Whereas the media, the police and layers of government focus on the criminalisation of trafficking by prosecuting both traffickers and 'illegal' migrants, NGOs have persistently campaigned for the recognition of trafficking as a human rights issue. Of course, human rights can also be approached by emphasising the punishment for violations: however, the punishment angle in international human rights law is arguably less important than and should at least be accompanied by prevention of the violation in the first place and adequate provisions for the support of victims. Moreover, whereas the first internationally agreed definition of trafficking was developed in an optional protocol to the Transnational Organised Crime Convention, there is a host of human rights instruments that are violated when trafficking occurs. Moreover, researchers are increasingly noticing that the transnational organised crime networks may not play the largest role in the trafficking of human beings (Obokata 2006).

Having set out how this chapter fits awkwardly in the context of the present book, it is opportune to acknowledge that many people still mainly approach trafficking from a 'sex and crime' angle. For example, Amnesty International, in their press release welcoming the UK decision to sign the European Convention Against Trafficking (2005),[3] say that 'Trafficking in people is a vicious and well organised crime which is causing untold human misery around the world and right here in the UK.' This illustrates the lack of awareness that traffickers can be small-scale opportunists who are experienced by the trafficked person as a 'helper'. Nowhere in the press release is trafficking shown to be occurring in other industries. Instead, the only background information given to the journalists relates to the sex industry:

> Home Office research due to be published this year suggests that at any one time during 2003 there were in the region of 4,000 victims of trafficking for forced prostitution in the UK. Trafficked women and girls, from countries including Moldova,

Romania, Albania, Thailand and Nigeria have been forced to work as prostitutes in London. Victims of trafficking are tricked or violently coerced into leaving their homes.[4]

This feeds the stereotypical images of women and girls as vulnerable victims rather than agents who make choices under constrained conditions. The demand for jobs abroad is high in many countries and the deception is not in being taken abroad but in the circumstances and types of work offered once there. The agency of trafficked persons needs to be acknowledged without taking away from the fact that neither the situation in the country of destination nor the (sexual) violence or force used on the way there is part of what the migrant opted for.

This chapter aims to provide a different perspective in order to break through the automatic identification of trafficking in human beings with sex and crime. The chapter first gives an indication of the wide range of human rights violations in the area of trafficking, showing that what was known for a longer time about the occurrence of human rights violations in cases of trafficking for sexual exploitation is often also true for cases of trafficking into 'other industries'. It then assesses existing approaches to trafficking, such as restricting migration and a human rights-based approach. The final section then sets out a cosmopolitan approach necessary to recognise duties across national borders beyond state obligations to implement human rights only in their own countries.

Human rights violations in the practice of trafficking in human beings

The cases of trafficking with the highest media profile and the most extensive action by government, police and NGOs are those of trafficking for the purpose of sexual exploitation. The growing awareness about human rights violations in these cases since the mid-1990s has resulted in the development of new international law and a host of national and international initiatives. The Palermo Protocol (2000) provides the first internationally agreed definition of trafficking in human beings. The disputes surrounding the phrasing of the definition have been well-documented and the definition raises some pertinent questions. However, the framework provided by the Palermo Protocol carries the obligation to be implemented nationally. The definition consists of the following three elements:

- recruitment, transfer, harbouring or receipt;
- threat or use of force, other forms of coercion, abduction, fraud, deception, the abuse of power or of vulnerability, giving or receiving payments or benefits to achieve consent;
- having control over another person for the purpose of exploitation, including at a minimum: sexual exploitation, forced labour or services, slavery or similar practices, servitude or the removal of organs.

The immediate questions raised by this definition are, for example: to what extent do all three elements need to be present for trafficking to have occurred? And to what extent does the victim's consent take away from the violation of the Protocol (Davidson and Anderson 2006)? The consent of the person trafficked is irrelevant if exploitation is present and the means set out in the definition are used.

Increasingly, difficulties in implementation of the Protocol are being discovered. First, people usually don't self-identify as trafficked due to the belief that their consent disqualifies them and because of their perspective that their circumstances will get better over time. Secondly, agencies prioritise people's undocumented status, not the human rights violations they have experienced. Thirdly, there is a lack of internationally compatible definitions at the national level, even though the Protocol is from 2000. Even in countries where new legislation exists, there is often a lack of use of new trafficking legislation in court cases. In many countries we[5] observed the lack of inclusion of other industries in the system of criminalisation. Finally there is an overall lack of victim support systems which prevents survivors of trafficking from testifying in court. This is especially true for victims of trafficking into 'other industries'.

In order to develop a list of some of the human rights violations that occur in trafficking cases, I present here four individual case studies from recent research. The first case study is from the Czech Republic where researchers interviewed 25 professionals and 19 migrant workers. Trafficking for forced labour was found in construction, agriculture and the service sector. There was a clear gender division into separate sectors of work. There was no obvious separation between trafficking for the sex industry and other industries as is illustrated in the case study below. There seemed to be a sequence in using different forms of coercion from more subtle to more violent.

Case study 7.1

A group of young Vietnamese women were assisted to come to the Czech Republic to work in a family shop. One of them was forced to work in prostitution at night while working in the shop during the daytime. Others ended up having to work in prostitution to repay their debts.

This case study violates the Palermo Protocol in that it involved the recruitment and harbouring of the trafficked persons, it relied on force to make them do the work and it exploited them through violations of several ILO Conventions by violating limits to working hours and using forced labour. *La Strada* states that:

> It is evident from the research that violence and threats of violence are not rare in the environment of exploitation of migrant workers. Hence, the provision of article 16 of Migrant Workers Convention is important in this context. This provision gives the migrant workers the right to personal freedom and safety and further states that they are entitled to effective protection from the state against violence, maltreatment and threats, regardless of whether they come from public authorities or private persons. (Cited in Burcikova 2006)

The second example is taken from a UK country report (Skrivankova 2006). In the UK 23 professionals and 19 migrant workers were interviewed and 300 cases from Citizens' Advice Bureaux were analysed. The industries where cases of trafficking for forced labour were reported included agriculture, construction, the food industry, care and restaurants. Several different forms of coercion were used. There were a lot of difficulties reported with support from the authorities: the irregular migration status of victims generally dominates the response and leads to lack of identification as a trafficked person, whereas the immigration and work permit regulations are complex. Migrant workers arriving from newly acceded EU countries need to register with the police in order to work legally. This is expensive and gives employers a chance to withhold documents or pretend registration has happened while later on threatening with deportation as registration was not done.

Case study 7.2

Polish workers in food packaging were brought to a house. They had no idea where they were; they spoke no English. They were subcontracted in a complex chain of labour agencies. Inside: no furniture, mountains of rubbish, soiled mattresses on the floor and a terrible smell.

> They were threatened with eviction and loss of two weeks' wages if they spoke out. Pay: withheld; no minimum wage paid; deceit at recruitment stage. Tax deducted at a high rate, yet tax office has no record. Most did not register since the £50 required was an impossible amount. This made them undocumented. Health and safety regulations: the electric cooker had no plug, its wires pushed straight into the socket.

This case study illustrates a myriad of violations supposedly designed to protect this group of people. Labour laws, for example, were violated in a number of ways, e.g. non-payment of the national minimum wage, making illegal deductions from pay, etc. The workers were not treated in a just and fair manner, their rights of movement were infringed and they were not enjoying freedom from psychological abuse and threats.

A case study from Ireland shows further that in a very different work situation similar human rights violations occur. In Ireland the research for the same project included 46 completed questionnaires from professionals, five interviews with professionals and 15 interviews with migrant workers. Trafficking was reported in restaurants, agriculture, domestic workers and construction. Forms of coercion were often subtle: late payment, confiscation of papers, threat of not renewing work permits or threats of denunciation to the authorities followed by deportation. Trafficked people frequently enter the state legally and many of the victims do not identify themselves as trafficked (Coghlan 2006).

Case study 7.3

Rana (from Bangladesh) worked for two years in a household where she was constantly verbally abused and at times physically abused. She was locked in a bathroom if her employer felt she had not listened or completed her work properly or if she became upset and cried.

Rana became exhausted and very frightened. She had no English and no one to turn to. She had no knowledge of the Irish work permit system. She decided to try to leave and asked a regular visitor to the house for help.

Ireland has not yet ratified the Palermo Protocol, yet many other international treaties that protect human and/or workers rights have been transposed into Irish law. In addition, Ireland has substantial employment rights legislation. This story demonstrates the extent to which human rights have none the less been violated.

While laws offer some protection to workers the reality is that, in the absence of the implementation of the Palermo Protocol, victims can be viewed as undocumented workers and are in danger of being deported. (Coghlan 2006)

The final case study is from Portugal. Here the researchers interviewed 18 migrant workers, five of whom were professionals; in addition 17 questionnaires were received from professionals. The common thread among the responses of the migrants was the wish for a better life and social isolation. Most migrants entered the country legally yet were not permitted to work. Most victims failed to identify as such due to lack of legal provisions governing forced labour trafficking.

Case study 7.4

A, B and C, Romanian nationals, lived all their lives in an orphanage and came to Portugal to pick fruit. They were promised work abroad by a local. Their transportation (with seven others) was arranged and on their arrival they were sold to Portuguese Roma families. Their passports were taken; they were beaten every day.

They were paid by the farmers, but their money was taken away by the traffickers. They lived in constant fear. Although only one spoke English, they distracted the traffickers and escaped with help from one of the farmers.

APAV (the Portuguese Association for Victim Support) states:

In this case, the workers were not paid a fair wage and there was no guarantee that they receive the benefits to which they were entitled. [...] Because of [inspections not being carried out], there was a failure to ensure that workers' physical integrity was respected and that they were not subject to physical abuse. They were also discriminated against in relation to access to social benefits and services. The workers' right to freedom of movement was not respected (they worked confined to the workplace) and there was no guarantee of respect of workers' rights by ensuring that their documents were not removed, their choice of residence or of employment. (Cited in Amaral 2006)

Human rights violations in this case again included violations of the international legislation on slavery, trafficking, forced labour and general civil and political rights.

A few conclusions can be drawn from these case studies and the overall research on which they are based. First, in the case of trafficking in human beings, human rights violations occur beyond those set out in anti-trafficking and anti-slavery legislation. ILO Conventions are regularly violated as well as the general basic set of human rights represented in the Universal Declaration of 1948, the twin covenants of 1966 and the specific conventions on women's, children's and migrants' rights. Secondly, human rights violations generally are more likely to stack up against people in vulnerable groups who are often discriminated against in more than one respect. Well-recognised root-causes of trafficking include gender-based violence and discrimination against women and girls, discrimination on the basis of skin colour, ethnic group, religion or caste and marital status. If human rights violations are this central to cases of trafficking it is no surprise that NGO campaigns have lobbied governments to pay more attention to the rights of trafficked persons rather than the current widespread practice of deporting them on the basis of their lack of legal residence documents. Moreover, the NGOs have not distinguished workers trafficked for sex from those other trafficked persons, since at this level the problems of all trafficked persons are much the same. In the following sections I will therefore compare and contrast the policy approaches to trafficking in human beings that have been developed or called for up to now. In the final section I then add my own pleas for a wider contextual view based on the underlying principle of human equality: a cosmopolitan approach to ending trafficking and other harms done within the present migratory regimes.

Policy approaches to combating trafficking

Generally, policy responses to trafficking in human beings have focused on restricting migration flows. This has had a contrary effect: when people cannot find legal ways to migrate they are not deterred and they do not stay at home. The circumstances at home that inspired their decision to migrate in the first place are often such that risks will be taken in trying to realise the goal of earning some money abroad. With decreasing options for legal migration research has found an increase in the numbers of people who pursue undocumented migration (Doomernik 2004).

By involving others to assist in travel arrangements to cross borders, there is always the chance that, despite paying large sums of money for such assistance, the helper will take advantage of the dependency of the migrant. The distinction made between smuggling and trafficking in policy circles is therefore not always that clear-cut in reality. For example, in a recent speech made by Maud De Boer-Buquicchio, Deputy Secretary General of the Council of Europe, on the occasion of the regional seminar on combating trafficking in human beings in Cyprus in February 2007, she stated that:

> Above all, contrary to illegal immigrants, victims of trafficking do not choose to be victims: they are often deceived or misled by the traffickers and in the end deprived of freedom and completely controlled by criminal gangs. Secondly, trafficking always aims at the exploitation of the victim. In short, while the main objective of those arranging illegal immigration is smuggling people across borders for a fee, the objective of trafficking is exploitation of human beings. This is a crime which may, or may not, involve an illegal crossing of a border.[6]

However, several aspects of this image need to be challenged. Firstly the distinction between smuggling and trafficking is often hard to make in actual cases. This is illustrated by van Liempt (2007) among others. Smuggling is regarded as different from trafficking in that it is with the consent of the migrant, yet smuggling will often leave migrants exposed to increased insecurity and vulnerability (Koser 2001). In other words, someone who may originally be smuggled may be more likely to end up in exploitative circumstances later on. Such circumstances include, but are not exclusive to, bonded sex work.

Our research shows that self-identification as a trafficked person is often not made in cases where the initial contact was made on the basis of the migrant's wish to get help in crossing a border. If the migrant consented to leaving the country, they often view the trafficker as a helper, even if they later become exploited by the same person or group. In addition, the exploitation is often not worse than circumstances people are used to at home and they are frequently seen as an initial phase that has to be endured in order to 'make it' abroad. Moreover, the huge pressure to be seen as a successful migrant and either returning home with money to do up the house or sending remittances also keeps people locked into exploitative situations.

There are several important factors for why trafficked persons are not identified as such by the relevant practitioners and for why they don't seek assistance from the authorities or NGOs. Among recent migrants, there is often a lack of knowledge of their rights: the migratory regimes in Europe are often not only restrictive, but they are so complex that it is hard to know precisely what to do about residency status and permits to work. The threat of deportation is often used to keep people in exploitative circumstances and it is regularly reported that Gangmasters in the UK and Ireland recruit specifically on the basis of lacking English language skills and even sack people if they learn English, in order to keep trafficked persons socially isolated (Anti-Slavery International 2006).

Secondly, the Deputy Secretary of the Council of Europe contributes to the location of trafficking as carried out by well-organised criminal gangs or transnational organised crime. This is challenged in the literature and some argue that it is more 'disorganised crime' that is involved in trafficking in human beings.[7]

Finally, the emphasis on the distinction between 'legal' and 'illegal' migrants in the quotation is upholding a perspective that is generally confusing the discourse on trafficking. Besides reducing human beings to 'legal' or 'illegal', and therefore granting or withholding the protection of the law, it is also factually unhelpful in the case of trafficking. It is often assumed that people enter the country illegally when they are trafficked, whereas our recent research shows that this is not the case. People often enter legally but are then vulnerable when they overstay their visa or are threatened by their employers with deportation. This also links in with the debate about asylum seekers and refugees. Increasingly migrants are seen as claiming asylum in order to become economically active in a country of destination. This contributes to stereotyping and contravening the universal legal principles of the presumption of innocence. The links between trafficking and asylum, however, are manifold. Refugees often cannot work at the level of their education at home, so become more vulnerable to low-skilled exploitative jobs; during the process of waiting for an asylum decision or if refused status, people often become destitute and therefore vulnerable to forced labour. Women, therefore, enter the sex trade voluntarily, although their decision to do so is constrained by their economic and political circumstances as documented migrants. In this, as in other matters, they are not markedly different from other women and men who are constrained into exploitative, sometimes illegal (undocumented) work in other trades.

Often, existing approaches in policy-making do not meet the international obligations of the receiving countries. Many states now position migration in the recently exponentially growing security debate and attempt to justify the restriction of migration flows. Yet, on the other hand, governments have to admit that there are skills gaps as well as unskilled vacancies that need to be filled. Governmental rhetoric in Europe on migrants is therefore often mixed and ambiguous.

Regulating migration leads inevitably to more complex and restrictive immigration regimes and regulations of migrants' right to work. These increase the risk of migrants falling prey to unscrupulous Gangmasters who will exploit their lack of knowledge of their rights. In the UK, for example, the Trades Union Congress now campaigns for abolishing the special registration schemes for the A8 (newly acceded EU countries) which make it harder to acquire legal status as a migrant due to the bureaucracy and cost involved. Registration duties also increase the chances of trafficking, as employers can hold on to documents which leaves employees vulnerable.

Recent migration policies across Europe have led to increased deportations of failed asylum seekers and incentives for return migration. This whole discourse shows the dilemma for governments across Europe. On the one hand, the electorate wants to see a tough stance on immigration, for fears of 'swamping' and competition for lower skilled jobs. On the other hand, European economies completely rely on the cheap labour of migrants, whether they are in possession of the correct documentation or not. Off-the-record agreements have been disclosed between local police and businesses relying on 'flexibility'. This acknowledgment of the structural reliance on cheap labour and therefore on the exploitation of migrant workers is illustrated by what Bhattacharya (2005) has called 'the underbelly of the global economy'.

Let us now turn to what a human-rights based approach offers to resolve the difficulties with the current anti-migration strategy to combating the sex trade and other trafficking in human beings.

Human rights-based approaches

A human rights-based approach to trafficking in human beings, for whatever purpose, would emphasise the development and local implementation of international law. Through the focus on the human rights of trafficked persons, the approach has highlighted calls for victim support, including housing, legal aid, reflection period, counselling and education. This would mean that on discovery by the authorities a person's legal status in the country or right to work would not be the main focus, but their experiences of human rights violations. In several countries this way of thinking has led to the establishment of a temporary visa, either related to the involvement as a witness in a case against the trafficker, or, in the case of Italy, without such conditions. (See for example Dormaels, Moens and Praet 2004.)

Human rights-based approaches also emphasise the need for short-term prevention campaigns, support for returnees and attempts to convict more traffickers. However, human rights-based approaches advocated by NGOs focus on short-term prevention, for example informing potential migrants of risks, yet as long as these campaigns are aimed at reducing migration, they are not working. In Moldova, as in many other countries, for example, the circumstances for young women, especially since the transition to the free market economy, are too limited for would-be migrants to be dissuaded from trying to emigrate by campaigns warning of the dangers. Many who reported that they felt that 'it would not happen to me' or who have paid well-known smugglers again and ended up being re-trafficked illustrate the lack of success of traditional warnings in prevention campaigns of the International Organisation for Migration (IOM) or UNICEF.[8]

Those NGOs that acknowledge the need for longer-term prevention focus mainly on gender inequality as a root cause for trafficking and consider trafficking mainly in the context of sex work. Recent long-term prevention proposals therefore include a wider context for thinking about counter-trafficking policies. The Brussels Declaration (2002) recognises both poverty and the demand side as important root causes, yet it does not mention conflict or discrimination other than gender-based. The argument of this paper has been precisely that gender must not be ignored, but also that the sex trade is not the only dangerous or gendered workplace. The SAARC Convention refers to the development and supervision of employment agencies, yet without international obligations to assist development this does not provide an effective long-term prevention strategy. The Organisation for Security and Cooperation in Europe (OSCE) (2003) in its Action Plan includes all of the above and social and economic measures to address root causes in origin and destination countries, yet again the plan mentions only national and no international obligations (van den Anker 2006b).

Some of the other drawbacks of human rights approaches are that states remain the primary actor in (a) signing up to conventions and (b) responsibility for implementation. Yet, as we have seen, even many liberal democracies don't sign up to the European Convention

(2005) due to its emphasis on victim support, including a 30-day recovery/reflection period, or to the Migrant Workers' Convention[9] due to its emphasis on the implementation of labour rights.

This 'statism' is also a drawback of the human rights approach precisely because the whole system of nation-states and their protective guarding of their borders is part of the problem that creates the inequality leading to vulnerability and to trafficking in human beings. The loss of life due to violence around borders is no longer necessarily related to wars, but to cross-border trafficking of people, arms, drugs and other commodities.

Still, a human rights-based approach would overcome the important factor of immediate deportation which keeps many migrants locked into exploitative employment conditions such as sex work. Some have even called for the wider of granting of asylum on the basis of the human rights violations suffered as a trafficked person. Although this is mostly worked out in the case of trafficking for sexual exploitation, this could also apply in other industries (see, for example, Gallagher 2006). Moreover, if long-term prevention could be taken more seriously, then a human rights-based approach could contribute to the human rights not only of trafficked persons but of potential migrants and their families in countries of origin. This would move the interpretation of human rights beyond a statist interpretation towards a cosmopolitan one which I develop in more detail in the final section below.

A cosmopolitan approach

Having observed the limits to a statist human rights approach to combating trafficking in human beings, I propose an alternative, which I call a cosmopolitan approach. In a cosmopolitan perspective on global politics the scope of justice is global, the boundaries of nation-states are not the boundaries of morality, and duties of justice are owed to all human beings. This position is backed up by the belief that moral principles are and should be universal in their application (Caney 2005). This may seem to contrast with notions of cosmopolitanism used more generally in migration discourse. For example, Ulf Hannerz (1996: 103) states that: 'A more genuine cosmopolitanism is first of all an orientation, a willingness to engage with the Other.' The contrast between the two conceptions of cosmopolitanism is in the identification of the cosmopolitan in Hannerz's view with mastery and control. This would link in with the perception of contextualists that cosmopolitanism as a political theory is imperialist in its universalism. The challenge in my cosmopolitanism is to bring together the engagement with injustice from a perspective of human equality while allowing arrogance towards the 'victims' to be exposed and eradicated. Instead, the engagement should be as equals and allies.

In the context of trafficking, a cosmopolitan approach would lead to aiming for the prevention of trafficking in a much more long-term perspective with attention to structural factors of global inequality and the most inclusive set of root causes. These would at least include:

- economic inequality: poverty and lack of opportunities – demand for cheap labour;
- gender inequality (especially single mothers);
- ethnic, religious, national discrimination;
- conflict, peacekeeping and post-conflict reconstruction.

A set of principles of global justice would form the basis for the development of policies. These principles would build on the human rights approach, but move beyond it in important ways. They would include at least the following:

1 respect for the rights of victims;
2 cosmopolitan impartiality (justice for all);
3 respect for the agency of victims;
4 commitment to long-term structural change in the global economy;
5 provision of support to develop viable alternative livelihoods (van den Anker 2004).

Cosmopolitanism would propose action plans that include international obligations to support social and economic measures in all affected countries. These would include duties beyond borders for states, civil society and individuals. For example, creating alternative livelihoods would move beyond the current training programmes for specific skills for potential or returning trafficked persons; it would involve investing in social development in which the political will in national governments as well as international redistribution would play a role.

A cosmopolitan approach to combating trafficking would galvanise efforts with existing cosmopolitan proposals. For example, in the long term the root causes of trafficking would be addressed by several concrete programmes. The ongoing campaigns for debt relief are important for some of the source countries of trafficked persons. In addition, fair trade can be of assistance to local livelihoods and the growth of the fair trade turnover is a sign that the principle of profit-making is no longer the only 'bottom line' of business. Of course, in the end the structure of the global economy needs to be addressed but fair trade is a good example of how a small bottom-up initiative can grow into a relevant campaign for trade justice more widely. This links into the context of sustainable human development; despite migrants often not being the poorest of the poor, remittances and family strategies involving migration often reach many more people who couldn't themselves move abroad. If the pressure on migrants of contributing to their family income was not so high, the risks taken would not be so great in their migration trajectories and the market for cheap labourers would diminish. A human rights approach that wanted to contribute to these longer-term changes, and to development, would need to emphasise the full range of human rights, including the economic and social ones. This would require a cosmopolitan outlook on the provisions required for these rights to be implemented for all. Finally, cosmopolitan theorists as well as activists have proposed several forms of global redistribution involving global taxation. An interesting and relatively popular example is the Tobin tax on currency speculation (Dowling 2004), but Thomas Pogge's (1998) resources dividend is also still worth considering.

Some cosmopolitans propose (nearly) open borders yet, if this leads to deregulation, it can be more harmful for migrant workers as working conditions may be harder to protect still. One way forward in thinking about borders would be to imagine a long-term project of working towards their gradual demise. The EU is often cited as an example in this respect. However, in the case of the European Union the harshest protection of borders simply moves to the outside borders with checks becoming possible anywhere within them, too. Others argue our energy should be focused on global equality, not borders. In the end we may meet in the same place: a world where there is equality of capability and no discrimination according to place of origin as well as a right to mobility.

In this section I have argued for a cosmopolitan approach to combating trafficking in human beings and sketched its outline. Some critics may argue that we cannot wait until we have created a just world in combating trafficking through intermediary measures. Others may argue that it is local responses that weigh more heavily, rather than some grand scheme. My response to those critics is that we do not have to wait for cosmopolitanism to be implemented fully or in its strongest institutional form to take action against trafficking in human beings. Moreover, we should not overlook the local ways in which practices differ, yet we recognise the commonalities in causes and means to work towards eradication. In developing policy responses taking a cosmopolitan perspective will lead to a stronger human rights-based approach, moving beyond its statism and building in international duties of support to countries of origin. Immigration, and especially more transitional lifestyles, is at present casually used to back up perceived trends towards cosmopolitan citizenship; however, transnationalism would only support embedded cosmopolitanism where local identities support overseas local groups as has been the case for many years with faith-based networks. So instead of waiting for a 'natural' process of the disintegration of nation-states and cosmopolitan citizenship to develop, structural and ad hoc measures and initiatives need to be taken to bring a just world about but from an overarching cosmopolitan long-term perspective.

Conclusion

Current approaches to combating trafficking in human beings fail to address prevention adequately as they focus too much on sex and crime. Even organisations that do address prevention too often focus on short-term measures. Those that address longer-term prevention stop at national measures. Current policy responses to trafficking are not working if they are simply focusing on restricting migration or on a statist account of human rights. Instead, I propose a cosmopolitan approach to the long-term prevention of trafficking. This includes an analysis of global root causes as well as local; prevention strategies need to consist of local, national and international components. Implementing human rights to address trafficking in human beings effectively needs to strengthen international duties.

I conclude this chapter with the acknowledgment that despite recent recognition of a cosmopolitan approach in international policy documents the argument still requires campaigning for. Setting it out very clearly in volumes like this one may assist in that task. Some people working on global justice start from a particular theory; others start by addressing a specific issue. In my case, working on the issue of contemporary slavery and especially trafficking in human beings for forced labour – has assisted me in seeing the process of setting norms and creating effective policies, and has helped me to see where more abstract theories of justice need to be contextual in order to suggest more helpful solutions to relevant issues of global justice.

Acknowledgments

The author wishes to thank the editorial team for their feedback and patience, Anti-Slavery International for permission to publish the results of our collaborative research project, funded by the AGIS programme during 2005–2006, and the new friends who allow reflection on the ways of being cosmopolitan together.

Notes

1 Protocol to Prevent, Suppress and Punish Trafficking in Persons, Especially Women and Children, often referred to as the Palermo Protocol, supplements the United Nations Convention against Transnational Organised Crime. The full text is available from http://www.ohchr.org.
2 For the full list see Anti-Slavery International (2006).
3 For the full text and background documents see http://www.coe.org.
4 http://www.amnesty.org.uk, accessed January 2007.
5 The discussion here draws on collaborative research in the UK, Ireland, Portugal and the Czech Republic, as well as on discussions on the theme of trafficking in women and girls in the context of the Network for European Women's Rights.
6 James Korovilas, Researcher in Kosovo and Bosnia-Herzegovina (personal communication).
7 Cezara Nanu (personal communication).
8 For the full text of the Migrant Workers Convention, see http://www.ohchr.org.
9 See Antoine Pécoud and Paul de Guchteneire (2006).

References

Amaral, C. (2006) *Trafficking for Forced Labour in Portugal*. Lisbon: APAV, p. 31.
Anderson, B. and Rogaly, B. (2004) *Forced Labour and Migration to the UK* (study prepared for COMPAS in collaboration with the Trades Union Congress, available at http://www.tuc.org.uk/international/tuc-9317-f0.pdf).
Anti-Slavery International (2006) *Trafficking for Forced Labour in Europe*. London: Anti-Slavery International.

Bhattacharya, G. (2005) *Traffick: The Illegal Movement of People and Things*. London: Pluto Press.

Burcikova, P. (2006) 'Trafficking in human beings and forced labour exploitation in the Czech Republic', *La Strada*. Available at http://www. strada.c2/download/files/LS_report_ENG_20_10_06.pdf.

Caney, S. (2005) *Justice Beyond Borders*. Oxford: Oxford University Press.

Coughlan, D. (2006) *Trafficking for Forced Labour in Ireland*. Dublin: Migrant Rights Centre.

Davidson, J. and Anderson, B. (2006) 'The trouble with trafficking', in C. van den Anker and J. Doomernik (eds) *Trafficking and Women's Rights*. Basingstoke: Palgrave, pp. 11–26.

Doomernik, J. (2004) 'Migration and security: the wrong end of the stick', in C. van den Anker (ed.) *The Political Economy of New Slavery*. Basingstoke: Palgrave, pp. 37–54.

Dormaels, A., Moens, B. and Praet, N. (2004) 'The Belgian counter-trafficking policy', in C. van den Anker (ed.) *The Political Economy of New Slavery*. Basingstoke: Palgrave, pp. 75–90.

Dowling, E. (2004) 'Strategies for change: the Tobin tax', in C. van den Anker (ed.) *The Political Economy of New Slavery*. Basingstoke: Palgrave, pp. 201–16.

Gallagher, A.M. (2006) 'Triply exploited: female victims of trafficking networks: strategies for pursuing protection and legal status in countries of destination', in C. van den Anker and J. Doomernik (eds) *Trafficking and Women's Rights*. Basingstoke: Palgrave.

Hannerz, U. (1996) *Transnational Connections: Culture, People, Places*. London: Routledge.

ILO (2005) *A Global Alliance Against Forced Labour*. Geneva: International Labour Organisation.

Koser, K. (2001) 'Smuggling asylum seekers to Western Europe: contradictions, conundrums, and dilemmas', in D. Kyle and R. Koslowski (eds) *Global Human Smuggling: Comparative Perspectives*. Baltimore, MD: Johns Hopkins University Press, pp. 58–73.

Obokata, T. (2006) *Trafficking of Human Beings from a Human Rights Perspective*. The Hague: Nijhoff.

Ould, D. (2004) 'Trafficking and international law' in C. van den Anker (ed.) *The Political Economy of New Slavery*. Basingstoke: Palgrave, pp. 55–74.

Pécoud, A. and de Guchteneire, P. (2006) 'International migration, border controls, and human rights: assessing the relevance of the right to mobility', *Journal of Border Studies*, 21 (1): 69–86.

Pogge, T. (1998) 'A global resources dividend', in D. Crocker and T. Linden (eds) *The Ethics of Consumption*. Oxford: Rowman & Littlefield, pp. 501–36.

Skrivankova, K. (2006) *Trafficking for Forced Labour in the UK*. London: Anti-Slavery International.

van den Anker, C. (2004) 'Contemporary slavery, global justice, and globalization', in C. van den Anker (ed.) *The Political Economy of New Slavery*. Basingstoke: Palgrave, pp. 15–36.

van den Anker, C. (2006a) 'Trafficking and women's rights: beyond the sex industry to "other industries"', *Journal of Global Ethics*, 2 (2): 163–82.

van den Anker, C. (2006b) 'Trafficking in women: a cosmopolitan approach to long-term prevention', in C. van den Anker and J. Doomernik (eds) *Trafficking and Women's Rights*. Basingstoke: Palgrave.

van Ellemeet, H. and Smit, M. (2006) 'Trafficking for exploitation outside the sex industry', in C. van den Anker and J. Doomernik (eds) *Trafficking and Women's Rights*. Basingstoke: Palgrave.

van Liempt, I. (2007) *Navigating Borders*. Netherlands: University of Amsterdam Press.

Chapter 8

The sexual intentions of male sex workers: an international study of escorts who advertise on the web

Victor Minichiello, P.G. Harvey and
Rodrigo Mariño

Introduction

In the past twenty years or so new discourses about the sex industry have emerged. They include a 'gender industry' discourse that openly acknowledges that there exists both a female and a male sex industry. The evidence suggests that male sex work is a growing enterprise and the male body is increasingly seen as a commodified product. The expansion of men's participation as sex workers is complemented by the growing eroticisation of men's bodies in popular culture (Minichiello and Harvey 2007). For example, male-to-male pornography constitutes a sizable segment of the US pornography market, about one-third to one half of the $2.4 billion adult industry (Watson 2000). A decriminalisation and professionalisation of the sex industry has occurred as a 'sex' as 'work' discourse has also emerged. Here we see government and health and community agencies introducing, for example, professional standards for the industry through codes of practice, licensing requirements, professional guidelines for safe sex and client–worker interactions, health education and community outreach programmes. Likewise, a large number of sex workers are adopting a professional identity with regard to the quality of the services they provide to clients and how they promote themselves as workers in the recreation industry on the internet and via advertisements.

AIDS is the world's fastest spreading epidemic and this is true of developing as well as Western countries (UNAIDS/WHO 2005). In the United States there is one AIDS-related death every 15 minutes, and someone is infected with HIV every 13 minutes. It is estimated that 80 per cent of Americans infected with HIV do not even know they are infected (Centers for Disease Control 2005). About one in every 30 gay adults in New York (or 3.3 per cent) is infected with HIV (Gay Men's Health Center 2006; New York Department of Health and Mental Hygiene 2003).

Within this context the reported rise of HIV infection in the general community and among men who have sex with men (MSM) needs to be understood and the purpose of this chapter is to provide information on the intention of sex workers to have safe sex. There are a number of obvious and important public health reasons why understanding the sexual behaviour of sex workers is important to contemporary societies. First, recent data show a trend towards an increase in AIDS diagnosis (UNAIDS/WHO 2005). In the United States, the CDC HIV/AIDS Surveillance Report (CDC 2004) shows that during the mid-to-late 1990s, advances in treatment slowed the progression of HIV infection to AIDS and led to dramatic decreases in AIDS deaths. However, while the decrease in AIDS deaths continues, the number of AIDS diagnoses is increasing along with the reported number of new infections. For example, data released from the Centers for Disease Control and Prevention from 25 states in the United States show a 14 per cent increase in the number of HIV diagnosed men who have had sex with men from 1999 to 2001 (CDC 2005). This pattern is also found in other countries (UNAIDS/WHO 2005). In the state of Victoria, Australia, the newly diagnosed HIV cases were steadily declining and had reached a low level in 1999. However, this statistic has increased, reaching the highest rates since 1994 in 2002 (Department of Human Services, Victoria 2002). More recently, the Australian National HIV/AIDS Strategy 2005–08 reports that the rates of HIV and STIs (sexually transmissible diseases) among MSM have shown marked increases during the last five years (Commonwealth of Australia 2005).

Second, commercial sex is transmitting HIV/AIDS and, because of its activity (recreational paid sex), requires monitoring as a public health issue. In the early years of HIV, a study of 1,396 female sex workers (FSWs) in six US cities found an HIV positive result ranging from 12 per cent to 47.5 per cent (Centers for Disease Control and Prevention 1987) and a study of 234 male sex workers (MSWs) in Atlanta found a 29.4 per cent seroprevalence (Elifson, Boles and Sweat 1993). Generally speaking, prevalence studies show that male sex workers have higher rates of HIV and STI than female sex workers. In more recent years, studies conducted in several countries reveal a prevalence of HIV between 6.5 and 27 per cent among the male sex worker populations (Belza 2005; Estcourt *et al.* 2000; Leuridan *et al.* 2005; Minichiello *et al.* 2000; Ziersch *et al.* 2000). Studies, however, have reported that there are differences with regard to the transmission of HIV/AIDS through the sex industry depending on how regulated the industry is by government (Harcourt and Donovan 2005). Countries such as Thailand, India and Nepal, where the sex industry is unregulated, report much higher rates of transmission of HIV through the sex industry (Brown *et al.* 1998). In a study that examined the sexual behaviour of 6,661 male sex workers in India in order to determine the probability of acquiring and transmitting HIV for men who sell sex to men, it was found that over half had unprotected anal sex and 27 per cent of the men sold sex to men. The study predicted that for every 1,000 men who sell sex to men in a year 146 would acquire HIV and HIV would be transmitted to 43 male clients who do not sell sex and to twelve women. These figures are 6.7 times higher for acquiring HIV and 2.5 times higher for transmitting HIV to sex partners than those for women who sell sex (Dandona *et al.* 2006).

Third, in 2003 male sex workers in the United States represented the largest proportion of HIV/AIDS diagnoses (MMWR 2004), and this is true of many other Western countries (Hart and Williamson 2004; UNAIDS/WHO 2005). Despite the success of the early intervention in curbing the rise of new infections, studies are reporting an increase in unsafe anal sex and a new phenomenon known as 'bareback sex' (unprotected anal intercourse). A central component associated with barebacking is extreme sexual gratification as an intentional decision and lifestyle choice (Ridge 2004), although the literature identifies different types of barebackers: 'ignorant', 'misinformed', 'issue avoiders', 'Russian Roulette' and 'HIV is inevitable barebackers' (Outspoken 2006). It is worth stating here that extreme bareback sex is also popular in the heterosexual community where it has been applied to describe any type of penetrative sex without the use of a condom.

Research emerging on the topic of barebacking reveals that this term is understood by many people and that people engage in this sexual behaviour. For example, Gordon Mansergh *et al.* (2002) in a survey of 554 men who have sex with men found that 70 per cent were aware of barebacking and among those who had heard the term, 14 per cent had barebacked in the previous two years. A sizable proportion of men reported barebacking partners of a different or unknown HIV status. Perry Halkitis and Jeffrey Parsons (2003), in a sample of

112 HIV-positive gay men, found a significant correlation between defining masculinity as sexual prowess and intentional unprotected anal sex. In another study, Halkitis, Parsons and Wilton (2003) found that of the 448 men who were familiar with the term 'barebacking', 45.5 per cent reported bareback sex in the past three months. Alex Carballo-Dieguez and José Bauermeister (2004) reviewed messages posted on an internet message board and found that out of the 130 messages reviewed, 48 per cent could be coded as pro-barebacking. Within this context it is timely to conduct an analysis of whether male sex workers engage in the phenomenon of 'barebacking'. Using a rich source of data to capture a large sample of male sex workers who advertise their services on the internet, this chapter describes the sexual practices and intentions of male sex workers as reported to clients.

Methods

The source of data used for this study was the website http://www. rentboy.com. This website contains information on men who sell sex for money listed by cities across the world. Each escort is advertised with a picture and a message of up to 100 words describing him and what sexual services he offers. A further 'statistical card' can be clicked for each escort that provides a standard list of information on a number of items, including race, age, weight, height, hair and eye colour, body type, sex preference, safe sex practice, smoking status, penis size and status of foreskin. Information provided by the webmaster shows that this website receives over 10,000 hits per day and totals over 13 million hits to the site.

The website was accessed for data collection between May to June 2005. During this period 1,426 escorts were listed. The top 14 cities were included in the sample and all escorts listed in these cities were analysed for information. The 14 selected cities included a total of 1,015 escorts and this represents 71 per cent of the total escort sample on the website at the census time of this study.

Each escort profile was read and data recorded for the following variables: age, body weight, masculinity, safe sex practice and sexual intention. *Sexual masculinity identity* was categorised in terms of the individual's definition of self, and respondents identified themselves as either 'Top', 'Versatile' or 'Bottom', common lay terms used in the gay community and sex literature to denote whether the person gives (top) or receives (bottom) anal intercourse. Participants provided information about their *body weight*, and indicated whether they practised safe sex. This was coded as 'Sometimes or never', 'Prefer not to say' and 'Always'.

Finally, a sexual intention variable was derived from the participants' written statements consisting of no more than 50 words provided to clients about themselves and what they would do sexually to distinguish between what people report as a result of ticking the fixed answer category 'safer sex' and the message they provide to clients about what they are prepared to do in terms of the sexual services they offer. Two researchers read the male sex workers' descriptors on the web and coded it into one of the following categories. If the statement clearly indicated that they would only provide safe sex then this was categorised as 'safe sex intention', if the statement was unclear about this subject, then this was categorised as 'ambiguous sex intention', and if the statement was clear that the sex worker would consider unsafe sex, then this was categorised as 'unsafe sex intention'.

Table 8.1 provides examples of statements that were coded as unsafe sex intention. Where there was a difference between the researchers about the assigned coding a discussion took place to reach a consensus. To cross check the reliability of this variable, the researchers randomly selected from those male sex workers classified under the 'unsafe sex intention' category and called them via telephone to ask them if they would offer bareback sex (unprotected anal sex).

Descriptive statistics were used to summarise the data. Chi-square analysis was used for nominal and ordinal variables, while continuous variables were compared using one-way analysis of variance (ANOVA) and post-hoc comparisons using Tukey's Honestly Significant Differences test. Data were analysed using SPSS v.13.0. To better understand the relationship between the combination of socio-demographic variables and safe-sex practice, the relationships were studied using automatic interaction detection procedures (AID) (McKenzie *et al.* 1993), using the KnowledgeSEEKER software program (Firstmark Technologies 1990). KnowledgeSEEKER is a multivariate stepwise decision-making procedure which selects combinations of independent variables that best separate groups on the basis of statistical significance. This is a method for partitioning data into homogeneous groups which allows the identification of combinations of predictors and non-linear relations between them and the outcome variable (Biggs, DeVille and Suen 1991; Firstmark Technologies 1990).

Table 8.1 Examples of unsafe sexual intention from descriptive statements

---

'I just say wot ya wantin n ya will get it'
'Your wish is my command on demand no matter what it is'
'Whatever you desire'
'Walk on wild side'
'Cater to all scenes, just ask'
'Special requests, bring it on!'
'See where it goes'
'Can do everything you imagine'
'Everything is negotiable'
'Fulfill your every desire … just ask'
'Always up for new things … test my limit … so just ask and lets do it'
'I promise I do as I am told … no limits'
'And remember no thoughts … just do'
'Ask me what I am into … chances are I probably do it … you won't know unless you ask'
'Open to all fantasy … open to anything'
'Whatever does it for you'
'Am totally open to your suggestion'
'Able to do what you want'
'Making all wild fantasies come to reality'
'You name your fantasy'
'All scenes considered, including raw'
'All scenes open to negotiations, including rough and raw sex'
'Ask and it will happen and come true'
'Enjoy going to the limit'
'Pig in bed, all is possible'
'Can play bareback'
'Because this is what some men want'
'I will do what makes you happy, just tell me'
'No scene out of the question'

A detailed explanation of this method will not be attempted here. However, in order to better interpret the results it must be noted that KnowledgeSEEKER splits data sets into new, homogeneous subsets of data (nodes) (Biggs, DeVille and Suen 1991). At each node all predictor variables are considered to further split the node. The node of best partition is based on the selection of that variable which produces the highest level of significance. This process continues until no more significant splits can be found (Biggs, DeVille and Suen 1991). To determine if the relationship between the dependent variable and the independent variable was significant, the significance level was set at 0.2, the exploration level. This method resulted in a 'bushy' decision tree. In the next step, in order to avoid association patterns that may be found by chance, the resulting tree was pruned back until the significance level of the lowest branch was lower than 0.01. This method has been shown to be robust under cross validation when the nominal type I error is set at the 0.01 confidence level (McKenzie *et al.* 1993).

Results

A total of 1,015 male sex workers were included as part of the dataset – 318 participants were from New York City (31.3 per cent), 149 were from Los Angeles (14.7 per cent), 74 were from Miami (7.3 per cent), 67 from Paris (6.6 per cent) and 63 were from Chicago (6.2 per cent). The remaining 33.9 per cent were from the other nine locations. Table 8.2 presents the distribution of the men in the sample by location.

Age, masculinity and body weight

The men's ages ranged from 18 to 52 years, with an overall mean of 28.5 years (s.d. 5.7). Of the men in the sample 395 (38.9 per cent) were aged between 25 and 29, with the second largest group being aged between 30 and 35 (23.7 per cent), followed by the 20–24 age group (23.5 per cent), the over 35 group (2.3 per cent) and the under 20 age group representing less than 2 per cent. With the exception of male sex workers from Milan, who were significantly younger (25.7 years) than those from Washington (30.5 years) and San Francisco (30.3 years) ($F(13,1001) = 2.60$; $p < 0.001$), there were no differences in age by locations.

More than half of the participants (55 per cent) self-assessed themselves as 'versatile', 5.6 per cent as 'bottom' and 39.1 per cent self-identified as 'top'. The overall mean bodyweight was 171.31 pounds (s.d. 22.9). The majority of the sex workers weighed between 160 and 199 pounds (65.5 per cent), with 11.6 per cent having a body weight of over 200 pounds usually associated with the hypermasculine muscular male (Minichiello and Harvey 2006). A significant association was found between preferred sexual position (masculinity) and body weight ($F(2,1012) = 21.06$; $p < 0.001$), with those who self-identified as 'top' significantly heavier than 'versatile' and 'bottom'. In addition, 'versatiles' were significantly heavier than 'bottoms'.

Table 8.2 Percentage distribution of MSWs by city, age, body weight, sexual masculinity identity and stated safe sex practices (N = 1,015)

Variables	%
City	
New York	31.3
Los Angeles	14.7
Miami	7.3
Paris	6.6
Chicago	6.2
San Francisco	5.7
Boston	5.3
Washington	4.5
London	4.3
Milano	3.6
Atlanta	3.5
Madrid	3.3
Toronto	2.4
Sydney	1.3
Age	
Less than 20 years	1.5
20–24	23.6
25–29	38.9
30–35	23.7
More than 35 years	12.3
Body weight	
Less than 160 pounds	22.8
160–199 pounds	65.5
200 or more pounds	11.7
Sexual masculinity identity	
Bottom	5.6
Versatile	55.3
Top	39.1
Stated safe sex practice	
Never/sometimes	2.4
Prefer not to say	46.0
Always	51.6
Sexual intention	
Safe sex intention	17.1
Ambiguous sex intention	62.8
Unsafe sex intention	20.1

Sexual intention

As shown in Table 8.2, most respondents (62.8 per cent) indicated an ambiguous sex intention with regards to safe sex, followed by an unsafe sex intention in 20.1 per cent of the cases. A few, but nevertheless a significant number, of the male sex workers indicated a safe sex intention (17.1 per cent). When ambiguous and unsafe intention were collapsed into one group, no significant differences were present by location in the odds of reporting that outcome. In the bivariate analysis, a significant association ($p < 0.05$) was found between responses to masculinity identity and sexual intention. Although the majority in each masculinity group fell in the ambiguous categories, those who self-identify as 'top' were less likely to describe an unsafe sex intention (15.4 per cent) compared with versatile (23.4 per cent) and bottom (21.1 per cent).

Responses to these two variables were cross-tabulated to evaluate whether concordance existed between safe sex practice and sexual intention. Table 8.3 reveals the distribution of responses according to safe sex practice and sexual intention. The level of agreement of responses was evaluated using the kappa statistic. The result revealed that, although there was a good agreement among those who indicated that they would always practise safe sex with a safe sex intention (94.3 per cent), the majority of those who were found to have an ambiguous sex intention also indicated that they always practised safe sex (52.7 per cent), and of those who were classified with an unsafe sex intention, 11.8 per cent reported that they always practised safe sex. This represents a kappa lower than 0.2, indicating that the self-reported safe sex was significantly different from the participants' sexual intention.

Safe sex

As shown in Table 8.3, the majority of the participants (51.6 per cent) indicated that they always practised safe sex, while 46 per cent indicated that they preferred not to indicate their safe-sex practice and only 24 (2.4 per cent) reported that they practised safe sex sometimes or never. When the last two categories were collapsed into one (48.4 per cent), the multivariate analysis showed that the combination of four variables (age, practise safe sex, by weight and sexual intention) explained 60.5 per cent of the variance ($\chi^2 = 0.605$) in reported safe-sex practice (see Figure 8.1).

Those who were younger than 34 years of age were significantly more likely to indicate a safe sex practice (54.0 per cent) than those

Table 8.3 Relationship between self-reported safe sex and sexual intention

| | Sexual intention | | | |
	Safe sex intention (N = 174)	Ambiguous sex intention (N = 637)	Unsafe sex intention (N = 204)	Total
Safe sex				
Sometimes/never	0 (0.0%)	0 (0.0%)	24 (11.8%)	24 (2.4%)
Prefer not to say	10 (5.7%)	301 (47.3%)	156 (76.4%)	491 (46.0%)
Always	164 (94.3%)	336 (52.7%)	24 (11.8%)	524 (51.6%)
Total	174 (17.1%)	637 (62.8%)	204 (20.1%)	1,015 (51.6%)

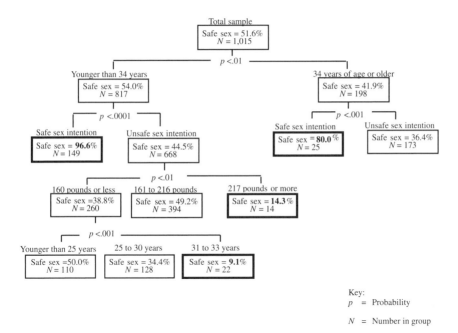

Figure 8.1 Pruned decision tree showing the predictive model for self-reported safe sex practice

34 years or older (41.9 per cent) ($\chi^2(1)$ = 9.28; p < 0.01). When considering these two age groups independently, the older subgroup was further split by their sexual intention. The majority of those with a safe-sex intention (80 per cent) actually practised safe sex, while only 36.4 per cent of those with an ambiguous or unsafe sex

intention actually practised safe sex ($\chi^2(1) = 17.04$; $p < 0.001$). Among those who were younger than 34 years, safe-sex intention was the next variable to be split. The great majority (96.6 per cent) of those with a safe-sex intention actually practised safe sex, compared with 44.5 per cent of those with an ambiguous or unsafe sex intention who actually practised safe sex ($\chi^2(1) = 133.54$; $p < 0.0001$).

For those with an ambiguous or unsafe sex intention (n=668), weight was then split ($\chi^2(1) = 12.12$; $p < 0.01$). Those weighing between 161 and 216 pounds (n = 394) reported a significantly higher proportion of safe-sex practice than those weighting 217 pounds or more (49.2 per cent versus 14.3 per cent). The subgroup of participants weighing less than 161 pounds (n = 260) was further split by age. Half of those younger than 25 years of age practised safe sex. However, of the participants aged between 25 and 30 years of age, only 34.4 per cent actually practised safe sex. This proportion decreases to 9.1 per cent when MSWs were aged between 31 and 34 years ($\chi^2(1) = 15.04$; $p < 0.001$). The lowest proportion of self-reported safe-sex practice was in this group.

What next?

The results of this study are interesting with respect to two issues. First, they provide evidence that there is a male sex industry out there of some significance and that these men present themselves openly to the public as providing a sex service. Similar to findings in other studies, the profile of male sex workers is diverse. The stereotypical image of an effeminate gay persona is challenged by the number of escorts in this study who display the body image of the hypermasculine body builder and the diversity of sexual practices and sexualities found among these men.

Second, while it is encouraging to see that over half of the sample reported always practising safe sex, it is of concern that a little under half of the sample equally reported that they preferred not to say what their sexual practise was or that they never/sometimes practised safe sex. The data was also able to detect significant differences by age and body image (as measured by weight) with regard to safe sex practice suggesting that we need to better understand how the biography context of people shapes their sexual histories. This may suggest that a person's age does matter as older workers and clients may be more willing to engage in riskier behaviour as they become less attractive or desirable or clients may feel less at risk with a worker who has a well defined muscular body because they assume good health.

A new phenomenon has emerged since the early days of the AIDS epidemic where people were concerned to even touch someone with HIV, let alone people advocating that they would consider having unprotected sex with a person who held the view that they would not indicate their safe sex-practices. This phenomenon is reflected in the finding that the majority of the sex workers revealed an ambiguous sex intention to clients and a significant number went as far as to reveal an unsafe sex intention. Perhaps this reflects that what is likely to occur in a commercial sexual encounter is highly sexual in nature and cannot be predicted in advance. Both workers and clients may realise that what the transaction will look like is partly situational related and unpredictable and negotiated as the event unfolds, sometimes over several encounters with the same client. It may also reflect that clients are making requests for barebacking (Bimbi and Parsons 2005). But are these the only explanations? To isolate this to the sex industry and requests from clients would miss the point of connecting the phenomena of barebacking to a much larger context.

'Barebacking' has increased during the mid-1990s and has achieved something of a fetish status with the phenomenon being widely documented and debated in some sections of the popular press (Agosto 2001). It should not be a surprise to also find an increase in this practice among a sample of male sex workers. It may well reflect client demand for this sexual practice as well as a sexual practice preference by the sex worker under certain circumstances. Increase in this practice has been attributed to 'AIDS optimism' and 'condom fatigue'. The evidence in Australia, for example, is that 'fatigue/optimism' may be common among men who were young in 1985–90 and who are now 40 years and older (the common age profile of clients of MSWs) and have lived with HIV all of their sexual lives (Commonwealth of Australia 2005). This is partly the product of the short-term crisis of HIV/AIDS becoming a long-term challenge, the use of recreational substances before and during sexual activity and the introduction of new drugs for the treatment of HIV infections (Carballo-Dieguez and Bauermeister 2004). It is argued that some men intentionally engage in unsafe sex because they want to and it is closer to their notion of the male sexual psyche (Gendin 1997). Unsafe sex is also supported by discourses in amateur and professional pornography, internet sites and chat rooms devoted to barebacking, personal advertisements, private parties and the number of men seeking sexual partners who bareback. Others argue that some men are informally utilising harm reduction strategies (e.g. assessments of risk with long-term clients and clients with long-term sex workers). Others will bareback as long as they are the top partner because there is a myth that it is safe to bareback as the top.

Barebacking, raw and skin-to-skin sex have been extolled as 'feeling better' and being more pleasurable, spontaneous and intimate. Specific jargon and slang terminology has developed, some of which highlights the pleasure of intentional infection with HIV and the unrestricted exchange of bodily fluid as a shared act of bonding (i.e. 'gift giver', 'gifting' and 'bug chaser'). These are complex issues that need unpacking at both the social and individual level as they reveal that barebacking is not restricted to the male sex industry or a response to anti-retroviral treatments altering the perception of the risk of contracting HIV. Drawing on Foucault's work (1990) regarding attempts to regulate the relationship between sexual behaviour and identity, the focus on anal sex as a risk activity can have symbolic meaning as an act of profound intimacy and context for the expression of masculinity, power, sex as an expression of a certain kind of interaction and the changing nature of men's relationships with each other.

Despite twenty years of safer sex education 'barebacking' has emerged, and it also seems prevalent among male sex workers. At a time when reinvigorated HIV/STI prevention strategies are required particularly for MSM, the sexual health promotion needs of the less mainstream groups of society such as MSWs and their clients, especially those who bareback, require urgent and specific attention. It is important for strategies to recognise that many male sex workers do not have a gay self-identity and are reluctant to attend sexual health services, or if they do, do not reveal to staff their involvement in selling sex to other men. As David S. Bimbi and Jeffrey T. Parsons (2005) have argued, intervention efforts for this population need to understand the issues around intentions for engaging in sexual risk behaviours and the reasons behind those intentions. Such knowledge is critical to informing new and appropriate behavioural interventions. Some have argued that HIV/AIDS harm reduction programmes designed for gay men (e.g. small groups, individual counselling, community building activities conducted at gay and lesbian community centres) would not suit some of the people in this population. New intervention programmes that utilise anonymous and confidential forms of technology such as the internet and other venues in which some workers and clients prefer to operate may be required to engage their attention, together with exploring ambivalence about safer sex practices and HIV/STI infection. The use of language and context appropriate to their lives is critical here. If we can understand how they make sense of and give meaning to their experiences perhaps this information may be useful in developing appropriate interventions to curb the risk of HIV spreading even further among MSM. It is for this reason that we need more innovative strategies such as utilising the skills of 'indigenous' peer educators that include sex workers and clients. For example, the World Health Organisation guidelines for STI control in the sex industry recommends the involvement of peer sex workers as educators and coordinators of outreach community programmes (Ziersch *et al.* 2000). Such programmes may bring together the totality of the worker's experiences and lives rather than just their sexual behaviour, and be fundamentally more effective as they are less likely to be judgmental.

References

Agosto, M. (2001) 'Barebacking is back: the controversy of unprotected sex', *Genre*, 97: 50.

Belza, M. (2005) 'Risk of HIV infection among male sex workers in Spain', *Sexually Transmitted Infections*, 81: 85–8.

Biggs, D., DeVille, B. and Suen, E. (1991) 'A method of choosing multiway partitions for classification and decision trees', *Journal of Applied Statistics*, 18: 49–62.

Bimbi, D. and Parsons, J. (2005) 'Barebacking among internet based male sex workers', *Journal of Gay and Lesbian Psychotherapy*, 9: 85–105.

Brown, T., Chan, R., Mugrditchian, D., Mulhall, B., Plummer, D., Sarda, R. and Sittitrai, W. (eds) (1998) *Sexually Transmitted Diseases in Asia and the Pacific*. Honolulu, HI: Venereology Publishing, East-West Center and Thai Red Cross.

Carballo-Dieguez, A. and Bauermeister, J. (2004) '"Barebacking": intentional condomless anal sex in HIV-risk contexts. Reasons for and against it', *Journal of Homosexuality*, 47: 1–16.

CDC (2004) *HIV/AIDS Surveillance Report, 2003* (Vol. 15). Atlanta, GA: US Department of Health and Human Services.

CDC (2005) *HIV/AIDS Surveillance Report: HIV Infection and AIDS in the United States, 2004*, Atlanta, GA: US Department of Health and Human Services, available at http://www.cdc.gov/hiv//topics/surveillance/basic.htm, accessed 4 February 2006.

Centers for Disease Control and Prevention (1987) 'Antibody to human immunodeficiency virus in female prostitutes', *Morbidity and Mortality Weekly Report*, 36: 157–61.

Commonwealth of Australia (2005) *National HIV/AIDS Strategy: Revitalising Australia's Response 2005–2008*. Canberra: Attorney General's Department.

Dandona, L., Dandona, R., Kumar, G., Gutierrez, J., McPherson, S., Bertozzi, S. and ASCI FPP Study Team (2006) 'How much attention is needed towards men who sell sex to men for HIV prevention in India?', *BioMed Central Public Health*, 6: 31, available at http://www.biomedcentral.com/bmcpublichealth.

Department of Human Services, Victoria (2002) *New Plan Tackles Rising HIV Tally*. Melbourne: Department of Human Services, Victoria.

Elifson, K., Boles, J. and Sweat, M. (1993) 'Risk factors associated with HIV infection among male prostitutes', *American Journal of Public Health*, 83: 79–83.

Estcourt, E., Rohrsheim, R., Marks, C., Johnson, A., Donovon, B., Tidemon, R. and Mindel, A. (2000) 'HIV, sexually transmitted infections and risk behaviours in male commercial sex workers in Sydney', *Sexually Transmitted Infections*, 76: 294–8.

Firstmark Technologies (1990) *KnowledgeSEEKER User's Guide*. Ottawa.

Foucault, M. (1990) *The History of Sexuality, Volume 1: An Introduction*. New York: Vintage Books.

Gay Men's Health Center (2006) *HIV/AIDS Statistics*, available at http://www.gmhc.org/health/statistics.html, accessed 4 February 2006.

Gendin, S. (1997) 'Riding bareback: skin-on-skin sex been there, done that, want more', *POZ*, February: 50.

Halkitis, P. and Parsons, J. (2003) 'Intentional unsafe sex (barebacking) among HIV-positive gay men who seek sexual partners on the internet', *AIDS Care*, 15: 367–78.

Halkitis, P., Parsons, J. and Wilton, L. (2003) 'Barebacking among gay and bisexual men in New York City: explanations for the emergence of intential unsafe behavior', *Archives of Sexual Behavior*, 32: 351–7.

Harcourt, C. and Donovan, B. (2005) 'The many faces of sex work', *Sexually Transmitted Infections*, 81: 201–6.

Harcourt, C., Marks, C., Rohrsheim, R. *et al.* (2000) 'HIV, sexually transmitted infections, and risk behaviours in male commercial sex workers in Sydney', *Sexually Transmitted Infections*, 76: 294–8.

Hart, G. and Williamson, L. (2005) 'Increase in HIV sexual risk behaviour in homosexual men in Scotland, 1996–2002: prevention failure', *Sexually Transmitted Infections*, 81: 367–72.

Leuridan, E., Wouters, K., Stalpaert, M. and Van Damme, P. (2005) 'Male sex workers in Antwerp, Belgium: A descriptive study', *International Journal of STD and AIDS*, 16: 744–8.

McKenzie, D.P., McGorry, P.D., Wallace, C., Low, L., Copolov, D. and Singh, B.S. (1993) 'Constructing a minimal diagnostic decision tree', *Methods of Information in Medicine*, 32 (2): 161–6.

Mansergh, G., Marks, G., Colfax, G., Gusman, R., Rader, M. and Buchbinder, S. (2002) 'Barebacking in a diverse sample of men who have sex with men', *AIDS*, 16: 653–9.

Minichiello, V. and Harvey, G. (2007) 'Men as sex workers', in M. Flood, J. Gardiner, B. Pease and K. Pringle (eds) *Routledge International Encyclopedia of Men and Masculinities*. London: Routledge.

Minichiello, V., Marino, R., Browne, J., Jamieson, M., Peterson, K., Reuter, B. and Robinson, K. (2000) 'Commercial sex between men: A prospective diary-based study', *Journal of Sex Research*, 37 (2): 151–60.

MMWR (2004) 'High-risk sexual behavior by HIV-positive men who have sex with men: 16 sites, United States, 2000–2002', *Morbidity and Mortality Weekly Report*, 53 (38): 891–4.

New York Department of Health and Mental Hygiene (2003) *HIV Surveillance and Epidemiology Program Quarterly*. New York: Department of Health and Mental Hygiene.

Outspoken (2006) 'Outspoken barebacking', available at http://www.outuk.com/content/features/bareback, accessed 4 February 2006.

Packald, R., Brown, P., Berkelman, R. and Frumkin, H. (2004) *Emerging Illnesses and Society: Negotiating the Public Health Agenda*. Baltimore, MD: Johns Hopkins University Press.

Ridge, D. (2004) '"It was an incredible thrill": the social meanings and dynamics of younger gay men's experiences of barebacking in Melbourne', *Sexualities*, 7 (3): 259–79.

UNAIDS (2004) *Report on the Global AIDS Epidemic: Executive Summary*, available at http://www.unaids.org/bangkok2004/GAR2004_html/ExecSummary_en/ExecSumm_en_01.htm, accessed 4 February 2006.

UNAIDS/WHO (2005) *AIDS Epidemic Update: December 2005* (Geneva: UNAIDS), available at http://www.unaids.org/epi/2005, accessed 4 February 2006.

Watson, J. (2000) *Male Bodies: Health, Culture and Identity*. Buckingham: Oxford University Press.

Ziersch, A., Gaffney, J. and Tomlinson, D. (2000) 'STI prevention and the male sex industry in London: evaluating a pilot peer education programme', *Sexually Transmitted Infections*, 76: 447–53.

Chapter 9

From the oblivious to the vigilante: the views, experiences and responses of residents living in areas of street sex work

Kate Williams[1]

Introduction

Much research into female street sex work concentrates upon the viewpoint and experiences of the women involved (e.g. Phoenix 2001; Sanders 2005). The views, experiences and responses of local residents in the geographical areas in which sex work takes place are therefore often overlooked. Notwithstanding this, there does appear to be a gradually increasing interest in and consideration of the viewpoint of residents – for example, in the impetus for the government's Coordinated Prostitution Strategy (Home Office 2006a) and also appearing in recent research (see, for example, O'Neill and Campbell 2006; Pitcher *et al.* 2006). Nonetheless, a greater and more critical focus is still required, not only on the views and experiences of local residents, but especially on their responses to street sex work in their area.

In this chapter, I present findings from my research and attempt to highlight and critically discuss some of the views, experiences and responses that local residents of two very different areas within a major English city have towards sex work on the streets of their neighbourhood. Based on my results I have divided residents into six 'types' according to how they respond to living in areas of street sex work. The first part of the chapter discusses residents who have little or no response. The views and experiences of six residents living in an area of street sex work who were collectively taking moderate to high levels of action against the activity are then explored, before detailing and analysing their responses and also those of another group who can arguably be described as 'vigilantes'.

Method

Data in the form of observations, tape-recorded semi-structured qualitative interviews and documentary analysis were collected using both 'snowballing' and theoretical sampling approaches in two areas of one English city over two main periods totalling approximately two years, primarily as part of an ethnographic doctoral study that focused upon Street Watch community crime prevention schemes (which will be discussed in some detail later in this chapter).

Since the reason for the inception of the Street Watches in the two residential areas studied was to reduce and/or eradicate street sex work from their localities, an element of my research involved eliciting the views and experiences on the issue not only from the scheme members, but also from other non-participating residents. The data presented in this chapter concentrate in particular on those gathered on the activities of the two Street Watch schemes (including a series of interviews with six members of the Street Watch scheme in one of the areas), together with the results of interviews with 15 local residents.[2] I gained access to the members of the Street Watch schemes through the local police. The local residents were identified through several sources: some were identified via recommendations of the friends and neighbours of both the Street Watch members and the sex workers that I interviewed (snowballing). Another source was via the police who told me about other residents who had contacted them regarding the problem (four residents). Finally I made contacts through local community or religious organisations (six residents).

I first studied an inner-city area with a high population of ethnic minorities, high unemployment and a standard of living lower than the local city average. The area had been renowned as a red-light district for decades, with claims from the police and local residents that at its height in the 1980s and early 1990s, up to 450 sex workers were plying their trade daily both on the streets and from windows, leading it to being compared with prostitution in Amsterdam.

In contrast, the second area that I studied is a predominantly white, middle-class, affluent 'leafy' suburb, where levels of street sex work have always been much lower, with an average of no more than twenty sex workers working at any one time.

The two neighbourhoods, although located adjacent to one another, are therefore highly different both in their composition and in their experiences of street sex work. This gave me a rich variety of views and experiences to interpret, although clearly such data cannot claim to be wholly representative.

My data also include observations, interviews with sex workers, and interviews and discussions with police officers. However, in this chapter only the residents' views are addressed.

Residents' views, experiences and responses

I identified a wide range of resident views about, experiences of and responses to local street sex work. As aforementioned and shown in Table 9.1, based on my data the residents have been separated into six categories. It is not my intention, however, to suggest that these are distinct types of response, since some respondents straddled or changed categories at different times. Nor do I claim that these categories are definitive or causal – indeed more research would be required in order to demonstrate any direct relationship or correlation between awareness/concern and action levels, or in fact between the different amounts of sex work in the areas and the views expressed. Indeed, examples of most responses could be found in both areas. Nonetheless, there were clearly discernible patterns of response in each of the areas, such that while some opinions and reactions were found in both places, there is ample justification for presenting the areas as having very largely distinct response patterns. This will be explained further below. It should also be noted that people in other areas may well cite different 'problems' from those stated in Figure 9.1 below, not only due to the level and nature of the local sex work, but also because of the differences in the urban geography of an area. Moreover, to some extent such views are socially constructed by conversations between neighbours.

Minimal or no response

A minority of individuals was completely unaware of local street sex work, appearing almost oblivious to its existence. I have called these Type 1 residents or the phlegmatic group, and only two of the leafy suburb area residents (out of the total of 15 residents in the two areas) fell into this category. However, explanations for this are not altogether straightforward; for example, it was not that the individual

Table 9.1 Resident responses to local street sex work

Resident type	Awareness of local street sex work	Concern about local street sex work	Action taken	Number of residents in leafy suburb	Number of residents in inner city
1. Phlegmatic	None	Not applicable	–	2	0
2. Tolerant	Yes	Yes	Inactive	1	2
3. Passive concern	Yes	Yes	Inactive	1	2
4. Passing the buck	Yes	Yes	Minimal and responsible:* e.g. attending community meetings	4	3
5. Actively dissatisfied	Yes	Yes	Moderate/high and responsible:* e.g. Street Watch scheme, involvement in gaining ASBO	6	N/A**
6. Proactive activists	Yes	Yes	Extremely high and autonomous:* e.g. vigilantism	0	N/A**

* Johnston (1996).
** It is not possible to provide a total amount for those within my research who fell into categories 5 or 6 from the inner-city area, as not only did the actions of those Street Watch members vary over time, but the nature of the fieldwork (for example, observations and documentary analysis) combined with the large scale of their actions does not lend itself to the calculation of numbers.

was housebound or spent large amounts of time working away. Often, he or she was concerned with other matters. For example, one man argued:

> I don't consider it [prostitution] a problem ... I've not witnessed anything that would suggest to me that it's a big problem ... there are much more serious problems: dog fouling. Seriously, I'm absolutely serious about that. I was told about the prostitution and that the place is littered with used condoms – I've seen three used condoms ... since I've been here, *every morning* there are three new, you know, deposits from people's pets.

Another minority of residents (one from the leafy suburb and two from the inner-city area) was aware of the existence of street sex work in their local area, but were tolerant of it. For example, one local resident of the leafy suburb explains:

> The girls occasionally have stood on the opposite corner to us here. We've minded our business, they've largely minded theirs.

One female resident in the inner-city area saw distinct advantages to the situation, describing it as:

> One of the safest streets, because we had the girls watching out for anybody dodgy, we had the police going up and down watching the girls, so you never got burglaries!

Some of the residents I interviewed (one from the leafy suburb and two from the inner-city area) were aware of street sex work taking place in their neighbourhood, and were concerned about it, yet they did not take any action with a view to altering the situation. Reasons for this varied – one individual cited lack of time, the other two had children and feared repercussions. This has been named the passively concerned group.

Other residents, however (four from the leafy suburb and three from the inner-city area), took some action, albeit minimal and 'responsible' (Johnston 1996), in order to attempt to express their concerns and effect some type of change. For example, some had attended a community meeting to voice their feelings or talked to the police when particularly concerned. This group hoped that someone else would deal with the problem on their behalf: they preferred passing the buck to active engagement, but they were concerned.

Moderate or high response

An extremely important proportion of residents in my research had taken action against local street sex work, and the impact had been and continued to be highly significant and at times damaging to both the sex workers and other residents.

These 'actively dissatisfied' residents were those individuals whose concern about local levels of street prostitution led them to take moderate to high yet 'responsible' (Johnston 1996) levels of action in order to attempt to combat what they perceived to be a problem. Although many residents of the inner-city area I studied fell into this category, here, I focus on a particular group of six residents in the leafy suburb. Before discussing their actions, I want first to explore their potential reasons by highlighting a few of their views and experiences as summarised by Figure 9.1. Some of these also concurred with the 'passively concerned', those 'passing the buck' and the 'proactive activists' (see below).

Views and experiences of those taking action against local street sex work in the leafy suburb area studied

Without doubt, for some local residents of areas in which street sex work takes place, it can constitute a significant problem, causing a

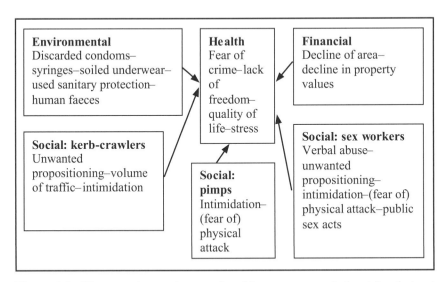

Figure 9.1 Views and experiences of residents concerned about local street sex work

range of stresses (see also Sion 1977; Matthews 1993; Pitcher *et al.* 2006). For the purposes of discussion and analysis, these have been grouped into four main concerns: environmental, financial, social (kerb-crawlers, pimps, sex workers) and health. Many of these concerns are overlapping and interconnected, although all impact upon health, as will be explained below.

Environmental concerns

One of the most obvious concerns cited by these suburban residents was the impact of street sex work on the physical environment, typically in the form of used condoms, syringes, soiled underwear and sanitary protection being discarded on the streets or in people's gardens. Some residents commented that their gardens were also used as toilets by the sex workers.

Sex workers have been regarded as a potential threat to public health throughout history (Phoenix 2001), and indeed it appears still to remain the case, as all the local residents I interviewed felt that these environmental effects presented a potential risk to physical health, together with clearly being generally unpleasant. A particular concern was about children picking up used condoms.

The feelings of the suburban residents are captured by one woman who lives in a local block of flats:

> You can't say we're affected here can you, on this top floor ... but when you [go] down the back onto your car park, and the girls have been using your car park, and you've got condoms on your car and you have to call the caretaker because they've defecated in your dustbin area, and there's soiled underwear and blood-stained underwear been left, and Tampax.

Furthermore, popular family areas such as parks may become restricted areas, according to residents, because of this type of litter, together with the risk of children viewing public sex acts. One retired woman explained:

> We used to go round the reservoir with the grandson to feed the ducks – we can't go round there now. We can't go in the park.

Financial concerns

Secondly, some residents believed that street sex work had caused their neighbourhoods to decline in terms of an increase in problems associated with drugs and crime. This had also had a harsh financial impact upon them, in that their properties were worth significantly less. Furthermore, some felt that they were unable to move away from the area, as properties could be difficult to sell as no one wanted to move into the neighbourhood. As one man of retirement age explained:

> Now, this particular house is too big for our needs. This problem has not only stopped us selling the house, it's had a great effect on the value of the house.

Social concerns
The potential social impact of street sex work as described by these residents can be divided into three separate issues: the kerb-crawlers, the pimps and the sex workers themselves.

The problems caused by kerb-crawlers are twofold. First, the disruption of the noise caused by the sheer number of vehicles which circle the streets to pick up the sex workers. This can be particularly disruptive at night, with residents being unable to sleep for example, as one woman explained:

> We used to get traffic first thing in the morning and then half four in the afternoon to about six. Now, it's constant. I've come to the stage when … I've had enough, I've got to go, I cannot stop here. You know, because it's night after night, day after day, seven days a week, twenty-four hours a day.

Kerb-crawling was also described by these local residents as being extremely intimidating at times for female residents of all ages, causing many to feel threatened and not want to walk down the street alone at any time of day for fear of being propositioned or accosted. One woman described how:

> They are just running your life. You've got no life even in your own house really … you can stand in your own garden … watering the plants … and I've got guys stopping and looking at me … it's intimidating, because you know what they're down here for.

The pimps associated with the sex workers are also a source of fear and intimidation for these residents. One woman recalled an incident where she was threatened and physically assaulted by a pimp outside her house, leaving her fearful now to leave her home at all:

> I still am frightened to go out the house ... I'm frightened that
> ... if I've got to walk up the road, if he sees me, he'll stop and
> he'll attack me. And I know because if I hadn't run away that
> night when I did, he would have physically hit me.

Male residents complained of being the target of verbal abuse and
unwanted propositioning from the female sex workers. A small
number of residents had also witnessed public sex acts. Some
residents also found the sex workers to be intimidating, again fearing
attack, as one woman described:

> That other Friday when we were out here ... she came past,
> and she spit all over the car, stood, and then starting shouting
> ... 'I'll smash your windows and your car'. We get that quite a
> lot ... you have to take these threats seriously, because it could
> happen, especially when they're high on the drugs.

Indeed, three others from the group claim that they have suffered
attacks from sex workers, including being kicked and punched.

Health concerns

All of these experiences can be argued to have a potentially alarming
impact upon health and overall quality of life. For example, the
presence of kerb-crawlers, pimps and sex workers may increase fear
of crime. One young woman stated:

> I don't feel safe going to the shops. I'm wary of people ... of
> who's around. It's all since the prostitutes have come.

Indeed, freedom may be impaired because of not feeling confident
or comfortable in walking the streets due to the fear of crime, or
perhaps fear of contamination from an unhygienic environment – and
one may not be able to move to a different area. Financial difficulties
may also further increase stress levels. One resident, who attributed
her heart attack and need for sleeping tablets to the stress of living
in the area, summed up its impact upon her life:

> Every day you get up now, there's nothing to look forward to,
> because you know what you're going to see outside your front
> door, day after day. And to me, that's no life. I feel personally

that my freedom has been deprived of me. All of the everyday things, that's all been taken away.

It can be seen, then, that the lives of some residents of the leafy suburb have been dramatically impaired by the presence of street prostitution in their neighbourhood. Given their feelings, opinions and frustrations, it is understandable that they wish to take some form of direct action in order to reduce levels of street sex work in their area and thus, in their opinion, improve their lives.

Furthermore, certain forms of action, including Street Watch schemes (discussed below), are encouraged by the police and overall government policies as part of the recent 'responsibilization strategies' (Garland 1996).[3] Moreover, these residents believed that tackling street sex work was not a police priority and so they had little choice but to take action themselves. Although many community crime prevention initiatives like Neighbourhood Watch have had debatable success rates (see, for example, Bennett 1994; Rosenbaum 1988), there is some evidence to suggest that Street Watch schemes can reduce crime (see Williams 2005).

Urban 'bird spotting': activities of those taking action against local street sex work in the leafy suburb area studied

Street Watch schemes

This particular group of six residents that I interviewed in the leafy suburb were members of a (larger) Street Watch scheme. Street Watch schemes were introduced in 1994 so that residents could be the 'eyes and ears' of the police as part of a police/community crime prevention partnership scheme. Now an extension of Neighbourhood Watch, it is estimated that around 20,000 such schemes exist in the UK. They may be created to combat a variety of crimes or anti-social behaviour. The defining feature of Street Watch schemes is that members patrol the streets in small groups in order to gather information for the police, together with providing a visible deterrent (Home Office 2000).

Street Watch schemes are therefore popular, yet they were met with considerable controversy at their inception, with fears over the management and accountability of untrained citizens voluntarily patrolling their own streets and thus the risk of vigilantism. As will be described below, some of these concerns have materialised.

The members of the Street Watch scheme in the leafy suburb area spent a considerable amount of their time and energy – and, many would claim, took significant personal risks – in order to target both 'demand' and 'supply' to help reduce the volume of street sex work in their neighbourhood. First, they attempted to tackle demand by targeting the kerb-crawlers. In order to do this, while patrolling either on foot or by vehicle, the group noted down details of cars seen kerb-crawling – including the registration number, make and colour of the vehicle, a description of the occupants, together with the date, time and location of the sighting. This information would then be handed to the local police, enabling them to send out letters to the registered keepers of the vehicles, warning them that they would be liable to prosecution if they were seen in similar circumstances again. The police also maintained a kerb-crawlers database in order to record this information. This method was successful in the sense that several kerb-crawlers were prosecuted partly due to the information provided to the police by the Street Watch group. The Street Watch scheme also lobbied their MP and local councillors, claiming some responsibility for making kerb-crawling an illegal offence as part of the Criminal Justice and Police Act 2001.

The Street Watch group was also instrumental in securing road closures in their area in order to make circuiting the area more difficult for kerb-crawlers. Although effective in breaking the potential circuits, this method can of course be frustrating for local residents as well, often meaning that a simple journey can become quite complex.

The other major activity which the Street Watch scheme undertook was to focus upon the sex workers themselves. Besides the presence on the streets of members of the scheme, which at times served to deter potential clients and thus profitable trade, the Street Watch scheme also gathered information for the police about the sex workers, to be used as evidence against them in the process of serving an Anti-Social Behaviour Order (ASBO).[4]

The Street Watch members viewed this gathering of information as a necessary albeit time-consuming task, yet during my observations, I noted that it sometimes involved somewhat dubious, questionable and possibly intimidating methods. For example, the group would patrol the area by vehicle most evenings in order to 'spot' a sex worker. When a (at least suspected) sex worker was found, a member of the group would drive near to her (often simultaneously instructing her to 'move on' or 'go home') in order to shine a lamp on her and take a photograph. The photographs, together with times and dates of sightings, formed what the group jokingly referred to as the 'tart log' and were then also handed over to the police. Several sex workers were served with ASBOs with the help of the Street Watch group.

Although usually associated with youth crime, ASBOs have been widely used against street sex workers due to the alleged 'harassment, alarm or distress' that they may cause to residents, as described above. Potentially banning a sex worker from entering a particular area for significant amounts of time and resulting in a possible prison sentence if breached, the 'punitive populism' of the ASBO has been severely criticised (for example, Muncie 1999; Budd and Sims 2001; Wood 2004), most notably for not addressing any underlying causes of behaviour. With regard to street sex work, however, ASBOs can result in an array of serious and potentially life-threatening repercussions. For example, although police officers may argue that ASBOs break the traditional cycle of sex workers being arrested, fined and returning to the streets to earn money to pay off that fine, the use of what amounts to a costly and cumbersome order may instead force the sex worker to work in a new and unfamiliar environment. This raises the possibility of even more dangers for the sex worker, including taking increased risks due to not being familiar with the local kerb-crawlers and not being able to access health services such as crucial HIV prevention projects.

Overall, Helen Jones and Tracey Sagar (2001: 879) argue that ASBOs are inappropriate and discriminatory:

Exclusion is not an effective deterrent against street prostitution and its use merely resurrects the (past) legislative predilection for social segregation and discrimination towards female members of the sex industry ... the privileging of public sensibility over personal welfare will result in danger and isolation for prostitutes.

Without doubt, the 'notoriously slippy' (Kelling 2005: 140) notion of 'community' is open to question in situations such as this: small groups of individuals such as those forming the Street Watch scheme may claim to represent the 'community', yet in so doing may discriminate further against other, often more vulnerable and already victimised, sections of the 'community'. As Adam Crawford (1998: 125) argues, schemes such as this may not be representing 'communities as collective entities' but rather 'aggregates of individuals or households' and can therefore be regarded as 'collective individualism'. One must therefore ask whose community is being served in these situations and, furthermore, whose justice? Doubtless, the activities of the Street Watch scheme – albeit understandable – may have indeed contributed to compromising the personal welfare of the sex workers. Nonetheless, and crucially, residents would respond that the sex workers are also compromising their personal welfare in many significant respects as described above. It can be argued that it is not the responses of groups of residents in schemes such as Street Watch that divide and alienate sections of communities, but rather the government which is responsible for providing such opportunities for the much encouraged notion of active citizenship, yet at the same time failing to offer any long-term and/or realistic solutions to the problems of either the sex workers or, as a result, of the residents.

Vigilantism: activities of those taking action against local street sex work in the inner-city area studied

Finally, the group I have called 'proactive activists' are those who sometimes respond with threats and force. They may take autonomous (Johnston 1996) action against sex workers in their neighbourhood, which might be deemed as vigilantism. This section concentrates upon the activities of some of the residents in the inner-city area studied. Although officially a part of a separate Street Watch scheme and undertaking approved activities (including some of those as described above), some members of this inner-city group took other actions which could be argued to be vigilantism.[5]

Vigilantism is a complex term that is difficult to define. Les Johnston (1996) provides a framework which specifies that the individuals must be voluntarily involved, as well as being private citizens without the state's support, who intend an act that either uses or threatens force. According to this definition of vigilantism, the act needs to arise as a reaction to deviance and also to offer assurances of security to others.

In this inner-city area, the Street Watch scheme reduced levels of street sex work dramatically (and more dramatically than in the leafy suburb, although it should be noted that the former originally had much higher levels of street sex work). However, there were many alleged incidents of vigilantism against sex workers. These incidents have been denied by the Street Watch group, yet the accusations were made and the activities reported. For example, *The Guardian* newspaper (11 February 1998) reported a response from the English Collective of Prostitutes (ECP) to an article:

> The activities of the Street Watch organisation ... were glorified in these pages, with photos of elderly men sitting by the roadside with placards, illustrating the power of 'community

action'. But from the point of view of prostitute women and others who oppose Street Watch, this is not 'community action'. It is mob rule ... women from our network were terrorised by bricks through their windows, beatings and threats.

Furthermore, according to some female residents, the actions taken by this particular group in order to move street sex work from the area were worse than living with the sex workers. Indeed, the 'vigilantes' themselves were causing fear and dividing the community. As one female resident explained to me:

The Street Watch people ... you'd have a group of ten men ... standing there ... but also harassing women ... whether they were prostitutes or not. They didn't know who was a prostitute and who wasn't ... it was very intimidating ... in fact, I felt more intimidated walking past them than I did walking past kerb-crawlers ... with the kerb-crawlers, if they asked you if you were working and you said 'no', then that was fine, but with the vigilantes, they wouldn't believe you weren't working ... I got stares.

It is not possible to provide clear-cut reasons as to why 'vigilante' behaviour allegedly took place in this area and not the leafy suburb. Indeed, it is arguably not simply due to the levels of street sex work having been much higher in this area (indeed, as I have indicated, some residents were tolerant, passively concerned or took responsible action); rather it was a complex mix of different factors. Of course, another issue which may influence the reactions of residents to street sex work which has not been mentioned above is cultural, religious or moral beliefs. Some of these factors may be applicable to the inner-city area studied, due to its high Muslim population, where according to Marie Macey (2002: 27):

Under the concept of izzat (honour), central to Islamic culture, women carry the entire burden of upholding family and community honour ... and 'appropriate' female dress and behaviour are taken to signify not only their honour, but that of their families and the wider community ... the result is that in defence of honour, men go to inordinate lengths to monitor the appearance and behaviour of women.

Indeed, there were comparable events in Lumb Lane in Bradford, where it was alleged that residents were also involved in violent actions towards sex workers. *The Guardian* newspaper (18 June 1995) reported the claims of a sex worker:

> Two of them got a bit of wire and put it around my neck. One of them picked up a machete. When I put my hand up to defend myself, they chopped into it. I had to have 11 stitches.

Overall, this type of violent behaviour – for whatever reason it may be caused – clearly places sex workers in yet more violent, dangerous and unacceptable situations, together with having the potential to intimidate other local residents and to be generally divisive. Furthermore, although this type of action may be successful in terms of eliminating street sex work from a particular neighbourhood, it is of course merely displaced to another area or region and thus provides no overall 'solution'.

Conclusions

A number of conclusions, albeit tentative, can be drawn from this exploratory research. Community responses to sex work can certainly be extremely varied, ranging from people who are oblivious or passive to others who take direct and sometimes violent and/or potentially damaging actions against the women involved. However, at the same time, given the difficulties experienced by many residents and the sometimes extremely upsetting effect that street prostitution as described above can have upon their lives, it is possible to sympathise with their frustrations.

Sex work which occurs in residential areas is therefore an extremely complex, sensitive and often highly controversial matter, impacted upon by so many different factors. The status quo is clearly unacceptable, with both local residents and sex workers suffering. Invariably, when areas of street sex work are displaced or constantly in a state of shift, partly as a result of resident actions, this at best merely moves the problems experienced by residents to a different area; at worst it causes greater exclusion and danger to the women who are selling sexual services.

At present, however, it appears to be too early to assess fully the potential impact of the government strategy (although see Phoenix, this volume). The fact that this is the first such review of the prostitution laws in 50 years is progress that in itself should be welcomed. However, the results of my research underline the longstanding unacceptability of the current arrangements and the need to take every possible measure to devise a solution which solves the problem for both aggrieved parties.[6] While some of the key aims of the strategy – focusing on prevention, tackling demand, developing routes out of prostitution, and addressing off-street prostitution – may hold promise, the controversial concept of a managed area where sex workers would be allowed to work, which has been understandably popular with residents of red light areas, has currently been dismissed. What is needed is a policy which seeks to resolve this contradiction, recognising both the rights of residents to a quiet environment without the litter of sexual intercourse, and also the right of sex workers to be protected as they sell their services. However, what is crucial is that all parties, including residents, are listened to and heard, within the current context of 'modernising' the prostitution laws.

Notes

1 This chapter is based upon research for a PhD (ESRC Award No. R00429934471). The author would like to thank the other editors for their most helpful feedback on this chapter.
2 Although some of the residents interviewed had lived in both areas and therefore gave their views and experiences of both, the 15 can be split into seven from the inner-city and eight from the leafy suburb.
3 For example, the Together We Can action plan (Home Office 2005a), the Anti-Social Behaviour Act 2003, the Respect Action Plan (Home Office 2006b), the National Community Safety Plan 2006–2009 (Home Office 2005b) and the police reform White Paper (Home Office 2004).
4 ASBOs were created by the 1998 Crime and Disorder Act. They are civil orders which can be served upon an individual who is causing harassment, alarm or distress to local residents. ASBOs can restrict movement and behaviour, can last for life, and if breached can result in a prison sentence of up to five years.
5 Clearly, the use or threat of vigilantism within a police/community partnership questions the accountability and legitimacy of any such scheme, in that the state cannot be seen to support unauthorised violence. Although not the focus of discussion here, please refer to Williams (2005).
6 In the meantime, Pitcher et al. (2006) have suggested tactics to ease the current situation, including mediation and awareness raising, as part of an integrated response.

References

Bennett, T. (1994) 'Community policing on the ground: developments in Britain', in D. Rosenbaum (ed.) *The Challenge of Community Policing*. London: Sage, pp. 224–6.

Brady, P. (1999) '"Vice girls" litter "a risk to health"', *Birmingham Evening Mail*, 23 July.

Budd, T. and Sims, L. (2001) *Antisocial Behaviour and Disorder: Findings From The 2000 British Crime Survey*, Home Office Findings 145. London: Home Office, Research, Development and Statistics Directorate.

Crawford, A. (1998) *Crime Prevention and Community Safety: Politics, Policies and Practices*. London: Longman.

Garland, D. (1996) 'The limits of the sovereign state', *British Journal of Criminology*, 36 (4): 445–71.

Hancock, L. (2001) *Community, Crime and Disorder*. Basingstoke: Palgrave.

Home Office (1994) *Guidelines for Street Watch Schemes*. London: Home Office Public Relations Branch.

Home Office (2000) *Welcome to Neighbourhood Watch*. London: Home Office Communications Directorate.

Home Office (2004) *Policing: Building Safer Communities Together: Summary of Consultation Responses*. London: Home Office Communications Directorate.

Home Office (2004/5) *Welcome to Neighbourhood Watch*. London: Home Office Communications Directorate.

Home Office (2005a) *Together We Can*. London: Home Office, Civil Renewal Unit, Communities Group.

Home Office (2005b) *National Community Safety Plan 2006–2009*. London: Home Office.

Home Office (2006a) *A Co-ordinated Prostitution Strategy and a Summary of Responses to Paying the Price*. London: HMSO.

Home Office (2006b) *Respect Action Plan*. London: Home Office Communications Directorate.

Johnston, L. (1996) 'What is vigilantism?', *British Journal of Criminology*, 36 (2): 220–36.

Jones, H. and Sagar, T. (2001) 'Crime and Disorder Act 1998: prostitution and the Anti-Social Behaviour Order', *Criminal Law Review*, November, pp. 873–85.

Kelling, G. (2005) 'Community crime reduction: activating formal and informal control', in N. Tilley (ed.) *Handbook of Crime Prevention and Community Safety*. Cullompton: Willan.

Macey, M. (2002) 'Interpreting Islam: young Muslim men's involvement in criminal activity in Bradford', in B. Spalek (ed.) *Islam, Crime and Criminal Justice*. Devon: Willan.

McElvoy, A. (1995) 'The battle for the streets of Bradford', *The Times*, 13 June.

Matthews, R. (1993) *Kerb-Crawling, Prostitution and Multi-Agency Policing*, Police Research Group Crime Prevention Unit Series Paper 43. London: Home Office Police Department.

Mills, H. (1998) 'From vice town to vigilante hell', *The Observer*, 6 December.

Mitchell, C. (1998) 'Community action: street dread', *The Guardian*, 11 February.

Muncie, J. (1999) 'Institutionalised intolerance: youth justice and the 1998 Crime and Disorder Act', *Critical Social Policy*, 19 (2): 147–75.

Narayan, N. (1995) 'Asians see red over streetgirl "toleration"', *The Guardian*, 18 June.

O'Neill, M. and Campbell, R. (2006) 'Street sex work and local communities: creating discursive spaces for genuine consultation and inclusion', in R. Campbell and M. O'Neill (eds) *Sex Work Now*. Cullompton: Willan.

Phoenix, J. (2001) *Making Sense of Prostitution*. Basingstoke: Palgrave.

Pitcher, J., Campbell, R., Hubbard, P., O'Neill, M. and Scoular, J. (2006) *Living and Working in Areas of Street Sex Work: From Conflict to Coexistence*. York: Joseph Rowntree Foundation.

Rosenbaum, D. (1988) 'Community crime prevention: a review and synthesis of the literature', *Justice Quarterly*, 5 (3): 323–95.

Sagar, T. (2005) 'Street watch: concept and practice: civilian participation in street prostitution control', *British Journal of Criminology*, 45 (1): 98–112.

Sanders, T. (2005) *Sex Work: A Risky Business*. Cullompton: Willan.

Sion, A. (1977) *Prostitution and the Law*. London: Faber & Faber.

Williams, K. (2005) 'Caught between a rock and a hard place: police experiences with the legitimacy of a Street Watch partnership', *Howard Journal*, 44 (5): 527–37.

Williams, K. (2006) 'A Question of Legitimacy: an Ethnographic Study of Two Street Watch Schemes' (unpublished PhD thesis, Keele University).

Wood, M. (2004) *Perceptions and Experiences of Antisocial Behaviour*, Findings No. 252. London: Home Office, Research, Development and Statistics Directorate.

Part 2

Sex as Violence

Philip Birch, Maureen Cain, Kate Williams and Gayle Letherby

The second part of this volume brings together eight original and innovative chapters on the theme of 'sex as violence'. The chapters cover a number of areas including rape, sex offenders, trafficked sex and child abuse via the internet; however, there are three overarching themes all eight chapters encapsulate. These themes are:

- sex crime policy;
- offending behaviour;
- public protection and public communication systems.

These chapters offer a critique of current policies, debates and interventions surrounding the issue of sex as violence, and suggest that not all of them have been effective and that some may have been positively harmful. Among other issues the following questions are raised by the chapters in this section of the book:

- How do we protect victims of sex-related violence, and are current policies and interventions really maximising protection?
- Has the state inadvertently supported sexed violence by implementing policies and interventions based on false theorising, strategies which have therefore been ineffective and possibly at times harmful?
- How can we better understand the nature and extent of such violence?

As with the first part of this collection, this introduction to Part 2 addresses the ambiguous and ambivalent nature of the responses to 'sexed violence'. For example, one of the issues which emerges about popular conceptions of sex as violence is that victimisation is highly feminised: to be a victim implies a female status,[1] it seems. A similar discursive reduction, this time relating to age, is found in the processes described by Jenny Davidson and Elena Martellozzo and by Jenny Kitzinger (see below), whereby in the one case adolescent victims of sex offences are infantilised and therefore offered inappropriate help, and in the other mature men who have sex with younger teenagers are demonised as if they had had sex with a small child. Again, two oversimplified categories are allowed to stand for complex social and psychological processes, thereby once again making it unlikely that any party will receive appropriate help tailored to their specific needs. Indeed, the victimisation of sex workers themselves is also signed by the ambivalence and ambiguity which characterise discourses about sex as violence, as sex workers who are raped and sexually assaulted are viewed differently from women in other occupations and financial circumstances. Indeed, the papers collected here suggest that sexual assault may be regarded as an 'occupational hazard' of sex work. Women, it seems, are natural victims of sex crimes, and not least when they are, quite legally, selling sexual services.

This image of women as normal victims is demonstrated by those exceptional and high-profile cases involving, for example, convicted child murderers such as Myra Hindley and Rose West, or accessories to such murders such as Maxine Carr. Clearly these are not women at all but demons! How else could the normalcy of women as essentially *victims* be discursively maintained? This discourse matters: it ensures that whether women are perpetrators or victims of violent, sex-related crimes, they do not get the help they need: these often desperate individuals can only be approached through a prism of cultural mythology. Another common myth is that strangers are the most common perpetrators of rape, whereas the evidence is that, war zones excepted, family members are most frequently perpetrators, followed by friends as the next most frequent group of perpetrators. This further highlights a widespread and seemingly deep cultural reluctance to recognise the by now incontrovertible evidence about the forms and frequencies of sex as violence. One of the opening papers in this part of the collection, by Adrian Howe (see below), addresses this issue head on. In light of the mounting evidence about the intrinsically, if variously, gendered nature of sex as violence the ambiguity, the ambivalence and the outright obfuscation which constitute both the official and the media discourses suggest a very deep level of denial, an almost intended obtuseness. This needs to be stated clearly here, since much of this part of the book is (yet another) attempt at demystification, while the rest is concerned with the fact that in the case of female as well as male perpetrators, a response in terms of these widespread ideological misunderstandings means that perpetrators will be inappropriately treated and the undeniably serious problems thereby exacerbated. These are the reasons we have collected these papers together in the second part of this volume. Below we consider how the three substantive themes and the three policy-related questions identified above are addressed by our contributing authors.

Sex violence policy is, as indicated above, first considered by Adrian Howe in Chapter 11 – 'Yes Minister, "sex violence policy *has* failed": it's time for sex, violence and crime in a postmodern frame'. Howe focuses on the UK government's announcement in March 2006 that a rethink of how best to tackle rape is needed, with a focus on challenging the attitudes of men in relation to sex. Howe considers that previous policy on domestic violence, for example, has done very little to overcome the 'pervasive culture of permissiveness towards men's violence' or to change the fact that women and children are far more likely to be killed or otherwise victimised (by men) in the domestic sphere than men are. The notion of gender equality is persistently used to obscure this major and enduring inequity. Therefore, she argues, it is time to rethink 'sex violence policy'.

The theme is picked up by Liz Kelly in 'Contradictions and paradoxes: international patterns of, and responses to, reported rape cases' (Chapter 13). She reviews the extensive reforms of statute, procedure and agency guidelines in relation to rape, which many nations undertook in the 1970s and 1980s. Despite the shared ambition among these countries to protect women by securing more convictions in rape cases, nowhere has this outcome been achieved. In fact the reverse effect occurred, with falling rates of prosecutions, convictions and a decline in willingness to report. Rapes still occur with relative impunity, and this has to be acknowledged and more effectively addressed.

In Chapter 16 – 'Sexual offenders and public protection in an uncertain age' – Bill Hebenton reviews the historical background to the regulatory and registration arrangements on both sides of the Atlantic in relation to this offending group. The profanation of a child, constructed as the epitome of innocence, is itself constructed as unforgivable. In actuarial terms the risk of a second profanation, a reoffending, is calculable but unpredictable in the individual case. This is the actuarial dilemma confronting policy-makers and practitioners. In the end the risk to responsible agencies in the event of a mistake is more readily calculated, and there is a risk that the offender is left with the burden of proving that he is no longer dangerous. Hebenton's paper reveals that there is no solution to this dilemma in the United States either, just skilled professional judgment based on available best evidence. The popular demand for certainty is understandable but misplaced.

The final paper which addresses policy questions directly is Chapter 12 written by Jen Marchbank. In 'War and sex crime' she documents the mass rape and other violent crimes against women which have occurred in wartime. Again women are targeted. Here the male 'ownership' of women is also turned against rival men, when rape is itself used as a weapon of war, intended to demoralise the rival army for example. Are men always the key audience for male actions, whether the sex is willingly and satisfactorily purchased from a sophisticated and equally willing online vendor or alternatively savagely stolen in the aftermath of war? It seems so … This is a double objectification, by both sides. International law in this area is exposed as just as ineffective as the national legal systems discussed by Kelly.

Offending behaviour

Under this theme we begin with Philip Birch's 'Attachment styles, emotional loneliness and sexual offending' (Chapter 14). Birch explores the impact of these personality characteristics on sexual offending. While earlier research from outside the UK has found a strong relationship between sexual offending and insecure attachment styles and high levels of emotional loneliness, Birch's research comparing carefully matched samples of sexual offenders and a sample of non-offenders drawn from the staff of a local authority in the UK shows *no* relationship between these personality variables and sex offending. The relationship is dynamic and undeniably complex. Moreover, the relationships found may be culturally specific given that sexual expression is integrally related to the cultural variable of gender. These findings indicate a need for considerable caution both in the development of generalised explanatory theory and in the formulation of treatment policies.

In Chapter 15 – 'Understanding women who commit sex offences' – Amanda Matravers draws on in-depth research with female sex offenders and her research indicates a similar need to avoid premature generalisations and treatment programmes based upon them. In exploring the motivations of a sample of 48 women convicted of serious sex offences she questions the assumptions typically made about this offending population: that they were coerced by men or that previous victimisation by men plays a role in their sex offending. Through lifestory interviews Matravers reveals a number of competing narratives offered by the women themselves, including that '[a]ll five lone offenders experienced abusive or inadequate mothering' … four had been abused in childhood, but, tellingly, one had not. Abuse carried out with partners, she goes on, is best conceived as a *folie à deux*, to which each partner makes a contribution; group offenders share with their victims economic disadvantage and life in a socially isolated community. There is no denial of agency by the women themselves. Rather, through their stories, Matravers reveals the complexity of individual circumstance leading up to their offending. From this she argues that both theoretical and practical work needs to be done in order to develop intervention styles which allow women themselves to explain their offending and to develop strategies for behavioural change which give due weight to the particularities of each woman's story. As pro-feminist scholars ourselves we note the risk, which Matravers avoids, of denying agency to the women we may most wish to assist. As in the case of teenaged victims of underage sex discussed by Lyvinia Rogers Elleschild in Chapter 10 – 'Why do "young people" go missing in "child prostitution" reform?' – well intentioned help misfires when the theory is inadequate for the job it must do if 'real' female sex offenders and 'real' child victims, with all their complex motivations and emotions, are to be allowed true agency in their pasts and hoped for futures.

Marchbank's chapter, discussed in the previous section above, also addresses the theme of offending behaviour. She reveals that while the majority of genocidal rapes, such as those committed in Bosnia in the 1990s, are perpetrated upon women, men and boys may also on occasion be targeted. Such sex crimes can best be explained using concepts of gender construction and deconstruction, nationalism, ethnic dominance and ethnic cleansing, and cultural genocide, as well as the more obvious connections between militarisation and masculinity. From the editors' point of view, the question arises whether perhaps similar issues may play a larger part in 'everyday rape' than has hitherto been recognised. It may be hoped that applying these theoretical propositions to research on 'everyday rape' might lead to more culturally sensitive theory and perhaps, as a result, to more effective preventive strategies – although Kelly's analysis, discussed earlier, leaves little room for confidence.

Public protection and public communication systems

At this stage of the discontinuous argument constituted by these papers we turn our full attention to the issue already raised obliquely by the work of Hebenton, Birch and Matravers: the issue of what to do, or public protection.

In 'The "paedophile-in-the community" protests: press reporting and public responses' (Chapter 18) Jenny Kitzinger considers the plight of sex offenders who are released into the community, focusing in particular on the lurid language of media campaigns. She analyses what motivates communities to mount aggressive and high-profile responses. In her conclusion Kitzinger reminds us that only a minority of 'paedophiles' lives in the community in this way. Most live in the same familial household as their victims. Of that minority living 'in the community' post-release from prison, the majority do not reoffend. Nonetheless, Kitzinger does not demonise the press and concerned citizens either: their fears are real, if statistically disproportionate, and we can learn from the fact they are expressed. What is necessary is to analyse carefully these moments of disproportionate anger/ fear for what they reveal about the structure of communities, about citizens' sense of powerlessness and about the press. Certain it is that aftercare services have responded to these fears here as in the United States (Hebenton, this volume).

Finally, in Chapter 17 Julia Davidson and Elena Martellozzo explore 'Protecting children online: towards a safer internet'. The chapter presents findings from two studies, one which is based on a programme attempting to educate children and their parents about safe internet use, with the second exploring police practice in combating indecent online images of children and in the prosecution of online groomers. The findings reveal that while children do have a basic understanding of 'Stranger Danger' this is not necessarily applied in cyberspace. However, in relation to actual and potential abuses to children in and resulting from cyber contacts, the problem is not too much or misplaced parental alarm, but insufficient realisation by carers of the extent of the problem (one US study suggests a quarter of children who use the net have had 'an unwanted exposure to inappropriate sexually explicit pictures', or of the dangers in the 'real' world that can result. Here the authorities, and in particular the police, are in advance of public concern, and their early recognition of the problem and willingness to devote resources to it is to be applauded. For parents the authors' advice is low key and sensible: treat an online session like going out: ask your son or daughter which sites they will visit, how long they expect to stay there and whom they will meet. As a matter of routine interest, ask about it when they 'return'. This way it will not become an issue.

The message from this second half of the book is that deductive theories about engendering, sex and crime are of little value. Instead, where data do exist – as they overwhelmingly do in relation to rape and 'everyday' violence against women for example – they must be used in the construction of policy. Data now also exist in relation to many other sex crimes. Well designed research which listens carefully to both offenders and victims – research which may be qualitative as well as quantitative and which is culturally as well as psychologically sensitive – reveals both general patterns of vulnerability and specific reasons for perpetration. Both are needed. Statistical trends reveal the unspoken presence of socio-political and ideological/cultural structuration, which must be addressed by public education and acknowledged by policing policy. This socio-cultural context provides an enabling environment for potential offenders. When an ideology of stereotyped extreme behaviour is to be found both in the community and, in more sophisticated forms, at the professional level, it means that those sex offenders who wish to desist may be unable to receive either the skilled casework help they need or the protection to which they, as citizens post-release, are entitled. It also means that past victims are shortchanged and future victims put at even greater risk.

Meanwhile, as Part 1 showed, substantial resources are still being devoted to the harassment of street workers who must be seen, post-Ipswich 2006, as undeniably more sinned against than sinning. Our policies and practices in relation to sex as crime are in serious need of rebalancing. The point, after all, is to change them.

Note

1 Not a reduction because to be female is less, but a reduced way of thinking which refuses to acknowledge the complexities of victimisation and in so doing normalises the victimisation of women.

Chapter 10

Why do 'young people' go missing in 'child prostitution' reform?

Lyvinia Rogers Elleschild

Introduction

Traditionally, academic analyses of social policy formulation focus on the motivations and interactions of political actors rather than the representational strategies deployed. As a consequence, little attention has been given to how the criminal justice and welfare policy processes work to constitute particular subjectivities. In this chapter I describe how youth prostitution has been reconfigured as a form of sexual violence, namely child sexual abuse, and how, through this process, those involved in youth prostitution are reconfigured as 'sexually abused *children*'.

Through the discourse of welfare protection the young person as the subject of policy 'goes missing' and is reconfigured as a 'child'. Yet 'youth' is a necessary concept to hold on to because it distinguishes 'youth' from 'childhood', and differentiates children from young people. This is important because if welfare subjects are categorised as 'children' then it is feasible to suggest that policy responses will be suited to meeting the assumed welfare needs of 'children'. I argue that the discursive framing of 'child prostitution' in *Safeguarding Children Involved in Prostitution: Supplementary Guidance to Working Together to Safeguard Children* (DoH *et al.* 2000) and the Sexual Offences Act 2003 is counter-productive for some young people, constituted as subjects by an infantalising discourse that positions them as *children*.

I have documented elsewhere the influences of a range of contributory actors and agencies on the policy formulation for *Safeguarding Children Involved in Prostitution* (Elleschild 2004). Here

I focus specifically on Barnardo's Street and Lanes 'Model For Understanding Abuse Through Prostitution' because this model is based on a procuring strategy and sexual violence which work to redefine youth prostitution as child sexual abuse. I trace thinking about 'procuring strategy' back to radical feminist analyses,[1] drawing particularly on the work of Sheila Jeffreys, who argues that prostitution constitutes sexual violence, and Kathleen Barry, who develops a 'procuring strategy' model. Barnardo's model is then described, showing how it gained popularity through media coverage and influenced policy formulation. Questions are then raised about the infantalisation of young people, configured through this model as 'children'.

Redefining youth prostitution: the context

In the 1990s Barnardo's, the Children's Society and radical feminists all argued that 'child prostitution' should be a priority for government policy. Barnardo's and the Children's Society mounted separate campaigns to redefine youth prostitution as an act of child sexual abuse perpetrated by child sex offenders and 'abusing adults'. This was motivated by concerns that young people were being wrongly punished by criminal law, and that adults engaged in procuring young people or purchasing sex should be criminalised rather than those 'being abused and exploited through prostitution' (Barnardo's 1998: 91).

Prostitution as sexual violence

Radical feminists have argued that prostitution is a practice that constitutes sexual violence and/or sexual slavery (Barry 1979; Jeffreys 1985). Prostitution is an expression of male sexuality, which is 'a perversion because its primary motivation is not pleasure, individual or mutual, or the enhancement of personal relationships, but control of and power over women' (Jeffreys 1985: 68). Prostitution is necessary because:

> men need practice and must hone the valuable weapon of sexual aggression and contempt which is needed for the job of social control of women. Men need the reinforcement of their woman-hatred if they are to be effective. (Jeffreys 1985: 68)

Some men are 'casualties' who can 'only perform with prostitutes'; for these 'casualties' prostitution 'serves as a *guerrilla training camp and rehabilitation centre for sexual terrorists*' (Jeffreys 1985: 68, original emphasis). Jeffreys (1997: 243) argues that it is 'unreasonable to omit prostitution from the feminist understanding of violence against women'. From this point of view rather than change the conditions of prostitution men's demand for prostitution must be eliminated. This could be achieved through conceptually redefining the act of prostitution as being sexually abusive and criminalising the men who purchase sex. Jeffreys (1997: vii) acknowledges Barry for 'providing the framework of ideas and organization that has made it possible for me and feminists in other countries to challenge prostitution'. Barry's analysis has made a significant contribution to how prostitution is understood and influenced international policy formulation on 'child prostitution' (Barry 1995; Kempadoo and Doezema 1998).

Kathleen Barry, sexual slavery and procuring strategies

Barry wrote *Female Sexual Slavery* to expose the 'slavery and exploitation of women in prostitution' (1979, 1984: 38). She develops a 'model for understanding the victimization of women in prostitution', and reveals a 'victimization process', 'an invisible reality ... that has no name' (1984: xi, 118). Conceptual redefinition is strategically deployed so that 'victims of sexual slavery' can identify themselves as 'victims' of male coercion, for:

> When victims have no way of naming what has happened to them, they cannot understand themselves as victims.
> Because sexual slavery is not perceived as a reality, young women are easily vulnerable to it, particularly if their history or background has been one of abuse. (1984: 118)

What is particularly relevant to the contemporary discourse on 'child prostitution' is Barry's identification of 'procuring strategy'. This involves the strategic performance of 'romantic love' by pimps who masquerade as boyfriends in order subtly to coerce young women into 'sexual slavery'. Extracts are drawn from Barry's 'model for understanding the victimization of women in prostitution' because this thinking re-emerges in Barnardo's model.

The narrative of 'procuring strategies'

The definition of 'sexual slavery' is based on the 'objective conditions of enslavement' and the 'procuring strategies' used to involve women in street prostitution (Barry 1984: 12). Pimps deploy particular strategies targeted at 'young girls, who appear to be naïve, lonely, bitter or rebellious' (1995: 204). Females:

> ... may be procured through seduction by being promised friendship and love. Conning a girl or young woman by feigning friendship or love is undoubtedly the easiest and most frequently employed tactic of slave procurers (and one that is also used for procuring young boys) and is the most effective. (1984: 5)

For Barry, the following pimp procuring scenario is typical:

> Suddenly he appears, he is friendly, he offers to buy her a meal and, later, he gives her a place to spend the night. She hears compliments for the first time in ages, as well as promises that he will buy her new clothes and have her hair done. This romantic-movie scenario is played out. But it may be days, weeks, or even months before she figures out what has happened to her. (1984: 89–90, 1995: 204)

Barry implies that pimping operates through a simple formula. A pimp identifies his victim but:

> He will not introduce prostitution immediately ... When a sexual relationship between them is established and he is sure she loves him, he employs the 'If you love me, you'll do anything for me' line. To prove her love she must have sex for money with someone she does not know. If she resists or refuses, he will likely pout, create a scene, and insist that she does not truly love him. To restore his affection, she finally agrees to do what he asks, believing that one time won't hurt. He has her hooked. After she turns one trick, he starts pimping her, giving her nightly quotas, taking the money she earns, and making her believe she is really a slut ... (Barry 1984: 91)

This process is strategically deployed on 'vulnerable' females by the 'pimp' in order to foster an emotional dependency that in turns leads to a situation where he controls her behaviour and she prostitutes herself for his financial gain. The female becomes totally dependent on the 'pimp', a situation that Barry (1984: 12) describes as 'sexual slavery'. 'Procuring strategy' conceals the victimisation involved, making it difficult to recognise by the female 'victim'. This leads to the denial of prostitution as being 'sexual terrorism' and renders the slavery dynamic 'hidden' (1984: 13). Prostitution appears then to be something that the woman freely chooses to do. The assumption that prostitution is freely entered into makes 'the victim responsible for her own victimization' (1984: 42). Patriarchal control and 'sexual slavery' is managed though this mechanism: the illusion of 'choice' legitimates female involvement and obscures male 'sexual terrorism'. An awareness of 'sexual terrorism' is 'passed down' by mothers to their daughters:

> Terror – sometimes openly expressed, more often tacitly understood – permeates lives, often through something 'known' but never stated. Such is the way a legacy of terror passes from mother to daughter. Many inner-city mothers wait and worry, knowing their daughters must return home from school through streets with cruising pimps. Suburban parents wait at the school or bus stop to ensure their children's safe return home. And mothers explain to teenage daughters why it is unwise for them to go out at night even though their brothers do. Sexual terrorism has become a way of life for women …. *Will he turn to my child next?* (Barry 1984: 43)

'Procuring strategy': the explanatory model for youth prostitution

This analysis of sexual exploitation has influenced international social policy and human rights law (Barry 1995). However, Barry's 'sexual slavery' analysis has been criticised for being a 'figment of neo-Victorian imagination', constructing a 'damaged other' as a powerful metaphor to justify interventionist impulses (Doezema 1998: 44, 2001: 16). Barry has been accused of manipulating discourse to 'advance certain feminist interests' through deploying:

> … narrative elements of 'White Slavery': innocence, established as youth and sexual purity, helplessness, degradation and death… the rhetorically explosive combination of sex and slavery served

to whip up public support for the abolitionist cause. (Doezema 2001: 24)

The narrative of the 'pimp-victim' relationship is told in an authoritative and unambiguous way, raising questions about the evidence used to support her analysis. In *Female Sexual Slavery* (Barry 1984) only 'victims ... who had either escaped or left prostitution' were interviewed (1984: 7). Evidence to support the prevalence of 'procuring strategies' is largely drawn from Steven Barlay's *Sex Slavery: An Investigation into the International White Slave Trade* (1975). This book is written in the style of sensationalist socio-journalism and claims to be an 'international bestseller' (1975, back cover). It is a 'horrifying undercover report' about the procuring strategies deployed by 'sex slavers' (ibid.). Barlay (1975: 16), who refers to his female respondents as 'bed fodder', coins the term 'sexual slavery' because it is 'more appropriate and less ambiguous than 'white slavery'. Procuring strategy is central to 'sexual slavery', which exists because of 'the attitude of men' and:

the consent of women who – due to lack of power and to the fact that education, ... has penetrated their minds but has not yet dissolved in their blood stream – accept sex slavery as a natural way of life. (Barlay 1975: 220)

Alongside Barlay's *Sex Slavery*, Barry draws from Iceberg Slim's (1969) *Pimp, The Story of My Life*, papers confiscated by police from a pimp in 1977 and transcripts from an undercover police officer (Barry 1984).

Regardless of the limited evidence that it is drawn from, Barry establishes 'procuring strategy' as being the main route into prostitution for young women. However, this 'procuring strategy' narrative begs questions about romantic discourse, and how this can be used as a script to coerce young women into prostitution. It also raises questions about the extent to which this narrative is described as the main, or only, route into prostitution for young women.

'Procuring strategy' is one that is probably familiar to most readers, drawing from the archetype of heterosexual seduction strategies through which an unsuspecting, innocent female is conned through male manipulation of romantic discourse. This is a story made familiar through popular fiction, soap operas, movies and chat shows. The male manipulation of romantic discourse is a 'truth' that is difficult to dispute because it is so familiar. It may be understood by some as an archetypal 'imaginary fiction' or by others as a well used script of patriarchal coercion. Barry applies this script to the particular context of pimping, identifying 'procuring strategy' as the central route into prostitution. Her narrative centralises maternal anxiety: the public sphere holds the risk of 'sexual terrorism' that necessitates the close surveillance of daughters. It is these two aspects of her work that I argue are particularly important in understanding the formative ideas that underpin Barnardo's 'child prostitution' campaign.

Barnardo's 'model for understanding abuse through prostitution'

In Bradford, 1992, a project called ACE was established in order to work with 'vulnerable young people at risk of, or engaged in, abusive relationships, which may involve prostitution' (ACE 1993). In *I'm Not a Prostitute* ACE (1992: 2) claim:

> Many young women are sought out by 'boyfriends' who 'seductively groom' them offering an attractive lifestyle and claiming to love them. Completely enthralled she is then persuaded to have sex with other men in order to help her boyfriend out of some situation, e.g. car repairs. Soon she finds herself working as a prostitute for the boyfriend and when she seeks a way out, is offered violence.

In 1995 the children's charity Barnardo's took over the ACE project, renaming it 'Street and Lanes' (SALs). SALs describes its purpose as a '"life-line" and "rescue" service' (Barnardo's 1997: 22, 1998: 19). SALs' drop-in service was used by 45 young women from April 1995 to March 1996 and by 56 young women from April 1996 to March 1997 (Barnardo's Annual Reports 1996, 1997). In 1995/96 13 of the 45 project users had been involved in sex for money, while in 1996/97 24 of the 56 project users had been involved in sex for money (Barnardo's, 1997: xv). The ages of the project users are given in Table 10.1.

Barnardo's SALs 'model for understanding abuse through prostitution' (Swann 1998) has contributed to the conceptual framework for how 'child prostitution' is understood, and informs a range of police and social services policy documents, including

Table 10.1 Ages of SALs Project Users

Age in years	1995/6	1996/7
12	1	0
13	3	2
14	12	9
15	13	12
16	10	12
17	6	10
18	0	3

Source: SALs Annual Reports.

Safeguarding Children Involved in Prostitution (Home Office *et al.* 2000) and the Sexual Offences Act 2003. It is therefore important to consider this model and to trace the processes through which it 'assumes authority' and through which its 'truth claims' are legitimised and become 'known as "true"' (Hall 1997: 45).

The SALs model is based on a four-stage process, beginning with 'ensnaring':

> When a girl meets her 'boyfriend' he impresses her through his maturity, good looks, money, car and lifestyle. He makes her feel special and important, lavishing attention on her, buying her clothes and jewellery. He begins a sexual relationship and she falls 'head over heels' in love. (Barnardo's 1996: 2)

The other stages are 'effecting dependency', 'taking control' and 'total dominance'. A process of conceptual redefinition is central to the model. This is presented in diagrammatic format ('the triangles') and used in policy campaign presentations from 1995 onwards, including the campaign report and video *Whose Daughter Next? Children Abused Through Prostitution* (Barnardo's 1998).

The model provides a discursive reconstruction of those involved in prostitution. It is based on the premise that a young woman is coerced by a young man between 18 and 25 years old who recognises the signs and symptoms of vulnerability and begins a relationship with her (Swann 1998a: 11). The young woman is unaware of being exploited; rather, she perceives those involved in the sexual exchange as her 'boyfriend' and 'his friend'. However, others generally perceive this as 'the prostitution triangle', involving a 'young prostitute', 'a pimp' and a 'punter':

The supply side (the pimp) and the demand side (the punter) together ensure that the child is abused and exploited. (Swann 1998a: 14)

This 'prostitution triangle' is reconfigured to describe the 'reality': 'the abuse triangle', composed of an 'abused child', an 'abusing adult' and a 'child sex offender' (Swann 1998a: 20). The status of 'young woman' has been changed to that of 'abused child':

There is a child who is being abused and sexually exploited [...].

As there is no such thing as a child prostitute then it follows that there is no such thing as child prostitution, youth prostitution or young people involved in prostitution. Rather than defining Prostitution – we need to look at defining abuse and exploitation.

It also follows that there is no such thing as a 'pimp'. There are abusing adults who control and coerce, who assault, who rape, who in extreme cases torture, who give addictive drugs, who humiliate and degrade and yes they do make a lot of money ...

It also follows that we don't have punters or curb (*sic*) crawlers or customers. These exist in the world of prostitution in the 'sex industry'. Is it a curb crawler who winds down his window and ask(s) for sexual services from a 12 year old child? Is this the same as a curb crawler who winds down his window and enters into an agreement with an adult to purchase services?

... we have a child victim. When a man seeks to satisfy his sexual desires on a child, he is not a curb crawler ... he is quite clearly a child sex offender.

...we do not blame or identify causes for this abuse in Social Services or the Care System, or the Education System, or even as I have heard mentioned Poverty.

Without a basic shift in understanding that this is an issue about child abuse, not about prostitution, then we will never even begin the real debate that SALs is asking for. A debate that is urgently needed and concerns the prevention of this abuse and the protection for these extremely vulnerable children. (Barnardo's 1997: 24–5)

Sara Swann argues that while society's perception is influenced by the 'prostitution triangle' child abuse will continue to take place and abusing adults and child sex offenders will continue their actions (1998a: 20). Furthermore:

> Language is important as it underpins our assumptions, attitudes and perceptions that relate to prostitution. Referring to a child as a prostitute and the men as 'pimps and punters', implies that children are making informed choices and decisions...
>
> Children will continue to suffer this abuse while attitudes, legislation and statutory responses remain in the 'prostitution triangle'. When the reality is understood, then the prevention of this abuse, the prosecution of the abusers and the protection of these vulnerable children will begin. (1998a: 20)

The discourse of 'child protection' has been used to justify a change of category: the 'young woman' becomes 'an abused child'. This reconfiguration makes it possible to deploy the descriptors 'child sex offender' or 'child sex abuser'. This categorical shift allows interactions to be explained differently: there is a subtle change in sexual scripts and subject positions that is intentional and strategic:

> ... the term 'prostitution' has tended to obscure the fact that what we are dealing with is the sexual abuse of children ... Changing the language used in this way helps to reveal the true nature of these relationships. (Swann 1999: 5)

This discursive refiguration is important. It is now possible to talk about the welfare subject as a child, even though her[2] temporal age remains the same. The process of representing the subject as 'not being a prostitute' seemingly necessitates the reconfiguration of the subject as 'an abused *child*'. It is possible that this discursive shift is made because contemporary child welfare legislation, the Children Act 1989, constructs its subjects as 'children' rather than 'children and young people'. Furthermore, it may be more acceptable to appeal to protect 'children' rather than 'young people', as the former signifies a range of qualities: innocence, virginity, purity, vulnerability. The iconography of 'childhood' is strategically used by charities in their campaigns for donations (Critcher 2003): Barnardo's deploys particular representations of 'stolen childhood' in this campaign (Barnardo's 2002).

This reconfiguration of the objectified subject from young person to child is not wholly consistent, as two narratives are deployed in the project literature: 'youth empowerment' and 'child protection'. The 'empowerment narrative' situates the subject as a 'young woman'. For example, SALs aims 'to empower young women to make decisions to achieve more settled and safer lifestyles' (Barnardo's 1998: 22). Alongside this a 'protectionist narrative' situates the subject generally as a 'child', although at times both subject positions are used to describe the same subject:

> The blindness to the actual harm suffered by *these young women*, and the lack of agreed co-ordinated responses, have in the past led to the prevention of protection of these children. (Swann 1998b: 30)

> Crucial to this facility is creating an atmosphere of warmth and a safe space, so young women can be themselves and often be 'children'. Art and craft sessions, which include basic colouring books … encourage a sense of play. (Swann 1998b: 22).

The latter suggests a young woman with an 'inner child', who can be cared for through emotional nurture and play activities. Furthermore, Barnardo's *Whose Daughter Next? Children Abused Through Prostitution* (1998) configures the female subject as a 'daughter' and implies that *all* daughters are at risk of being coerced into prostitution. In appealing to parents it assumes that the risk is in the 'public sphere' (Swann 1998a). This is at odds with research that suggests that the home is an unsafe place for some young women who run away because their fathers have sexually, physically or emotionally abused them and subsequently become involved in prostitution to manage their financial needs (Gordon 1989).

Too immature for sex?

It is worth noting that SALs frequently draws attention to the age of sexual consent and 'sexual immaturity'. The reconfiguration of 'young woman' as 'abused child' is justified on the grounds that those under the age of 16 years cannot give consent to sexual intercourse thus 'a child cannot consent to her own abuse and should not therefore be labelled as a prostitute' (Swann 1998a: 19). *Whose Daughter Next?* points out that:

> No exception has been made in the case of the child, notwithstanding the guiding principle of the criminal law in

its endeavour to protect children under 16 from sexual activity and the protectionist imperative of the Children Act 1989 which regards sexual activity by adults with children as a form of abuse and 'significant harm'. (Edwards, in Barnardo's 1998: 73)

However, this raises general issues about sexual activity by those under the age of sexual consent: the subject of the protectionist discourse slips from those specifically involved in underage prostitution to *all* 'children' involved in 'sexual activity'. All sexual interactions become highlighted as 'illegal' and 'adult abusers' are aged 16 years and over. The child protection discourse is contradictory: on the one hand child protection legislation (the Children Act 1989, the Children Leaving Care Act 2000) constructs those under 18[3] (or under 21 if 'in care') as 'children', while legal discourse configures those between 16 and 21 who have consensual sexual activity with those under 16 years as 'sex offenders'. Furthermore, the subject position of 'abused child' sits uneasily with figures that indicate a high number of sexually active young women: during 1996–7 approximately 107,000 females under 16 years used family planning services in England (Social Exclusion Unit 1999: 53). Positioning the subject as 'child' and highlighting the illegality of sexual acts under the age of 16 reinforces concerns raised in 'age of consent' debates about *any* under-age sexual activity (Epstein *et al.* 2000; Gorham 1978).

Concerns about 'teenage pregnancy', the 'increase in 'unmarried females and males' who have had sexual intercourse between the ages of 15 and 19' and 'the harm of early sex to human development' are articulated by Barry (1995: 61–2):

If the prostitution of sexuality, the reduction of oneself to sexual object, is increasingly demanded of adult women, it is an even more pressing requirement of teenagers. With the sexualization of society, first sex is occurring at earlier ages, in the teenage years. Sexual norms in high school and college dating are expressed now in the language of prostitution: 'hooking up' identifies dating for the purpose of having sex.

... sexual development of teenagers initiates female sexual subordination in the early years and cuts off female potential for development. (Barry 1995: 63)

While Barnardo's expresses the following anxieties:

There is an enormous amount of pressure on 12–13 year old girls in our society to 'have a boyfriend', and if you've got one who is older, good looking and materially successful then you've made it. He very quickly becomes the most important person in her life. (Barnardo's 1996: 2)

... we can't make up our mind about sex and children. The models are getting younger and younger, so are we saying sex is okay with a ten-year-old? What's the message? (Swann, *The Guardian*, 21 August 1996)

To recap, Barnardo's model redefines 'youth prostitution' as 'child sexual abuse'. The narrative that underpins the model is similar to Barry's (1984) 'model for understanding the victimization of women in prostitution'. Both describe stages of procuring and the deployment of romantic discourse as a means to 'ensnare victims'. They appeal to maternal/parental anxiety about 'at-risk daughters' and articulate wider anxieties about young people and sexual activity.

Procuring strategy and the media

SALs generated media publicity through issuing a press release to media agencies and hosting a press briefing on 20 August 1996. Twenty-three newspapers featured the SALs news story 20–24 August 1996 and 26 radio and television news programmes covered the feature on 20 August 1996 (Barnardo's 1997: xvi–xxiv). The media reportage constructs the subjects as 'children', 'pimps' and 'paedophiles':

Pimps and *paedophiles* across West Yorkshire are imprisoning, raping and forcing *children* into prostitution.

... horror stories of *child sexual abuse* will be documented by Home Office Minister [...] aiming to go to *war against paedophiles*.

Barnardo's, which has been studying the *street styles of children* across West Yorkshire, says vulnerable victims of perverts are being let down and abandoned by both society and the law.

Barnardo's says that in West Yorkshire it has found *girls as young as 12* being sold and abused in a way normally associated with the far-east. West Yorkshire Chief Constable Keith Hellawell has pledged to target the *pimps and paedophiles preying on the children* ... ('Children trapped in life of vice', *Yorkshire Evening Post*, 20 August 1996, emphasis added)

The article cites Swann, SALs' coordinator:

The whole thing is horrifying, yet it is going on under our noses. It's not just Bradford where our project is operating, every town and city needs to be concerned. Everybody knows of the child prostitution places such as Thailand, but it is going on under our noses. (*Yorkshire Evening Post*, 20 August 1996)

The article draws on the discourse of child sexual abuse. It frames those who purchase sex not as 'clients' or 'punters' but as 'paedophiles'. Barnardo's configures this subject position as 'child sex offender' in its model; however, 'paedophile' is a populist and powerful journalistic descriptor. Reference to the 'street styles of children' invokes the image of 'street children', a powerfully iconic image generally used to suggest a feral lifestyle involving begging and foraging in 'Third World' countries. Meanings attributed to sex tourism and 'street children' 'over there' appear to be imported in order to influence the construction of an urgent problem 'over here'.

The Guardian ran a front-page story 'Abused. Beaten. Raped. Sold for Sex. Aged 15':

A pioneering project on *child sex abuse* in Bradford has found that *children as young as 12* are being kept prisoner, tortured and pushed on the street as prostitutes. (*The Guardian*, 21 August 1996, emphasis added)

It describes a young woman who, from 15 to 17 years, was kept locked in an attic room:

Her work as a prostitute in Bradford did not begin until 6pm when she was unlocked from her room by her pimp, ready for the men who leave their city offices and stop off on their way home for tea to buy *sex from children*. (*The Guardian*, 21 August 1996, emphasis added)

Her story is the story of hundreds, perhaps *thousands of British children* exposed by a pioneering Barnardo's project.

It reports that 'her journey to the attic [...] began when she was drunk at a party and had sex with Dealer, a Pakistani drugs dealer', and that:

> She gave birth to a daughter, now three, in the front room with his mother, sister, aunt and granny to help her. There was no midwife or doctor at the birth, which was never registered. After the birth, the baby was taken away ... Dealer's sister said she had registered the baby as hers and her baby was going to Pakistan. (*The Guardian*, 21 August 1996)

This narrative introduces 'otherness'; a Yorkshire landscape with exotic golden mosques is described, inhabited by Asian families who steal babies, deal drugs and imprison young white women, forcing them to work in prostitution. This account is not supported by evidence or by calls to further investigate how someone could illegally register a baby and then abduct the baby to Pakistan. This can be compared to the narratives of 'white sexual slavery' told by prostitution reformers in the nineteenth century (Gorhan 1978; Jeffreys 1995).

The media reportage outlined the SALs model in several articles. For example, in 'Girls as young as 12 "sold for sex"':

> Sara Swann, the project manager, said that interviews with the girls had revealed a pattern in the way they had become ensnared into prostitution.
>
> Men, usually aged between 18 and 25, would court a young girl and lavish her with attention and gifts. She would soon become dependent on him and regard him as her boyfriend.
>
> The girl, who would invariably cut ties with her family, would be willing to do almost anything to safeguard the relationship – even agreeing to have sex with her boyfriend's friends.
>
> Ms Swann said: 'They are not selling sex to feed a drug habit or because they are sex mad. They are doing it because they regard their boyfriends as special and love them very much. They never consider that these men are exploiting them." (*The Daily Telegraph*, 21 August 1996)

Swann discounts the need to finance drug usage as a causal factor for involvement in prostitution, yet the exchange of sex for drugs was recorded in Barnardo's profiles (Barnardo's 1996, 1997). Through SALs' well orchestrated press release procuring strategy achieved legitimacy as the causal factor for involvement in 'child prostitution', as illustrated by 'Barnardo's calls for the protection of child prostitutes':

> Barnardo's, which is helping 45 girls in Bradford, found that *all* had been *enticed into prostitution by older 'boyfriends'* who had sexual relations with them when they were *as young as 12*. (*The Times*, 21 August 1996, emphasis added)

This prevalence of procurement does not necessarily correlate to the project data in SALs' 1995–96 Annual Report (Barnardo's 1996). The user-profiles recorded that 13 respondents had 'involvement in sexual activity' for money but the profile questions do not ask if boyfriends had been involved in this (ibid.: 16). Furthermore, the media reportage on 'child prostitution' focuses on '12-year-olds' yet SALs' Annual Report 1995–96) noted that only one 12-year-old had used their project (see above, 1996: 16). No 12-year-olds used the project in the following two years (Barnardo's 1997, 1998). This focus on '12-year-olds' legitimates this issue as being one of 'child prostitution' and directs attention away from the complex range of factors that lead to involvement in prostitution by young people.

Procuring strategy and policy reform

> The Bradford and Airedale Child Protection… 'now regards this as an issue of child protection, which is due in a large part to the powerful analysis that has emerged from the work of SALs project' (Chair of ACPC, SALs, 1997: 12).

As well as achieving significant media coverage the SALs model successfully influenced local and national policy reform. The children's safeguard review, *People Like Us*, formulated policy recommendations on 'child prostitution' and graphically reproduced the model, recommending its adoption by all those working in this area (Utting 1997: 9.37). The position statement of the Association of Directors of Social Services *Child Victims as Child Prostitutes* draws substantially from the model (ADSS 1997). Consequently, many of the local protocols compiled following the ADSS position incorporate a procuring strategy.

Safeguarding Children Involved in Prostitution describes the model and although it does recognise other routes into prostitution, 'procuring strategy' is identified as an explanatory model (DoH *et al.* 2000: 15). It also categorises young people under the age of 18 as 'children', and states that 'child prostitution' is an issue to be dealt with under the legislative framework of the Children Act 1989 rather than the criminal justice system. However, 'if the child continually and of his or her choice continues to solicit, loiter or importune in a public place for the purposes of prostitution, criminal justice action may be undertaken' (DoH *et al.* 2000: 27, 6.21–6.30). The construction of prostitution as 'child sexual abuse' now means socio-economic factors for involvement in prostitution are obscured: youth prostitution becomes either child abuse or a 'free choice'. Prostitution has not been decriminalised; rather, the Sexual Offences Act 2003 defines prostitution in statute and intervenes more harshly than previous legislation.[4] A person is categorised as a 'prostitute' even if they were *compelled* to offer or provide 'sexual services', and if they had done so on only one occasion (s.51). Furthermore, the Act increases the age of sexual consent for paid 'sexual services' to 18 years (s.47)

Why age matters

It might seem that my focus on the life-course status of the policy subject is trivial, particularly in relation to the discourse of sexual violence and sexual slavery. Yet it is important to think about what age signifies: chronological age, physiological age and social age interconnect (Hendrick 1997). The transition from 'childhood' to 'youth' involves rejecting a range of cultural and social practices synonymous with 'childhood' and participating in those that signify 'not being a child'. While recognising that this transition is not simply a matter of biological reductionism, embodiment does have a role in the construction of identity for children and young people. It was central to constructing the 'fundamental categories' of 'childhood-adulthood' in debates of the 1830s when

> … in 1833 a Royal Commission, drawing upon physiological evidence concerning puberty and having identified the associated change in social status, declared that at the age of 13 'the period of childhood ceases'. (Driver 1946: 244, in Hendrick 1997: 42)

If the period of 'childhood' ceased at 13 years in the 1830s, why, in the early twenty-first century, are young people up to the age of twenty-one[5] being categorised in policy texts and legislation as 'children'?

It matters that those aged between 13 years and 18 years are discursively situated as 'young people' rather than 'children' because the meanings attributed to the categorical concepts of 'child' and 'young person' differ substantially. A four-year-old is very different from a 17-year-old yet both are conceptually merged. The deployment of the category 'child' and the meanings that it invokes is a useful rhetorical device at a time when moral panics about sexuality are prolific. Evoking the category 'child', which presupposes a set of assumptions in relation to welfare needs and dependency, erases the specific social, economic, cultural and political context in which young people negotiate their identity and well-being. Yet the attribution 'child' to denote a 17-year-old often goes unremarked in 'child prostitution' discourse. There are exceptions to this:

> ... many people assume that what is being described is involvement of prepubertal children in sex work. This sensationalises the issue quite unjustifiably ... it is my experience that the vast majority of people involved in sex work, whether sex workers or their clients, share these taboos. (Kinnell 1999: 2)

Furthermore, research does exist on youth prostitution and sexual exploitation that constructs its subjects as young people rather than as children and recognises a range of routes into prostitution (Harper and Scott 2005; McNeish 1998).

A cultural shift in the 'conditions of youth' is marked by an 'infantilisation discourse' that frequently and uncritically categorises young people as *children* in welfare discourse. Issues of financial autonomy, sexual agency and privacy without surveillance are not part of the discourse of child welfare. Accordingly, in welfare discourse the young person is frequently represented as a child, in criminal discourse as an adult.

Some young people are involved in prostitution because of coercion and sexual violence. But it is important not to overlook other reasons for involvement in prostitution, including failures in state welfare policy. The Children Act 1989 has been operational during the same period in which eligibility to income support has been removed from most 16- and 17-year-olds and the youth labour market has diminished. The contradictions in 'promoting and safeguarding welfare' for the same group for whom the welfare 'safety net' has been removed cannot be overstated.

Notes

1 Typologies simplify and homogenise strands of thought, so that different, even conflicting, viewpoints become subsumed within a singular typology. This is the case with the typology 'radical feminism', which encompasses a range of diverse thinking.
2 In Barnardo's model and *Whose Daughter Next?* (1998) the subject is explicitly female.
3 This includes clinics and GPs providing family planning services, and these figures may include some double counting. It is difficult to estimate numbers of sexually active under-16s as condoms can be obtained commercially and lesbian and gay young people may not use family planning services.
4 The Street Offences Act 1959 allowed two cautions before categorising women as 'common prostitutes'.
5 The Children Act 2004 includes provision for those 'in care' under the age of 21 and for those under 25 with learning difficulties (2004, Part 1, s.10: 9).
6 Paradoxically, there is a noticeable shift in criminal justice discourse where the distinction between 'young people' and 'adults' is becoming eroded. This has been described as an 'adulteration of youth justice' (Fionda 1998: 84). 'Youth' is increasingly used to denote 'anti-social minors' and legitimise punitive policies to those between ten and 14 years: in criminal justice discourse 'the 1990s saw children metamorphose into dangerous youths' (Piper 2001: 32).

References

ACE (1992) *I'm Not a Prostitute* (ACE Project, Bradford).
ACE (1993) Project Information Pack.
Association of Directors of Social Services (ADSS) (1997) *Child Victims as Child Prostitutes*, Position Statement, March.
Barlay, S. (1975) *Sex Slavery: An Investigation into the International White Slave Trade.* London: Coronet.
Barnardo's (1996) *The First Year: Lessons Learned, Street and Lanes Annual Report, 1995.* London: Barnardo's.
Barnardo's (1997) *Street and Lanes Annual Report, 1996–97.* London: Barnado's.
Barnardo's (1998) *Whose Daughter Next? Children Abused Through Prostitution* (video and report). Essex: Barnardo's.
Barnardo's (2002) *Stolen Childhood.* London: Barnardo's.
Barry, K. (1979) *Female Sexual Slavery.* Engelwood Cliffs, NJ: Prentice-Hall.
Barry, K. (1995) *The Prostitution of Sexuality: The Global Exploitation of Women.* New York: New York University Press.

Critcher, C. (2003) *Moral Panics and the Media.* Buckingham: Open University Press.

Department of Health, Home Office, Department of Education and Employment, National Assembly of Wales (2000) *Safeguarding Children Involved in Prostitution: Supplementary Guidance to Working Together to Safeguard Children.* London: DoH.

Doezema, J. (1998) 'Forced to choose: beyond the voluntary v. forced prostitution dichotomy', in K. Kempadoo and J. Doezema (1998) *Global Sex Workers: Rights, Resistance and Redefinition.* London: Routledge.

Doezema, J. (2000) 'Ouch!': Western feminists "wounded attachment" to the "third world prostitute"', *Feminist Review,* 67: 16–38.

Edwards, S. (1998) 'Abused and exploited – young girls in prostitution: a consideration of the legal issues', in Barnardo's *Whose Daughter Next? Children Abused Through Prostitution.* Essex: Barnardo's.

Elleschild, L.R. (2004) '"Missing Youth": A Discourse Analysis of Policy Formulation on Child Prostitution'. Unpublished PhD: Plymouth University.

Epstein, D., Johnson, R. and Steinberg, D.L. (2000) 'Twice told tales: transformation, recuperation and emergence in the age of consent debates 1998', *Sexualities,* 3 (1): 5–30.

Fionda, J. (1998) 'The age of innocence? The concept of childhood in the punishment of young offenders', *Child and Family Law Quarterly,* 10 (1): 77–87.

Gordon, L. (1988) 'The politics of child sexual abuse: notes from American history', *Feminist Review,* 28: 56–64.

Gordon, L. (1989) *Heroes of Their Own Lives: The Politics and History of Family Violence.* London: Virago.

Gorham, D. (1978) '"The maiden tribute of modern Babylon" re-examined: child prostitution and the idea of childhood in late-Victorian England', *Victorian Studies,* 21 (3): 353–79.

Hall, S. (ed.) (1997) *Representation: Cultural Representations and Signifying Practices.* London: Sage.

Harper, Z. and Scott, S. (2005) *Meeting the Needs of Sexually Exploited Young People in London.* Essex: Barnardo's.

Hendrick, H. (1997) 'Constructions and reconstructions of British childhood: an interpretative survey, 1800 to the present', in A. James and A. Prout (eds) *Constructing and Reconstructing Childhood.* London: Falmer Press.

Jeffreys, S. (1985) 'Prostitution', in S. McNeill and D. Rhodes (eds) *Women Against Violence Against Women.* London: Onlywoman Press.

Jeffreys, S. (1997) *The Idea of Prostitution.* Melbourne: Spinifex Press.

Kempadoo, K. and Doezema, J. (1998) *Global Sex Workers: Rights, Resistance and Redefinition.* London: Routledge.

Kinnell, H. (1999) *Some Reflections on Terminology in Relation to Sex Work and Young People,* Briefing Paper delivered to National Working Group: Young People and Prostitution (held on 1 October at the Royal South Hants Hospital, Southampton, hosted by the Working with Prostitutes Group).

McNeish, D. (1998) 'An overview of agency views and services for young people abused through prostitution', in Barnardo's *Whose Daughter Next? Children Abused Through Prostitution*. Essex: Barnardo's.

Phoenix, J. (2002) 'In the name of protection: youth prostitution reforms in England and Wales', *Critical Social Policy*, 22 (2): 353–75.

Piper, C. (2001) 'Who are these youths? Language in the service of policy', *Youth Justice*, 1 (2): 30–9.

Social Exclusion Unit (1999) *Teenage Pregnancy*. London: TSO.

Swann, S. (1998a) 'A model for understanding abuse through prostitution', in Barnardo's *Whose Daughter Next? Children Abused Through Prostitution*. Essex: Barnardo's.

Swann, S. (1998b) 'Barnardo's street and lanes project', in Barnardo's *Whose Daughter Next? Children Abused Through Prostitution*. Essex: Barnardo's.

Swann, S. (1999) 'Children involved in prostitution: the government's draft guidance', *ChildRight*, 154: 15–16.

The Daily Telegraph (1996) 'Girls as young as 12 sold for sex', 21 August.

The Guardian (1996) 'Abused. Beaten. Raped. Sold for sex. Aged 15', 21 August.

The Star (1996) 'Sad girls of 12 forced into vice', 21 August.

The Times (1996) 'Barnardo's calls for protection of child prostitutes', 21 August.

The Yorkshire Evening Post (1996) 'Children trapped in life of vice', 20 August.

Utting, W. (1991) *People Like Us: The Report of the Review of the Safeguards for Children Living Away from Home*. London: HMSO.

Chapter 11

Yes, Minister, 'sex violence policy *has* failed': it's time for sex, violence and crime in a postmodern frame

Adrian Howe

Introduction

In March 2006, *The Guardian* filed a report on a Home Office proposal for dealing with violence against women under the arresting headline: 'Sex violence policy has failed – minister'. The policy in question was rape prevention. Speaking about a new £500,000 advertising campaign urging men to get women's consent to sex, the then Home Office minister, Fiona McTaggart, pronounced that the government had to challenge men's attitudes to sex because other attempts at tackling rape such as changes to the law and improvements to support services had failed to stem men's attacks on women. Further, she insisted that the government needed to focus more on 'men's behaviour and teach men they have some responsibility ... We have done a lot of things to help victims of rape ... and it still keeps happening.' More crucially, what was needed, she said, was 'some really active crime prevention' (Branigan and Dyer 2006). Yes Minister, and so feminists have been saying, and your government promising, for years.

Indeed, just three years earlier, Solicitor-General Harriet Harman had pronounced the Blair government's new proposals on domestic violence to be an important step in ending the 'culture of excuses' for men's violence against women. She also spearheaded a campaign against the provocation defence, law's premier excuse for men's murderous violence against women, and indicated that she favoured abolishing it. Moreover, it was reported that ministers were secretly meeting to review the defence, going so far as to condemn it for perpetuating 'a medieval view of marriage that blackened the victim's name, painting her as a bad wife' (Hinsliff 2003). Yet the law of provocation survived a Law Commission inquiry which declared it to be eminently capable of reform, thereby enabling men to continue to get away with murdering women on the grounds of provocation and other equally feeble excuses.[1] As if that weren't enough cause for concern, the so-called 'attrition rate' in rape cases is at a record high level, with only 5.6 per cent of rape allegations ending in a conviction (Kelly *et al.* 2005), and in early 2006, the Sentencing Advisory Council recommended both that jail terms for rapists be slashed and that men convicted of domestic violence offences escape custodial sentences in order to relieve pressure on Britain's overcrowded prisons (Branigan and Dyer 2006).

This all flies in the face of the Blair government's new millennium promises to deal with the problem of men's violence against women in Britain. What had puzzled Minister McTaggart was the 'strange' way in which 'victims commonly feel responsible, and perpetrators sometimes feel victimised' by rape allegations, but it was clear to her that 'what we are doing so far isn't working'. As we shall see, there is nothing strange about the reversal of perpetrator and victim when it comes to speaking about men's violence against women – that's the way hegemonic masculinist discourses work. Still, the minister was surely right to declare that it was past time to implement some really active crime prevention – prevention that challenges the still pervasive culture of permissiveness toward men's violence in western societies. It's time, that is, to rethink 'sex violence' policy along the lines proposed in my forthcoming book, *Sex, Violence and Crime in a Postmodern Frame*.[2] In this book I provide an answer to the minister's prayers by pointing the way towards a crime prevention strategy that is pitched at the deeper level of the cultural scripts that narrate and normalise violence against women. In this article, I revisit and rework arguments I have made before about what happens when men's violence against women is named. These arguments will underpin a critical analysis of some recent very pertinent legal events, namely reviews of partial defences to murder conducted in England and Australia. As ever, my focus will be on these the latest legal responses to persistent calls for the radical reform or, better still, abolition of the law of provocation.

Sex, violence and crime in a postmodern frame

Here, as in the book, I begin with a question: what happens when you sex crimes of violence – when you demand of acts of criminal violence that they declare their sex or, as some folk still prefer to call it, their gender? What happens, more specifically, when you take men's violence against women as an analytical object, perhaps making it the focus of scholarly attention or a guest lecture? The short answer is: tread very, very carefully because all hell is about to be let loose, such is the explosive nature of any query – no matter how casual or innocent – about men, women and violence. Instead, I jump into the fray by exploring how men's violence against women has been named and un-named as a significant social problem in western countries over the past 30 years. During that time, some western governments, most recently in Britain, have made violence against women a policy priority (see Howe 2006). Yet questions remain about how that violence should be understood and thus more effectively resisted. Remarkably, a question also remains about whether it is culturally permissible to hold men (and not their mothers, wives, girlfriends or children) responsible for their own violence. I call this 'the man question' because it opens an inquiry into the discursive place occupied – or more usually vacated – by men in accounts of men's violence against women. Asking whether explanations can be provided for men's violence that do not discursively erase it or worse deteriorate into excuses for it, I take non-feminist criminologists to task for faltering on the man question. But while criminology is the primary target, the critique applies to any attempt in any field or in any discourse to deny or explain away the unpalatable evidence of men's pervasive violence against women. In short, I explore the discursive possibilities for and the prohibitions against speech acts about men's violence against women today.

For these reasons *Sex, Violence and Crime in a Postmodern Frame* is bound to be a controversial book. Even calling men's violence 'men's violence', thereby giving responsibility for that violence to men, incites outrage, whether the setting is a university tutorial, a dinner party, a family gathering, or a casual pub conversation. One is met immediately with qualifying 'buts': *but* not all men are violent; *but* women are violent too; *but* the victim had it coming. She, always already *she*, 'asked for it', provocation being the most deeply culturally ingrained and widely accessed sex-specific excuse for violence in western societies. And do not expect non-feminist criminological reactions to feminist investigative research demonstrating the asymmetry of violence 'between the sexes' to be any more sophisticated. So-called 'expert' explanations for men's violent acts invariably deteriorate into apologies for violent men. Here it pays to emphasise that this is not some sort of male conspiracy to defend men against unsavoury allegations. Much more commonly, the explanation takes the form of an unselfconscious agent-deleting manoeuvre that presents the violence as a weird kind of disembodied abstraction, yet at the same time manages somehow to trace a causal chain back to a woman, almost always the violent man's hapless mother. Moreover, if mainstream criminology's erasure of men from violent narratives is astonishing, the speedy scramble to unsay men's near-monopoly on violence is electrifying even in the array of so-called 'critical criminologies'. Indeed, in some sections of the academy in the United States, and now in Britain, it is argued that, contrary to feminist claims, women are equally if not more violent than men (see Howe 2004a). If there is one thing that has remained constant over the two decades that I have taught criminology, it is that even the simple act of naming men as the main perpetrators of most forms of violence is not culturally permissible in any non-feminist forum.

Sex, Violence and Crime in a Postmodern Frame deploys an engaging type of discourse analysis that I call spotting discursive manoeuvres. It is borrowed from Hilary Allen's (1987) brilliant analysis of British social work and psychological reports on women charged with serious offences in the 1980s. As she shows, the discursive manoeuvres deployed in the reports had the effect, albeit unintentionally, of erasing women's guilt and their responsibility for their violent acts and their potential dangerousness, thereby 'rendering them harmless'. Interestingly, Allen found that the kinds of discursive constructions made in reports on women offenders, for example that they were mothers and therefore presumed to have loving, maternal and 'harmless' personalities, were 'absent or untypical in cases involving males' (Allen 1989: 82). While not wishing to deny the problems raised for feminism by Allen's examination of the sanitation of violent women defendants in professional reports, I believe it is productive to draw on her insights about the operation of discursive manoeuvres for a very different purpose – that of exploring the erasures, that occur inside and outside the discipline of criminology, of men's responsibility for their violence against women. Some of these discursive strategies are well-known, such as the victim-blaming narratives routinely invoked in criminal courts, in the media and in supposedly 'objective' criminological texts to excuse men who kill 'provocative' women. But there are others, notably 'strategies of recuperation' which channel resistant voices into 'non-threatening outlets', for example by labelling feminist speech about men's violence as 'extreme' or dismissing as hysteria women's allegations about violent men (Alcoff and Gray 1993: 268).

By way of example, last year I sent my undergraduate criminology students at the University of Central Lancashire out into the world armed with one of the most frequently reported statistics in the English media over the last few years. The statistic was the one about two women being killed by their (male) partners every week ('male' is placed in parentheses because it usually did not appear in mainstream media outlets). The students' task was to monitor people's first reactions to the statement: 'Did you know that two women are killed every week in this country by their male partners?' My favourite of all the responses collected by the students was this – 'Are you a feminist?' What the students came to realise through direct experience was that such a response is not a *non sequitur* in a society where violence against women is normalised by cultural permissions and prohibitions on speech acts about men's violence.

Making excuses for men's violence is as endemic in western culture as blaming women for it. It took one leading non-tabloid English newspaper just a month to find boyhood photographs of one of the men alleged to have flown a plane into the World Trade Center. The headline evinced the standard criminological agenda of searching for underlying causal factors: 'Do these snapshots of a teenage boy in Cairo contain clues to what turned him into a killer?' Beneath it is a photo that shows a boy being hugged by his mother. The adjoining text quotes his father describing him as a pampered mummy's boy: 'I used to tell her that she is raising him as a girl' (Buncombe 2001). The inference is obvious: mums have much to answer for when pampered sons turn into enraged killers.

Sex, Violence and Crime in a Postmodern Frame extends the sexing-sex-crime project that I commenced in *Sexed Crime in the News* (1998a). That project aims to disturb the complacency and self-evidence of sex crime. Even if sex crime is narrowed down to crimes involving sexual violence, definitional problems persist. Sexual assaults followed by murder are treated as sex crimes in criminology texts and in the media, but what does murder have to do with sex? Is family violence sex? Paedophilia would appear on most conventional lists of sex crime, but would father-daughter rape? What about marital rape? Why are these much more prevalent forms of men's violence never reported as sex crime? What makes violence sexual, and to whom? Asking questions about the taken-for-granted 'sex' of sex crime by reading all interpersonal violence as sexed helps to break down the arbitrary division separating public from privatised forms of sexual violence. Asking sex crime to declare itself helps to destabilise it, ensuring that some crimes involving sexual violence can no longer be classified quite so simply as 'sex crime' while others, notably the domestic or private variety, are left out of the equation. Calling sex crime 'sexed crime' not only problematises the 'sex' of crimes of violence; it also acknowledges that women are not the only sex. Men have a sex too. Thus, speaking about 'sexed crime' or 'sexed violence' helps to sex violence by raising questions about its fundamental, though usually ignored, sexed and sexual aspects.

Sexed violence then covers all forms of violence in which the gender or sexed status of the perpetrator or victim is relevant to the violent act. It includes so-called 'domestic' violence and 'sexual intimacy killings' – which I will get back to – also child sexual assaults in the home, whether or not these are reported. Moreover, in the public sphere, sexed violence is not confined to rape or sexual assault of women; it includes sexual assaults on men, sexual harassment of women and attacks on sexual minorities. Cases in which heterosexual men kill men they claim made sexual advances to them are also instances of sexed violence, whether or not the dead victims identified themselves as homosexual men. Sexed violence then is violence that can only be fully understood in the context of human relationships that are profoundly sexed, but are not often recognised as such, precisely because they are dismissed as having something to do with a vaguely defined, amorphous 'gender' (Howe 1998a).

But that's enough about the book. What has it got to do with so-called 'sex violence policy' and with formulating some really active crime prevention? Everything. To take a most relevant example – my all-time favourite – let us return to what is perhaps the most vexed sex violence policy of recent times. I refer to the recent inquiries in western jurisdictions, notably England and Wales and, in a happy coincidence, in my home state of Victoria, Australia, into the operation of partial defences to murder. Our focus will be the defence that has most taxed the minds of law commissioners in Australia over the last two decades and in England over the last three or four years – that of provocation.

Provocation under the hammer

Now here I need to introduce myself as a stakeholder, albeit a marginal, or better still marginalised player in the heated debates that have taken place about the law of provocation in Anglophone jurisdictions over the last 25 years, debates culminating in several reviews of partial defences to murder.[3] I have made submissions to several of the reform bodies, most recently to the Law Commission in England during its wide consultation in 2003 which culminated in its very problematic report of partial defences to murder published in 2004, and its most unfortunate recommendation that the defence of provocation be reformed rather than abolished (see Howe 2004b). But it should be made clear from the start that my submissions and work in the field have had close to zero impact on law reformers. While my submission to the UK Commission was completely ignored, the Options Paper of the Victorian Law Reform Commission (VLRC) dropped my articles on provocation into a footnote – an appropriate fate given the very limited consideration of the argument contained therein (VLRC 2003: 102). The footnoted article (Howe 1999), just one of several available, sets out my root-and-branch abolitionist position advocating the abolition of provocation as a defence to murder and as a mitigating factor to be considered in sentencing. Abolitionism unmodified, while it may focus on the operation of provocation defences in criminal courts, is much bigger than that; it is a full-frontal assault on the enunciation of the she-asked-for-it cultural script, any time, anywhere. It is intent on banning the deployment of every kind of cultural excuse for violence against women and against sexual minorities. More broadly, it plots the annihilation of the cultural script of provocation – that antiquated idea of provocation as partial excuse for violence, as explanatory factor, as mitigation – in its entirety.

Such an approach was evidently too extreme for the VLRC which recommended instead that the defence be abolished yet retained it as a sentencing discretion, and the Victorian parliament concurred. Now, while I may sound rather miffed, not to stay bitter and twisted, at this cavalier dismissal of my work, I am actually quite content with being relegated to the margins. For against the odds, I remain optimistic, and still very much committed to the view put forward by Carol Smart nearly 20 years ago, that for all its limitations as a feminist strategy, 'law, understood in its widest meaning' remains one of 'the most important sites of engagement and counter-discourse' (Smart 1999: 392). Moreover, law is still a site of struggle not simply between feminists and apologists for men's violence, but between feminist activists and law scholars many of whom take a reformist stance, one that starts with the seemingly intractable problem of what to do about battered women killers who kill sleeping men. Marginality also provides a happy site for continuing that very modest, always already Foucauldian project of shifting thresholds of tolerance, in this case thresholds of tolerance for homicidal rage dressing itself up as provoked violence (Foucault 1981: 11–12; Howe 1998: 32).

Marginality, as bell hooks argued so lucidly two decades ago, can be conceptualised as a 'space of radical openness' in which 'those of us who would participate in the formation of counter-hegemonic cultural practice … begin the process of re-vision' (hooks 1990: 145). It is in this space of radical openness – this 'profound edge' that 'comes from lived experience' (hooks 1990: 149–50) – that we find the resources to continue hammering away at the execrable tales of 'provocation' told in cases of sexed homicide, notably femicide and homosexual advance cases. Sexed homicide covers all cases in which sex is the stubborn driver of homicidal violence, sex being understood in two senses – first, sex in the sense of having, or rather not having it (departing sex, inadequate sex or unwanted sex occupy centre place in most men's accounts of homicidal violence); and second, sex in the sense of having *a* sex. Sexed homicide then includes all cases in which the violence turns on or is premised on the sexed identities of the players, on what it means to be sexed as a man or a woman. Abolitionism unmodified refuses to countenance sexed excuses for homicidal violence whatever form it takes.

I have taken this position in numerous writings bordering on the obsessive about two sorts of cases in which provocation defences loom large. The first type of case that attracted my attention was femicide cases, in which men kill their wayward, 'taunting' or departing wives and women partners. The second type was that of the so-called homosexual advance cases, in which self-defining heterosexual men claim they needed to respond with lethal violence to alleged non-violent sexual advances made by other men (Howe 1994, 1997, 1998b, 1999, 2000, 2002). It is true that I have been known to modify my position. Following recommendations of Canadian feminists who have put the abolitionist case at its highest, I would now allow provocation to be considered as a mitigating factor during sentencing, but only if so-called 'egalitarian guidelines' are introduced requiring a non-discriminatory understanding of provocation, and only if these guidelines can be shown to prevent both group-based prejudice against women or gay men and the systematic undervaluing of their lives creeping back in under the mantle of judicial discretion (National Association of Women and the Law 2000: 41–7; Howe 2004b). However, as I still insist on a total ban on men raising excuses for killing in sexed cases at any stage of the criminal justice process, my position remains, effectively, one of abolitionism unmodified.

227

Well, you might ask, so what, and why all the fuss about a single partial defence to murder? First, the received, historically mandated idea that homicidal violence that takes the form of a provoked hot-blooded killing is a lesser crime than a cold-blooded killing lies at the heart not only of sex violence policy, but of the recent Law Commission inquiries into the operation of defences to murder held in England and Wales and in Victoria at the beginning of the twenty-first century. Indeed, the UK Law Commission was still talking about provocation in its far-reaching recommendations to reform the law of murder published in November last year (Law Commission 2006). Second, and this point was quickly lost on the English law reformers, the recent English and Australian inquiries both came about through feminist campaigning against the operation of provocation defences in femicide or woman-killing cases, not because of so-called 'domestic homicide' cases (code for cases in which battered women kill their male partners after a long history of violence). Third, both sets of recommendations – the reformist ones in England and the modified abolitionist ones in Australia – are destined to fail because they do not address the core problems which lie with provocation scripts in sexed violence cases.

Disappearing acts – the English law review

Focusing on developments in England, the spark for the review of criminal defences to murder was media uproar over three cases decided in the summer of 2002 in which three men got away with murdering their wives. By far the most notorious case was that of Humes, in which a successful but overworked lawyer killed his wife in 'a red mist' when she confessed to being in love with another man. The case caused an outcry not only because he stabbed his wife repeatedly in front of their children, one of whom frantically called 999 as her mother bled to death, but because he negotiated a manslaughter plea, on the basis of provocation, with the Crown Prosecution Service. He received a seven-year sentence. Media outrage propelled senior law officers into action. The Attorney-General launched an appeal against the sentences handed down to the three wife-killers on the grounds of leniency. The appeals failed.[4] The following year, the Law Commission was asked to hold an inquiry into the law and practice of partial defences to murder and to have 'particular regard to the impact of those defences in the context of domestic violence' (Law Commission 2003). After a wider-range consultation, the Commission came up with a profoundly flawed recommendation for the reform of the law, thereby rejecting the abolitionist position outlined in my submission.

To understand why this particular sex violence policy is destined for failure, it pays to take a close look at the Commissioners' recommendations. Briefly, they decided that the law of provocation was 'capable of reform in ways which would significantly improve it' (Law Commission 2004: 3). Their 'improvements' extended the defence so that that it was potentially available to defendants who kill in response to fear of serious violence; drew it more tightly so as to prevent it being advanced 'in certain cases where presently it is available'; and gave judges an explicit power to withdraw provocation from the jury. While 'considered desire for revenge' is now out of the question, a person – say a battered woman who kills her husband in fear of further violence – may avail herself of the defence even if she was angry towards the deceased at the time (Law Commission 2004: 5–9). If this sounds like a great leap forward, it is to be noted that the five (male) Commissioners supported their decision to retain the defence on a supposedly 'moral basis'. This turned out to be the traditional and much criticised notion that the defendant had legitimate ground to feel seriously wronged by the person at whom his or her conduct was aimed, and that this lessened the moral culpability of the defendant reacting to the outrage in the way that he or she did. It is the justification of the sense of outrage which provides a partial excuse for their responsive conduct. For them:

> … the moral blameworthiness of homicide may be significantly lessened where the defendant acts in response to gross provocation in the sense of words or conduct (or a combination) giving the defendant a justified sense of being severely wronged. (2004: 44–5)

But what, in their view, might constitute legitimate grounds for feeling seriously wronged? The initial impression given is that it would not be an unfaithful or departing wife, inasmuch as the Commissioners confirmed that they agreed with Lord Hoffmann in *Smith (Morgan)* that:

> Male possessiveness and jealousy should not today be an acceptable reason for loss of self-control leading to homicide, whether inflicted upon the woman herself or her new lover.[5]

It followed that they believed that 'provocation should not be left to the jury in such a case'. After all:

> More than fifty years ago in *Holmes* Lord Simon said that Othello would be guilty of murder, even if Iago's insinuations had been true, and we think this should be so. (2004: 65)

And yet, for all this grandiose posturing, the Commissioners' recommendations will still allow male possessiveness and jealousy to found a provocation defence. For a belief that male possessiveness and jealousy 'should not' be permitted as grounds for a provocation defence is not strong enough to ban them altogether. Should stories of unfaithful or departing wives prove insufficient, defence barristers can resort instead to the tale of the taunting woman – for it is always a woman who taunts and torments a man in a domestic homicide case. Consider, for example, the following homicide scenario, one of several put to 62 respondents in one of the empirical studies conducted for the inquiry. In this one, a husband who is being taunted by the deceased about his sexual inadequacy confronts her about an affair she is having and kills her. Just over half the respondents thought this lessened the gravity of the crime. So too did the Commissioners, declaring it to be 'a sad commonplace that when relationships break up there are often arguments and mutual recriminations'. While they believed it would be rare that a taunting case could meet their new test of provocation, there might be cases 'where one party torments another with remarks of an exceptionally abusive kind' (2004: 66). Given that none of the cases they provide as examples of ones below the threshold of the new test are wife-killing cases, it is made clear, by omission, which cases would be likely to involve 'exceptionally abusive' remarks. Infidelity cases would not make the grade, apparently, at least not those in which a brooding jealous husband kills a woman who says she will leave for another man by poisoning her tea, for this 'implies premeditation'. Nor would a cuckolded husband case, where a husband decides to kill his unfaithful wife if she has one more affair, and does so, for that would be 'a prima facie case of murder'. But a taunted husband case – where on discovering his wife is having an affair, he confronts her, she taunts him about his sexual inadequacy (as so many women seem to do when confronted with men's homicidal violence) and he kills her – that is a different matter. In the Commissioners' view, the wife's taunts may 'constitute some provocation' and the husband may well be said, at law, to have lost his self-control if he kills her in such circumstances (Law Commission 2004: 191–3).

Thus did the Commissioners make it clear that the law of provocation protects the interests of heterosexual men by making a sex-specific concession to their emotional health. In the process, they reinscribed as 'natural' a profoundly violent status quo in which men claim mitigation where women 'make' them kill them and criminal courts indulge them. Battered women who kill men in fear of further violence may now be able to avail themselves of a provocation defence, but a highly circumscribed and patently heterosexist and misogynist idea of 'passion' – say, for example, a violent, traumatised response to a battered or otherwise desperately unhappy wife leaving her husband and 'taunting' him in the process – will be retained as mitigation to murder. The unfortunate effect of such 'reasoning' is that the whole point of reviewing the operation of partial defences to murder because of concern over the lenient sentencing of men who kill women is lost.

This was hardly surprising – it was destined in the Commission's very terms of reference, namely that it pay particular attention to the impact of partial defences 'in the context of domestic violence'. 'Domestic violence' functions here as a discursive manoeuvre, diverting attention away from the problem that had led to the inquiry – the problem of men killing women and then getting away with lenient sentences for manslaughter. A reference framed more clearly in terms of domestic homicide, rather than domestic violence, might have had a better chance of highlighting the sexed asymmetry in the matter of who is killing whom in the 'domestic' contest. It might have helped to remind the Commissioners that the controversy over provocation in England was sparked not by a 'domestic violence' case, but by the spate of femicide cases in the summer of 2002. For they seem to have forgotten that they received their reference to review the operation of partial defences because of concern that the provocation defence was 'allowing men who kill their wives in a burst of anger to receive lenient sentences but not battered women who kill violent husbands' (Dyer 2003). The problem of male killers appears to have slipped the Commissioners' minds. By narrowly construing their brief to take account of 'domestic violence' homicides as signalling cases of battered women killers, they were able to gloss over the far more frequent incidence of 'domestic' homicides involving men killing women. In doing so, they lost sight of the crucial issue – law's complicity in profoundly subjugating provocation tales of unfaithful, taunting or departing women who deserve to die.

Furthermore, it needs to be re-emphasised that the proposal to abolish the defence yet retain provocation as a sentencing discretion – the limited abolitionist option considered by the Commission and adopted by the Victorian Law Reform Commission (2004) – is an utterly inadequate response to the problem of men's lethal violence against women, two of whom are killed each week in the UK by their angry male partners or former partners. This simply sets the stage for defence barristers to raise the same old tired narratives of excuse for 'provoked' violent men in pleas in mitigation of sentence. These pleas would be heard by an overwhelmingly non-feminist judiciary that still appears to subscribe to the idea that adultery is the 'highest invasion of property',[6] or at least to its derivative idea that men who kill 'their' women deserve some compassion.

Thus, provocation – western societies' most deeply ingrained cultural excuse for violence against women – has managed to survive inquiries into its operation in western criminal courts at the turn of the new millennium. It has also survived the Law Commission's recent and even more far-reaching inquiry into the law of murder in England and Wales. In its report, published in November 2006, the Commissioners revisit their earlier recommendations for reform of the provocation defence. Rejecting the argument of some feminist groups that the defence should only apply to excessive self-defence scenarios where there is fear of serious violence, they concede that the current law could be seen to be 'especially user friendly to men ... because they are more likely to lose their temper or respond violently to such matters', thereby permitting lenient sentencing in cases where the provoked murder 'may have been little more than a reflection of the continuing cultural acceptability of men's use of violence in anger' (Law Commission 2006: 91). They remain satisfied, however, that their restriction on the use of the defence to cases where there is a justifiable sense of being seriously wronged will put a stop to the more controversial cases where men have got away with murdering women.

Crucially, their final argument for permitting a provocation defence to apply beyond cases in which the defendant was responding to a threat of serious violence is that the door must be left 'ajar for cases where a real injustice would be done' if the defence was not available. Tellingly, their example, based apparently on an actual North American case, is that of an Asian woman who chases and kills a white man who has taunted her with racial abuse after she found him attempting to rape her daughter (2006: 93). What passes the Commissioners by is that by putting the spotlight on the exceedingly rare case of a woman killing in such sympathetic circumstances, the door is left ajar for all those male defendants whose feeble excuses for killing women prompted the review of homicide trials in the first place. They scarcely get a mention in the hundreds of pages of consultation papers and reports on defences to murder and the law of murder published by the Law Commission over the last three years. What more powerful testimony could there be to the key contention in *Sex, Violence and Crime in a Postmodern Frame* that even today it is still not culturally permissible to keep the focus steadfastly on men's violence in any non-feminist forum.

Victorian 'abolitionism'

This proposition holds true whether the reform body is composed entirely of men – as it was in England[7] – or is headed by a woman and is fully informed of feminist objections to the use of provocation defences in femicide cases, as it was in Victoria. In its final report, in which it advocated the abolition of the provocation defence but its retention as a sentencing discretion, the VLRC emphasised the importance of considering 'the social context of killing'. This turned out to be the context in which men and women kill each other. Unlike the English Law Commission which managed to almost completely lose sight of the question of men in its review of the law of murder, the VLRC duly listed its own research findings, notably that homicides are overwhelmingly committed by men – 84 per cent of the accused in their study of late twentieth-century prosecutions in the state of Victoria – that both men and women were most likely to kill 'in the context of sexual intimacy' – just over 30 per cent of homicides involved situations where a person killed his or her partner or former partner or sexual rival – and that men and women killed in the context of sexual intimacy for different reasons. Their findings confirmed other research which has demonstrated that while men were motivated by jealousy or a desire to control their partners, women were most likely to kill in response to violence (VLRC 2004: 15).

And yet, when the VLRC came to consider the issue of sentencing, specifically the question of how judges might consider provocation as a factor in mitigation, its only real concern seemed to be that with the abolition of the provocation defence, convictions for murder might attract higher sentences than would have been the case with a manslaughter conviction. That the Court of Appeal might need

233

to articulate principles which should apply 'when the killing is an escalation of prior violence by the offender' is mentioned only as a secondary consideration. It is not until the next sentence that it becomes clear that the VLRC is referring here to men, when it expresses satisfaction that Victorian courts 'appear to be placing increasing emphasis on the seriousness of domestic killings and the need to deter men from resorting to violence' (VLRC 2004: 290–1). Once again, the problem of men – the social group making up 84 per cent of the killers in their study – is downplayed, relegated almost to an afterthought.

It was all very well for the VLRC to congratulate itself on making radical recommendations for the reform of the law of homicide, and for the Victorian Attorney-General to announce – in impeccably gender-neutral terms – that the defence of provocation was to be abolished because it promoted 'a culture of blaming the victim and had no place in a modern society'. Attorney-General Hulls made it clear that it was 'people' (read: men) who kill in circumstances where they lose control, such as killing in anger at discovering a spouse has been unfaithful, who would no longer have the defence of provocation to rely on. This emphasis on cases involving the killing of 'unfaithful' spouses (read: women) serves as a useful reminder that it was concern about precisely this sort of killing that led to the Law Commission inquiry in the first place.[8] However, the VLRC failed to mention the need for egalitarian sentencing guidelines such as those formulated by Canadian feminists to ensure a non-discriminatory understanding of provocation, one which prevents group-based prejudice against women and a systematic undervaluing of their lives creeping back in under the mantle of judicial discretion. It also provided no guarantee whatsoever that the same old provocation tales told by violent homicidal men and their apologists, criminal barristers, will not creep back at the sentencing level in Victorian courts.

Conclusion

The VLRC's proposal to abolish the defence of provocation might be an improvement on the English Law Commission's proposal to reform it, but I predict that because the VLRC failed to adopt a root-and-branch abolitionist agenda, its recommendations will do little to dent the enduring cultural script that women frequently provoke men to violence. Nothing less than abolitionism unmodified will work; nothing less than a refusal to entertain any excuse for lethal violence against women – at any stage of a criminal trial – will suffice. This point must be made crystal clear: every single judgment that 'provocative' behaviour on the part of women mitigates the culpability of their killers reinforces the cultural message that these men deserve some compassion. Every concession to men's homicidal anger – by a jury or a sentencing judge – is a postmortem slander on their allegedly badly behaved victims. More, it perpetuates a 'social injury' against us all, dead or alive (Howe 1987).

In conclusion, reformist tinkering with the provocation defence will not dent the potent provocation cultural script which provides no hope whatsoever of delivering that really active crime policy that the Home Office minister so yearned for when she cast her eye over the failure of two decades of 'sex violence' policy to reduce sexual assaults on women. Nor will tweaking sentencing guidelines so that infidelity may not count as 'strong provocation' (Dyer 2005). Only a root and branch assault on the she-asked-for-it cultural script, one that refuses to resort to agent-deleting discursive manoeuvres that shift the blame for interpersonal violence, from the rapist or homicidal man to the short-skirted or taunting or departing woman in his sights, stands a chance of getting to the core of the problem. But that, as we have just seen in the case of law reform bodies charged with the task of examining the operation of provocation defences, is still a bridge too far. Perhaps the publication of this article, and of *Sex, Violence and Crime in a Postmodern Frame*, can help kick start yet another movement against the risible stories of sexed violence told by violent men and their apologists. Perhaps it won't. Once again, only time will tell.

Notes

1 For a critical account see Howe (2004b). For the lengths that criminal barristers will go to defend homicidal violence against women see the account of a defence of reasonable belief in demonic possession in Howe and Ferber (2005).
2 Routledge-Cavendish 2008 (forthcoming).
3 Reviews were held in Australia in Victoria in the late 1980s; in New South Wales in the 1990s; at the federal level by the Model Criminal Code Officers Committee in the late 1990s; more recently by the Victorian Law Reform Commission and the English Law Commission, and currently by the New Zealand Law Commission.
4 Attorney General's Reference (No. 74) [2002] EWCA Crim 2982.

5 [2001] 1 AC 146. Lord Hoffmann noted that Australian judges were able to withdraw these cases from the jury, but English judges were unable to do so.
6 *Mawgridge* [1707] Kel J 119 136–7.
7 It is notable that while the composition of the Law Commission has changed since the inquiry into partial defences to murder in 2003, they are still all men.
8 Press release, October 2005.

References

Alcoff, L. and Gray, L. (1993) 'Survivor discourse: transgression or recuperation?', *Signs*, 18 (2): 260–90.

Allen, H. (1987) 'Rendering them harmless: the professional portrayal of women charged with serious violent crimes', in P. Carlen and A. Worrall (eds) *Gender, Crime and Justice*. Milton Keynes: Open University Press, pp. 81–94.

Branigan, T. and Dyer, C. (2006) 'Sex violence policy has failed – minister', *The Guardian*, 13 March.

Buncombe, A. (2001) 'Do these snapshots of a teenage boy in Cairo contain clues to what turned him into a killer?', *The Independent*, 12 October.

Dyer, C. (2003) 'Law on provocation in killings a "mess"', *The Guardian*, 31 October.

Dyer, C. (2005) 'Men who kill partners face tougher sentences', *The Guardian*, 29 November.

Foucault, M. (1981) 'Questions of method: an interview with Michel Foucault', *Ideology and Consciousness*, 8 (6): 3–14.

Hinsliff, G. (2003) '"Crime of passion" is no defence', *The Observer*, 19 January.

hooks, b. (1990) *Yearning*. Boston: South End Press.

Howe, A. (1987) 'Social injury revisited: towards a feminist theory of social justice', *International Journal of the Sociology of Law*, 15: pp. 428–38.

Howe, A. (1994) 'Provoking comment: the question of gender bias in the provocation defence – a Victorian case study', in N. Grieve and A. Burns (eds) *Australian Women: New Feminist Perspectives*. Oxford: Oxford University Press, pp. 225–35.

Howe, A. (1997) 'More folk provoke their own demise (revisiting the provocation defence debate courtesy of the homosexual advance defence)', *Sydney Law Review*, 19: 366–84.

Howe, A. (1998a) *Sexed Violence in the News*. Sydney: Federation Press.

Howe, A. (1998b) 'The provocation defence – finally provoking its own demise?', *Melbourne University Law Review*, 22: 466–90.

Howe, A. (1999) 'Reforming provocation (more or less)', *Australian Feminist Law Journal*, 2: 127–36.

Howe, A. (2000) 'Homosexual advances in law: murderous excuse, pluralised ignorance and the privilege of unknowing', in D. Herman and C. Stychin (eds) *Sexuality in the Legal Arena*. London: Athlone.

Howe, A. (2002) 'Provoking polemic: provoked killings and the ethical paradoxes of the postmodern feminist condition', *Feminist Legal Studies*, 10: 39–64.

Howe, A. (2004a) 'Managing "men's violence" in the criminological arena', in C. Sumner (ed.) *Blackwell's Companion to Criminology*. Oxford: Blackwell.

Howe, A. (2004b) 'Provocation in crisis – law's passion at the crossroads? New directions for feminist strategists', *Australian Feminist Law Journal*, 21: 55–77.

Howe, A. (2006) 'New policies for battered women: negotiating the local and the global in Blair's Britain', *Policy and Politics*, 34 (3): 407–27.

Howe, A. with Ferber, S. (2005) 'Delivering demons, punishing wives – false imprisonment, manslaughter and other marital duties', *Punishment and Society*, 7 (2): 123–46.

Kelly, L., Lovett, J. and Regan, L. (2005) *A Gap or a Chasm: Attrition in Reported Rape Cases*. Home Office Research Study 29. London: Home Office.

Law Commission (UK) (2003) *Partial Defences to Murder*, Consultation Paper No. 173. http://www.lawcom.gov.uk

Law Commission (2004) *Partial Defences to Murder*, Report No 290. http://www.lawcom.gov.uk

Law Commission (2006) *Murder, Manslaughter and Infanticide: Project 6 of the Ninth Programme of Law Reform*. http://www.lawcom.gov.uk

National Association of Women and the Law (2000) *Stop Excusing Violence Against Women: NAWL's Position Paper on the Defence of Provocation*. Ottawa: NAWL.

Smart, C. (1999) 'A history of ambivalence and conflict in the discursive construction of the "child victim" of sexual abuse', *Social and Legal Studies*, 8 (3): 391–409.

Victorian Law Reform Commission (2003) *Defences to Homicide: Options Paper*. Melbourne: Victorian Government Printer.

Victorian Law Reform Commission (2004) *Defences to Homicide: Final Report*. Melbourne: Victorian Government Printer.

Chapter 12

War and sex crime

Jen Marchbank

Introduction

Rape in wartime has occurred since antiquity (Trexler 1995). It came to public attention most recently in the West with the genocidal rapes of Bosnian women in the 1990s. Yet the Bosnian case is far from exceptional. Mass rape and other sex crimes have been used systematically throughout history and across geography: over 100,000 women were raped in Berlin in the Second World War (Seifert 1994); over 20,000 Chinese women were brutalised by Japanese soldiers during the 1937–8 'rape of Nanking' (Copelon 1994) and, during the Bangladeshi War of Independence from Pakistan in 1971, it is estimated that 200,000 women were raped (Brownmiller 1975). Research by Karen Parker and Jennifer Chew (1994) estimates that each Japanese Comfort Woman[1] was raped at least five times a day and that there were at least 20,000 women at any one time, meaning that there were at least 100,000 rapes per day organised by the Japanese authorities and conducted by soldiers. They further calculate that in the five years of the Comfort Woman programme over 125 million rapes were enacted against women from the Philippines, Burma, China, Korea, Indonesia, Taiwan and the Netherlands.

Although rape and other sex crimes during war are predominantly enacted upon women, men and boys are also targeted (Chang 1997; Hague 1997; Pettman 1996; Trexler 1995) both for rape and sexual mutilation (Goldstein 2001) and to conduct sexual acts upon their own communities (Liebling 2004) to destroy the social fabric of the 'enemy'. Adam Jones (2006) points out that sexual violence against males only results in the actual penetration of the victim in a minority of cases, often inflicted by a fellow detainee rather than captor. Rather, severe sexual torture predominates, frequently followed by murder.

However, rape and sexual exploitation during war have only recently come to be seen as part of the casualties, with history showing us that military occupation and conflict tend to permit, even sanction, the sexual exploitation of local women by military men (Hynes 2004).

As already shown, the extent of rape in times of conflict and war is immense. And these are the documented figures; women and girls do not always report rape for many reasons, including fearing family rejection, even by their husbands (Stiglmayer 1994), being ostracised, fear of the rapist and deep feelings of shame among women of many cultures (Hynes 2004). Men also under-report rape (Pino and Meier 1999), often for similar reasons. Stephanie Chester's study (referred to in *Oxford University Gazette* 1998) of male victims of rape in peacetime found that reasons for non-reporting included fears of rejection by wives and being seen as homosexual. As Shana Swiss and Joan Giller (1993) document, even when women do seek out medical assistance they often withhold the fact that they have suffered rape, even though their bodies display the evidence through their injuries. Explaining why rape testimonies had not been collected from Rwandan women, the Deputy Prosecutor explained that African women do not like to talk about rape, telling Human Rights Watch, 'We haven't received any complaints. It is rare in investigations that women refer to rape' (Human Rights Watch 1996: 95). As such, it is clear that what evidence we have on war rape probably under-represents the true rates, due to social and cultural factors which silence the testimony of many. Some survivors prefer silence to further victimisation, while in other cases there is no systematic collection of data, with figures deriving from the observations of health professionals, aid workers, churches, etc.

However, we do not need to know exact figures to know that sexualised violence occurs in times of war and other armed conflicts or to challenge these crimes. In this chapter I discuss various explanations of the causes of war rape and other sexual crimes. This is followed by an exploration of the linkages between gender and the military and the implications for the construction of masculinity. I end with a summary of the history of the development of international law on sexual crimes and war rape.

Explaining war rape

The international rules of war define rape as a criminal act as do individual countries' codes of military justice (Brownmiller 1975), yet as Susan Brownmiller wrote over three decades ago, '[r]ape in war is a familiar act with a familiar excuse' (Brownmiller 1975: 32). Brownmiller summarises a number of explanations for rape in war and notes that during conflict 'ordinary men' rape. She concludes that rape is part of victory as it is enacted upon the bodies of the defeated community as an act of conquest. Rape is a crime of domination (Goldstein 2001). It is also gendered.

Feminist-informed analysis of gender violence during war refuses to see it as different from gender violence in other contexts – simply that sexual violence in the context of armed conflict intensifies already existing attitudes and behaviour. As Brownmiller has argued a 'female victim of rape in war is chosen *not* because she is a representative of the enemy but precisely because she is a woman, and *therefore*, the enemy' (Brownmiller 1975: 64, emphasis in the original). However, other explanations of war rape do point to the desecration of women's bodies, and those of men and boys, precisely because they represent a particular group, ethnicity, religion or class (Seifert 1994; Goldstein 2001). Ruth Seifert (1994) points out that the meaning of rape in wartime has many dimensions and motivations, some conscious acts of individuals, some policies of armies and some unconscious acts of aggression. Like others, Seifert claims that the first explanation for war rape is simply that rape is part of the generally understood 'spoils' of war, yet other dimensions exist. Rape is also employed to send particular messages to the men of the raped women's community, messages of humiliation, emasculation, terror and vulnerability. Rape tells the defeated men that they were too weak to protect their women. As Joshua Goldstein (2001) summarises:

> Rape arises from different specific motivations in various ways – revenge for Russian soldiers in Berlin in 1945, frustration for US soldiers in Vietnam, ethnic cleansing in Bosnia. Historically, the main point of rape in war seems to be to humiliate enemy males by despoiling their valued property. (Goldstein 2001: 362)

On the other hand, women are not always perceived as passive property. It is the very fact that women are viewed as the cultural gatekeepers of their communities (Yuval-Davis and Anthias 1989) through their roles as mothers and socialisers of future generations that precipitates further classes of war rape. These are genocidal rape for the purposes of impregnating 'enemy' women with the sperm of the victor (Diken and Bagge Lausten 2005) and a deliberate assault on women as cultural symbols. 'Sexual violence against women is likely to destroy a nation's culture. In times of war, the women are those who hold the families and the community together. Their physical and emotional destruction aims at exterminating social and cultural stability' (Seifert 1996: 39).

Before turning to further discussion of both genocidal and cultural rape it is worth noting that several other dimensions exist, from rape to terrorise whole communities to submission (Grech 1993) to individual acts of brutality by those men who find rape sexually arousing and take war as an opportunity to act upon these desires without fear of prosecution (Lohr, Adams and Davis 1997). In addition, the disruption of social norms within wartime facilitates sexual violence (Goldstein 2001: 333).

Writing about the conflicts in the former Yugoslavia, Bulent Diken and Carsten Bagge Lausten (2005) contend that the primary aim of 'war rape is to inflict trauma and thus to destroy family ties and group solidarity within the enemy camp. Apart from demoralization of the enemy war rape can also become an integral aspect of ethnic cleansing' (Diken and Bagge Lausten 2005: 111). Some of the most shocking crimes during the war in Bosnia-Herzegovina were those of extreme sexual violence and systematic rape, including a policy of 'genocidal rape' followed by the military and paramilitary units of the Serb and Bosnian Serb nationalist forces (Hague 1997). This policy was based on the relationships among power, gender and ethnic nationalisms.

Cultural cohesion is affected when women's bodies are violated (Seifert 1996), and it appears that cultural destruction was a deliberate strategy of the Serb forces in former Yugoslavia. Seifert details the steps following Serbian occupation of an area: first, symbols and artifacts of cultural significance were destroyed. Secondly, intellectuals were imprisoned and frequently killed due to their role in the preservation of traditions and cultures. The final step was the establishment of rape camps and, according to Seifert, women were not randomly selected. In fact, women of high status and higher education were among the first to be interred in these camps.

Nira Yuval-Davis and Floya Anthias (1994) have shown the intricate connections among gender, nationalism and culture. They argue that women not only perform the functions of cultural cohesion but are

241

also viewed as the embodiment of the nation. In fact, the role of gender in ethnonationalism is clear: the nation is gendered female while the state is male (Goldstein 2001: 369), and as such women represent the whole community in a symbolic manner. As such, when violence is enacted upon the bodies of women it is also aimed at the destruction of that national or ethnic community. 'The rape of women of a community, culture, or nation can be regarded – and is so regarded – as a symbolic rape of the body of that community' (Seifert 1996: 39). Further, as Joyoti Grech (1993: 18–19) explains: '[T]here are clear national-political implications to war rape that revolve around manipulations of national honour, racial purity and national integrity. These make it so terrifyingly effective and widespread as a weapon of war.'

So rape embodies cultural meanings. In cultures where honour is a core value, the meaning of rape for each individual woman, and her family, is filtered through this discourse. In former Yugoslavia many believed that following rape a woman's honour, and that of her family, could only be regained through suicide. Countless women across the world face the choice of silence or stigma, and life choices are restricted when such women are known to have been raped.

In addition to the above, war rape can contribute to ethnic cleansing by the strategy of deliberately impregnating 'enemy' women and girls to dilute the supposed ethnic purity of their community. During the Bosnian war women in camps were continually raped until medics declared that pregnancy had been achieved. They were then held until an abortion was no longer possible (Diken and Bagge Lausten 2005). As such, not only are these acts of torture but of a war strategy aimed at ethnic annihilation. Although the most commonly known cases of systematic war rape occurred in Bosnia and Kosovo, similar cases have also been documented during the civil wars in Liberia, Uganda, Rwanda and against the Jumma people of Bangladesh:

> The officer ordered them to start killing men but to take women away so that at least the next generation of Chakmas [an ethnic minority] will behave like good Bangladeshis. (Grech 1993: 20)

This indicates that one explanation for war rape is that it is a deliberate 'weapon of war' (Diken and Bagge Lausten 2005: 112) and, as such, is not merely a crime committed by individual members of the military but condoned and even planned by military hierarchies and governments.

Cultural and social destruction have also been attempted by the forcing of members of defeated communities to conduct sexual and other taboo acts upon each other either for the amusement of the victorious soldiers, as occurred during the 'rape of Nanking' (Chang 1997) or to tear apart the social fabric of that community. There are many documented cases of family members and neighbours being forced either to watch or to conduct rape (Pettman 1996) and of prisoners being forced to perform oral sex on each other, even being forced to bite off each other's testicles (Human Rights Watch 1993). Helen Liebling's (2004) study of the victimisation of the people of the Luwero Triangle of Uganda details multiple examples of intergenerational rape and sexual mutilation by family members forced by soldiers at the point of a gun. Liebling argues that such forced transgressions of cultural taboos were attempts to diminish the social and cultural capital of the Luwero communities.

In all of these cases gender is an aspect of the explanation. Whether one accepts the arguments of Brownmiller (1975) and Seifert (1994) that war rape is an expression of male contempt for women that is permitted in chaotic times or not, it remains the case that gender is a major factor in the performance of war. This is hardly surprising given that war is conducted by military forces, politically legitimated or otherwise, whose very structure encourages and encompasses a very particular form of masculinity. It is to this that I now turn.

Gender, military and the construction of masculinity

In the following I argue that the role of the military in the construction of masculinity provides further explanations for the occurrence and legitimisation of war rape. War rape can both reinforce the masculinity of the aggressor while, as already stated, emasculating and taunting the men of the oppressed society. All rape is an experience of power, domination, degradation and humiliation. The rapist takes a position of power, no matter if the victim is male or female, adult or child, a position of power that, Euan Hague (1997) argues, is masculine, allowing the rapist to torture, attack and brutalise the victims whom the rapist, or the policy, deems as inferior. So in Bosnia-Herzegovina men and boys were also raped to show them they were inferior – that is feminine. Through such practices of humiliation Bosnian Serbs not only bolstered their own masculinities and identities as Serbs but eroded the identities of non-Serbs by the extreme shame and dishonour associated with the rapes. This is not a new phenomenon, however. Goldstein (2001) details examples of feminising the enemy, like war rape itself, occurring from the ancient world onwards. The subjugation of the enemy as 'feminine' is central to a masculinity the perpetrator conceives as superior:

> One of the most intriguing elements of male-on-male rape and sexual violence is the gendered positioning of the rapist and victim: the way in which victims are feminized while *rapists are confirmed in their heterosexual, hegemonic masculinity*. This reflects more broadly on patterns of intermale sexual relations. It is a well-established fact, for example, that in highly patriarchal societies such as those in Latin America and the Balkans, as well as in the hypermasculine environment of men's prisons worldwide, feminine status is assigned to the 'passive' (receptive) partner in anal intercourse but not to the 'active' (penetrating) one. Indeed, the latter finds his masculinity *and his heterosexual identity* actually reinforced. (Jones 2006: 459, emphasis in the original)

Masculinity is the product of social practices and discourses rather than of genetics (Marchbank and Letherby 2007). As Michael Kimmel (1994) argues, masculinity acquires its meaning in opposition to other categories, in particular femininity. The relationship between gender and the military, which exists whether conflict is present or not, has become a significant aspect of investigation by feminists and in critical studies of masculinity. Cynthia Enloe (1987) shows how both the military and other security services are dependent upon masculinity and maleness, both cross-culturally and historically. As Frank Barrett (2001: 97) argues, '[t]he military is a gendered institution. Its structure, practices, values, rites and rituals reflect accepted notions of masculinity and femininity. But it is also a gendering institution. It helps to create gendered identities.'

Of course, the masculinity the military constructs is one which fits its requirements. The military require soldiers to be physically tough, to endure hardships and to be aggressive. Other traits required by the military are those of logic, emotional indifference and heterosexuality. As Robert W. Connell has described, the military is an '… oppressive but efficient regime – emphasizing competition, physical hardness, conformity, and a sense of elite membership – designed to produce a narrowly defined hegemonic masculinity' (Connell 2002: 141). Little surprise then, in the midst of the aggressiveness of war, with its concomitant suspension of social norms, that war rape occurs. In fact, it has been argued that the combination of this aggression with the presence of 'exotic' women (that is women from the 'other' side) can encourage war rape, especially as it may make a soldier a 'double veteran' (Goldstein 2001: 365) to rape and then kill.

One way in which masculinity appropriate to the military can be attained is by the situating of anything outside of acceptable behaviour as the 'other', frequently through invoking images of femininity (Enloe 1990), the very practice that Hague contends explains the rape of men in wartime. It is not unusual in armies for it to be traditional to insult the enemy by calling them women or to 'encourage' military recruits by similar name-calling. As Barrett's (2001) research into the US military shows, basic training instructors sometimes refer to marine recruits as 'faggots' to insinuate that they are not aggressive enough. Likewise recruits that did not perform as required were also taunted with gendered insults such as being 'called girls, pussies, weenies, and wimps by the instructors' (Barrett 2001: 82). All of this not only reinforces 'appropriate' masculinity but also stipulates that that masculinity must be heterosexual.

In addition to the encouragement of a specific hegemonic form of aggressive, hetereosexual masculinity, the military encourages bonding between combatants, the creation of a notion of brotherhood. In times of war, however, when social norms have been temporarily suspended, rape has been used to solidify such 'brotherhood', as Diken and Bagge Lausten (2005: 123) refer to it, a 'brotherhood in guilt':

> What, within a closed community of soldiers, is understood as guilt (as a transgression which proves one's manhood and loyalty), is transformed into shame as soon as the soldier leaves this community – which is why he does not and why the officers force soldiers to break taboos. This also explains the frequent use of gang rape. By sharing the crime, a brotherhood in guilt was established. (Diken and Bagge Lausten 2005: 124)

Further, as Goldstein (2001) details, as war rape is often also gang rape, such acts can promote cohesion within groups of soldiers and involve men who would not normally rape individually to do so in order to display their connection to the group or to prevent becoming an outcast.

Many men who commit war rape do so under duress, either for fear of their own lives or for fear of not being seen as one of this brotherhood. Many of these men are not only reluctant participants in rape but also have not volunteered to be involved in the conflict, having been forcibly conscripted into the military through legal dictate. Further, in the context of the conflicts in former Yugoslavia it has been argued that by forcing soldiers to transgress social norms they were also forced to choose sides – to display whether they were Croats, Muslims or Serbs – creating instant ethnic enemies and immediately destroying previously existing cross-ethnic friendships and relationships. As Diken and Bagge Lausten (2005: 125) argue:

> This also explains why knives were a favourite weapon. By forcing unwilling soldiers to use a knife against their opponent (neighbour or friend), the act was intensified and personalized in a way that would not have been the case if a machine-gun had been used. The act of rape was used as a rite of initiation, which made men true Serbs (implying the rejection of multiculturalism in any form). Soldiers were not just soiled in blood but also baptized in it.

Over 30 years ago Susan Brownmiller (1975) detailed how the very maleness, and specific versions of masculinity, encouraged the spiritual bonding of men. She also has argued that this bonding, which we have seen may be forced or voluntary, in addition to the hierarchical nature of military authority, makes women peripheral and therefore, vulnerable. Yet war rape has been employed in other ways to amalgamate soldiers to a cause – as a call to soldiers to protect their women, a call to act as 'real' men and to rally men to the patriotic cause. As Brownmiller notes, propagandists use rape by the enemy as evidence of the enemy's viciousness and subhuman status citing evidence from the Duke of Cumberland's campaign at Culloden: 'the lairds of the Scottish Highlands ... used evidence of rape by English soldiers as proof of their enemy's efforts to destroy them as a national people' (Brownmiller 1975: 88). Similarly, Goldstein (2001: 369) details the use of reports of British propagandists utilising the theme of war rape and other atrocities to rally patriotism in both the First and Second World Wars by playing up gang rapes by German soldiers.

It would be inaccurate to argue that all war rape is the product of organised military policies, though some most certainly is as shown in the case of the Bosnian rape camps, in the attack on Nanking, in the case of the Japanese Comfort Women and in the sufferings of the people of the Luwero Triangle in Uganda and the Jumma minority in Bangladesh. Most war rape is not organised from above but is conducted by small units or individuals and while some officers may have tolerated and do tolerate this others are outraged.

Strange contradictions arise around war rape: during the Second World War the German military punished rape and plunder which occurred on the Western Front but not on the Eastern Front (Goldstein 2001: 368). In addition, not all armies rape. Brownmiller (1975) details the extreme prohibitions and severe punishments against war rape administered by the Vietcong during the Vietnam War. For the Vietcong rape was considered a serious crime and women who had been raped were recognised as national heroines by them. This may be due to the fact that women played a large role in the Vietcong, fighting as equals. However, Brownmiller (1975: 90–1) also suggests that the lust for rape was controlled due to the Vietcong soldiers' sense of dedication to the cause and to their community.

War rape and international law

The history of law surrounding acts of sexual violence during war is a long one. It is usually seen as beginning during the US Civil War when Abraham Lincoln signed an order specifically including rape as an offence punishable by death, as part of the Leiber Codes in 1863 (Women's Caucus for Gender Justice, undated). The 1907 International Peace Conference accepted the code as the basis for international law and this in turn became the foundation of the Hague Convention later that year. A significant change, however, was that rape was no longer specifically mentioned; rather, prosecutions were based upon Article 46 which protects family honour and the lives of persons (Women's Caucus for Gender Justice, undated). Further prohibitions against rape and sexual violence were included in the prosecutions following the Second World War with the presentation of evidence of rape to the International Military Tribunals held in Nuremberg and Tokyo. Although the Charters establishing the Tribunals did not contain mention of rape as a specific crime, the Tokyo War Crimes Tribunal did charge rape relying on Article 46 of the Hague Convention (Women's Caucus for Gender Justice, undated). However, as David Scheffer, a former US Ambassador-at-Large for War Crimes, has argued, this led to a legal blurring with rape being lost in the vast array of war crimes:

> Unfortunately, in the Tokyo Trials, acts of sexual violence and rape were not placed at a level that would allow them

to stand alone. The Tribunal and its lawyers, while deserving ample credit for presenting the evidence and recognizing the atrociousness of the offenses committed upon women in places such as Nanking, Borneo, the Philippines, and French Indo-China, lumped the acts of sexual violence under the residual umbrella of Crimes Against Humanity – Inhumane Treatment. (Scheffer 1999: unpaginated)

The legal instrument used to prosecute 'lower level Nazis" (Women's Caucus for Gender Justice, undated), the Allied Control Council Law No. 10, Punishment of Persons Guilty of War Crimes, Crimes Against Peace and Against Humanity, did however, include a specific reference to rape in its charter.

Rape has also been prohibited in the Geneva Conventions, and is specifically mentioned in Article 27 of the Fourth Geneva Convention: 'Women shall be especially protected against any attack on their honour, in particular against rape, enforced prostitution, or any form of indecent assault' (Geneva Convention relative to the Protection of Civilian Persons in Time of War, 1949). However, as we have seen above these seem to do little to dissuade those intent on abuse for whatever reason.

The first occurrence of sexual abuse and rape being specifically codified as a 'recognizable and independent crime' (Scheffer 1999: unpaginated) was within the statutes of the International Criminal Tribunals for Rwanda and the Former Yugoslavia (ICTR and ICTY respectively). The first decision was made within the ICTR in the case against Jean-Paul Akayesu, when the Chamber held that rape, as well as being a violation of personal dignity, is like torture when it is used to humiliate, punish, degrade and intimidate (Scheffer 1999: unpaginated). The legal decisions made by both these Tribunals mean that now rape and sexual and gender violence are recognised as among the most serious of offences. These decisions form the basis upon which these crimes are now prosecuted.

In addition, these Tribunals have established that rape and other acts of sexual violence can constitute genocide. Again this began with the Akayesu case 'when it held that rape or sexual violence can be prosecuted as genocide if there is evidence to prove that it is conducted with the intention of physically or psychologically destroying a group of people' (Scheffer 1999: unpaginated). As Scheffer (1999: unpaginated) states, the result is that:

... there is now solid case law holding that rape and sexual violence are a form of genocide. The ICTY and ICTR cases have also reinforced the legal basis for arguing that rape and sexual violence are individual crimes against humanity, and also constitute violations of the laws and customs of war. This jurisprudence handed down from both ad hoc tribunals has forever altered the landscape of criminal prosecution and affected the scope of the consequences that any potential perpetrators must consider.

Since then the Rome Statute of the International Criminal Courts, which came into force on 1 July 2002, has added further prohibitions to this case law. This Statute explicitly includes war rape under Article 7, Crimes Against Humanity:

> Rape, sexual slavery, enforced prostitution, forced pregnancy, enforced sterilization, or any other form of sexual violence of comparable gravity. (Article 7, 1g)

The Rome Statute also includes further articles ensuring that these prohibitions cover both internal and international armed conflicts. However, only crimes committed since this date can be prosecuted by the Hague-based International Criminal Court established by the Rome Statute.

Although both international case and statute law now exist to prosecute war rape and sexual violence this does not prevent it from occurring. Further, the mere existence of law does not mean that all victims will witness justice being done. Clotilde Twagiramariya and Meredith Turshen (1998) point out the limitations of law, in this case in Rwanda, but applicable worldwide:

> Both the International Tribunal and the Rwandan genocide law cover the crime of rape. Rape is also prosecutable under Rwandan criminal law, but few inspectors, and few women themselves, are aware of this; and there is a lack of female judicial investigators to whom women might speak more easily about being raped.

Following Human Rights Watch, Twagiramariya and Turshen advocate for special provisions to enable women to report rape. 'Special interview conditions of safety and privacy are necessary if women are to talk, and they must believe that telling their testimony will help bring about justice' (Twagiramariya and Turshen 1998: 113).

Conclusion

Sexual violence occurs in both peacetime and conflict, sometimes for the same reasons. However, during war other uses of rape and sexual violence are present. As I have argued rape is committed for a range of reasons: simply as war booty; to boost soldiers' morale; to force bonding among combatants; to keep them 'keen' to fight; to feed hatred of the enemy; to humiliate enemy men; to terrorise and intimidate a community; to degrade and destroy that community; to torture and for ethnic cleansing. In addition, it appears that women, in particular, are raped as war provides a form of social licence to rape. The disruption of social norms and, sometimes, also official sanction and planning are also influential. Unfortunately, despite the existence of legal instruments to prosecute sexual violence during conflicts, it is predictable that the justifications and excuses for rape will outweigh the prohibitions and it is likely that such crimes will continue to be committed.

Notes

1 Japanese Comfort Woman is used to identify those women captured and imprisoned during the Second World War. The women were used to provide sexual 'comfort' for Japanese soldiers.

References

Barrett, F.J. (2001) 'The organised construction of hegemonic masculinity: the case of the US Navy', in S. Whitehead and F.J. Barrett (eds) *The Masculinities Reader*. Cambridge: Polity, pp. 77–99.

Brownmiller, S. (1975) *Against Our Will: Men, Women, and Rape*. New York: Simon & Schuster.

Chang, I. (1997) *The Rape of Nanking: The Forgotten Holocaust of World War II*. New York: Basic.

Connell, R.W. (2002) *Gender*. Cambridge: Polity.

Copelon, R. (1994) 'Surfacing gender: reconceptualizing crimes against women in time of war', in A. Stiglmayer (ed.) *Mass Rape: The War Against*

Women in Bosnia-Herzegovina. Lincoln, NE: University of Nebraska Press, pp. 197–218.

Diken, B. and Bagge Lausten, C. (2005) 'Becoming abject: rape as a weapon of war', *Body and Society*, 11 (1): 111–28.

Enloe, C. (1987) 'Feminist thinking about war, militarism and peace', in B. Hess and M. Marx Ferree (eds) *Analysing Gender: A Handbook of Social Science Research*. Newbury Park, CA: Sage.

Enloe, C. (1990) *Bananas, Beaches and Bases: Making Feminist Sense of International Politics*. Berkeley, CA: University of California Press.

Geneva Convention (1949) available at Office of the High Commissioner for Human Rights, http://www.unhchr.ch/html/menu3/b/92.htm, accessed December 2006.

Goldstein, J. S. (2001) *War and Gender*. Cambridge: Cambridge University Press.

Grech, J. (1993) 'Resisting war rape in Bangladesh', *Trouble and Strife*, 26: 17–21.

Hague, E. (1997) 'Rape, power and masculinity: the construction of gender and national identity in the war in Bosnia-Herzegovina', in R. Lentin (ed.) *Gender and Catastrophe*. London: Zed.

Human Rights Watch (1993) *War Crimes in Bosnia-Hercegovina*, Vol. 2. New York: Human Rights Watch.

Human Rights Watch (1996) *Shattered Lives: Sexual Violence during the Genocide and Its Aftermath* (New York: Human Rights Watch).

Hynes, P.H. (2004) 'On the battlefield of women's bodies: an overview of the harm of war to women', *Women's Studies International Forum*, 27 (5–6): 431–45.

Jones, A. (2006) 'Straight as a rule. Heteronormativity, gendercide, and the noncombatant male', *Men and Masculinities*, 8 (4): 451–69.

Kimmel, M.S. (1994) 'Masculinity as homophobia: fear, shame, and silence in the construction of gender identity', in H. Brod and M. Kaufman (eds) *Theorizing Masculinities*. Thousand Oaks, CA: Sage.

Liebling, H. (2004) 'A Gendered Analysis of the Experiences of Ugandan Women War Survivors' (unpublished PhD thesis, Warwick University).

Lohr, B.A., Adams, H.E. and Davis, J.M. (1997) 'Sexual arousal to erotic and aggressive stimuli in sexually coercive and noncoercive men', *Journal of Abnormal Psychology*, 106: 230–42.

Marchbank, J. and Letherby, G. (2007) *Introduction to Gender: Social Science Perspectives*. Essex: Pearson Education.

Oxford University Gazette (1998) 'Study of victims of male rape', http://www.ox.ac.uk/gazette/1998-9/weekly/011098/news/story_4.htm, accessed December 2006.

Parker, K. and Chew, J. (1994) 'Compensation for Japan's World War II rape victims', *Hastings International and Comparative Law Review*, 17: 524.

Pettman, J.J. (1996) *Worlding Women: A Feminist International Politics*. London: Routledge.

Pino, N. W. and Meier, R. F. (1999) 'Gender differences in rape reporting', *Sex Roles*, 40 (11–12): 979–90.

Rome Statute of the International Criminal Courts, available at http://www.un.org/law/icc/statute/99_corr/2.htm, accessed December 2006.

Scheffer, D. J. (1999) *Remarks – Rape as a War Crime*, to Fordham University, New York, http://www.converge.org.nz/pma/arape.htm, accessed December 2006.

Seifert, R. (1994) 'War and rape: a preliminary analysis', in A. Stiglmayer (ed.) *Mass Rape: The War Against Women in Bosnia-Herzegovina*. Lincoln, NE: University of Nebraska Press, pp. 54–72.

Stiglmayer, A. (1994) 'The rapes in Bosnia Herzegovina', in A. Stiglmayer (ed.) *Mass Rape: The War Against Women in Bosnia-Herzegovina*. Lincoln, NE: University of Nebraska Press, pp. 82–169.

Swiss, S. and Giller, J.E. (1993) 'Rape as a crime of war – a medical perspective', *Journal of the American Medical Association*, 5: 612–15; also at http://www.phrusa.org/research/health_effects/humrape.html.

Trexler, R. (1995) *Sex and Conquest: Gendered Violence, Political Order and the European Conquest of the Americas*. Ithaca, NY: Cornell University Press.

Twagiramariya, C. and Turshen, M. (1998) '"Favours" to give and "consenting" victims', in M. Turshen and C. Twagiramariya (eds) *What Women Do in Wartime*. London: Zed, pp. 101–17.

Women's Caucus for Gender Justice (undated) *Treatment of Sexual Violence in International Law*, available at http://www.amicc.org/docs/Sexualviolence_history.pdf, accessed December 2006.

Yuval-Davis, N. and Anthias, F. (eds) (1994) *Women–Nation–State*. London: Macmillan.

Chapter 13

Contradictions and paradoxes: international patterns of, and responses to, reported rape cases

Liz Kelly

Introduction

Rape was one of the first issues second-wave feminists took into the public sphere in the 1970s. Alongside 'speak-outs' in which women gave testimony of their experiences of coercive heterosexuality (Connell and Wilson 1974), innovative responses such as women-only telephone helplines, self-help support groups, reclaim the night marches, and self-defence classes mushroomed (Seith and Kelly 2003), creating new social spaces in which it became possible to speak about rape. This space for action also enabled knowledge creation, with early research and foundational texts (see, for example, Brownmiller 1975; Clark and Lewis 1977) documenting ways in which the legal process denied credibility and dignity to women.

The heady combination of activist protest, passionate polemic and more considered research and commentary led governments to embark on reforms of statute and procedural responses to rape and sexual assault. These changes gathered momentum in the 1980s and 1990s, informed by detailed critical legal commentary and rigorous research on the process of reporting rape and rape trials (see Bargen and Fishwick 1995; Kelly 2002). Some aspects of the reform process were common – for example removing unique evidential requirements such as the corroboration rule (Temkin 2002) – others, including how rape was defined, varied across jurisdictions. A shared ambition among reformers, however, was to increase reporting and confidence in the criminal justice system, with feminist and critical legal theorists also committed to the removal of explicit and implicit gender bias in the letter and practice of law.

This chapter presents data on patterns of reporting, prosecution and conviction across Europe, which support arguments made in Australia and the US (Bronitt 1995; Schulhofer 1998; Spohn and Horney 1996), that rape law reform has not had the outcomes intended. After exploring this challenging data, possible explanations are canvassed drawing on recent critical scholarship. Some of the paradoxes and contradictions, and their implications for social, feminist and criminological theory, are highlighted in the final section.

Theorising coercive sex

There is no doubt that feminist theory and research has had a profound influence on how sexuality and sexual crime are understood. At the same time some of the challenges have been the most resisted and contested arenas in contemporary feminist ideas. In this context it is worth revisiting the way the discursive construction of sexual violence has developed.

In the early feminist texts, while the role of rape in the social control of women is an emergent theme, rapists are still implicitly understood as deviant. These relatively rare events were connected, by some, to more mundane 'petty rapes' (Greer 1971). The journey from this point to asking disturbing questions about heterosexuality and masculinity spanned two decades, and encompasses many key texts and argumentative engagements within and without women's movements. One of the earliest moves, however, was in the opposite direction – seeking to position rape as a crime of violence rather than sex, a claim that was intended to focus attention on the actions of the perpetrator. Catherine MacKinnon most succinctly pointed out that to define rape as a crime of violence was to avoid asking what the harms of 'sex as usual' were for women. The concept of sexual violence as a continuum (Kelly 1987) provided one route for theorising connections between taken-for-granted sexual pressure and criminalised violations. Social research provided both new information and confirmation of these shifts (Hanmer and Saunders 1984; Russell 1984), especially the recognition that most rapes are committed by known men, men whose normality challenged the clinical constructions of sex offenders.

During the 1990s the foundational challenges which radical feminist ideas encompassed (Richardson 2000) ricocheted through social theory and social research, leaving traces across disciplines and in methodological approaches to the study of sexuality and crime. This 'mainstreaming', combined with ongoing debates between feminists, has at times been reduced to a fatuous reference to 'sex wars'. The issues at stake were, and continue to be, profound and unresolved: what constitutes sexual consent? in what circumstances can women be said to exercise sexual agency? what is 'sexual liberation' when examined from the standpoint of women, including those in marginalised groups? to what extent are contemporary masculinities constructed through essentialist premises about male sexual drives? Alongside these explorations, in the realms of popular culture, moves back to the more comforting positions which had facilitated the 'othering' of sex offenders could be observed as the term 'paedophile' was rehabilitated (Cowburn and Dominelli 2001; Kelly 1996) and 'date rape' deployed as a shorthand to suggest incidents were not really rapes at all (McColgan 1996). There were, therefore, currents pulling in different directions, locating sexual violence (and rape in particular) within understandings of heteronormativity alongside the more traditional constructions of sex offenders and sexual offences as representing a break with social norms. Within feminist theory the victimhood/agency debate constituted a new fault line, with more thoughtful engagements exploring intersections (see, for example, Kelly *et al.* 1996; Lamb 1999) rarely acknowledged. Currently a notable re-emergence of critical scholarship on sexual violence seeks to transcend some of the recent binary constructions (see, for example, Gavey 2005; Jordan 2004).

This brief and necessarily oversimplified overview provides the backdrop against which the empirical data that form the core of this chapter can be understood. Other layers which are not explored include the de-radicalisation and/or professionalisation of groups such as rape crisis (Bevacqua 2000), the ways in which feminists have engaged with the state (Martin 2005) and the extent to which and how aspects of feminist thought find their way into mainstream policy responses (Walby 2004; Zippell 2006).

A forgotten issue

The data in this section draw on two projects funded by the European Commission addressing rape as a 'forgotten issue': eclipsed for over a decade by domestic violence (Kelly and Regan 2001; Regan and Kelly 2003). NGO partners from over 20 countries confirmed that in most countries rape rarely registered on the media and policy radar in the previous decade. Few of the now extensive European prevalence studies on violence against women[1] included sexual assault or sexual harassment (Hagemann-White, 2001). This analysis no longer applies to the UK in the twenty-first century, where research and critical commentary on the attrition process have captured media attention and raised public and policy concern (Kelly *et al.* 2005; HMCPSI 2007).

A number of commentators have argued that rape is a unique crime, not only because for centuries it has been the subject of unique evidential requirements (Temkin 2002), but also because of its specific characteristics (New South Wales Standing Committee on Social Issues 1996). Unlike other forms of assault, rape violates personal intimate and psychological boundaries – what in human rights language is designated human dignity and bodily integrity, and in feminist and critical theory is termed sexual autonomy or sexual sovereignty (Richardson 2000). The meaning of rape for women, within gender and generational relations and cultural contexts, underlies its emotional, psychological and social impacts and consequences. For example, while it is shaming in all cultures to have been raped, in those based in traditions of honour it can carry heavy burdens, including at the extreme the threat of death (Sen 2005). Some claim it is a distinctive crime because of the potential physical and health consequences, including pregnancy, infertility, STDs and HIV infection. Unlike many crimes, rape is surrounded by durable cultural myths and stereotypes all of which function to deny the legitimacy of women's and children's accusations (Jordan 2004) and/or define what happened as their responsibility. From a criminological perspective, one of the distinctive features of sexual crimes against women and children is that they are most commonly committed by someone the victim knows. Many of these elements combine with the potential for being blamed/held responsible, acting as a powerful disincentive to making an official report or even telling anyone (Kelly 2002).

Uncovering attrition

Following two waves of law reform – addressing the unique evidential requirements and redefining rape[2] – attention turned to other issues in policy and the academy, reflecting an implicit presumption that the changes would translate into enhanced access to justice and redress (see, for an overview, Kelly 2002; for specific countries – Department of Women 1996; Jordan 2001; McGregor *et al.* 2002; Spohn and Horney 1996). Where reforms were more extensive, including procedural changes that enhanced support, one could expect to see increased rates of prosecution and conviction, since what were considered significant impediments had been removed. This should be followed by higher levels of reporting, as confidence in the system was enhanced. Whether due to arrogant confidence, indifference or simply other priorities, statistical offices, justice departments and academics failed to track trends in the relationships between reporting, prosecution and conviction rates.

This made the two projects in Europe unique: the first – *Rape: The Forgotten Issue?* (Kelly and Regan 2001) – presented comparative data on legal reforms, reporting, prosecution and conviction rates. This was updated as *Rape: Still a Forgotten Issue* (Regan and Kelly 2003). Selected charts from the second report are used in this chapter to illustrate the key patterns.

Justice ministries in EU member states and accession countries were asked to provide raw numbers for reported rapes and those that resulted in prosecutions and convictions from 1971 to 2002. Where the full time series was difficult to provide, data at five-year intervals was requested. Full data were available for a minority of countries, while some submitted no data across both projects.[3] Data were supplied, however, for 21 countries, which was sufficient to explore commonalities and differences and document trends over time.

The starting point for these studies was data collated in 1997 for England and Wales[4] documenting the attrition process (the proportion of cases that fail to result in prosecution and/or conviction). This revealed an unbroken increase in reporting for over two decades, coupled with a slight rise in prosecutions and a virtually static number of convictions. These trends have continued up until 2004, the last year for which full data are available (see Figure 13.1), when there was an all time low conviction rate of 5.3 per cent. What was unexpected was not just the low conviction rate (less than one in ten in 1997) but the dramatic fall since the late 1970s, when one in three reported rapes resulted in a conviction. That attrition had increased so markedly was not well known until this tracking of trends. The data also question the assumptions underlining legal reform, since reporting has increased despite a falling proportion of prosecutions and convictions, suggesting that reporting and confidence in the criminal justice system are not linked in a straightforward or unidirectional way.

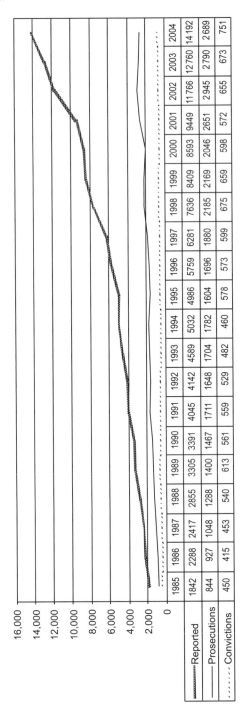

	1985	1986	1987	1988	1989	1990	1991	1992	1993	1994	1995	1996	1997	1998	1999	2000	2001	2002	2003	2004
Reported	1842	2288	2417	2855	3305	3391	4045	4142	4589	5032	4986	5759	6281	7636	8409	8593	9449	11766	12760	14192
Prosecutions	844	927	1048	1288	1400	1467	1711	1648	1704	1782	1604	1696	1880	2185	2169	2046	2651	2945	2790	2689
Convictions	450	415	453	540	613	561	559	529	482	460	578	573	599	675	659	598	572	655	673	751

Figure 13.1 Attrition in reported rape cases in England and Wales

The European study was designed to discover if increasing attrition was evident beyond England and Wales. Similar stark increases in attrition were evident in all the countries with adversarial legal systems, the most extreme example being Ireland (Figure 13.2), where just one in a hundred reported rapes resulted in a conviction in 2001.[5] While less marked, the fundamental trends of increased reporting accompanied by falling prosecution and conviction were apparent in some investigative legal systems, including Sweden and Finland (see Figures 13.3 and 13.4). The patterns identified in England and Wales were, therefore, identified in societies with varied legal definitions of rape and contrasting histories of legal reform and approaches to gender equality. Thus not only had the promises of rape law reform failed to deliver, but also rising attrition was evident in two of the Scandinavian countries considered to have achieved most with respect to gender equality.[6]

This was not the only pattern, however, in the time series data. A specific trend emerged across six Eastern European countries:[7] a – in some instances sharp – decrease in reporting throughout the 1990s. The data from Hungary (see Figure 13.5) illustrate this, alongside the fact that by 2000 this trend was reversing. NGO partners explained the decline through reference to the decreased capacity of the state infrastructure following the collapse of the Soviet Union, prompting a loss of confidence in the justice system. The small upward movements noted in the second wave of data collection reflect transition processes, specifically the stabilisation of emergent state formations. These data offer both a window on the gendered impacts of transition and support a strong relationship between state capacity[8] and reporting of sexual crime.

Across the German-speaking countries (Austria, Germany, Switzerland), reporting remained flat with rates of prosecution and conviction relatively constant, although the data here are not as complete as they could be (see Regan and Kelly 2003). Germany offers an intriguing exception to rising or flat attrition, in that since 1999 a sustained increase in prosecutions and convictions has taken place (see Figure 13.6). More detailed research is needed to account for this (welcome) anomaly.[9]

While there is no consistency in patterns of reporting across Europe, in most countries conviction rates have fallen in the 1990s, particularly in Western Europe where the most extensive legal reform took place. The changes in statute law, evidential rules and even police procedures which activists campaigned for in the 1970s and 1980s have failed to convict more rapists, and could be argued to

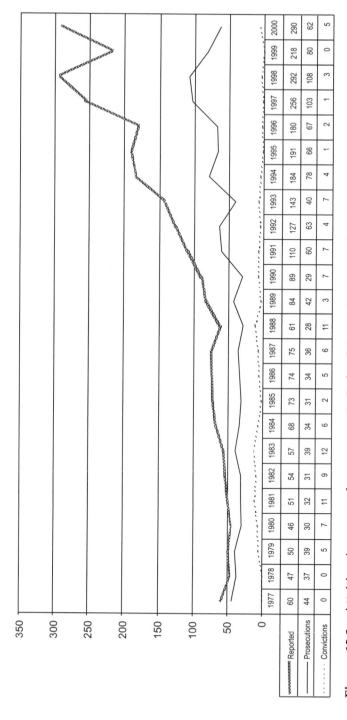

	1977	1978	1979	1980	1981	1982	1983	1984	1985	1986	1987	1988	1989	1990	1991	1992	1993	1994	1995	1996	1997	1998	1999	2000
Reported	60	47	50	46	51	54	57	68	73	74	75	61	84	89	110	127	143	184	191	180	256	292	218	290
Prosecutions	44	37	39	30	32	31	39	34	31	34	36	28	42	29	60	63	40	78	66	67	103	108	80	62
Convictions	0	0	5	7	11	9	12	6	2	5	6	11	3	7	7	4	7	4	1	2	1	3	0	5

Figure 13.2 Attrition in reported rape cases in Ireland (cases include minors)

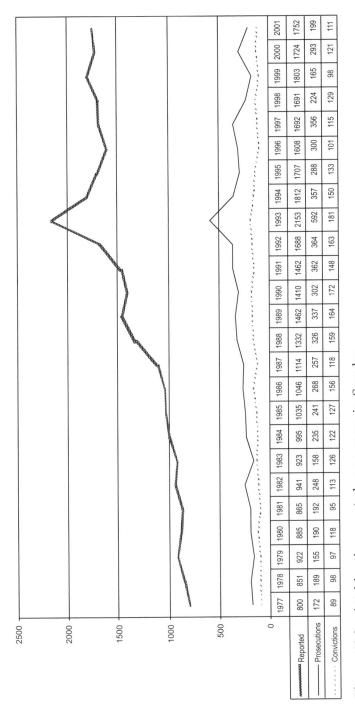

	1977	1978	1979	1980	1981	1982	1983	1984	1985	1986	1987	1988	1989	1990	1991	1992	1993	1994	1995	1996	1997	1998	1999	2000	2001
Reported	800	851	922	885	865	941	923	995	1035	1046	1114	1332	1462	1410	1462	1688	2153	1812	1707	1608	1692	1691	1803	1724	1752
Prosecutions	172	189	155	190	192	248	158	235	241	268	257	326	337	302	362	364	592	357	288	300	356	224	165	293	199
Convictions	89	98	97	118	95	113	126	122	127	156	118	159	164	172	148	163	181	150	133	101	115	129	98	121	111

Figure 13.3 Attrition in reported rape cases in Sweden

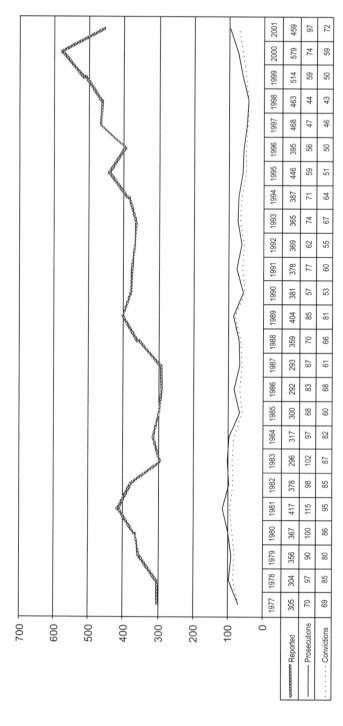

	1977	1978	1979	1980	1981	1982	1983	1984	1985	1986	1987	1988	1989	1990	1991	1992	1993	1994	1995	1996	1997	1998	1999	2000	2001
Reported	305	304	356	367	417	378	296	317	300	292	293	359	404	381	378	369	365	387	446	395	468	463	514	579	459
Prosecutions	70	97	90	100	115	98	102	97	68	83	67	70	85	57	77	62	74	71	59	56	47	44	59	74	97
Convictions	69	85	80	86	95	85	87	82	60	68	61	66	81	53	60	55	67	64	51	50	46	43	50	59	72

Figure 13.4 Attrition in reported rape cases in Finland (cases include minors)

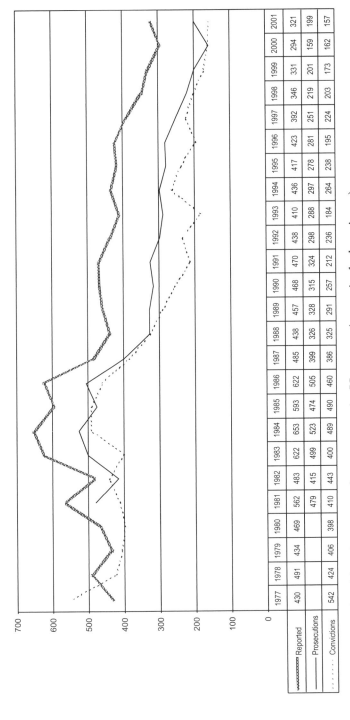

	1977	1978	1979	1980	1981	1982	1983	1984	1985	1986	1987	1988	1989	1990	1991	1992	1993	1994	1995	1996	1997	1998	1999	2000	2001
Reported	430	491	434	469	562	483	622	653	593	622	485	438	457	468	470	438	410	436	417	423	392	346	331	294	321
Prosecutions				398	479	415	499	523	474	505	399	326	328	315	324	298	288	297	278	281	251	219	201	159	199
Convictions	542	424	406	398	410	443	400	489	490	460	386	325	291	257	212	236	184	264	238	195	224	203	173	162	157

Figure 13.5 Attrition in reported rape cases in Hungary (cases include minors)

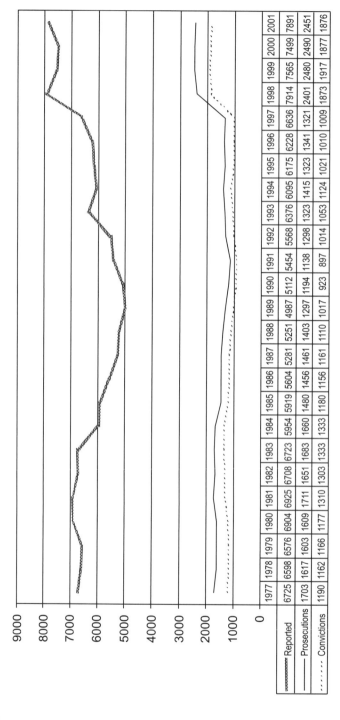

	1977	1978	1979	1980	1981	1982	1983	1984	1985	1986	1987	1988	1989	1990	1991	1992	1993	1994	1995	1996	1997	1998	1999	2000	2001
Reported	6725	6598	6576	6904	6925	6708	6723	5954	5919	5604	5281	5251	4987	5112	5454	5568	6376	6095	6175	6228	6636	7914	7565	7499	7891
Prosecutions	1703	1617	1603	1609	1711	1651	1683	1660	1480	1456	1461	1403	1297	1194	1138	1298	1323	1415	1323	1341	1321	2401	2480	2490	2451
	1190	1162	1166	1177	1310	1303	1333	1333	1180	1156	1161	1110	1017	923	897	1014	1053	1124	1021	1010	1009	1873	1917	1877	1876
Convictions																									

Figure 13.6 Attrition in reported rape cases in Germany (cases include minors)

have had the paradoxical outcome of holding fewer men to account. These findings transcend legal systems, since falling conviction rates – now referred to by the British government as a 'justice gap' (Kelly *et al.* 2005) – appear across adversarial and investigative systems.

Examining attrition

While it is not the primary ambition of this chapter to explain attrition rates (see Kelly *et al.* 2005; HMCPSI 2007), some broad conclusions can be drawn from the current knowledge base which primarily addresses adversarial systems (Australia, Canada, New Zealand, the UK, the USA). We currently have the most detailed information on these processes for England and Wales (Harris and Grace 1999; HMCPSI 2002, 2007; Kelly *et al.* 2005). The analysis presented below draws on a research review (Kelly 2002) and an in-depth exploration of attrition processes in England and Wales (Kelly *et al.* 2005).

In *A Gap or a Chasm?* (Kelly *et al.* 2005) 3,527 cases were tracked prospectively, and a range of other data collected, including interviews with complainants and professionals. Attrition through the criminal justice system was explored through a sub-sample of 2,284 cases, which were reported to the police and where the eventual outcome is known. The conviction rate of 8 per cent across this sample is marginally higher than the national rates for 2001 and 2002, when the cases were dealt with.

The first attrition point is the actual decision to report, with various sources suggesting that between 6 and 15 per cent of rapes are reported to the police (Johnson and Sacco 1995; Myhill and Allen 2002). Whatever the proportion, it remains the case that the majority of sexual assaults are still not reported to the police or indeed anyone (Kelly 2002). Reasons for not making official reports are a combination of personal circumstances and resources (relationship to the perpetrator, not wanting others to know, wanting to forget) and anticipated responses (disbelief, blame and the CJS process). Those reports appear to act from more social motives, stressing the need to protect others and that the perpetrator should be sanctioned (Kelly *et al.* 2005).

Once a report is made the highest attrition occurs in the early phases of investigation (see Table 13.1), with more than three-quarters – in this study 80 per cent – of cases falling at the first hurdle. While there are matters such as failure to identify offenders in play here, the vast majority of cases drop out due to decisions made by the complainant

Table 13.1 Attrition at the police/investigation stage

Reason for case not proceeding	Number N = 2,284	Percentage
Insufficient evidence	386	21
Victim withdrawal	318	17
Victim declined to complete initial process	315	17
Offender not identified	239	13
False allegation	216	12
No evidence of assault	83	5
No prospect of conviction	37	2
Not in public interest	20	1
Other	67	4
Reason unknown	136	8
Attrition total	1,817	80

or criminal justice personnel. It is here that the contested matter of no/not criming is evident, alongside over a third (34 per cent) of victims declining to complete aspects of the process or withdrawing their complaint. While there are many valid reasons why someone might withdraw, there are also failures within the investigative process – such as the lack of (female) forensic examiners and having to wait hours for a specially trained officer (STO) to be available to take a statement (HMCPSI 2007; Lovett *et al.* 2004) – which act as disincentives for those who are already ambivalent. Very significant to some are the messages they get from police officers. Ethnographic research in a USA police station (Kersetter 1990) and interviews with complainants in the UK (Kelly *et al.* 2005) reveal the ease with which police officers, acting in good and bad faith, can steer complainants away from pursuing cases. These data suggest that increased reporting is an inadequate index of confidence in the CJS, since early withdrawal implies withdrawal of trust in the process and a loss of confidence that the integrity and dignity of the complainant will be dealt with respectfully.

Deficiencies in police investigations and their own decision-making accounts for the next layer of case attrition: they may fail to find/ identify the attacker; they may label the complaint 'false'; or they may decide that 'no further action' should be taken since the evidence is not, in their opinion, strong enough. This final decision may involve an assessment of the strength and/or credibility of the complainant, and is often applied where she is a prostitute, has learning difficulties or mental health problems (Kelly *et al.* 2005). Some police decision-making is made in good faith – officers believe that it would be more harmful to the woman to proceed. Much is, however, rooted in clichés about rape, stereotypes and prejudices about who counts as a 'deserving' victim (Kelly 2002). An overestimation of false allegations remains a significant barrier to improved practice (Kelly *et al.* 2005; Jordan 2004), meaning that cases are abandoned before a thorough investigation has been undertaken.

The stage at which cases reach prosecutors varies across Europe, and thus the number of cases over which they exert a determining influence is not consistent. Table 13.2 suggests that in England and Wales the CPS are responsible for only 6 per cent of attrition; this belies their influence on police decision-making through offering advice at early stages. Their influence will become even more significant through new joint charging decisions (HMCPSI 2007). While prosecutors explain their decision in terms of evidential matters, research in the USA (Frohmann 1991) and the UK (Kelly *et al.* 2005) reveals that supposedly objective reasoning can act as a smokescreen for subjective assessments of the credibility of complainants, linked to constructions of acceptable femininity. There is also a sense among many lawyers that rape cases are 'difficult' and that where a consent defence is in play, it is 'one person's word against another'.

Cases that reach court, therefore, have been through winnowing processes which ensure not only that the complainant is determined to pursue the case, but on evidential grounds these are the 'strongest'. This skews the kinds of cases that appear in court, with a higher proportion of the stereotyped stranger case, with visible injuries, making it through the process (Kelly 2002). Judges in both investigative and adversarial systems can 'throw cases out' at early stages if they

Table 13.2 Attrition at CPS/prosecution stage

Reason for case not proceeding	Number N = 145	Percentage
Caution/final reprimand	9	6
Discontinued	38	26
Victim withdrawal	25	17
Suspect fled prior to PDH	1	1
Pending trial	72	50
Attrition totals, calculated on base N, 2,284	145	6

feel the evidence is weak, and they and/or juries can reach a 'not guilty' verdict at the end of a trial (Table 13.3). The proportion of the tracked sample cases which resulted in a conviction at trial was 3.4 per cent – guilty pleas made up a higher proportion of convictions. Despite the selection process noted above, the ratio of acquittals to findings of guilt in contested trials involving adults was 2:1, with highest rates for adult women, compared with both adult men and/ or minors (Kelly *et al.* 2005, 2006). Contemporary research concurs that extra legal factors influence much decision-making in rape cases (see Department of Women 1996 for Australia; Jordan 2004 for New Zealand; Kelly *et al.* 2005; McGregor *et al.* 2002 for Canada).

Rewriting the script

This section draws on a review of sexual offences law (Home Office 2000) and two major legislative reforms – the Youth Justice and Criminal Evidence Act 1999 and the Sex Offences Act 2003. The latter reworked the entire framework of sexual offences law through the philosophical principles of justice, fairness and equality.

The Youth Justice and Criminal Evidence Act 1999 introduced procedural changes to enable those designated 'vulnerable' and intimidated witnesses to give 'best evidence', including: to record evidence in chief on video,[10] or to give evidence in court behind a screen or through a video link. While victims of serious sexual

Table 13.3 Attrition at court/trial stage

Reason for case not proceeding	Number N = 322	Percentage
Trial to be rearranged, suspect fled	1	<1
Victim withdrawal	15	5
Discontinued/withdrawn at court	19	6
Acquittal	104	32
Guilty plea	89	28
Not clear if guilty plea/conviction	17	5
Part conviction	11	3
Conviction	66	20
Attrition		14
Total convictions		
[both calculated on base N, 2,284]		08

offences were formally defined as 'vulnerable', all protections remain at the discretion of the trial judge. Sections 41–43 of this statute introduced a new regime to limit the use of the complainant's sexual history evidence in sexual offence cases (Temkin 2002). The scheme begins from a presumption that such evidence should be excluded, except where it falls into one of four exceptions. Clear rules for how applications should be made (in writing and before trial) were introduced. An evaluation (Kelly *et al.* 2006), however, documents both circumvention of the court rules and a consensus across the legal practitioners that sexual history is relevant in more contexts than the legal reform intended.

The first wholesale review of sexual offences law for a century began in January 1999 and was undertaken by two groups,[11] with members selected to encompass both expertise and special interests.[12] The groups were tasked with creating a modern coherent code resting on four pillars: justice, fairness, equality and protection of the vulnerable. Previously sexual offence law made unjustifiable distinctions depending on the sex of the perpetrator and victim, not to mention criminalising some acts only when they involved homosexuality. From the outset the government made clear that their priorities were to enhance protection of children and vulnerable people (those with physical or mental impairments). This immediately raised the question of how women's over-representation as victims of sexual crime was to be addressed, since defining them either as children or vulnerable was unacceptable. At an early stage the work of US legal professor Stephen Schulhofer (1998) was used to set a framework for adults rooted in the right to 'sexual autonomy'.

The deliberations and conclusions were published in 2000, as *Setting the Boundaries*,[13] and following a consultation proposed changes appeared in November 2002 entitled *Protecting the Public*.[14] The new law, the Sexual Offences Act (SOA), was passed in 2003 and implemented in May 2004, and contains most of the recommendations from the original review.

The section covering general sexual offences against adults redefines the crime of rape for the third time in 15 years[15] to include penetration of the mouth, alongside the vagina[16] and anus. Unlike in many other jurisdictions the word rape has been retained and the crime has not been made gender neutral: while males, females and transgendered people can be raped, rapists are male, since the offence is committed with a penis. A second, equally serious, gender-neutral offence was created – sexual assault by penetration – to cover penetration by objects, fingers and fists. While some have criticised this construction (see, for example, Phoenix and Oerton 2005) the alternative – creating levels and layers of sexual assault as has been done in other jurisdictions – has not delivered hoped-for increased conviction rates and has reinforced the construction (not supported by research evidence) that rapes by known perpetrators are less harmful than those by strangers (Kelly 2002). Alongside a raft of new offences and reflecting the current knowledge base on sexual offending, other definitional and procedural issues were addressed, not least introducing a positive consent standard in statute.

With respect to children, the stated intent was to address the realities of sexual abuse which had emerged since the last reform efforts in the 1950s. A specific set of offences was elaborated, designed either to have different evidential thresholds or to enable recognition of contexts and/or to allow aggravating factors, such as abuse by a family member. The strong message that sexual contact with children is not acceptable and represents a breach of rights and trust can be seen in the creation of 'strict liability' offences where the child is under 13: if the prosecution can prove that the defendant did what they are accused of there is no defence. Reflecting the tension between a focus on the realities and populist constructions of sexual violence, these offences and contexts have received far less attention in the media – and by politicians – than the offences introduced to address sexual exploitation and grooming over the Internet.[17] While the legal reforms were anchored in perspectives that owed much to feminist ideas, what politicians, children's charities and the media combined to promote emphasised the risk from the quintessential stranger – one who could prowl in cyberspace and need not even live in the same country as children they targeted. This took the 'othering' of child sex offenders (Kelly 1996) into new realms, especially since the comparative risks of this event compared with someone in a child's everyday landscape being the perpetrator were minute. Paradoxically, therefore, the new framework of law was built upon a strong evidence base, but this has not translated into wider public and especially populist engagement.

The knowledge base documenting the extent of sexual abuse of adults with disabilities underpinned the need to enhance their protection, while at the same time respecting the right of adults with disabilities to engage in chosen sexual activity – the sexual autonomy principle – has gained recognition. Drawing a boundary required defining two areas – capacity to consent and breach of relationships of trust. Where a person is, in law, seen as having no capacity to consent, a strict liability offence was created. A series of lower level offences which focus on issues of inducement, threat or deception (with or without breach of a relationship of care) set out sexual ethics for those providing care in residential and other settings. The hope and intention was that these offences might be prosecutable without having to rely on the testimony of this category of victims, who have persistently been defined as lacking credibility by UK courts.

While an unpublished internal stocktake has been undertaken on the SOA, the lack of an external evaluation means we have limited evidence as to what the impact of the changes has been on how cases are investigated, prosecuted and presented in courts. The data presented in Figure 13.1 show that the earliest data have not reversed the progressive increase in attrition, although the rate of fall on the conviction rate seems to be slowing for England and Wales. Government policies have also sought to reverse the falling conviction rate through: supporting the establishment of sexual assault referral centres (SARCs); specialisation in police and prosecutors; codes of guidance for police investigators and the CPS; and a range of other more generic reforms (HMCPSI 2007). While SARCs undoubtedly make the process of reporting and forensic examinations in particular less daunting, their contribution to reversing attrition is limited (Lovett *et al.* 2004). Research with complainants reveals that reporting rape need not be the trauma that it invariably was in the past: at the same time the emphasis on 'victim care' (HMCPSI 2002) has had minimal impact on the number of cases proceeding to trial (Kelly *et al.* 2005). We face, therefore, something of a contradiction: that despite extensive reform of statute and procedural rules, evident commitment at policy levels and sustained media interest, the conviction rate continues to fall. Some argue that the problem here is one of political will, that because rape has not been specified as a priority within Policing Plans and Public Service Agreements (PSAs) for the justice agencies, there are no incentives for improving performance. There is some support for this position in the variations in conviction rates across police force areas (Kelly *et al.* 2005) and the emerging findings that lower attrition is associated with local prioritisation and senior oversight, at least in the police (HMCPSI 2007).

Cultures of scepticism and pessimism

That successive legal and procedural reforms have failed to reverse attrition suggests that deeper social and cultural processes are at play. One is undoubtedly the paradoxical way in which feminist knowledge both informs reform processes and is simultaneously disavowed. In a similar vein it is evident that practitioners draw more on the safety of clichés and long-held beliefs than evidence in their assessments of cases and individuals. Consider these statements by police officers, all of whom were considered specialists in the sexual offence arena:

> *In theory, I would say that somebody who has been raped is going to stick quite rigidly to the account that they give, and that might be an account they give to a uniform police officer and then to us and then perhaps the doctor as well... whereas sometimes those that have made a false allegation, the story may well change.* (Female detective constable)

> *... I have dealt with hundreds and hundreds of rapes in the last few years, and I can honestly probably count on both hands the ones that I believe are truly genuine.* (Male detective constable)

Both reflect what we have called a culture of scepticism that suffuses rape investigations, something also evident to a worker at a SARC, with many years' experience of the early stages of the reporting process:

> *One of the things that comes up, time and time again, is their automatic disbelief of a complainant. I'd be getting details off the officer, and they'd say 'Ooh, so what did they say to you in there? What do you think's happened? Sounds a bit dodgy to me' ... It seems to be a natural cynicism, and I am sure that along the way they have met complainants who have made false allegations ... everybody then suffers because they happen to have met one or two or maybe more who've told lies ... I think they disbelieve, apart from what fits their stereotype of a rape.* (SARC worker)

Having appropriate statutes and procedures is only one part of the equation needed to address the justice gap. So long as all those who implement laws retain outmoded understandings of rape, masculinity, femininity and sexuality law in practice will retain many of the orthodoxies reform seeks to move on from.

The culture of scepticism draws on one of these orthodoxies, which operates in a series of explicit and implicit ways, the notion of 'real rape' (Estrich 1987). This concept refers to a constellation of expectations without which a case may not be included in the category 'rape': a 'real rape' takes place outside, at night and the attacker is a stranger with a weapon. While many professionals no longer discount rapes by known assailants they do treat them as less credible (Jordan 2004; Kelly *et al*. 2005). Despite the fact that only a minority of reported rape cases fit the stereotype, they are still the most likely to be reported, investigated and prosecuted.

Contradictions and paradoxes

A number of contradictions and paradoxes have already been alluded to; these are revisited along with further observations with respect to the shifts in thinking and trends in criminal justice responses.

One paradox about which no conclusions can be drawn is the different pattern in reporting rates for rape across Western Europe, since the reasons underpinning the flat rates in the German-speaking countries are yet to be adequately explained. The countries with increased reporting (see Figures 13.1–13.4) can claim to have achieved one of the intentions in the reform process and in so doing have brought the profiles of rape in community surveys and official reports closer together. At the same time attrition is highest for these countries, with 'real rapes' still more likely to make it through into the courtroom. Thus despite an acceptance of the wider definition of rape in statute and to some extent in public attitudes, a narrower meaning continues to be reinscribed through the criminal justice process and populist media: a process noted in early feminist scholarship (Gavey 2005).

One potential contradiction these data show is that the achievement of formal gender equality appears to have minimal impact on either gender violence in general (Kelly 2005) or the attrition rate in rape. This leads in several possible theoretical directions: that violence against women needs to be introduced as a key measure in equality indices; that it has a relative independence from other aspects of formal equality; or that it is a mechanism which some men use to resist changes in gender orders (Kelly 2005b).

While the law in a number of jurisdictions has endeavoured to provide more clarity about sexual autonomy and consent, this is yet to be translated into wider social attitudes, especially among young people (Amnesty International 2005). The resilience of constructions of 'real rape', 'date rape' and deserving/credible victims attests to the limited progress to date. Some reformers have given up on being able to fill consent with feminist meaning and have opted for an entirely new approach to defining rape: in South Africa and the International

Criminal Court it is defined as 'sex in coercive circumstances' (Kelly 2005a), the intention being to shift the emphasis onto the actions/ agency of the accused.

Another paradox which has received limited attention is the unintended consequence of the construction of rape as a heinous and intrinsically traumatising event. While it may well be both, it also takes place in the messiness of everyday lives and can be far more mundane than many representations of it allow for. This both encourages many women to not define their experiences of forced sex as rape and also ensures that expectations of damage and distress determine whether complainants will be accorded the status of victim.

From 'real rape' to real reform

Real reform of the criminal justice system will have begun when reports of sexual crime by known offenders, including in contexts where the complainant could be seen as 'taking risks' (such as accepting a lift, an invitation for a cup of coffee or having consumed alcohol voluntarily), are not dealt with as an 'exercise in scepticism', but rather as a report of a serious crime which requires dedicated investigation and thoughtful evidence gathering. Further evidence of the social science data and feminist critique having taken deep roots will be when defence barristers can be observed choosing not to invoke sexist stereotypes, however effective they might be, in their advocacy (Temkin 2000), and prosecution lawyers confidently presenting an account of what happened, in which they assert the right of women who do not fulfil expectations of conventional femininity to sexual autonomy.

> The inability to engage with cultural narratives and macho adversarialism explains rape law reform's failure. These primary mechanisms by which rape jurors determine credibility are unchanged. Consequently, unjustified acquittals mount. (Taslitz 1999: 154–5)

What is needed to address the attrition rate is a change in culture – not just in the justice system, but across societies – such that 'the word of a woman' as Jan Jordan (2004) refers to it is no longer treated as less worthy of belief when what she speaks about is sexual victimisation. A feminist contribution to this process must include transcending the victim/agency opposition which has suffused contemporary theory and critique. One useful place to start would be the voices of women who have lived to tell, and reflect upon, their experiences of sexual violence. Susan Brison (2002) in a moving account of how rape changed her, including how as a philosopher she theorises the self, challenges simplistic constructions of rape victims in ways that offer a route out of at least one paradox – while victimisation denies forms of agency, dealing with the aftermath necessitates regaining it.

> I develop and defend a view of the self as fundamentally relational – capable of being undone by violence, but also of being remade in connection with others … [the] tension between living to tell and telling to live, that is between getting (and keeping) the story right in order to bear witness and being able to rewrite the story in ways that enable the survivor to go on with her life. (xi–xii)

Notes

1 While aware that some men and boys are raped and sexually assaulted this chapter will refer to victims/survivors/ complainants as female, since that represents the vast majority of reported and unreported cases.

2 Definitions were always extended, including a variable combination of: penetration of anus and mouth; penetration by fingers and objects; rape of men; removing the marital rape exemption.

3 At least five formal requests were made by letter and one direct follow-up telephone call, often by the NGO partner from the country in question. The dearth of data from southern Europe was notable.

4 Data is not compiled for the UK as a whole, since Scotland has a separate and subtly different legal system, as to a lesser extent does Northern Ireland. The Scottish data mirrors that for England and Wales, but we have been unable to obtain the Northern Irish data.

5 One explanation proffered for this pattern was the large number of historic abuse cases reported to the police in the 1990s. This claim has yet to be explored with reference to case data.

6 Most measures focus on the public sphere – employment, equal pay and political representation.

7 Data was available for Bosnia, Hungary, Latvia, Poland, Slovenia, Romania.

8 Capacity here refers not just to the ability to take and record reports but also to respond appropriately to them.

9   A project, led by the author, began in mid-2007 to prospectively track reported rape cases in eight European countries, while simultaneously documenting legal and procedural changes on a time line.

10 This element has yet to be implemented.

11 The author was one of two academic members of the External Reference Group.

12 Children's charities, Rape Crisis, Sexual Assault Referral Centre, groups representing the elderly, lesbians and gay men, adults and children with disabilities, faith groups, lawyers and academics.

13 This report can be accessed at http://www.homeoffice.gov.uk/cpd/sou/vol1main.pdf.

14 This can be accessed at http://www.official-documents.co.uk/document/cm56/5668/5668.pdf.

15 Previous revisions in the early 1990s included male rape and rape in marriage.

16 Vagina includes reconstructed ones, making it possible for the first time for rape of a transsexual to be prosecuted as rape.

17 This was an offence added at a late stage and did not form part of the original recommendations.

References

Amnesty International (2005) *Sexual Assault Research*. London: Amnesty International.

Bargen, J. and Fishwick, E. (1995) *Sexual Assault Law Reform: A National Perspective*. Canberra: Office of the Status of Women.

Bevacqua, M. (2000) *Rape on the Public Agenda: Feminism and the Politics of Sexual Assault*. Boston: Northeastern University Press.

Brison, S. (2002) *Aftermath: Violence and the Remaking of a Self* (Princeton, NJ: Princeton University Press).

Bronitt, S. (1995) 'The direction of rape law in Australia: toward a positive consent standard', *Criminal Law Journal*, 18: 249–53.

Brownmiller, S. (1975) *Against Our Will: Men, Women and Rape*. Harmondsworth: Penguin.

Clark, L. and Lewis, D. (1977) *Rape: The Price of Coercive Sexuality*. Toronto: Women's Educational Press.

Connell, N. and Wilson, C. (1974) *Rape: The First Sourcebook for Women*. New York: New American Library.

Cowburn, M. and Dominelli, L. (2001) 'Masking hegemonic masculinity: reconstructing the paedophile as the dangerous stranger', *British Journal of Social Work*, 31 (3): 399–415.

Department of Women (1996) *Heroines of Fortitude: The Experiences of Women in Court as Victims of Sexual Assault*. Sydney: New South Wales Department of Women.

Estrich, S. (1987) *Real Rape: How the Legal System Victimizes Women Who Say No* (Boston: Harvard University Press).

Frohmann, L. (1991) 'Discrediting victims' allegations of sexual assault: prosecutorial accounts of case rejections', *Social Problems*, 38 (2): 213–26.

Gavey, N. (2005) *Just Sex? The Cultural Scaffolding of Rape*. London: Routledge.

Greer, G. (1971) *The Female Eunuch*. London: Paladin.

Hagemann-White, C. (2001) 'European research into the prevalence of violence against women', *Violence Against Women*, 7 (7): 732–59.

Hanmer, J. and Saunders, S. (1984) *Well Founded Fear*. London: Hutchinson.

Harris, J. and Grace, S. (1999) *A Question of Evidence? Investigating and Prosecuting Rape in the 1990s*. London: Home Office.

HM Crown Prosecution Service Inspectorate and HM Inspectorate of Constabulary (2002) *A Report on the Joint Inspection onto the Investigation and Prosecution of Cases involving Allegations of Rape*. London: HMCPSI.

HM Crown Prosecution Service Inspectorate and HM Inspectorate of Constabulary (2007) *Without Consent: A Report on the Joint Review of the Investigation and Prosecution of Rape Offences*. London: HMCPSI.

Home Office (2000) *Setting the Boundaries: Reforming the Law on Sex Offences, Volumes 1 and 2*. London: Home Office.

Johnson, H. and Sacco, V. (1995) 'Researching violence against women: Statistics Canada's national study', *Canadian Journal of Criminology: Special Issue: Focus on the Violence Against Women Survey*, 37 (3): 281–304.

Jordan, J. (2001) 'Worlds apart? Women, rape and the police reporting process', *British Journal of Criminology*, 41(4): 679–706.

Jordan, J. (2004) *The Word of a Woman: Police, Rape and Belief*. London: Palgrave.

Kelly, L. (1987) *Surviving Sexual Violence*. Cambridge: Polity Press.

Kelly, L. (1996) 'Weasel words: paedophiles and the cycle of abuse', *Trouble and Strife*, 33, published online at http://www.cwasu.org.

Kelly, L. (2002) *A Research Review on the Reporting, Investigation and Prosecution of Rape Cases*. London: HMCPSI.

Kelly, L. (2005a) *Promising Practices: Addressing Sexual Violence*. Expert paper commissioned by UN Division for the Advancement of Women.

Kelly, L. (2005b) *How Violence is Constitutive of Women's Inequality and the Implications for Equalities Work*. Paper commissioned for the Equality and Diversity Forum Seminar, Seminar 2: Different Forms of Prejudice, November (London: Equality and Diversity Forum, online at http://www.edf.org.uk/).

Kelly, L. and Regan, L. (2001) *Rape: The Forgotten Issue? A European Attrition and Networking Study*. London: Child and Woman Abuse Studies Unit.

Kelly, L., Burton S. and Regan L. (1996) 'Beyond victim or survivor: sexual violence, identity and feminist theory and practice', in L. Adkins and V. Merchant (eds) *Sexualizing the Social: Power and the Organization of Sexuality*. London: Macmillan, pp. 77–101.

Kelly, L., Lovett, J. and Regan, L. (2005) *A Gap or a Chasm? Attrition in Reported Rape Cases.* London: Home Office.

Kelly, L., Temkin, J. and Griffiths, S. (2006) *Section 41: An Evaluation of New Legislation Limiting Sexual History Evidence in Rape Trials.* London: Home Office, online at www.homeoffice.gov.uk/rds/pdfs06/rdsolr2006.pdf.

Kersetter, W. (1990) 'Gateway to justice: police and prosecutorial response to sexual assaults against women', *Journal of Criminal Law and Criminology*, 81: 267–313.

Lamb, S. (ed.) (1999) *New Versions of Victim: Feminists Struggle with the Concept.* New York: New York University Press.

Lovett, J., Kelly, L. and Regan, L. (2004) *Sexual Assault Referral Centres: Maximising Potentials.* London: Home Office.

McColgan, A. (1996) *The Case for Taking the Date Out of Rape.* London: Pandora.

McGregor, M., Du Mont, J. and Myhr, T. (2002) 'Sexual assault forensic medical examination: is evidence related to successful prosecution?', *Annals of Emergency Medicine*, 39 (6): 639–47.

Martin, P. (2005) *Rape Work: Victims, Gender and Emotions in Organisations and Community Context.* Abingdon: Routledge.

Myhill, A. and Allen, J. (2002) *Rape and Sexual Assault of Women: The Extent and Nature of the Problem – Findings from the British Crime Survey*, Home Office Research Study 237. London: Home Office.

New South Wales Standing Committee on Social Issues (1996) *Sexual Violence, Volume 1.* Sydney: Department of Justice.

Phoenix, J. and Oerton, S. (2005) *Illicit and Illegal: Sex, Regulation and Social Control.* Cullompton: Willan.

Regan, L. and Kelly, L. (2003) *Rape: Still a Forgotten Issue.* London: Child and Woman Abuse Studies Unit/Rape Crisis Network Europe, online at http://www.rcne.com/downloads/RepsPubs/Attritn.pdf.

Richardson, D. (2000) *Rethinking Sexuality.* London: Sage.

Russell, D. (1984) *Sexual Exploitation.* Beverley Hills, CA: Sage.

Schulhofer, S. (1998) *Unwanted Sex: The Culture of Intimidation and the Failure of Law.* Boston: Harvard University Press.

Seith, C. and Kelly, L. (2003) *Achievements Against the Grain: Self-Defence Training for Women and Girls in Europe* (London: Child and Woman Abuse Studies Unit).

Sen, P. (2005) '"Crimes of honour" values and meaning', in L. Welchman and S. Hossain (eds) *'Honour': Crimes, Paradigms and Violence Against Women.* London: Zed books.

Spohn, C. and Horney, J. (1996) 'The impact of rape law reform on the processing of simple and aggravated rape cases', *Journal of Criminal Law and Criminology*, 86 (3): 861–84.

Taslitz, A. (1999) *Rape and the Culture of the Courtroom.* New York: New York University Press.

Temkin, J. (2000) 'Prosecuting and defending rape: perspectives from the bar', *Journal of Law and Society*, 27 (2): 219–34.

Temkin, J. (2002) *Rape and the Legal Process.* Oxford: Oxford University Press.

Walby, S. (2004) 'The European Union and gender equality: emergent varieties of gender regime', *Social politics: International studies in Gender, State and Society*, 11 (1): 4–29.

Zippell, K. (2006) *The Politics of Sexual Harassment: A Comparative Study of the United States, the European Union, and Germany.* Cambridge: Cambridge University Press.

Chapter 14

Attachment styles, emotional loneliness and sexual offending

Philip Birch

Introduction

This chapter explores the relationship between attachment styles and emotional loneliness in relation to sexual offending. Research into attachment styles, for example John Bowlby (1969), has suggested that the types of attachments formulated in early childhood are a blueprint for the type of relationships we develop in adulthood. While secure attachment styles in early childhood will result in positive adult relationships, insecure attachment styles in childhood will result in negative adult relationships. Furthermore, links between emotional loneliness and attachment styles have been made in the work of Dan Russell *et al.* (1980) where it is has been argued that there is an association between insecure attachments and emotional loneliness. An individual who cannot form secure attachments will feel isolated and cut off from peers, thus leading to a lack of emotional intimacy within a relationship. William Marshall (1989) conducted the first research into attachment styles and sexual offending and concluded that sex offenders demonstrate insecure attachment styles and high levels of emotional loneliness. From this, the following chapter investigates the styles of attachments and levels of emotional loneliness of a sample of male sex offenders in custody in comparison with a group of males who were not sex offenders within the UK. The research challenges the results from previous research in relation to attachment styles: first the assumption these are static and secondly the claim that sex offenders display insecure attachment styles and high levels of emotional loneliness.

Background

Attachment theory and emotional loneliness

Attachment theory 'conceptualises the propensity of human beings to make strong affectional bonds to particular others' (Bowlby 1977, cited in Ward *et al.* 1996). This research has suggested that the types of attachment styles formulated in early childhood with our main caregivers are important to our psychological development and the social relationships we develop throughout our lives.

Attachment theory originally focused upon relationships between maternal loss and subsequent personality development. The main aim of attachment theory was to 'regulate behaviours designed to obtain proximity to an infant's attachment figure, protector and main caregiver, usually the child's parents' (Gross 1992). Bowlby (1969) reported that attachments are thought to lead to either positive emotional states such as good interaction with others or negative emotional states such as poor interaction with others/loneliness. Regardless of whether an attachment is positive or negative, attachment styles are considered to provide growing children with a template to develop future relationships and interact with the social world in adulthood (Bowlby 1973, cited in Ward *et al.* 1996).

Mary Ainsworth *et al.* (1978), who based their work on Bowlby's earlier work, identified three types of attachment styles in their research: secure, anxious/ambivalent and avoidant. Ainsworth and colleagues (1978) argued that secure attachments develop when parents are sensitive to the needs of their child and respond in a warm and receptive manner. This results in a child that does not have to stay in close proximity to their parents, but shows signs of distress when, for example, the mother becomes absent. Securely attached infants tend to react happily with a stranger in the presence of their parents but will become distressed when parents are absent. Anxious/ambivalent attachments develop when parents respond inconsistently to a child's needs and this results in a child becoming impulsive, attention seeking and helpless. An infant who is identified as having anxious/ambivalent attachment styles usually cries a lot and will seek to have constant contact with their parents. However, when contact is achieved it will be in the form of aggression towards the parents. In addition an anxious/ambivalent attached child will tend to resist any efforts of a stranger (Ainsworth *et al.* 1978). Finally, Ainsworth *et al.* (1978) stated that avoidant attachment occurs when the parent is detached from the infant, fails to show emotion to the child and is unresponsive to the child's needs. The child pays no attention to their parent's presence or absence and does not show distress in the presence of a stranger. Characteristics of anti-social behaviour and lack of empathy are associated with avoidant attachment styles. Ingrid Bretherton (1992) reviewed the origins of attachment theory and stated that the attachment bond between a child and its main caregiver can be disrupted by a variety of means such as separation, bereavement and deprivation. Bretherton recognised that early family relationships affect personality development and as a result lends support to the research of John Richters et al. (1991), who analysed a number of secondary sources such as Farrington's longitudinal studies (1940s through to the 1980s). They suggest that such longitudinal studies demonstrate a correlation between criminal behaviour in general and parental characteristics. Parental characteristics such as lack of warmth and low levels of supervision of their child are prominent in the childhood of offenders thus suggesting less secure attachments have been formed during childhood.

In my own research in a prison setting (Birch 2001) I studied both male and female offenders aged 18–21 in order to investigate the nature and extent of criminogenic factors that influence their offending behaviour. Contrary to expectations I discovered that 60.3 per cent of the sample identified their mothers as the closest person to them in their lives, thus suggesting that those who become offenders do form secure attachments with their main caregivers. The second closest people identified in these young offenders' lives were their current partners, which suggests that the respondents had formed secure attachments in their childhood that are reflected in their attachment style in adulthood.

It is claimed that 'particular forms of social behaviour develop as a means of adapting to the environment' (Morris 1969, cited in Taylor et al. 1995). These, according to some sociologists, are learnt within the family unit. Paul Taylor et al. (1995) highlighted that there are a variety of family types in UK society, which include the nuclear family, extended family, lone-parent families and reconstituted families. Jacqueline Burgoyne and David Clark (1984, cited in Taylor et al. 1995) suggest that the experiences of reconstituted families can be more difficult than in other family types. These can include lack of boundaries and issues of contact with ex-spouses. Furthermore, divorce rates within the UK are also rising: in 1911, 859 petitions for divorce were filed compared with 183,000 in 1987 (Taylor et al. 1995). Arguably this suggests the instability of family life within contemporary society. In light of the changing nature of family life and the 'instability' of the family, could it be suggested that attachment styles are affected by the changing nature of the family?

Cindy Hazan and Phillip Shaver (1987) were pioneers in assessing childhood attachment styles and how they influence attachment styles in adulthood. They found a correspondence between attachments observed in infants and in adults. In their initial study, between 55 per cent and 65 per cent of adults are classified as having secure attachments. Further to this study a second study with adults asked respondents to choose the attachment styles that best fitted their feelings in relationships. Based on their results, Hazan and Shaver (1987) suggested that particular attachment styles lead to the development of particular styles of relationships. For example, adults that demonstrated an avoidant attachment style admitted feeling distant from other people, while adults that demonstrated secure attachment styles were able to seek support from others and hold more positive attitudes about interpersonal relationships. Eleonora Feher and Stuart Perlman (1985, cited in Ward *et al.* 1998) stated that 'intimacy involves mutual self disclosure in relationships, warmth, affection, closeness and interdependence between partners'. A failure to achieve these skills in interpersonal relations can lead to emotional loneliness.

The area of emotional loneliness has been primarily focused on by Russell *et al.* (1980), who describe emotional loneliness as 'chronic distress whereby an individual feels estranged from peers and starved of the emotional intimacy in relationships' (Weiss 1973, cited in Russell *et al.* 1980). They argue that lonely individuals are driven to establish new relationships in order to eradicate the distressful state they endure. It is suggested that this is caused by the end of a significant relationship in early childhood such as the end of an attachment with a main caregiver. The authors suggest that insecure attachments formed in early childhood result in the prevention of positive interpersonal relationships in adulthood. Relationships established are uncooperative, unsociable and non-compliant, thus leading to unstable relationships. Others argue that 'adolescence is a period when intimacy is a prime issue in the development of interpersonal relationships' (Goodrow and Lim 1998: 151). According to Kenneth Goodrow and Mee-Gaik Lim attachment bonds are a powerful influence on intimate relationships and patterns of secure and insecure attachments formulated in childhood impact on relationships in adolescence and in relationships in later life.

Attachment theory and emotional loneliness applied to sexual offending

Marshall (1989) was the first researcher to introduce the concept of attachment theory to the discussion of sexual offending. Marshall suggested that sex offenders failed to achieve secure childhood attachment bonds and as a result fail to have secure attachments in adulthood. This results in a failure to develop interpersonal skills and self-confidence, which is necessary to develop intimacy with others, and in turn this leads to 'difficulties in engaging in appropriate courtship behaviour and therefore achieving intimacy in adult relationships' (Marshall 1989, cited in Smallbone and Dadds 1998: 558).

Marshall (1989) added that sex offenders seek emotional intimacy through sex, owing to the fact that they experience the closeness they desire through the act of sex. This leads to their offending behaviour. Thus he indirectly labels sex offenders as having insecure attachments in order to explain their difficulties in engaging in appropriate courtship behaviour and attempting to achieve emotional intimacy through sexual contact. Tony Ward *et al.* (1996) explored insecure attachment styles, and offered a classification:

• Anxious (Preoccupied) Adult Attachment – may lead to predisposition to sexual emotional relationships with children.
• Avoidant Adult Attachment – may be associated with offences involving physical contact.
• Fearful Adult Attachment[1] – may lead to no emotional investment.
• Dismissive Adult Attachment – may lead to sadistic and aggressive acts.

In his later work, which focused on male sex offenders, Marshall (1993) recognised that adult intimacy is linked to the emergence of inappropriate sexual dispositions. He argued that secure child–parent relationships lead to the formation of effective loving relationships in adulthood, whereas disruptive attachments formed through insecure child–parent relationships lead to adults being lonely in later life. Poor quality childhood attachments are understood to lead to a sense of alienation as an adolescent and adult. According to Marshall (1993), loneliness is a critical factor in the initiation and continuation of sexual offending. His argument is that good attachment bonds lead to a child displaying greater self-reliance and greater ease in establishing good quality peer relations. However, when parents are rejecting towards their children, difficulties in parent–child relations will emerge and this will interfere with relations during the shift from parental to peer relations during puberty and beyond. In addition difficulties in developing relationships with peers, alongside boys' new-found sexual and aggressive drives, will cause frustration. In turn, this will lead boys to any source they can to achieve a degree of satisfaction, such as sexual deviancy. Poor attachments not only lead to difficulties during adolescence but also during adulthood. The difficulties faced during adolescence due to insecure attachments and in forming relations will lead to loneliness and a lack of intimacy in relationships formulated in adulthood. This loneliness and lack of intimacy, Marshall (1993) argues, is the platform for the onset of sexual offending.

Emotional loneliness for Marshall (1993) constitutes:

- permanently feeling alienated from others;
- unable to form effective relationships which satisfy personal needs for intimacy.

His conclusion is that these limitations stem from poor childhood attachments; he suggests that prosocial skills in childhood, achieved through secure attachments, lead to the formation of good relationships. On the other hand, poor quality attachments are a critical feature in delinquency, especially sexual offending. This builds on the work of Elizabeth Fegan and Kenneth Wexler (1988, cited in Marshall 1993) who claim that social isolation is a common feature in the lives of sex offenders.

Marshall (1993) cites the research of a number of authors as evidence of the fact that sex offenders report loneliness, isolation, difficulties with peers and parental neglect in youth (for example, Tingle *et al.* 1986; Davidson 1983). Loneliness has also been found to be related to lack of confidence, social ineptitude, self-centredness, hostility and aggression (Bowlby 1977; Marshall and Barbaree 1990). More recent work suggests that similar factors relate to both non-violent and extremely violent sex offending, including offending against children (Russell *et al.* 1980; Seidman *et al.* 1996).

Smallbone and Dadds (1998) take the discussion further. Their findings suggest that child molesters and stranger rapists demonstrated different types of attachment styles. Child molesters were reported to demonstrate dismissive and preoccupied attachment behaviour, while 'stranger' rapists mainly demonstrated avoidant attachment behaviour. This is supported by Charles Farrugia and colleagues (1998) who report that adult attachment relationships are meant to be reciprocal and, as a result, sex becomes an integral part of attachment within the relationship. However, if a person has experienced insecure attachments during childhood, they will be less likely to engage within a reciprocal relationship due to their personal characteristics, which could include hostility and aggression.

Smallbone and Dadds' methodology enabled them to compare sex offender and non-sex offender attachment styles. They found that sex offenders were significantly less secure in their childhood attachments than non-sex offenders. Furthermore, they found that sex offenders reported less secure attachments to their fathers compared with the non-sex offenders. They suggest that early insecure attachments place some men at risk of later offending, especially sex offending.

These results have been supported by Ireland and Power (2004) who have studied attachment style, emotional loneliness and bullying behaviour between adult male offenders and young male offenders. Their research demonstrates how reported attachment styles and emotional loneliness impact on bullying behaviour, which is an aggressive form of behaviour as is sexual offending. They found that bullies/victims demonstrate an anxious/avoidant attachment style, with these types of individuals finding it difficult to engage with their peers. As a result of this poor engagement with others, the authors reported that bullies/victims target their aggression at others. In relation to emotional loneliness bully/victims demonstrated high levels of loneliness compared with other offenders within the study. The authors explain this finding as due to the experiences of rejection bullies/victims face from their peer groups.

Methodology

A sample of 60 adult males was obtained for the purpose of my own study; the sample included 30 adult male sex offenders and 30 adult male non-sex offenders. The male sex offender sample was obtained from a Category 'C' adult male prison in North England. In order to ensure that the sample size of 30 sex offenders was obtained for the research, all sex offenders housed on one wing within the prison were targeted. Upon collection of the data, only 30 completed questionnaires were used and the remaining completed questionnaires were destroyed. The male non-sex offender sample was obtained from employees within a local authority in North England; one service was randomly selected from a list of services in order to gather the data. This approach was adopted due to time constraints of the study.

In order to ensure that the demographics of both groups were similar, known demographics were matched. These demographics were gender and age.[2] A week before the research measures were distributed to the randomly selected sample, I distributed an information sheet explaining the purpose of the study to all single-occupancy cells on one sex offender wing in the prison, and to all males within a randomly selected service within the local authority.

All prospective sample members were asked to read the information sheet and read, as well as sign, the 'record of consent' form. Upon completion of these forms, the prospective sample members were to keep the two documents safe until the following week when I was to return to collect the signed 'record of consent' form and distribute the three self-reporting measures. From this procedure, the following week I randomly selected 40 males in each location to collect the 'record of consent' form and distribute the self-reporting measures. This extra collection would allow any spoilt returns to be disregarded, yet still obtain the desired sample size. Once 30 completed questionnaires were obtained, the remaining ten were destroyed and not used in the study.

The instruments used for the data collection within the research were self-completion questionnaires. A description of each of the questionnaires can be found below.

The first self-reporting measure used in the study was the 'Forced choice, three attachment style' measure by Hazan and Shaver (1987). The 'Forced choice, three attachment style' measure aims to measure the concept of adult attachment. It relies heavily upon the established infant–caregiver attachment styles as identified by Ainsworth et al. (1978), which are believed to be mirrored in adult relationships. The measure is made up of one section that presents a number of statements. Each statement relates to one of the three attachment styles, secure, anxious/ambivalent or avoidant. Respondents are required to show how much each statement applies to them by using the Likert scale attached to each statement. The 'Forced choice, three attachment style' measure contains 11 items. This measure aimed to identify the attachment styles of the sample. The measure is also recommended for use in a secure setting such as a prison.

The second self-reporting measure used in the study was the 'Revised UCLA loneliness scale' by Russell et al. (1980). The scale was initially devised as an assessment instrument to measure loneliness. The scale consists of 20 items with 10 items focusing on satisfaction with relationships, e.g. 'I "feel in tune" with the people around me', and 10 items on dissatisfaction, e.g. 'I lack companionship'. Participants are directed to indicate how often they feel the way described in each of the items using the Likert scale attached to each statement. The total is the sum of all items, 1 = never, 2 = rarely, 3 = sometimes and 4 = often. However, the scoring of item 4 is reversed, therefore, 1 = 4, 2 = 3, 3 = 2 and 4 = 1. This questionnaire was used to link the types of attachment styles identified in the first questionnaire to the types of relationships the participants have in adulthood. The 'Revised UCLA loneliness scale' has also been used in secure settings, such as a prison, in previous research, for example Ireland and Power (2004).

The third self-reporting contained questions that obtained data on demographic details.

Due to the use of the self-reporting measures in previous prison studies (Ireland and Power 2004; Birch 2001), it is appropriate to state that the measures used in the study reported on here are valid; they measure what is purported to be measured within the current research.

The research design was based on two independent samples, sex offenders and non-sex offenders. An independent sample design, rather than a matched sample, was selected for the purpose of this research primarily due to time constraints of the study and other related practical issues. A sample of 60 participants was chosen for analysis. These data were collected to allow for descriptive statistics to be obtained and analysed. The statistical data were analysed using SPSS.

The data collected were continuous interval data. The data collected using the questionnaire on demographics were used in the data analysis as independent variables (IV) while the data collected using the two self-reporting measures were used in the data analysis as the dependent variables (DV). A descriptive analysis is given of the demographics of the sample as well as a descriptive analysis of the individual responses given by sample members to each of the two self-reporting measures.

Findings and implications

The sample was mainly made up of males aged 21–40, with 85 per cent of the sample being Caucasian. Furthermore 83.3 per cent of the sample identified themselves as heterosexual. The sample was educated to a high level with 41.7 per cent of the sample holding an undergraduate degree or higher and 81.7 per cent of the sample having employment.[3]

In relation to attachment styles, the data suggest that the sex offender sample identified more with the secure attachment style in comparison with their non-sex offender counterparts, with the mean scores of 16.50 and 13.77 respectively. This result is further supported by the fact that the sex offender sample scored lower mean scores in relation to the two types of insecure attachment styles, anxious/ambivalent and avoidant, in comparison with the non-sex offender sample.

From these results, the implication is that the sex offender sample would demonstrate lower levels of emotional loneliness in comparison with the sex offender sample if there was a correlation between attachment styles and emotional loneliness. However, this was not to be the case. The sex offender sample demonstrated higher levels of emotional loneliness in comparison with their counterparts, with mean scores of 47.67 and 36.70 respectively.

From the analysis of the research the findings can be summarised as:

* prison-based sex offenders identified more with secure attachment styles, 53.3 per cent, in comparison with insecure attachments;
* non-sex offenders identified more with insecure attachment styles in comparison with the sex offender sample;
* non sex offenders identified more with avoidant attachment styles than anxious/ambivalent attachment styles, 60 per cent and 53.3 per cent respectively;

Table 14.1 Summary of findings – highest mean scores of variables for sample groups

	Sex offender sample (mean scores) n = 30	Non-sex offender sample (mean scores) n = 30
Secure attachment style	16.50	13.77
Anxious/ambivalent attachment style	11.63	13.60
Avoidant attachment style	11.93	13.10
Emotional loneliness	47.67	36.70

Table 14.2 Summary of findings – highest percentage score of variables for sample groups*

	Sex offender sample (%) n = 30	Non-sex offender sample (%) n = 30
Secure attachment style	53.3	46.7
Anxious/ambivalent attachment style	43.3	53.3
Avoidant attachment style	43.3	60
Emotional loneliness	53.3	43.3

*Significance tests were not carried out due to the small number of the sample.

- the sex offender sample demonstrated higher levels of emotional loneliness than their counterparts, 53.3 per cent and 43.3 per cent respectively.

What, therefore, are the implications of such findings? Research by Bowlby (1969) and Ainsworth *et al.* (1978) has suggested that the types of attachment we formulate in early childhood with our main caregiver impact on our social and personal development and as a result on the attachment styles we have in adulthood. Furthermore, the attachment styles we have in adulthood impact on the relationships we have throughout our lives. Marshall (1989) demonstrated that sex offenders failed to establish secure attachment styles in childhood and as a consequence failed to have secure attachments in adulthood. Marshall therefore claims that this deficit leads to difficulties in engaging in appropriate and intimate behaviour in relationships, and this leads to more forced relationships, thus implying sexual offending. My study, in which this phenomenon was investigated by assessing attachment styles of sex offenders and non-sex offenders, does not support the previous arguments and findings suggested by researchers such as Marshall.

Previous research within this field which has occurred outside of the UK, primarily in Australia and Canada, such as Smallbone and Dadds (1998), implies that sex offenders demonstrate insecure attachment styles. However, the opposite results were found in my study. My research findings are that the sex offender sample had a stronger association with secure attachment styles than with less secure attachment styles.

According to Ainsworth *et al.* (1978) secure attachment styles are associated with characteristics such as empathy and social inclusion. A securely attached child experiences a warm and receptive relationship with their main caregiver. They are happy to explore the social world without being in the close proximity of their main caregiver and interact well with strangers in the presence of their main caregiver. However, less secure attachment styles are associated with characteristics linked to offending behaviour such as anti-social behaviour, aggression and lack of empathy. However, in the current research this theory was not supported. There are a number of reasons, which could explain the current findings.

- The work of Marshall (1989, 1993; and Barbaree 1990) was conducted in Canada; it could therefore be argued that such findings are culturally influenced. The way children are reared in Canada could be different from in the UK, and therefore other explanations need to be explored to investigate why sex offenders commit such a crime within UK society.

- The work of Bowlby (1969) and Ainsworth *et al.* (1978) and their definitions of attachment styles could be dated and not suitable for application in twenty-first century UK. The ways children are raised and the many different recognised family structures within the modern-day UK, such as reconstituted families, are significantly more varied than were recognised in the 1960s and 1970s.

- From the sample of sex offenders used in my research, a large proportion of the offenders were serving a sentence of more than five years (60 months or over) – 53.3 per cent, furthermore, 93.3 per cent of these offenders had been sentenced, only 6.7 per cent were on remand. Also, these offenders were in a Category 'C' prison, which implies that a majority of this sample had already served a number of years of their sentence in custody. This finding implies that due to the fact a large proportion of the sample had spent a number of years in prison, they had become securely attached to their environment and their counterparts due to the close proximity experienced between the inmates in a prison environment and the sense of social inclusion. This argument is supported by Hazan and Shaver (1987) who suggest that adults who demonstrate secure attachment styles are able to seek support from each other and thus hold positive attitudes about interpersonal relationships. The sex offender sample may have experienced this support within their setting due to the close proximity and similarity between those in the prison.

It can be deduced from this finding that attachment styles are not static but dynamic, and that the type of attachment style demonstrated in a particular moment is a reflection of the current situation an individual finds himself in. Furthermore, if many of the sex offenders had personally admitted to themselves they had committed a sexual offence and completed the SOTP (Sex Offender Treatment Programme), then this experience could have impacted on the attachment style they demonstrated.

My data did not allow me to explore:

- how long the sex offender sample had served of their current sentence;
- if they had experienced a prison setting prior to the current sentence, as a previous experience of a prison setting could have impacted on their attachment style;
- if they had completed the SOTP;
- if the sex offender sample were in an intimate relationship currently, whether with another inmate or a person outside of the prison;
- if the sample was institutionalised and the stability the prison setting offered led to the display of characteristics associated with secure attachments.

The above factors could have influenced the findings of this research and therefore offer an explanation for the difference in findings compared with previous research findings. Furthermore, it could be argued that conducting this research with a sample of sex offenders that lived within the community may have led to different findings. However, Ireland and Power (2004) explored attachment styles of adult offenders in a prison setting in relation to bullying behaviour and the mean scores of attachment styles found in their research were similar to the mean scores found in my research. It is important to note that Ireland conducted her research with a range of offenders within a prison setting, not just sex offenders. However, due to the similar findings between the two studies it could be suggested that the work of researchers who imply a correlation between sex offending and attachment styles has been falsified and that attachment style is linked more to general rather than specific offending behaviour.

In my study an interesting finding in relation to attachment styles and the non-sex offending sample was also found. Within this group, it was demonstrated that this sample identified with a range of attachment styles, with no particular attachment style being significant. Following Marshall (1989) and his findings relating to attachment styles and sexual offending, it was anticipated that the non-sex offender sample would clearly demonstrate significant association to the secure attachment style in comparison with less secure attachment styles. However, this was not the case. Furthermore, it was expected that the non-sex offender sample, compared with the sex offender sample, would associate more with the secure attachment style than the less secure attachment styles. Again, this was not found.

In analysing the findings a key factor could be used to explain this last finding:

- The non-sex offender sample had experienced difficulties in relationships either in the past or currently, such as divorce. Bowlby (1977) suggests that negative emotional states are the product of attachments that have been lost or threatened. In the modern-day UK where the divorce rates and promiscuity are high such explanations could be suggested for the results of the non-sex offender sample. My research did not investigate the current marital status/previous relationships of the non-sex offender sample group, thus preventing an in-depth analysis.

Another aspect investigated within the current research was emotional loneliness. As argued in the work of Russell *et al.* (1980) insecure attachment styles formulated in childhood resulted in poor interpersonal relationships in adulthood, characterised by non-compliance and uncooperative and non-stable characteristics. Linking this to the work of Marshall, it is therefore suggested that sex offenders should demonstrate insecure attachments and have higher levels of emotional loneliness. A significant proportion of the sex offender sample in my research, while not revealing a significant relationship with insecure attachments, scored above the median score in relation to emotional loneliness, thus implying that they were emotionally lonely. This finding does not support the findings of Marshall (1989, 1993) who implies that sex offenders would be emotionally lonely as a result of the insecure attachment style associated with their offending behaviour. Another explanation for emotional loneliness becomes necessary.

Analysis of the two sample groups shows that the sex offender sample demonstrated higher levels of emotional loneliness than their non-sex offender counterparts. The mean score for the sex offender sample for emotional loneliness was 47.67 compared with 36.70 for the non-sex offender sample. It was expected that the sex offender sample would have scored a mean score higher than the non-sex offender sample in relation to emotional loneliness. However, due to the attachment style data this finding was surprising. A number of factors, however, could be used to explain the finding that the sex offender sample appears to be more emotionally lonely than the non-sex offender sample, for example:

- the sex offender sample are in an artificial social setting, one in which they have no choice in leaving;
- the sex offender sample do not get to interact with people who form part of their social network in the community;
- the sex offender sample experience no social reward for being in custody.

This contrasts with the non-sex offender sample who:

- have a choice to leave their environment, e.g. find a new job, move house;
- do not have to go for long periods without interacting with people who form their social network within the community;
- do get social rewards for being in their environment, e.g. payment from work, socialising with friends.

Ireland and Power (2004) also investigated emotional loneliness within their adult prison sample and the mean score for emotional loneliness in this prison sample was similar to that identified here. Again, this similarity between mean scores in Ireland's research and the research reported on here is an example of cross validation and support for the findings of the current research.

Reflections

The research reported here suggests that the environment in which the two sample groups found themselves has impacted on their attachment styles and the level of emotional loneliness demonstrated. This finding supports a claim cited in Paul Taylor *et al.* (1995) that our behaviour adapts to the environment we find ourselves in (see also Morris 1969), and through my research I have demonstrated that this is true in relation to attachment styles and levels of emotional loneliness. Although previous research claims a strong relationship between attachment styles and emotional loneliness, the current research questions the strength of this association. The research argues that levels of emotional loneliness and attachment styles can be dynamic and individuals can shift between insecure and secure attachment styles and be emotionally lonely depending on the particular circumstances and environments individuals find themselves in. This therefore implies that attachment styles are not static based on the experiences of childhood and levels of emotional loneliness do not always reflect an association with insecure attachments. In 1992 Bretherton claimed that attachment styles in childhood can be disrupted by a variety of means. My research can be used to argue the fact that this disruption can take place in adulthood too. Furthermore, it can also be argued that positive influences in adulthood can also impact on the attachment style an adult finds himself (or herself) identifying with at any given time.

There are number of implications here.

1 Work such as Bowlby (1969) and Ainsworth *et al.* (1978) is not valid, at least within contemporary UK society. Due to the changes in society such as unstable family life, humans evolve and adapt to the environment they currently find themselves in regardless of previous experience. Therefore if a child has secure attachments in childhood but finds him or herself in a situation in adulthood where such attachments are not suitable then insecure attachments will become manifest and vice versa.

2 The attachment styles we formulate in childhood (as suggested by Ainsworth) are not static throughout a person's life. Therefore it can be argued that attachment styles formulated in childhood are merely a learning tool for future relationships which are adapted to particular relationships throughout our lifetime. This supports the claim that humans can fluctuate between secure and insecure attachment styles throughout their lives.

3 Levels of emotional loneliness do not always correlate with attachment styles.

4 If all humans have attachment styles which are dynamic, and if at the time a sexual offence takes place the sex offender is likely to be displaying insecure attachments, this would suggest that all humans have a predisposition to sexual offending at moments of insecure attachment in the life course.

My study suggests the need for further research and investigation relating to the phenomenon that attachment styles are dynamic and the evidence that attachment styles formulated in childhood do not always mirror those in adulthood. Furthermore, the link between emotional loneliness and attachment styles must also come under scrutiny. This type of research would benefit from a longitudinal study in order to ensure that our current knowledge around this issue is accurate. Finally, in order to argue that there is a positive association between attachment styles, emotional loneliness and sex offending, then it would be necessary to assess all sex offenders on these variables at the time the offence takes place, where and if applicable, in order to confirm that at the time the offence took place the offender was insecurely attached with high levels of emotional loneliness. I suggest that current research within the area has taken a 'leap of faith' in assuming that insecure attachments will be deviant/criminal, while a further assumption is made in arguing that emotional intimacy is achieved purely through the act of sex.

This research is the first piece of research to investigate attachment, emotional loneliness and sexual offending within the UK. It is hoped that it will inspire further research around this phenomenon in order to allow for a better understanding of sexual offending and to demythologise the so-called enduring effects of childhood.

Notes

1 Fearful and Dismissive Adult Attachment Styles are viewed as a subcategory of Avoidant Attachment Styles.
2 Gender (males) and age (21 and over) were the only demographics used. No other demographics were used in order to 'match' the sample, e.g. social class, due to the time constraints attached to the research.
3 In relation to the sex offender sample, this question related to employment status before coming into prison for their current offence.

References

Ainsworth, M., Blehar, M., Waters, E. and Wall, S. (1978) *Patterns of Attachments*. Hillsdale, NJ: Erlbaum.

Birch, P. (2001) *Factors Associated with Offending Behaviour within a Young Prison Population*. Presented at the 11th Annual Division of Forensic Psychology Conference, University of Manchester, 3–5 April 2002.

Bretherton, I. (1992) 'The origins of attachment: John Bowlby and Mary Ainsworth', *Development Psychology*, 28 (5): 759–75.

Bowlby, J. (1969) *Attachment and Loss: Vol. 1, Attachment.* London: Hogarth Press.

Farrugia, C.E. and Hohaus, L. (1998) *Conceptualising the Pair Bond: Attachment, Care Giving and Sexuality as Predictors of Intimacy in Adult Romantic Relationships.* Presented at Changing Families, Changing Futures, 6th Australian Institute of Family Studies Conference, University of Melbourne, 25– 27 November 1998.

Goodrow, K. and Lim, M-G. (1998) 'Attachment theory applied to juvenile sex offending', *Journal of Offending Rehabilitation*, 27(1–2): 149–65.

Gross, R.D. (1992) *Psychology: The Science of Mind and Behaviour* (2nd edn). London: Hodder & Stoughton.

Hazan, C. and Shaver, P. (1987) 'Romantic love conceptualised as an adult attachment process', *Journal of Personality and Social Psychology*, 54: 511–24.

Ireland, J.L. and Power, C.L. (2004) 'Attachment, emotional loneliness and bullying behaviour: a study of adult and young offenders', *Journal of Aggressive Behaviour*, 30: 298–312.

Marshall, W.L. (1993) 'The role of attachments, intimacy and loneliness in the etiology and maintenance of sexual offending', *Sexual and Marital Therapy*, 8: 109–21.

Marshall, W.L. (1989) 'Intimacy, loneliness and sexual offending', *Journal of Behaviour Research and Therapy*, 27: 491–503.

Marshall, W.L. and Barbaree, H.E. (1990) 'An integrated theory of etiology of sexual offending', W.L. Marshall, D.R. Laws and H.E. Barbaree (eds) *The Handbook of Sexual Assault: Issues, Theories and Treatment of the Offender.* New York: Plenum Press, pp. 257–75.

Richters, J. and Waters, E. (1991) 'Attachment and socialisation: the positive side of social influence', in M. Lewis and S. Feinman (eds) *Social Influences and Socialization in Infancy: Genesis of Behavior Series.* New York: Plenum, pp. 185–213.

Russell, D., Peplaw, L.A. and Cutrona, C.A. (1980) 'The revised UCLA loneliness scale – concurrent and discriminate validity evidence', *Journal of Personality and Social Psychology*, 39: 472–80.

Seidman, B., Marshall, W.L., Hudson, S.M. and Robertson, P.J. (1996) 'An examination of intimacy and loneliness in sex offenders', *Journal of Interpersonal Violence*, 9: 518–34.

Smallbone, S.W. and Dadds, M.R. (1998) 'Childhood attachment and adult attachment in incarcerated adult male sex offenders', *Journal of Interpersonal Violence*, 13(5): 555–73.

Taylor, P., Richardson, J., Yeo, A., Marsh, I., Trobe, K. and Pilkington, A. (1995) *Sociology in Focus.* Ormskirk: Causeway.

Ward, T., Hudson, S.M. and Marshall, W.L. (1996) 'Attachment style in sex offenders: a preliminary study', *Journal of Sex Research*, 33(1): 17–26.

Ward, T., Hudson, S.M., Marshall, W.L. and Siegert, R. (1998) 'Attachment style and intimacy deficits in sexual offenders: a theoretical framework', *Journal of Research and Treatment*, 7: 317–35.

Chapter 15

Understanding women who commit sex offences

Amanda Matravers

Introduction

Sex offending is a multi-faceted phenomenon, no less in women than in men. Recent theoretical explanations of women's sexual offending focus on the contributions of individual psychology and male-dominated (or 'patriarchal') society to the development of sex offending in women. This chapter describes an integrated model that builds on existing research by expanding the theoretical focus to a range of individual, relational, socio-cultural and structural factors.

The model is centred round a three-category classification scheme based on the number of offenders involved in an offence: lone offenders committing offences alone; partner offenders with one male co-offender; and group offenders as part of a group.

The mode of offending classification was applied to a sample of 22 women convicted of sex offences in the United Kingdom. Although none of the cases lent themselves to single-factor explanations, there was a correspondence between the mode of offending and the factors that contributed to the development of sex offending. Lone offenders were primarily associated with individual factors; partner offenders with relational factors; and group offenders with socio-cultural and structural factors. These findings relate to a specialised sample, but their consistency with previous research underlines the relevance of offending mode to theoretical explanations of women's sex offending.

Classifying women sex offenders

The classification process contributes to theory development by identifying the shared characteristics that contribute to offending. Classification schemes also inform decisions about the treatment, management and release conditions of incarcerated offenders. Classifications are widely used in research on male sex offenders, although some authors question their clarity and empirical validity (Knight *et al.* 1985; Knight and Prentky 1990).

Women sex offenders rarely come to official attention and most studies rely on small samples derived from an eclectic range of sources including criminal justice databases, clinical referrals, police reports, media stories and word of mouth. The validity of some classification schemes is undermined by their reflection of cultural stereotypes of women and mothers. According to these (dearly held) stereotypes, women are innately caring, sexually passive and victims rather than perpetrators of sexual violence.

In a study of 26 incestuous mothers, L.M. McCarty (1986) develops a classification consisting of three categories: the independent offender, the co-offender and the accomplice. The categories are associated with distinct offence dynamics, but none is explicitly linked to sexual motivations. On the contrary: McCarty states that none of her subjects displayed a primary sexual interest in children or had a history of sexually deviant behaviour.

For McCarty, it is the women's relationships – or lack of relationships – that explain their offending. Co-offending women are associated with emotional dependence on male co-offenders: 'Like most of the women in this study', McCarty observes, 'Mrs J. was looking for someone to take care of her' (1986: 451). Paradoxically, male dependence is also identified as a motivation among independent offenders. In the absence of age-appropriate males, three independent offenders co-opted their young sons into the role of intimate partner. Independent offenders who sexually abused their daughters were associated with a different motivational source. The women denied the girls a separate existence, treating them as extensions of themselves. The identification of a motive grounded in psychoanalytic theory offers an alternative way of explaining women's sex offending, namely as the outcome of unconscious inner conflicts.

Faller (1987) studied the motivations of a clinical sample of 40 women sex offenders. She distinguished five offender types: polyincestuous abusers, who abuse at least two victims with at least one co-offender; single-parent abusers, who treat their older children as surrogate intimate partners; non-custodial abusers, who abuse their children during visiting times with them; psychotic abusers, whose behaviour is related to psychotic episodes; and adolescent abusers, who abuse children placed in their temporary care.

The single-parent abuser resembles McCarty's independent offender, but her co-offender and accomplice are subsumed under Kathleen Faller's polyincestuous type. The category includes women who abuse with a single male in the context of a nuclear family (like McCarty's co-offenders and accomplices) and women who form part of an elaborate network comprising different generations, extended family members and victims and offenders from outside the family circle. This is a rare instance of a category incorporating more than one mode of offending, and the result is unhelpfully comprehensive. The polyincestuous category absorbs 29 women, leaving the remainder of the sample (11 women) spread sparsely across the four single-offender categories.

Like McCarty, Faller attributes a high proportion of female sexual offending to male coercion and dependence. Women are identified as initiators in just two cases. Faller's surmise that women's roles in polyincestuous abuse may be 'yet another illustration of the unfortunate effects of male dominance' (1987: 274) draws on the feminist interpretations of women's sex offending that gained momentum during the 1980s.[1]

David Finkelhor and Linda Williams (1988) focus on the sexual abuse of children in day-care facilities. These authors too distinguish between women who offend with others and those who offend alone. They identify two basic female offender types: lone abusers and multiple perpetrator abusers. As with Faller's polyincestuous category, the multiple perpetrator category accounts for almost three-quarters of the sample. Here it is subdivided into initiators and followers, subtypes that echo McCarty's co-offender and accomplice, although the authors acknowledge that in some cases the distinction is difficult to substantiate.

Ruth Mathews *et al.* (1989) studied 16 women on a community sex offender programme in Minnesota. The authors identify themselves as feminist psychologists and explain that in conducting the research they have 'drawn on their foundation in feminist thought' (Mathews *et al.* 1989: 8). The three categories that constitute their classification scheme are consistent with an understanding of women's sexual violence as a crime that has its origins in male-dominated society.

Mathews and colleagues (1989) make an implicit rather than direct distinction between solo offenders and co-offenders. One of their single-offender categories is the rather inappropriately named teacher/lover offender, who targets adolescent males in an effort to escape 'the brutality of men' (Mathews *et al.* 1989: 33). The second single-offender type is the intergenerationally predisposed offender, who has a history of severe sexual abuse and whose offending is motivated by the desire for safe intimacy. The third type, the male-coerced offender, resembles McCarty's co-offender and accomplice. She acts primarily with one male co-offender who has previously abused children and is characterised by passive and dependent behaviour.

Jacqui Saradjian (1996) uses a slightly adapted version of the Mathews *et al.* (1989) model in her UK-based study of 50 women who sexually abused children. The study draws on a range of sources, including criminal justice professionals, clinicians, survivors and the author's own client base. Saradjian gives the three categories slightly cumbersome new names that allow for changes in the women's offending behaviours and underline their culpability. Teacher/lover offenders become women who initially target adolescents; intergenerationally predisposed offenders become women who initially target young children; and male-coerced offenders become women who were initially coerced into offending by men. Aside from these changes in nomenclature, the categories are essentially those used in the American study.

Saradjian (1996) shares the feminist perspective of the US authors. At the same time, she outlines a model of female sexual abuse of children that connects behavioural, physiological and environmental factors. Saradjian suggests that women abused in childhood internalise negative models of themselves and others, models that lead them to associate abusing behaviours with the fulfilment of key biological and social needs. The women's victimisation histories and their social isolation prevent them from replacing these negative models with more positive alternatives.

In marrying a feminist perspective with a framework that incorporates psychobiological and social structural factors, Saradjian is moving towards an integrated approach. However, the model's assumption of the foundational significance of previous victimisation obscures the relevance of other factors and leaves a question mark over the motivations of women without histories of abuse. The lack of fit between the adopted framework and Saradjian's expansive approach is revealed by the exclusion of 14 'atypical offenders' – almost the entire sample of the 1989 study – from the classification.

Summary of existing classifications

Classifications of women sex offenders rely on small samples for the generation of types and subtypes. The basis for offender categories varies between studies, but includes offender characteristics (single-parent abuser); offender motivations (male-coerced offender); offending roles (accomplice); and victim target groups (women who initially target adolescents). Some classifications base all their categories on a single factor (for example, McCarty's (1986) offending role typology), while others combine two or more factors (for example, Mathews *et al.*'s (1989) offender motivation/victim target group-based typology).

The separation of women who committed their offences alone from those who offended with others is a common factor among the classifications. Single-offender categories tend to be smaller and more numerous than multiple-offender categories, suggesting that solo offending requires more complex, individuated explanations than co-offending. This is in keeping with an understanding of female perpetration as largely the result of male coercion and oppression; the presence of a male co-offender is effectively an explanation in itself.

An integrated theory of women's sexual offending

The aim of the study was to develop a theoretical framework for understanding women who commit sex offences. The main sample consisted of 30 women identified as sex offenders by the UK criminal justice system. Access to the women and their files was negotiated via prison governors and chief probation officers and facilitated by designated staff at each location. In-depth, life history interviews were carried out with 22 women and documentary data were gathered from prison and probation files.

The integrated approach combines psychological and structural perspectives with relational and socio-cultural level explanations. All these levels of explanation are pertinent to women's sexual offending, although their relevance varies in accordance with offender type.

Life experiences and characteristics of convicted women sex offenders

The women's lives were marked by adverse childhood factors, problem relationships and socio-economic disadvantage. The extent to which these factors played into the development of sex offending behaviours is discussed in the next section.

Childhood

Childhood was traumatic for most of the women. Previous studies focus on the prevalence of child sexual abuse among women sex offenders; here, sexual victimisation was just one of a cluster of adverse childhood experiences.

Difficult and distorted family relationships affected all but three women (one of whom grew up in a children's home). Thirteen women were sexually abused by male relatives. A minority of mothers were abusive, one mother sexually. Relationships with mothers and stepmothers were undermined by absence, illness, domestic violence and addiction. Ten women were not close to their mothers; of these, four said their mothers had actively disliked them. Four women described themselves as the 'black sheep' among their siblings.

Family breakdown was another source of childhood trauma. Nine women spent time in local authority and foster care homes during childhood, five for prolonged periods. Four were taken into care in early adolescence because they were deemed to be beyond their parents' control.

Three women – all partner offenders – described more positive aspects of childhood. None of the three reported violence or abuse within their families and all could name a family member to whom they had been close. Interestingly, none of these was a mother; two women described themselves as 'daddy's girl' and the third named an uncle and aunt who lived locally.

Adolescence

Adolescence was a period marked by turbulence and change. School-related issues such as learning difficulties, bullying, truancy, fighting and disruptive behaviour affected 21 women; six were permanently excluded from school and only three gained any formal qualifications. Eight women ran away from local authority and family homes in adolescence; of these, six left to escape sexual victimisation. Four subsequently became involved in underage prostitution.

Drug and alcohol misuse affected ten women as teenagers; six were group offenders. Women who worked as prostitutes used drugs to cope and to maintain what they considered a desirable bodyweight. For five women, funding their increasing drug habits became their key motivation for involvement in prostitution.

Sex and relationships were issues for most of the women during adolescence. Two women (both group offenders) were 12 years old when they became street prostitutes, working for pimps who were also their sexual partners. Two partner offenders were involved in exploitative relationships with older men in early adolescence. Nine women were involved in violent relationships as teenagers; eight went on to have children with their abusive partners. By contrast, four women reported no adolescent involvement in relationships; of these, three were sexually abused in their families of origin.

Current offences aside, 12 women were involved with the criminal justice system in their teens. Eleven committed property offences including criminal damage, theft, fraud, driving offences, burglary and drug-related offences. Three were also convicted of violent offences and one was convicted of a sex offence with a male co-offender. Relationships with offending men brought many women into contact with criminal networks during adolescence, although in some cases the process worked in reverse: involvement in criminal networks brought the women into contact with offending men.

Adulthood

The women's pre-conviction lives were characterised by social isolation and economic disadvantage. Their employment histories ranged from chaotic to non-existent. Three women were in work on arrest; one woman had a full-time job in a factory and two worked as part-time childminders. The work experience of six women was limited to youth training schemes; seven had never been employed in any capacity.

As their employment histories suggest, most of the women were strangers to the legitimate economy. Six were earning money from prostitution and two from dealing drugs. Seven had convictions for acquisitive crimes including theft, shoplifting and burglary. Even women without direct involvement in offending tended to be linked to criminal lifestyles via male partners, neighbourhood contacts and friends.

Substance misuse and mental health problems affected half the sample. All the women who were or had been involved in prostitution were drug users. Twelve women had histories of dependence on prescription drugs. Eleven described episodes of depression and mental disturbance; five had been assessed by psychiatric professionals and received treatment for depression and problem drug use.

The women were socially homogeneous, belonging to the low end of the social scale and seldom if ever mixing with people beyond it. The majority lived in urban neighbourhoods, often in areas with poor reputations and few amenities. Some women attempted to leave these 'bad areas', but the transition was invariably emotionally or economically impossible.

Relationships with men as boyfriends, husbands, punters and pimps were a focal point of nearly all the women's lives. Outside the context of prostitution, these relationships observed traditional role divisions, with the men overseeing financial concerns and the women looking after the children and the home. Most of the women who were mothers became pregnant in their mid to late teens; only two were in their 20s when they had their first child. None of the women worked after the birth of their children, and while this wasn't necessarily against their wishes, it limited their social networks at an early age. It also prevented women whose partners were involved in crime from developing ties to non-offending individuals.

The women's social isolation was exacerbated by loss of contact with their families of origin. Fifteen women had little or no contact with family members. Although some women had been estranged from their families since childhood, others said their partners deliberately separated them from their relations. Deliberate or otherwise, the severing of family bonds left the women economically, socially and emotionally dependent on their male partners.

Summary

The women resemble female sex offenders in other studies. They also diverge from them in some notable ways. Their childhoods were commonly though not invariably troubled and sexual victimisation was one of a cluster of adverse early experiences. Poor and abusive relationships with mothers were an unanticipated childhood theme. Another unexpected issue was the level of criminal involvement and prior offending among the women. Finally, while male violence was a common experience, men play a diverse range of roles in the lives of women whose intellectual, social and economic resources are negligible.

The mode of offending model of convicted women sex offenders

The key influences on the women's sex offending are individual psychology and life experiences, relationships with co-offending men and social structural factors. In some previous research these complex influences have been reduced to previous victimisation, male coercion and patriarchal society. The mode of offending model revisits these familiar explanations, drawing on concepts and ideas from beyond the sex offender literature.

The individual factors that influence lone offenders are discussed from a psychoanalytic perspective that emphasises the significance of a range of early experiences. The offences committed by partner offenders are conceptualised as *folies à deux* or joint delusions that require the acceptance of both co-offenders. Group offending is associated with the build-up of 'angry aggression' (Bernard 1990) in deprived and socially isolated communities.

Lone offenders: powerlessness, perversion and psychoanalysis

Maggie, Lesley, Ivy, Ginger, Ellie

The name lone offender avoids the assumption of previous victimisation that is made in some classifications. Four lone offenders were severely abused in childhood, three by multiple abusers. But the existence of even one non-victimised solo offender shows we need to look beyond childhood sexual abuse for the causes of the women's offending behaviour.

Sexual abuse was one of a cluster of adverse experiences that marked the women's childhoods. Their early lives were dominated by family violence and distorted relationships, and they saw themselves as helpless, powerless and overwhelmed: like minnows shut up with whales, to paraphrase a literary victim of sexual abuse.[2] The absence of a nurturing relationship with their mothers intensified the women's sense of isolation. Lesley was sexually or physically abused by every one of her close relatives: 'There was no love or affection in my family,' she explained. 'All you ever saw was violence and disrespect.'

Lone offenders committed a range of offences from non-contact indecency to murder. The offences differed in terms of severity, duration, location and victim type, but all were associated with distorted sexuality. Three women targeted very young victims aged between two and five years; the other victims were nine and 13. The two women who targeted older victims used cognitive distortions in their accounts of the offences, describing the girls as 'promiscuous' and 'experienced'. One woman abused and murdered her two-year-old daughter during a psychotic episode. Two lone offenders said they had been sexually attracted to their victims; they were the only women in the study to admit this.

In previous studies, psychological theories have been used to explain the influence of women's mental states on their behaviour. Here, a psychoanalytic perspective derived from Freudian psychology explains the link between adverse early experiences, female sexuality and sex offending. According to Sigmund Freud, personality and behaviour are determined by unconscious as well as conscious mental processes, particularly those developed in early childhood. Individuals who experience trauma and abuse as young children will be subject to unconscious conflicts and distorted relationships in later life.

Psychoanalytic theory has been applied to abused and abusing women (see Motz 2000), but it is equally applicable to women who are not mothers and to those whose childhoods were marked by parental neglect and family disruption. Following John Bowlby (1997), many psychoanalytic theorists associate healthy child development with secure attachment to a primary caregiver. The failure to achieve an affectional tie with a parent is linked to a range of attachment disorders including anxiety and depression, eating problems, mistrust of others, relationship difficulties and inappropriate sexuality.

All five lone offenders experienced abusive or inadequate mothering and connected childhood with isolation and suppressed emotions. The women's attempts to communicate their distress to others never succeeded. Their mothers' responses to abuse disclosures ranged from unsupportive to sadistic, and outsiders always deferred to their mothers.

Suppression, repression and 'acting out' are regarded as common defence mechanisms both within and beyond psychoanalysis. Two women coped with childhood trauma by consciously suppressing their emotions. Lesley described herself as 'a robot, someone with no feelings' who 'grew up having to keep it all to myself'; Ginger said that she learned as a child to avoid her father's violence by holding her breath and pretending to be dead.

Repression occurs when traumatic experiences are unconsciously forced from consciousness: thus Ivy could not recall anything about her childhood beyond hearing her mother coughing and her father shouting, and Maggie 'forgot' why she had been removed from home at the age of 11.

'Acting out' behaviour is the flipside of repression, whereby painful feelings are expressed using behaviours rather than words. Ellie engaged in various kinds of acting out including aggressive begging near her home and hoax telephone calling. Ellie's sex offending itself could be conceptualised as an advanced form of acting out.

By the time they became pregnant in their teens, Lesley, Maggie and Ivy were problem drug and alcohol users. All three were also involved with multiple sexual partners. Within a psychodynamic framework, substance misuse and promiscuous sexual behaviour represent women's unconscious use of their bodies to communicate and resolve psychological distress (Motz 2000). Ivy was a 'terrible teenager' who was constantly beaten by her father for having sex with men she met at a local café. Her adolescent promiscuity evolved into a pattern of compulsive sexual activity that continued into middle age. Maggie became involved in prostitution as a 15 year old after running away from community care. Her avoidance of conventional relationships during this time suggests she was unable to detach female sexuality from exploitation and abuse.

The women's sexual promiscuity may also reflect their desire to compensate themselves for their deprived childhoods through pregnancy. The deprived woman does not see her unborn baby as a separate being, but as an extension of herself and a potential answer to her unmet needs. The birth of a child with its own competing needs and demands can be unbearably disappointing. Far from providing unconditional love and security, the baby may exacerbate the woman's awareness of her deprivation, triggering feelings of anger and frustration that give way to perverse assaults (Pines 1994; Motz 2000).

According to Welldon (1992), men and women express sexualised aggression (or perversion, to use the psychoanalytic term) in different ways. While men use their genitals to direct their hostility outwards, women's hostility is directed inwards, towards their entire bodies and those of their children. Maggie abused her eldest son from the age of two to late adolescence. By taking her son as her surrogate partner, Maggie finds a safe way to express her sexuality. She also finds an outlet for the hostility she feels towards her own abusers. Lesley's assertion that she wanted to give her babies everything she had lacked reflects her unconscious belief that they would provide her with unconditional love and a sense of being mothered. Tragically, the demands of small children seem to have triggered unbearable memories of her unmet needs and victimisation. Unable to separate her babies from herself, and in a perverse attempt to get rid of her feelings of helplessness and distress, Lesley subjected them to murderous violence and abuse.

The two women who abused older children displayed contrasting attitudes to sexual relationships in adulthood. Ivy had her first sexual experience standing up outside a roller skating club and said that 'ever since the first time I just carried on doing it with anyone'. Ginger, by contrast, repressed her sexuality altogether. In her early 20s she seriously considered becoming a nun; at 28 she married a man twice her age, but his health was poor and the marriage was never consummated.

Their distorted sexualities led the women to project their own desires onto their victims, and to misinterpret the children's needs and behaviour. In talking about their offences they used cognitive distortions about the girls, emphasising their sexual sophistication and attributing the offences to their seductive behaviour in bed. Ivy said her granddaughter 'insisted' on accompanying her home because she wanted a 'new experience'. Ivy clearly identified with the victim, describing her as 'just like me' and 'very grown-up for 13'. Ginger described her victim as 'provocative', adding that 'you can't call her a little girl, really. Well, only in age.' When asked whom or what she would blame for her offending, Ginger replied 'my naivety'.

Like Ginger, Ellie responded to her abusive childhood by avoiding sex and relationships. She communicated her distress not through drug misuse or promiscuity but through a string of minor offences and, finally, though a sex offence against a previously unknown child. Men who target unknown children are universally reviled as 'paedophiles'. In clinical terms, a paedophile is a person who has an exclusive or fixated sexual attraction to prepubescent children. There was nothing in Ellie's offending or psychiatric history to suggest such a sexual preference, although on her arrest at age 19 she had yet to form an age-appropriate relationship with another person. That Ellie's offending was a form of 'acting out' is indicated by her deliberate attempts to throw suspicion on herself. Her begging activities were confined to an area in which she was well known to local police, and her calls to the emergency services always sent them to her current or previous address. Through her assault on a random victim, Ellie acted out her anger and frustration at her stepfather's abuse and her mother's neglect. Before returning the victim to his home, she forced him to make a hoax call to the fire service.

Partner offenders: co-offending as *folie à deux*

If previous victimisation has sometimes been viewed as a prerequisite for solo offending, male coercion has been seen as synonymous with co-offending. The impression given by the literature is of a rather hydraulic process in which irresistible male pressure – physical and psychological – forces women to engage in sexual offending. Male coercion is an ideologically loaded concept that fails to convey the complexity of women's motives for committing sex offences with men. Partner offending is not the product of male desire and female submission; it results from the interaction of women's life histories and their social circumstances with the dynamics of a specific relationship.

Partner offenders share some adverse early experiences with lone offenders, notably abusive and distant maternal behaviour. But on the whole, the childhoods of partner offenders were not so uniformly bleak as those of lone offenders. Five women were sexually abused; four were not. Three women did not grow up in their own homes; three grew up with both parents. Six women saw childhood in broadly or very negative terms, but three emphasised happy times and positive family relationships.

If it is difficult to attribute partner offending to childhood trauma, it is equally hard to see it as entirely the result of male coercion. Partner offenders vary in their resemblance to the male coerced offender identified in the literature. In eight cases the women's co-offenders were their intimate partners; one was a male neighbour. Three women were in abusive relationships with their co-offenders, but the link between male violence and the women's offending was not straightforward. Male coercion in the sense of violent or threatening behaviour was not a feature of the other six cases, although one of the men was clearly manipulative.

Why would women put their often stormy relationships before everything else, including, in some cases, their children? The roles played by partner offenders vary from collusive observer to equal abuser, but there is no evidence that any of them committed sex offences in the absence of their co-offenders. Although this is a common finding, commentators tend to move too quickly to the assumption that women have no independent motives for participating in sex offending.

Emlyn Williams (1967) employs this reasoning in his renowned contemporary account of the arrest and trial of the Moors Murderers, Ian Brady and Myra Hindley. Williams's anachronistically sympathetic portrait of Hindley is based on his belief that had she never met Brady she would never have become a notorious sex murderer. But to say that she would not have committed the murders without Brady is not the same as saying that he coerced her into them. Neither is it certain, his violent record notwithstanding, that he would have committed them without her.

The fantasy world that Brady and Hindley created with their Nazi memorabilia, their endless, lurid, photographs and the books of the Marquis de Sade, defines the Moors Murders as a *folie à deux*, literally a madness between two. In the psychiatric literature, *folie à deux* refers to a syndrome in which a form of psychosis is shared between two closely associated people. In some cases, the disorder takes the form of a *folie simultanée* that occurs simultaneously in both parties; in others it is a *folie imposée*, whereby an inducer or principal imposes delusional ideas on an accepter or associate. In the first scenario, both individuals require treatment. In the second scenario, the accepter usually recovers on being separated from the inducer.

The concept of the *folie à deux* – not in the strict sense of a shared psychosis but rather a shared investment in jointly committed acts – is a useful one to apply to partner offenders. Even where the *folie* is imposed, the woman's reasons for accepting it need to be clearly elaborated.

Some partner offenders are an obvious fit for one or other of the *folie* categories; some are less easy to place. Taken together the cases are more appropriately arranged along a continuum than split between two groups.

The woman closest to the *imposée* end of the continuum is Olive, a 62-year-old registered childminder who was convicted of permitting indecent photographs to be taken of a child in her care. Her co-offender was a male neighbour who had befriended the victim over several weeks. When the little boy questioned the enterprise, Olive reassured him, saying that her neighbour needed to finish the film in his camera. At her co-offender's request she also helped the victim to remove his pyjamas. The next day Olive took the film to be developed and was arrested after the counter assistant alerted the police. The victim's mother described Olive as 'a naive person who did not equate nakedness with indecency'. Olive's unworldliness and her facility with children made her an ideal accepter. Beyond the offence, her behaviour was incomprehensible to herself and others, but her temporary acceptance of her co-offender's desires was crucial to their partnership.

Tina's offence is the most obvious instance of a *folie simultanée*. Tina met her co-offender when she was 15, and in spite of an age gap of ten years the two swiftly became inseparable. Tina gave birth to their first child at 16. The relationship was never physically violent, unlike those of the four other partner offenders who began long-term relationships in their mid-teens. The couple's sexual tastes were indiscriminate, florid and inclined towards sadism; their home was dedicated to the sexual torture of girls and young women. There seems little room for doubt that each found in the other the perfect foil for their *folie*.

The seven women remaining belong between these two extremes. Joy, Louisa and Mary associated their offending with male violence and coercion. Joy and Louisa were convicted of aiding and abetting rape and of separate offences against their daughters. They were cleared of engaging in independent acts of abuse, but there was nothing to suggest that violent coercion had preceded or accompanied their participation in offending. On the contrary, having reviewed a videotape showing Louisa sexually and physically abusing her daughter, the judge said he had received the 'strongest impression' she was enjoying the pain she was inflicting.

Male coercion is a potentially powerful defence for any woman. It was used by Joy and Louisa not so much to justify their offending as to justify their co-offending relationships. As described by the two women, the relationships developed in similar ways. Both were very young (Joy was 15, Louisa 17) when they met their partners. The men were domineering and possessive, and swiftly isolated the women from their families and friends. Violence and coercion followed any attempt to leave the relationships. Joy returned to her parents when she found herself pregnant at the age of 15. Her partner threatened to bomb the house, then lay in wait for Joy and beat her until she promised to go back to him.

The women's descriptions of the irresistibility of their husbands' violence are counterpoised by examples of their dedication to their children. Joy said she had received 'excellent reports' from her children's teachers and social work professionals: 'even social services were saying, like, I was always the one there for the children'. Louisa contrasted her own approach to mothering with those of other women prisoners who were inclined to 'dump' their children on other people: 'I've always taken my responsibilities seriously in that I wanted a family, it was my job to look after them.'

Accounts of domestic violence distance the women from their partners and allow them to situate themselves as their children's allies and fellow victims rather than their abusers. Joy referred to her husband's violence as 'part of all our lives'. What neither woman explained was that putting the needs of their offending partnerships before those of their children was also part of their lives. Both women were convicted not only of sex offences but also of cruelty and neglect. The house in which Louisa lived with her husband and five children was filthy and chaotic; electric wires protruded from the walls and lay in piles around the floors. The only clean corner of the house was an area containing computer and video equipment; here, Louisa's co-offender manufactured child pornography featuring his daughter, himself and his wife.

Mary's case falls towards the *imposée* end of the spectrum, and shows the combination of individual, relational and structural factors that play into partner offending. Mary explained that her co-offender had used violence and manipulated her drink problem to force her to participate in the abuse of her eldest daughter. If she protested, he threatened her with the loss of her younger children. At the same time, Mary admitted that she sometimes asked the victim to have sex with her partner to pre-empt his going to another woman. She lamented her inability to protect her daughter, explaining that she had thought she could not live without her partner.

Mary's failure to intervene on behalf of her daughter contrasts with her success, as a teenager, in retaliating against school bullies and her two sexually abusive brothers. Some of the reasons for her participation in this *folie à deux* lie in the structural aspects of Mary's situation: her social isolation, lack of economic power and the unchanging dearth of options faced by single mothers with dependent children. Others lie in her early experiences of sexual victimisation and maternal abuse. From a psychodynamic perspective, maternal physical abuse and neglect leaves women submissive, easily influenced and fearful of abandonment (Motz 1990). Mary's apparent willingness to sacrifice her daughter may be explained by her own resilience in the face of abuse. Having survived victimisation herself, she was able to convince herself that her daughter would be capable of doing the same. What she could not imagine surviving was the loss of her partner.

Male violence was not a feature of the remaining four partner cases in a direct sense. Three women had been married to violent men prior to meeting their co-offenders; the fourth, Jennifer, had been in numerous violent relationships. The absence of violence may have been one of the characteristics that led the women to place a high value on their co-offending partnerships.

Male violence and male coercion may make women's participation in sex offending more likely, but they are not the whole story. Conceiving of these offences as *folies à deux* helps unravel the contributions of each partner to the offending partnership.

Group offenders: angry aggression

Bella, Courtney, Lena, Dawn, Shelley, Alex, Tara, Amber

Unlike the other two categories, group offenders have no equivalent in existing research. The offenders, their victims and their offences are remarkably homogeneous, although they divide naturally into two subsets. Two women were involved in offences arising out of the coerced prostitution of girls between the ages of 13 and 15; the other six were members of loose social groupings convicted of the false imprisonment and torture of young women and girls. These latter offences were characterised by extreme violence and sexual misuse. Two women were convicted of the murder of their 16-year-old victim.

Group offenders shared characteristics with lone and partner offenders. Four women were sexually abused in childhood and all eight had been involved in violent relationships with men. Psychodynamic and relational perspectives round out the picture of these offenders, but their behaviour is best understood by reference to the exploitative street culture in which it originated.

The most striking aspect of group offending is the prominent role played by women. All eight group offenders were central to the instigation of the offences and were characterised as principals or 'ringleaders' in contemporary media coverage. Although men were part of all the offending groups save one, it was the women's anger and aggression that fuelled the offences.

A second notable factor is the similarity in offence settings and characteristics. All the offences took place in depressed urban neighbourhoods characterised by illicit drug use, prostitution and criminality. The victims were vulnerable young females who were held against their will and sexually misused by women with lifestyles and life experiences that closely resembled their own. The reasons given for these attacks were so trivial that several of the women apologised for their inadequacy. At the same time, they strongly objected to being described as sex offenders, maintaining that their actions constituted a reasonable response to the behaviour of their victims.

Thomas Bernard's (1990) article 'Angry aggression among the "truly disadvantaged"' investigates the phenomenon of violent incidents that arise out of seemingly petty conflicts and insults. He uses an individual or 'micro' level theory to explain the violent incidents and draws on a macro level theory to explain why they are concentrated among a narrow band of social groups. Bernard (1990) concludes that a subculture of angry aggression builds up in socially isolated communities and can only be targeted towards individuals within those same communities.

Bernard's 'angry aggression' theory is a useful way of thinking about the individual and social structural factors that shaped the lives and offences of group offenders. The women were the most economically and socially marginalised in the study. The only three minority ethnic women in the sample were group offenders and the category was also the only one to include minority ethnic victims.

At the individual level, the life histories of group offenders mirror those described by lone offenders. The women's childhoods were marked by abuse, neglect and upheaval. Four were sexually abused; two were working as prostitutes by age 12.

Other adverse childhood factors included family violence, care away from home, parental addictions and maternal absence and neglect.

From a psychodynamic perspective, women's early relationships with their mothers are a key influence on the development of their sexuality and their ability to form relationships in adulthood. Unlike the malevolent mothers described by lone offenders, group offender mothers were characterised by powerlessness and drug dependence. The ability of these mothers to provide care and security for their children was undermined by their own needs and problems.

Maternal neglect left the women to shoulder responsibility for themselves and vulnerable others. Lena looked after her little sister when their mother was high on drugs or in prison. Dawn 'acted as a mother' to her four young brothers when her father was away in the army and her mother was drunk. Some women mothered their mothers. Bella memorised her grandmother's telephone number so she could summon help when her father's violence got out of hand.

The women took their fragile autonomy and their frustration to school, where they identified with the bullies rather than the bullied. Courtney, Amber and Bella were all expelled from multiple schools for disruptive behaviour and fighting. The reputation of Bella's notorious family placed her at the top of the bullying hierarchy, as she explained: 'Of all the bullies, no one could ever touch us; we were the hard gang, even in junior school.'

In adolescence, the women began to rebel against the constraints of their stifling or abusive homes. Lena and her sister were forbidden to walk freely around their drug-dealing mother's house. Dawn and her siblings were not supposed to leave the house after school while their father was away in the army. Both made the most of every opportunity to get outside, often staying away for days at a time. Bella and Courtney too stayed out at night, using illicit drugs and progressing from promiscuity to underage prostitution. By the age of 12, and at their mothers' request, both had been taken into the care of the local authority. Ironically, it was the poor supervision they received in 'care' that sealed the women's commitment to street networks and criminal lifestyles. As Bella explained: 'I loved it; you could do anything. Just sign in and then go missing.'

The addiction, exploitation and abuse that characterised street life were routine experiences for the women and the people they lived among. Bella was devastated when her sadistic father abandoned the family; she couldn't cope, she explained, because it didn't feel 'normal'. Alex said she could not settle in a respectable suburb with her mother and new stepfather because she had lived among car thieves all her life. The women's lifelong proximity to violence and abuse enabled them to view their immersion in street life as a positive choice. Courtney said: 'I was just a street girl; I brought myself up on the streets. I chose to go out into the world and live my life.'

The women's fragile family ties were soon replaced by allegiances formed in residential care homes, open houses and on the streets. Like partner offenders, the women often found themselves in violent relationships. Unlike them, they generally responded by fighting back. Amber got rid of one abusive partner by hiring someone to hold a gun to his head. Shelley and Alex met men in their mid-teens who became increasingly violent and domineering. Unlike Joy and Louisa, Shelley and Alex left the relationships taking their children with them.

The women's troubled histories in interaction with the contingencies of street life generated the angry aggression that provoked their offences. The women grew up in disordered communities among people with few or no ties to conventional society and high tolerance for criminal behaviour. Their offending groups were microcosms of these communities, characterised by distorted and abusive relationships, illicit drug use and criminality.

The commodification of female sexuality is a key aspect of street life and of group offending. Four group offences were related to the control of women's sexual activity in the prostitution context.

Amber and Tara were convicted of controlling underage prostitutes. Tara and her associates 'trained' teenage runaways to perform a range of sex acts. The women's backgrounds inured them to the harmful effects of sexual exploitation on children; the nature of street life left them no one to exploit save other vulnerable and minority females. Amber insisted that she was a 'businesswoman', not a criminal.

Bella (16) and Courtney (20) were charged with the abduction and sexual assault of other young prostitutes. Bella was allegedly teaching the 14-year-old victim a lesson on behalf of the girl's pimp. Courtney said she was punishing the elder of her victims for having a sexual relationship with her 'husband' (as she referred to her pimp). Neither account gives a satisfactory explanation of the ferocity of the attacks – of Courtney's apparently unmotivated assault on the younger victim; of Bella's sadistic sexual attack on a girl whom she had been asked to 'beat up'. The significance of the relationship between women and pimps in the street context provides a rationale for the initial offences, but their escalation is related to the trauma the women experienced in early childhood.

In the remaining four cases involving five of the women, the victims were subjected to prolonged degrading and sadistic treatment. Their clothes were removed, their pubic hair was shaved, they were scrubbed with cleaning products and burned with cigarettes. One 16-year-old victim was tied to a bed frame and tortured over several days by a changing cast of abusers. Two of her teeth were pulled out using a pair of pliers and one of the women injected her with drugs.

In spite of the fact that men were involved in nearly all the cases, it was the women's grudges that the offences were intended to redress and their aggression that fuelled the violence. Lena explained that 'the boys weren't angry, only me and [her female co-offender]'. Courtney told her male co-offender to rape the older victim. When he refused, she made the two victims strip and perform oral sex on each other.

The antecedents to the cases were very similar, involving a build-up of tension over months and sometimes years between the women and their victims. Among the reasons for this tension were sexual transgressions (victims having sex with someone considered to be out of bounds), owing money for drugs, cheating pimps, calling someone a prostitute and stealing. Other reasons were failing to return a borrowed coat and leaving a woman's children standing near a busy street.

Idiosyncratic as some of these reasons seem, they are all associated with the retention of power, reputation and status within distressed, socially isolated communities. Whether they were drug dealers punishing bad payers, madams disciplining disobedient young prostitutes or prostitutes warning off other prostitutes, group offenders were all socially marginalised individuals whose angry aggression could only be taken out on similarly or even more marginalised victims.

The women struggled to justify their offences beyond the street context. They punctuated their accounts with phrases such as 'this is going to sound funny' and 'you're not going to believe this'. Acts that constitute logical responses to transgressive behaviour within exploitative cultures have different meanings for middle-class researchers and criminal justice agencies. Dawn said: 'If I look in my files, I think: my god, what a monster! And it's not like that, you know, they've blown it out of proportion.' Dawn's victim, whom she described as 'no angel', was forced to perform oral sex on one of Dawn's male co-offenders. As the victim's drug dealer, Dawn's perception of this offence was coloured by her knowledge that this was the way the victim financed her habit.

Group offences are not committed by offenders who are monsters against victims who are angels. The women and their victims alike are products of economically disadvantaged and socially isolated communities in which it is all too easy for subcultures of angry aggression to develop and thrive.

Notes

1 Feminist theorists characteristically emphasise the role of men and of male-dominated society in women's participation in sex offending, although some have emphasised the need to hold women responsible for sexually violent behaviour; see, for example, Kelly (1991).
2 Virginia Woolf (1985: 169).

References

Bernard, T. (1990) 'Angry aggression among the "truly disadvantaged"', *Criminology*, 28 (1): 73–96.

Bowlby, J. (1997) *Attachment and Loss: Attachment Vol. 1.* New York: Basic Books.

Faller, K.C. (1987) 'Women who sexually abuse children', *Violence and Victims,* 2 (4): 263–76.

Finkelhor, D. and Williams, L.M. with Burns, N. (1988) *Nursery Crimes: Sexual Abuse in Day Care.* Newbury Park, CA: Sage.

Kelly, L. (1991) 'Unspeakable acts', *Trouble and Strife,* 21: 13–120.

Knight, R. and Prentky, R. (1990) 'Classifying sexual offenders: the development and corroboration of taxonomic models', in W. Marshall, D. Laws and H. Barbaree (eds) *Handbook of Sexual Assault.* New York: Plenum.

Knight, Rosenberg and Schneider (1985) 'Classification of sexual offenders: perspectives, methods and validation', in A. Burgess (ed.) *Rape and Sexual Assault: A Research Handbook.* New York: Garland.

McCarty, L.M. (1986) 'Mother–child incest: characteristics of the offender', *Child Welfare,* 65 (5): 447–58.

Mathews, R., Matthews, J. and Speltz, K. (1989) *Female Sex Offenders: An Exploratory Study* (Orwell, VT: Safer Society Press).

Motz, A. (2000) *The Psychology of Female Violence: Crimes Against the Body.* London: Routledge.

Pines, D. (1994) *A Woman's Unconscious Use of Her Body.* New Haven, CT: Yale University Press.

Saradjian, J. (1996) *Women Who Sexually Abuse Children.* London: Wiley.

Welldon, E. (1992) *Mother, Madonna, Whore: The Idealisation and Denigration of Motherhood.* London: Guildford Books.

Williams, E. (1967) *Beyond Belief: A Chronicle of Murder and Its Detection.* London: Hamish Hamilton.

Woolf, V. (1985) *Moments of Being.* San Diego, CA: Harcourt Brace.

Chapter 16

Sexual offenders and public protection in an uncertain age

Bill Hebenton

Hamm: *I love the old questions.* (With fervour): *Ah, the old questions, the old answers, there's nothing like them! (Endgame: A Play in One Act* – Samuel Beckett)

All change (again...)

This chapter has been written against a background of further dramatic announcements in criminal justice policy by the British government (Home Office, July 2006). The hot temperatures of the summer of 2006 were closely paralleled by an equally heated debate in the media about law and order in general and paedophiles in particular: we had the Recorder of York, Judge Paul Hoffman, opining in the case of Robert Smith: 'If the sentence that is passed results in you dying in prison, that's no more than you deserve' ('UK's worst paedophile', *The Sun*, 10 August 2006); prospects of police looking for victims from 30 years ago in the Leslie Ford-Thrussell case ('Paedophile's garden to be dug up', *The Guardian*, 8 August 2006) and the 'tipping point' coming (arguably) with the Home Secretary's intervention on the sentence given to Craig Sweeney[1] (*The Observer*, 9 July 2006, 'Legal crisis erupts over paedophile sentencing'; *The Guardian*, 27 July 2006, 'Police criticised by watchdog over child sex kidnap'). Predictably and somewhat tiresomely the newspaper column inches among Britain's metropolitan 'finest' have mingled seamlessly with recorded interviews from government and opposition about 'unfinished business' in protecting the British public (see

Critcher 2002 for a cogent account of how the British media has revisited this all before; see also Kitzinger, this volume). While these latest concerns about serial predatory behaviour, inadequate police response and the judicial sentencing of child sexual offenders merit attention, my intent here is to take the opportunity to stand back from the summer of 2006 heat and light show and reflect a little. In an earlier attempt at this, I briefly considered the narrow issues raised by regulatory 'management' of offenders via risk assessment technologies (Hebenton 2003). My purpose here is wider. The chapter analyses how and why governments in Britain and North America have sought to 'protect' their publics from sexual offenders through the use of particular regulatory arrangements. The first part of the chapter charts both the background to and historical trajectory of regulatory efforts on both sides of the Atlantic, focusing in particular on registration and third-party disclosure and notification, and briefly reviews the criminological evidence about the effectiveness of such arrangements. My discussion considers how best to understand these American-UK policy developments.

Background

As has been noted:

> The 1990s has been the decade of the predatory sex offender, at least in terms of constructing a demon. Across the world a range of legislation has been put in place which seeks to single out this group of offenders for greater punishment, fewer rights and potential exclusion from society. (Nash 1999: 6)

Commentators have singled out a number of contributory factors underlying the emergence of the sexual offender 'problem' in the USA and Europe (see Jenkins 2001; also note Hebenton and Thomas 2003; and more generally for the British case see Thomas 2000). At a basic level, how sexual offences and sexual offenders are viewed relative to other kinds of offences and offenders in contemporary Western societies is a useful starting point. Much more than property offences or even physical assaults, sexual offending against persons is considered to involve violations of the self that damage the very core of victims. Such damage can often involve a sense of moral pollution. Here, the Durkheimian distinction (Durkheim 1964) between the sacred and the profane is often invoked. The more sacred, pure or innocent the victim, the more profane or unclean the assault and the person committing it are considered to be. In Western societies, there is no victim more sacred than a child victim and no offender more profane than one who spoils the innocence of children. This sense of the sacred and profane is recognised even in prison society, where child sex offenders are pariahs, unclean or inhuman beings deserving of all manner of verbal and physical assaults and humiliations. In addition to their perceived sacredness, another important feature of children is their perceived vulnerability. In modern Western societies, fear and anxiety about threats to children's physical and psychological well-being are pervasive. There is little correlation between the statistical risk of harm and the extent of fear of parents and the community at large. Indeed, the fear that one's children will be abducted and sexually assaulted is out of all proportion to the probability of the occurrence of this rare event – an indication that powerful, primal feelings are at work. So great is the sense of vulnerability and violation attached to the sexual victimisation of children and women that sex offenders in general, not just extremely violent ones, are considered to be highly dangerous. Our response to the perceived 'dangerousness' of these offenders – indeed our obsession with the protection of our children's moral and sexual innocence – has led us down a path strewn with inconsistencies (West 1987). Arguably, it is only through a thorough review of these conceptual frameworks of 'childhood sexuality' that drive contemporary responses to child sex offenders that we can even begin to understand these responses (but that, as they say, is a story for another paper – for those interested see a useful attempt by Kleinhans 2002).

If we simply consider the matter of perceived 'dangerousness' then clearly while historically there have been several approaches to dangerousness, including the clinical (for the background see Foucault 1977; Petrunik 1982, 1984) and the justice (see Hudson 2003) approaches, there has been only one hegemonic trope for criminal justice policy on both sides of the Atlantic in the last decade – namely, community protection.

The community protection approach emerged in response to the concern that the clinical and justice approaches gave insufficient attention to public safety and victims' rights. For proponents of community protection, treatment and offender rehabilitation, respect for the liberty, privacy and security of the person, rights of suspects, offenders and the principles of due process, proportionality and equity all had to take a back seat to public safety issues. Community protection developed in concert with the rise during the late 1980s nd early 1990s of various populist social movements calling for increased government attention to the rights of victims and their families and to citizens' fears about crime and calls for increased community participation in crime control (Hebenton and Thomas 1998; Scottish Executive 2001). In contrast with the justice model of social control, which emphasises avoiding false positives in risk assessments, the community protection approach prioritises public safety. Community protection advocates call for drastic means to avoid false negatives, particularly in those spectacular child sexual offender cases that arouse widespread public rage and fear. In contrast with the clinical approach (where there is also a concern about false negatives), community protection is unconcerned about treatment and other rehabilitation programmes intended to prevent offenders from reoffending and to help them integrate into the community. Interestingly, clinical approaches have been strongly influenced by the policy shift to community protection, with the result that clinicians now seem to be devoting as much, if not more, attention to issues of risk assessment and risk management than to treatment. The difference between clinicians and the proponents of community protection is that the latter tend to magnify considerations of risk, arguing for extreme caution in the loosening of controls, even when the results of actuarial and clinical assessments overwhelmingly indicate that risk of reoffence is minimal.

In the last decade of the twentieth century there was a wave of support for a community protection approach for dealing with predatory sexual offenders across the United States and, to a lesser extent, the Anglophone world (Canada, the United Kingdom, Australia, New Zealand) and parts of continental Europe (Jenkins 2001). At a micro-level, this demand for special community protection measures is a response to law enforcement officials' and victims' advocates' claims that the clinical and justice models of social control failed to protect the community from the enduring risk posed by sexual offenders. At a macro-level, the community protection movement has been seen as part of a shift in governance from welfarist approaches to remedying individual and socio-economic deficits to neo-liberal, state– community partnerships for managing all manner of perceived risks and associated fears (Brown and Pratt 2000). Within the community protection trope, the dominant contemporary image of sex offenders involves attributions of uncontrolled sexual compulsion, specialisation and persistence in behavioural patterns throughout their criminal careers. For example, Lisa Sample and Tim Bray (2003: 60) contended that current sex offender policies in the USA are predicated on a notion of 'once a sex offender, always a sex offender'. Similarly, Frank Zimring (2004: 27) identified four assumptions underlying current law and policies that project a comparable image of sex offenders. Elements of this image of sex offenders include (1) pathological sexual orientation, (2) sexual specialisation, (3) fixed sexual proclivities and (4) a high level of future sexual dangerousness. According to Zimring, these elements are interrelated and represent a collective portrait of the pathology-driven behaviour believed to characterise serious sex offenders (Zimring 2004: 32). The common belief that sex offenders exhibit specialisation and persistent behavioural patterns is clearly evident in public policies (e.g. community notification, sex offender registration, extended periods of civil commitment after serving criminal sentences; for a US review, see Lieb *et al*. 1998; Matson and Lieb 1997; Winick and LaFond 2003). In fact, the major assumption underlying these policies is that sex offenders will continue to repeat these offences unless they are controlled through greater public surveillance and monitoring. Within this context, Jonathan Simon (2003: 310) considered Megan's Law a 'long-term strategy for managing a permanently dangerous class'.

Community protection in the USA

The key initial event in the development of the community protection approach in the United States took place in Washington State in 1989. The residents of Washington were horrified when a seven-year-old boy was abducted, sexually assaulted and mutilated by Earl Shriner, a repeat child sex offender and alleged murderer, who had been involuntarily committed as a defective delinquent during his adolescence. As an adult, Shriner came under the ambit of the criminal justice system, where he fully served a fixed sentence for sexual assault. He failed to qualify for involuntary commitment under civil mental health legislation on his release, despite the discovery of plans he had made to torture and rape children. Not long after his release Shriner carried out the brutal assault that galvanised the people of Washington (Boerner 1992; LaFond 1992).

In response to intensive media coverage and to public outcry, Washington's governor immediately set up a community task force to develop special controls for dangerous sex offenders. The focus was not on intra-familial child abusers (the most common type of sex offender, with the lowest recidivism rates) but rather on predatory, extra-familial offenders. Such offenders, although few in number, struck fear into the heart of the community because of the random, compulsive nature of their offences, their multiple victims, their high recidivism rates and, occasionally, their shocking acts of violence. The Shriner case was of particular concern because he was representative of sex offenders who, following sentencing reforms in the early 1980s, had fully served fixed prison sentences for their crimes and had to be released. Complicating matters further, reforms of mental health law according to a justice model placed restrictions on the use and duration of involuntary civil commitment. This made it virtually impossible to confine, for an indeterminate period of time, individuals who were considered to have serious personality disorders and paraphilias but were not acutely psychotic and did not meet the standard of imminent danger (based on prior evidence of overt violent acts) to self or others (Boerner 1992: 542–4; LaFond 1992).

The task force, with strong representation from victims' advocates (including the mother of Shriner's victim), reported within six months. Only four months later a sweeping package of reforms, the Community Protection Act, was passed by Washington's legislature. Among the measures introduced were the following: a post-sentence civil commitment procedure for persons found to meet the criteria for a sexually violent predator (the SVP statute); a sex offender registry (SOR); and a tiered approach to notification of criminal justice officials, community groups and individual members of the community, based on three levels of perceived offender risk: high, moderate and low (Boerner 1992). In the case of individuals judged to be low risk, only the police were required to be informed. In the case of those judged to be at moderate risk, relevant community organisations such as schools and parks and recreation organisations were also informed. Most contentious was the category of high-risk offender, which required that members of the public living in the immediate vicinity of any person so designated be provided with his name, address and other pertinent information.

In 1994, the community protection movement gained impetus when several other states (including Kansas, Wisconsin and Minnesota) followed Washington's lead and introduced their own sexually violent predator commitment statutes. Indiana passed Zachary's Law (named after a child homicide victim named Zachary Snider), creating the first online sex offenders' register (Jenkins 1998: 200). New Jersey passed a comprehensive set of provisions called Megan's Law, only 89 days after the abduction and sexual homicide of seven-year-old Megan Kanka (Kanka 2000a, 2000b; Wright 1995).

That same year the US federal government enacted legislation to put pressure on states to set up their own sex offender registries.

President Bill Clinton, realising that the control of child sex offenders was an issue with almost universal public support, was instrumental in the passage of the Jacob Wetterling Act, named after a boy abducted in Minnesota in 1990 and never seen since. This legislation required all states to set up SORs or else face a 10 per cent cut in criminal justice funding (Lewis 1996; Logan 1999). Enactment of the Act was followed by the enactment of two related federal statutes in 1996. The federal Megan's Law required all states to carry out community notification according to federal standards or else face similar funding cuts. The Pam Lychner Act set up NSOR, a national sex offender registry and tracking system run by the FBI, and required lifetime registration for all offenders who had engaged in coercive penetrative sex or had had victims under the age of 12 (Lieb *et al.* 1998: 73). In 1998 the Commerce, Justice and State, the Judiciary and Related Agencies Appropriation Act was passed. This legislation mandated states to identify which sex offenders might be considered sexually violent predators and required that such offenders be subject to state and federal registration and notification requirements for life (Petrunik 2002: 494).

Victims' advocacy organisations (the Jacob Wetterling Foundation, the Megan Nicole Kanka Foundation and the Klaas Kids Foundation) and media personalities (Oprah Winfrey and John Walsh, the host of the television show *America's Most Wanted*) played a major role in promoting such legislation (Kanka 2000a, 2000b; Wright 1995; Jenkins 1998: 194). In response, politicians, both Republican and Democrat, acted swiftly (often within months) to enact legislation at the state and federal level memorialising child victims and seeking to appease an outraged populace.

In 1997 in *Kansas* v. *Hendricks*, the US Supreme Court upheld the constitutionality of Kansas's civil commitment statute for sexually violent predators, and in January 2001 Washington's statute was also upheld. Courts at various levels have also generally upheld the constitutionality of registration and notification provisions, although certain features, such as the absence of due process and retrospective application, have sometimes needed to be remedied (Petrunik 2002). In 2003, the US Supreme Court handed down two decisions on pending constitutional challenges – *Connecticut Department of Public Safety* v. *Doe*, and *Smith* v. *Doe* – which firmly implant Megan's Law as a mode of regulatory public policy.

The above policy responses (as well as other measures, such as three-strikes and two-strikes legislation and legislation mandating chemical castration) illustrate the development in the United States of a comprehensive community protection approach to sexual offenders (Matson and Lieb 1997; Lieb *et al.* 1998). These measures aim either to separate offenders permanently or for very lengthy periods from the community or to subject them to unspecified surveillance within the community. An innovative technological feature of this development, which allows members of the community to participate in surveillance, has been the establishment of databases on sexual offenders that are accessible to the public via the internet (World Wide Web) or CD-ROM. This vehicle for community participation in sexual offender surveillance, which began in 1994 with Zachary's Law, now exists in over 45 American states (see *http://www.mapsexoffenders.com* for an interesting example of 'entrepreneurial' action by the 'private' sector).

Community protection in England and Wales

The background, legislative framework and practice issues for England and Wales are now well documented (see the edited collection by Matravers 2003; Thomas 2000; Cobley 2000; Hebenton and Thomas 1996). Given space considerations, I wish here only to set out certain key milestones in the British 'career trajectory' of community protection – and also to note briefly how and why the policy outcomes differ in significant ways from the USA. Table 16.1 summarises developments in the civil regulatory community protection framework over the last decade.

A 1996 consultation document on the sentencing and supervision of sexual offenders (see Cobley 2000) advocated strengthening the arrangements for supervising convicted sexual offenders following their release from custody. These proposals have been embodied in a comprehensive range of measures which are founded on the basic premise that the best way to protect the community and potential victims is through increased restriction, surveillance and monitoring of sex offenders. One of the key measures in the community protection response is sex offender registration, which, perhaps as a result, has attracted considerable academic criticism and debate (for example, Hebenton and Thomas 1998; McAlinden 2006). Registration, initially provided for by Part I of the Sex Offenders Act 1997, requires certain categories of sex offender to notify the police of their name and address and any changes to these details within a specified period. Following calls for reform, the original registration requirements in the 1997 Act were first tightened by the Criminal Justice and Courts Services Act 2000 and later replaced by Part 2 of the Sexual Offences Act 2003. For example, initial registration is now required in person within three days as is any subsequent registration of changes to the offender's personal details. The conditions attached to registration for the offender and the degree of notification permitted to the community vary depending on the assessed level of risk. In England and Wales there are now Multi-Agency Public Protection Panels (MAPPPs) to carry out this activity; the Strategic Management Boards of MAPPPs, are corporately responsible for operational 'risk management' within a particular geographical area of England and Wales and produce a public annual statement of activities (for an early assessment of these 'risk-pooling' arrangements see Maguire *et al.* 2001; as usual these arrangements have been subject to policy and practice change – see Hebenton and Thomas 2004; Home Office 2005).

While the symbolic elements of 'policy rhetoric' and 'style' appear to have been remarkably similar on both sides of the Atlantic, the degree to which this rhetoric has been played out in concrete changes in community protection policy has been strikingly different in England and Wales. This appears to be due, in large part, to the resistance of key players in the criminal justice policy 'network' to public notification schemes. The abduction and murder of eight year old Sarah Payne in 2001 led to a high-profile media campaign for a 'Sarah's Law' that would allow for communities to be informed when a convicted sexual offender moved to their neighbourhood. Yet the Home Office has 'steadfastly refused to countenance a public right of access …' (Thomas 2003: 218). 'Controlled disclosure' by the police is permitted in a defined fashion – following case law (principally, *R* v. *North Wales ex parte Thorpe*, 1998, *The Times*, 23 March) and based on proportionality and risk. Both the National Probation Service and the Association of Chief Police Officers have, over the decade, opposed any direct application of 'Megan's Law'. The fact of this resistance, and the form that it took, speaks at least to a degree of difference between the extant cultures of control on the two sides of the Atlantic. It also shows, as Trevor Jones and Tim Newburn (2002) have argued, that institutional and political differences can mediate the practical impact of populist politics. Such differences, I would suggest, also include the culturally embedded issues of directly elected versus appointed criminal justice officials and the expectations coincident upon a society where direct democracy and cultural expectations of citizenship are rather different.

When we consider the 'evidence-base' of the core components of registration and notification, simply stated, not very much is known about how or to what extent sexual offender registries and Megan's Law contribute to public safety. No previous research has examined

Table 16.1 Community Protection (the civil law regulatory framework in England and Wales 1996–2006)

- **1996 Family Law Act** – introduced powers to make an abuser leave a given household when children were at risk (this was an amendment to the 1989 Children Act).

- **1997 Sex Offenders Act (Part 1)** – introduced the UK Sex Offender Register. Registration, initially provided for by Part 1 of the Sex Offenders Act 1997, required certain categories of sex offender to notify the police of their name and address and any changes to these details within a specified period.

- **1997 Police Act** – Part 5 of this Act introduced the concept of the Criminal Records Bureau as a centralised body to improve the pre-employment screening of workers with children and vulnerable adults. The Bureau started operating in 2002.

- **1998 Crime and Disorder Act** – introduced the Sex Offender Order (SOO), that is a civil order placed upon those with a history of sexual offending who look likely to reoffend. The Order required placement on the Sex Offender Register (if not already registered) and allowed for the specification of 'negative' requirements that the person desist from certain behaviours. Breach of the Order results in a criminal procedure.

- **1999 Protection of Children Act** – allows the Department of Health and the Department of Education to compile a national list of those considered unsuitable to work with children and vulnerable adults – even if there has been no previous conviction.

- **2000 Criminal Justice and Court Services Act** – introduced the Disqualification Order. This is made at the point of sentence for 12 months or more; it prevents the offender from working with children – thus even to apply for such work is a criminal offence. The Act also introduced the Multi-Agency Public Protection Panels – these are interagency arrangements (police, probation, local authority, private housing landlords and so on) which monitor and assess risk for violent and sexual offenders in their geographical area. The Act also introduced Restraining Orders – these are made at the point of sentence to prevent offenders going near certain named people or certain places. The Act tightened registration procedure under the Sex Offenders Act.

- **2002 Police Reform Act** – made it easier to obtain a Sex Offender Order and also introduced the emergency measure of the Interim Sex Offender Order.

Table 16.1 continues opposite

Table 16.1 continued

- **2003 Sexual Offences Act** – Part 2 replaces registration arrangements under the 1997 Sex Offenders Act. Both the Sex Offender Order and the Restraining Order have now been combined and replaced with a new expanded order – a Sexual Offences Prevention Order. The Act also introduces the risk of sexual harm order – a new civil preventative order which has been designed to protect children from sexual harm. It can be used to prohibit specified behaviour, including the 'grooming' of children. This term covers the situation where a potential offender will seek to make contact and become familiar with a child in order to prepare them for abuse either directly or, as is the case more recently, through internet chat rooms. The term has recently found expression in section 15 of the Sexual Offences Act 2003, which makes it an offence to 'meet a child following sexual grooming'. Foreign Travel Orders regulate an offender's travel activities overseas.

differences in experiences, recidivism or any other consequences based on a registrant's risk level (indeed Welchans' 2005 critical overview of the existing evaluation research in the USA reveals only two genuine 'outcome' studies; Hebenton and Thomas 1997 and Plotnikoff and Woolfson 2000 raise particular methodological issues in relation to England and Wales). In addition, arguably any regulatory activity of the 'Megan's Law' type is iterative in its impact. One decision follows another and the cumulative impact is simply the sum of those decisions. The overall outcome of Megan's Law is thus – multiplicity. The complexity of decision-making compounds at every point with the result that there is little guarantee of uniformity between cases as they proceed through the registration and notification process. Differences in implementation occur from state to state, county to county, official to official, neighbour to neighbour. The result is that offenders with identical records will, in all probability, fare differently as they pass through the process in different contexts. Thus any outcome 'evaluation' becomes highly problematic (Pawson 2002).

Discussion

The centrality of risk-based management to the regulatory framework of contemporary community protection described is well documented; its operational logic for policy and practice has also been subject to much critical scrutiny (see the collected papers in Matravers 2003; O'Malley 1998, 2004; McAlinden 2006; Simon 2003). In a previous piece, I briefly examined how criminal justice agencies in England and Wales had to alter their rhetorical strategies and practices to fit with expectations of emergent neo-liberal regimes and how they must now operate in the language of risk ('risk assessment', 'risk management', 'audit'), and experiment ('entrepreneur' may be a better term here) with new technologies of control such as satellite tracking of offenders or nanotechnology-based technologies (Hebenton 2003; for detailed developments on electronic monitoring see Nellis 2005; and for the role of innovation in crime control see Pease 2005). Analytically, risk in this sense is neither real nor unreal – rather, it is a way in which liberal governments render realities in order to govern (Pratt 2000; Ericson and Haggerty 1997; Rose 1999). As such, it is highly variable in both form and content. Realities are rendered by expert discourses and techniques for handling risk that present choices about how to approach the future. As Matravers' collection (2003) makes clear, a certain form of this risk penality has been particularly evident in relation to concerns over the risk posed by released sex offenders living in the community where assessing, managing and reducing those risks has become central (Matravers 2003).

The focus on regulatory measures and risk management is part of what has been termed the 'the preventive state' – rather than purporting to deal with an offender's past wrongdoing through a penal state sanction, the power of the state (and, in the case of Megan's Law and community notification, the power of civil society as well) is said to be deployed preventively, to anticipate future conduct rather than to exact sanctions for past events. The nature of this 'preventive' state and risk management (which never eliminates scientific 'uncertainty') has been recently explored by Richard Ericson – in particular the idea of the 'criminalization of uncertainty': how, in the face of limited knowledge about threats, criminalisation, more legislation, intensified surveillance, lower due process standards and greater punishment is often the preferred response (Ericson 2005). More generally, in articulating the scope and limits of the preventive state, we urgently need to engage in an exercise that identifies how such a state operates through regulation and law. What conceptual tools are relied upon and how do those tools give weight and credence to preventive practices? How, in short, is the preventive state constituted by law and its institutions? In other words, while the centrality of risk in its various forms has been well analysed, equal analytic attention now needs to be paid by criminologists to how risk management relates to the politics of 'uncertainty' and to what François Ewald refers to as the precautionary logic evident in contemporary society:

> Precaution starts when decisions must be made by reason of and in the context of scientific uncertainty. Decisions are therefore made not in a context of certainty, nor even of available knowledge, but of doubt, suspicion, premonition, foreboding, challenge, mistrust, fear, and anxiety … Precaution results from an ethic of the necessary decision in a context of uncertainty. (Ewald 2002: 294; for a recent overview of the precautionary principle, see Sunstein 2005)

Interestingly, the emergence of such a precautionary logic in relation to sexual offenders (and more widely in criminal justice as Ericson points out) arguably indicates the inherent limits of risk assessment and management. In this context, community notification arrangements like Megan's Law can be likened to attempts at reimagining risk (as non-expert and non-calculable) in the context of 'scientific uncertainty' – where the limits of expert assessment have been recognised and indeed supplanted. Thus the precautionary principle ('precautionary approach' may be a better term here in order to avoid an overly legal connotation and to emphasise technologies and discourses) applies where the risk assessment technologies for 'representing' the world find themselves surpassed by reality itself. The precautionary logic 'applies to what is uncertain – that is, to what one can apprehend without being able to assess' (Ewald 2002: 286). Precaution requires administrative decisions in situations of uncertainty. It can no longer rely on expert knowledge, on statistical and actuarial data. But in the precautionary imagination, the criminal Others' responsibility is also uncertain and a matter of decision. Whether the evidence about probability of reoffending is based on scientific premises is in itself immaterial. The 'burden of proof' is no longer on the state to show guilt, but on the offender to prove innocence. This changes the system of juridical responsibility to an a priori responsibility and guilt, even before any event has taken place. As a priori responsibility cannot be accommodated by normal juridical thinking, such impossibility often transfers judgements of responsibility to the sphere of 'administrative' policing. It is exactly at this point, under an 'ethic of the necessary decision in a context of uncertainty' that our contemporary soothsayers – the assorted risk managers – engage in the praxis of administrative work known as 'community protection'. Such praxis, one senses, draws part of its cultural sustenance from what Zygmunt Bauman describes as the garden culture:

> Modern culture is a garden culture. It defines itself as the design for an ideal life and a perfect arrangement of human conditions ... Apart from the overall plan, the artificial order of the garden needs tools and raw materials. It also needs defence against the unrelenting danger of what is, obviously, a disorder. (Bauman 1989: 92–3)

Yet equally, modernity ensures that such praxis cannot fully domesticate risk under the bounds of probabilistic calculations; modern science itself has undercut such certainty and all of us, paradoxically, recognise the moral and emotional limits to any such praxis (see Douglas 1992).

Note

1 Craig Sweeney from Newport in Wales was found guilty of the abduction and sexual assault of a three year old girl. His sentence was described as 'unduly lenient' by the Home Secretary. A debate between politicians and others followed.

References

Bauman, Z. (1989) *Modernity and the Holocaust.* Cambridge: Polity Press.
Boerner, D. (1992) 'Confronting violence in the act and in the word', *University of Puget Sound Law Review*, 15: 525–77.
Brown, M. and Pratt, J. (eds) (2000) *Dangerous Offenders: Punishment and Social Order.* London: Routledge.
Cobley, C. (2000) *Sex Offenders: Law, Policy and Practice.* Bristol: Jordans.
Critcher, C. (2002) 'Media, government and moral panic: the politics of paedophilia in Britain 2000–1', *Journalism Studies*, 3 (4): 521–35.
Douglas, M. (1992) *Risk and Blame: Essays in Cultural Theory.* London: Routledge.
Durkheim, É. (1964) *The Elementary Forms of Religious Life.* London: Allen & Unwin.
Ericson, R. (2005) *Criminalization and the Politics of Uncertainty*, John L.J. Edwards Memorial Lecture, University of Toronto, Toronto, Canada.
Ericson, R. and Haggerty, K. (1997) *Policing the Risk Society.* Oxford: Clarendon Press.

Ewald, F. (2002) 'The return of Descartes's malicious demon: an outline of a philosophy of precaution', in T. Baker and J. Simon (eds) *Embracing Risk: The Changing Culture of Insurance and Responsibility.* Chicago: University of Chicago Press.

Foucault, M. (1977) 'About the concept of the "dangerous individual" in 19th-century legal psychiatry', *International Journal of Law and Psychiatry*, 1: 1–19.

Hebenton, B. (2003) 'Risk and public protection: reflections on technology and oratory', *Criminal Justice Matters*, 51 Spring: 26–8.

Hebenton, B. and Thomas, T. (1996) 'Tracking sex offenders', *Howard Journal of Criminal Justice*, 35 (2): 97–112.

Hebenton, B. and Thomas, T. (1997) *Keeping Track? Observations on Sex Offender Registers in the USA*, Crime Detection and Prevention Series, Paper 83. London: Home Office.

Hebenton, B. and Thomas, T. (1998) 'Sex offenders in the community: reflections on problems of law, community and risk management in the USA, England and Wales', in P. O'Malley (ed.) *Crime and the Risk Society.* Aldershot: Dartmouth.

Hebenton, B. and Thomas, T. (2003) *Atlantic Crossings: The Emergence of the Sexual Offender Problem and Its Management on Both Sides of the Pond.* Paper presented to the Round-Table on 'Regulation of Sexual Offenders', American Society of Criminology, Annual Meetings, Denver, Colorado, 19–23 November.

Hebenton, B. and Thomas, N. (2004) *Introducing Lay People into Multi-Agency Public Protection Arrangements: A Pilot Study of Eight Areas.* London: Home Office.

Home Office (2005) *Strengthening Multi-Agency Public Protection Arrangements (MAPPAs)*, Home Office Development and Practice Report No. 45. London: Home Office.

Home Office (2006) *Rebalancing the Criminal Justice System in Favour of the Law-Abiding Majority: Cutting Crime, Reducing Reoffending and Protecting the Public.* London: Home Office.

Hudson, B. (2003) *Justice in the Risk Society: Challenging and Reaffirming Justice in Late Modernity.* London: Sage.

Jenkins, P. (1998) *Moral Panic: Changing Concepts of the Child Molester in Modern America.* New Haven, CT: Yale University Press.

Jenkins, P. (2001) 'How Europe discovered its sex offender crisis', in J. Best (ed.) *How Claims Spread: Cross-National Diffusion of Social Problems.* Hawthorne Creek, NY: Aldine.

Jones, T. and Newburn, T. (2002) 'Policy convergence and crime control in the USA and UK', *Criminal Justice*, 2 (2): 173–203.

Kanka, M. (2000a) 'How Megan's death changed us all: the personal story of a mother and anti-crime advocate', Megan Nicole Kanka Foundation, 28 March, available at http://www.apbnews.com/safetycenter/family/kanka/2000/03/28/kanka0328_01.html.

Kanka, M. (2000b) 'Child advocate in the making: lessons in the struggle for Megan's law', Megan Nicole Kanka Foundation, 27 April available at http://www.apbnews.com/safetycenter/family/kanka/2000/04/27/kanka0427_01.html.

Kleinhans, M. M. (2002) 'Criminal justice approaches to paedophilic sex offenders', *Social and Legal Studies*, 11 (2): 233–55.

LaFond, J. (1992) 'Washington's sexually violent predator law: a deliberate misuse of the therapeutic state for social control', *University of Puget Sound Law Review*, 15: 655–703.

Lewis, C. (1996) 'The Jacob Wetterling Crimes against Children and Sexually Violent Offender Registration Act: an unconstitutional deprivation of the right to privacy and substantive due process', *Harvard Civil Rights and Civil Liberties Law Review*, 39: 89–118.

Lieb, R., Quinsey, V. and Berliner, L. (1998) 'Sexual predators and social policy', in M. Tonry (ed.) *Crime and Justice: A Review of Research*. Chicago: University of Chicago Press, pp. 43–114.

Logan, W. (1999) 'Liberty interests in the preventive state: procedural due process and sex offender community notification laws', *Journal of Criminal Law and Criminology*, 89: 1167–231.

McAlinden, A. (2006) 'Managing risk: from the regulation to the reintegration of sexual offenders', *Criminology and Criminal Justice*, 6 (2): 197–218.

Maguire, M., Kemshall, H., Noaks, L. and Wincup, E. (2001) *Risk Management of Sexual and Violent Offenders: The Work of Public Protection Panels*, Police Research Series No. 139. London: Home Office.

Matravers, A. (ed.) (2003) *Sex Offenders in the Community: Managing and Reducing the Risks*, Cambridge Criminal Justice Series. Cullompton: Willan.

Matson, S. and Lieb, R. (1997) *Megan's Law: a Review of State and Federal Legislation*. Olympia, WA: Washington State Institute of Public Policy.

Nash, M. (1999) *Police, Probation and Protecting the Public*. London: Blackstone.

Nellis, M. (2005) 'Electronic monitoring, satellite tracking and the new punitiveness', in J. Pratt, D. Brown, S. Hallsworth, M. Brown and W. Morrison (eds) *The New Punitiveness: Trends, Theories, Perspectives*. Cullompton: Willan.

O'Malley, P. (ed.) (1998) *Crime and the Risk Society*. Aldershot: Dartmouth.

O'Malley, P. (2004) *Risk, Uncertainty and Government*. London: Glasshouse Press.

Pawson, R. (2002). *Does Megan's Law Work? A Theory Driven Systematic Review*, ESRC UK Centre for Evidence Based Policy and Practice, Working Paper 8. London: University of London.

Pease, K. (2005) 'Science in the service of crime reduction', in N. Tilley (ed.) *The Handbook of Crime Prevention and Community Safety*. Cullompton: Willan.

Petrunik, M. (1982) 'The politics of dangerousness', *International Journal of Law and Psychiatry*, 5: 225–53.

Petrunik, M. (1984) *The Making of Dangerous Offenders: The Origins, Diffusion, and Uses of Legislation for Dangerous Offenders in Europe and North America*. Ottawa: Programs Branch, Ministry of the Solicitor General.

Petrunik, M. (2002) 'Managing unacceptable risk: sex offenders, community response, and social policy in the United States and Canada', *International Journal of Offender Therapy and Comparative Criminology*, 46: 483–512.

Plotnikoff, J. and Woolfson, R. (2000) *Where Are They Now? An Evaluation of Sex Offender Registration in England and Wales*, Police Research Series Paper 126. London: Home Office.

Pratt, J. (2000) 'Sex crime and the new punitiveness', *Behavioral Sciences and the Law*, 18: 135–51.

Rose, N. (1999) *Powers of Freedom: Reframing Political Thought*. Cambridge: Cambridge University Press.

Sample, L.L. and Bray, T. M. (2003) 'Are sex offenders dangerous?', *Criminology and Public Policy*, 3 (1): 59–62.

Scottish Executive (2001) *A Review of the Research Literature on Serious Violent and Sexual Offenders*. Edinburgh: Central Research Unit.

Simon, J. (2003) 'Managing the monstrous: sex offenders and the new penology', in B.J. Winick and J.Q. LaFond (eds) *Protecting Society from Sexually Dangerous Offenders: Law, Justice, and Therapy*. Washington, DC: American Psychological Association.

Sunstein, C.R. (2005) *Laws of Fear. Beyond the Precautionary Principle*. Cambridge: Cambridge University Press.

Thomas, T. (2000) *Sex Crime: Sex Offending and Society*. Cullompton: Willan.

Thomas, T. (2003) 'Sex offender community notification: experiences from America', *Howard Journal of Criminal Justice*, 42 (3): 217–28.

Welchans, S. (2005) 'Megan's law: evaluations of sexual offender registries', *Criminal Justice Policy Review*, 16 (2): 123–40.

West, D.J. (1987) *Sexual Crimes and Confrontations: A Study of Victims and Offenders*. Aldershot: Gower.

Winick, B.J. and LaFond, J.Q. (eds) (2003) *Protecting Society from Sexually Dangerous Offenders: Law, Justice, and Therapy*. Washington, DC: American Psychological Association.

Wright, L. (1995) 'A rapist's homecoming' *The New Yorker*, September: 56–62, 64–9.

Zimring, F.E. (2004) *An American Travesty: Legal Responses to Adolescent Sexual Offending*. Chicago: University of Chicago Press.

Chapter 17

Protecting children online: towards a safer internet

Julia Davidson and Elena Martellozzo

Introduction

Media, public and political attention to the problem of child sexual abuse has risen in recent decades. Academic interest has also increased (Corby 2006; Davidson 2005; Beckett 2007; Pritchard 2004; Ashenden 2004; Goldson *et al.* 2002; Thomas 2000; Marshall 1997; Morrison *et al.* 1994). There is now a substantial and growing literature on the problem of child sexual abuse. However, one important type of child sexual abuse – that which takes place on and via the internet – remains under-researched.

Internet sex offenders[1] fall into two principal categories: those who use the internet to target and 'groom' children for the purposes of sexual abuse (Finkelhor *et al.* 2000); and those who produce and/or download indecent illegal images of children from the internet and distribute them (Quayle and Taylor 2002: Davidson and Martellozzo 2005).

In this chapter we explore online grooming and sexual abuse of children and the legislative and institutional measures being developed to prevent it. The discussion is informed by Tony Krone's (2005) typology of internet sex offenders, which identifies nine intersecting and overlapping categories of online sexually abusive behaviour. Case studies drawn from our ongoing research are used to illustrate and reinforce some of Krone's typological categories, while at the same time highlighting the complexities involved in policing online child sexual abuse. We conclude by suggesting that the education of children, parents and practitioners should be central to any sustained attempt to address this technologically driven form of twenty-first century criminality.

Criminalising the problem of 'online grooming'

A new offence category was created in the Sexual Offences Act 2003 in England and Wales: section 15 makes 'meeting a child following sexual grooming' an offence. This applies to the internet, other technologies such as mobile phones and to the 'real world'. 'Grooming' involves a process of socialisation during which an offender seeks to interact with a child (a young person under 18 in Scotland, England and Wales), possibly sharing their hobbies and interests, in an attempt to gain trust in order to prepare them for sexual abuse. The process, as we shall see, may also involve an attempt to normalise sexual relations between adults and children.

The concept of 'grooming' is also recognised in Scottish legislation. The Protection of Children and Prevention of Sexual Offences (Scotland) Act 2005 includes 'meeting a child following certain preliminary contact' (s.1); the English equivalent of 'grooming' and the definition is the same: where a person arranges to meet a child who is under 18, having communicated with them on at least one previous occasion (in person, via the internet or via other technologies), with the intention of performing sexual activity on the child.

Several countries are beginning to follow the Scottish and English lead in legislating against 'grooming' behaviour. Sexual grooming has also recently been added to the Crimes Amendment Act 2005 in New Zealand (http://www.legislation.govt.nz). In the United States it is an offence to transmit electronically information about a child aged 16 or under for the purpose of committing a sexual offence (US Code Title 18, Part 1, Chapter 117, AS 2425). The Australian Criminal Code (s.218A) makes similar restrictions, as does the Canadian Criminal Code (s.172.1). The legislation in Scotland, England and Wales differs in that the sexual grooming offence applies both to cyberspace and to the 'real world'; legislation in other countries addresses only electronic grooming via the internet and mobile phones. In reality it is extremely difficult to police and evidence grooming behaviour in the 'real world'. It is therefore unsurprising that few cases have been brought to court on this basis under the Sexual Offences Act 2003 or under the Protection of Children and Prevention of Sexual Offences (Scotland) Act 2005.

The concept of sexual grooming has in reality been drawn into legislation from the sex offender literature where it is well documented (Finkelhor 1984), and is now filtering into policy and crime detection and prevention initiatives. Note, for example, the Child Exploitation and Online Protection Centre (CEOP), a recently launched organisation (April 2006), funded by government and the communications industry, which includes representatives from the police and other criminal justice agencies. CEOP draws upon expertise from internet service providers (such as AOL and Microsoft) and children's charities such as the NSPCC in attempting to confront online abuse (http://www.ceop.gov.uk). This new centre aims to raise awareness among children and parents about the potential dangers of the internet and to create a database of known offenders. Police officers visit chat rooms posing as children in order to detect grooming behaviour. False websites will be set up to attract sex offenders seeking to groom children. These policing tactics are not new. The National High Technology Crime Unit Scotland and the London Metropolitan Police High Tech Crime Unit (HTCU), for example, have placed undercover officers in teen and other chat rooms likely to attract children since the introduction of the Sexual Offences Act 2003 (as have other HTCUs). These officers have been trained to act undercover and, through practice, have learnt how to pose as a child, as an adult or as a sex offender. They have learnt to mimic children's behaviour online, including their use of computer and mobile text language, in order to prompt and encourage conversation with child abusers seeking to groom a child. Several recent convictions have been secured on this basis and an increasing number of online groomers are being arrested.

Sex offenders' use of the internet

Sex offenders use the internet to access indecent images of children,[2] to select victims for abuse and to communicate with other sex offenders. Audrey Gillan (2003) has suggested that the demand for indecent images through, for example, the use of file-sharing technologies has expanded so much that law enforcement agencies are finding it increasingly difficulty to identify and track down child victims and the perpetrators involved (from interviews we conducted with London Metropolitan Police practitioners, June 2006).

Internet sex offender behaviour can include: the construction of sites to be used for the exchange of information, experiences and indecent images of children; the organisation of criminal activities that seek to use children for prostitution purposes and that produce indecent images of children at a professional level; the organisation of criminal activities that promote sexual tourism. Indecent images of children are frequently shared by sex offenders using the internet, and the industry which has emerged around the production and exchange of such images is becoming increasingly large and lucrative (Wyre 2003). Max Taylor, Gemma Holland and Ethel Quayle (2001) suggest that some online sex offenders are 'collectors' of indecent images of children who routinely swap images with other collectors. It is also suggested that some of these images are photographs taken by people known to the children, including members of their family (from interviews we conducted with London Metropolitan Police practitioners, June 2006).

Ethel Quayle and Max Taylor (2003) also comment on the possible motivations of online child sex abusers. It is suggested that sex offenders perceive the internet as a means of generating an immediate source of satisfaction for their fantasies. Factors including presumed anonymity, disinhibition and accessibility undoubtedly encourage offenders to go online. Quayle and Taylor (2003) also acknowledge, however, that the unique structure and protocols of the internet may play a major role in facilitating online child abuse.

Krone (2005) has developed a typology of internet child sex offenders, which has been adapted for use by Richard Wortley and Stephen Smallbone (2006) to guide the work of police officers in the United States of America. While some of the categories are questionable the typology does include those offenders targeting and grooming children online, a group largely excluded from other typologies. Nine categories of offender are identified, and these are outlined in Table 17.1.

These categories should not be seen as mutually exclusive. Clearly there are important areas of overlap between them, and further research is needed to explore the nature and extent of internet offending. However, Krone's (2005) work is useful in isolating different types of online sexually abusive behaviour and in beginning to elucidate the risks associated with different types of online activity, in terms both of the type of internet abuse which is likely to result, and the likelihood of further abuse in the 'real world', also known as 'hands-on abuse'.

The following case studies are provided to further illustrate some of the issues discussed above, and to demonstrate how the 'grooming' clause of the Sexual Offences Act 2003 can be applied in practice. The data were gathered by Elena Martellozzo as part of a PhD

Table 17.1 Typology of internet child sex offencers

Offender type	Typical behaviour
Browser	Offenders who accidentally come across indecent images and save them. In reality such images are either purchased via credit card or are swapped by collectors.
Private fantasy	Offenders who create digital images for their own private use.
Trawlers	Offenders who search for indecent images through open browsers and may engage in some networking.
Non-secure collectors	Offenders who look, by networking, for indecent images in open areas of the internet such as chat rooms and do not impose security barriers, such as password, minimum trade in images or encryption.
Secure collectors	Offenders who use security barriers in collecting child pornography and belong to an online hidden, paedophile network. These offenders are highly organised, likely to be collectors and employ sophisticated security to conceal their offending.
Online groomers	Offenders who have initiated online contact with a child with the intention of establishing a sexual relationship involving cyber sex or physical sex. These offenders may send indecent images to children as a part of the grooming process.
Physical abusers	Offenders who are actively involved in the sexual abuse of children and use indecent images of children to feed their sexual craving. The physical abuse may be recorded for the personal use of the abuser but it is not intended to be further distributed.
Producers	Offenders who record the sexual abuse of children for the purposes of distribution to networks and to satisfy their own fantasy.
Distributors	Offenders who distribute indecent images either for financial gain or as part of their collecting behaviour.

(Martellozzo, forthcoming) and are presented with the permission of the London Metropolitan Police. These cases have been selected from among many because of their illustrative potential within the specific context of the discussion presented in this chapter. Case study 17.1 illustrates the activities involved in online grooming. Case study 17.2 highlights the overlapping nature of different kinds of online sexually abusive behaviour. Case study 17.3 illustrates the variety of roles that the internet can play as a source, motivator and means of engaging in child sexual abuse. The details of these cases have been changed or generalised so as to maintain the anonymity of those discussed.

Case study 17.1: The online groomer

This case involved the 'grooming' of a 14-year-old girl from Canada by a 34-year-old businessman from South West England. The offender and victim spent six months chatting online before the offender began sending money to the girl for the purchase of phone cards so they could communicate also via text messages.

The girl's parents found out about their communication and became suspicious. They immediately contacted the local police, who in turn contacted the London Metropolitan police, when:

- he offered to go to see her in Canada;
- he was prepared to pay $500 to have sex with the girl;
- he offered to pay more money in exchange for sex with the girl's 10-year-old friend;
- he asked if she could post her underwear;
- he claimed to be an 'abuser of children'.

The suspect's behaviour was a clear act of 'grooming', as defined in the Sexual Offences Act 2003, and as such justified formal and immediate police intervention. The investigation revealed that the offender had other previous criminal convictions (for 'kerb-crawling', for soliciting a prostitute and for possession of cocaine). The suspect's computer was seized and analysed and it was found that he had previously met and sexually abused another child whom he had groomed online.

Also, around 6,000 images of children under the age of 16 were found in the suspect's computer, many of which were indecent. Of the total collection of images, 4,500 depicted children dressed in underwear or swimwear, and 1,117 portrayed children being physically abused. It was further discovered that the offender regularly discussed the sexual abuse of children with other like-minded individuals by logging on to dedicated websites, including a number of different child love forums. Clearly, sex offenders are aware of the dangers of downloading indecent

---

images of children and they are aware that there is a risk of being monitored. However, they support one another by providing advice on where to search for more indecent images and on how to behave when online so as best to avoid detection.

Furthermore, it emerged from interviews with the Canadian girl that the suspect had been sending her indecent images of other children. This represents another 'grooming' tactic whereby child abuse images are shown to the child to lower that child's inhibitions concerning sexual activity (Krone 2005) and to make the child believe that it can be regarded as 'normal' to have sex with adults or to pose naked in front of a camera. The suspect then asked the girl to send him indecent pictures of herself. He also offered to pay the girl money to produce and send indecent images of one of her younger friends.

While this chapter is particularly concerned with 'online grooming', it is important to remain cognisant of the interconnectedness between different forms of online sexually abusive behaviour. Reinforcing the importance of understanding the overlapping nature of the categories in Krone's (2005) typology of internet sexual abusers, the investigation revealed that the suspect was acting not only as an 'online groomer', but also as a 'non-secure collector' and a 'physical abuser'. His behaviour in relation to the latter two typological classifications is illustrated in Case study 17.2.

Case study 17.2: The on line groomer, the non-secure collector and the physical abuser

The same 34-year-old businessman discussed in Case study 17.1 arranged to meet one of the many victims he groomed online. The victim was a 15-year-old girl from the USA. She met the offender when she was in England on holiday with her mother and grandmother. The mother knew about the relationship between her daughter and the man, but did not at first suspect any indecent or criminal intent. She admitted speaking many times on the phone with the man, and they even agreed to meet during their visit to England.

After having spent some time together and gaining their trust, the man persuaded the mother to let him look after her daughter and promised he would bring her back to the hotel. The mother accepted on the condition he would have her back by 11 p.m. This process of ongoing interaction and negotiation further evidences the offender's manipulative capacity to groom not only the child, but also the parents (Finkelhor et al. 2000). It emerges that the offender needs to 'groom' two groups: the victim and those who protect the victim. He uses a variety of tactics including seduction, coercion and manipulation. Grooming tactics differ between varying offenders. However, once the victim has been manipulated and 'prepared' for the abuse, the perpetrator can proceed to the commission of the offence (Sullivan and Beech 2004).

It is alleged that he then invited the girl back to his house and took her to his bedroom, where he performed oral sex on her. Much later, the mother noticed love bites on the girl's body and took her immediately to the doctor, where it was discovered that she had contracted a sexually transmitted infection.

The suspect was then arrested and interviewed. During the interview with the police, the suspect claimed that he and the girl were very close and that, at the time of the investigation, he still felt close to her. The suspect admitted his 'unusual' close relationship with the girl, but attempted to transfer blame to the mother. The officer in charge of the case claimed that victim appeared to be naive and easily led (interview with officer, Metropolitan Police HTCU, 2 May 2005).

The forensic analyst in charge of the case described the suspect as leading a double life. On the one hand, he was involved with charities and participated in awareness campaigns for child amputees. On the other hand, these activities served as a means of increasing his access to disabled and/or vulnerable children for the purposes of abuse.

Conviction

The offender was subsequently charged with grooming, producing and distributing indecent images of children under the Sex Offences Act 2003, and was sentenced to two years in prison. He pleaded not guilty to sexually assaulting the young girl, and there was insufficient evidence to secure a conviction for this alleged offence.

Case study 17.3: the physical abuser

This case relates to a 55-year-old man who committed a series of serious sexual assaults against boys between the ages of 12 and 16 years. The offences were committed both in the UK and Ghana.

Briefly, the offender befriended a 12-year-old boy in the UK while working in a toy model shop. After a period of grooming he began sexually abusing the boy, having convinced him that this sexual activity was normal.

The offender also travelled to Ghana where his eldest son had been working for Voluntary Services Overseas as a teacher. Due to the extreme poverty in this country the offender was able to groom young boys with gifts and money in order to fulfil his sexual fantasies.

Following complaints by local people, authorities in Ghana interviewed the suspect about his activities. However, they did not have the technological facilities to analyse his computer and cameras, and he was released. British authorities were notified of his imminent return to the UK. Having been stopped at Heathrow Airport, the suspect was found to be in possession of hundreds of indecent images of children. He was arrested immediately by Customs officers, interviewed, charged with the importation of indecent images and remanded in custody. Police were then notified that the material seized was likely to contain evidence of hands-on abuse. Officers from the London Metropolitan Police Paedophile Unit commenced an investigation, which revealed that the man had:

- sexually abused a number of boys under the age of 16 in Ghana;
- sexually abused a boy under the age of 13 in the UK;
- abused boys in the UK both in a converted van and an office;
- recorded his sexual abuse of the victims;
- downloaded a quantity of indecent images of children from the internet;
- made indecent pseudo-images of children.

In June 2005 the offender was arrested and charged with:

- rape of a child under 13 years;
- the sexual penetration of a child;
- distribution of indecent images of children.

When he was interviewed by the police he gave a full admission of having sex with other boys in Africa. He also admitted downloading indecent images of children from the internet and also made a number of pseudo-images.

Conviction

The offender was successfully convicted of rape and sexual assault of young boys both in the United Kingdom and in Africa. He was sentenced to an indeterminate prison sentence in January 2006 under the new Sex Offences Act 2003 (section 72).

At this stage of our work (Martellozzo, forthcoming) it is unclear how typical these case studies are of cases likely to be brought forward under the Sexual Offences Act 2003. Nevertheless, they do illustrate some key issues raised by consideration of online child sexual abuse, and in particular the problem of online grooming. It is clear that the internet is more than just a medium of communication (Castells 2002, 2004). It constitutes a new virtual reality, or a cyberworld, with its own rules and its own language. It provides a supportive context within which the child sexual abuser is no longer a lonely figure, but forms part of a larger community that shares the same interests. The internet gives new meaning to the term 'paedophile ring', as the potential for offenders to organise to abuse children is so considerable. Audrey Gillan (2003) goes further, arguing that peer-to-peer file-sharing facilitates the most extreme, aggressive and reprehensible types of behaviour that the internet will allow.

Online sexual abuse: moves to protect children

Recent research demonstrates that in the past few years home internet access has rapidly grown and that school access has become a 'must have' facility. As a result, children spend more and more time online. Sonia Livingstone and Moira Bober (2004) suggest that one-fifth (19 per cent) of 9–19 year olds spend about 10 minutes per day online, half spend between about half an hour (25 per cent) and one hour (23 per cent) online, and a further fifth go online for between one (14 per cent) and three hours (6 per cent) each day. Only one in 20 (5 per cent) spend more than three hours on the internet on an average day (Livingstone and Bober 2004: 19).

These figures can be viewed positively if the internet is perceived as a vital tool for education and communication. Young people have embraced the new technology with enthusiasm by using interactive services such as games, chat rooms and instant messages which have almost transformed them into computer experts. However, the same figures can be viewed negatively if the risks and dangers that children may encounter when online are taken into consideration. According to Marni Feather (1999), the internet is acting as a new medium through which some commonly recognised forms of child maltreatment and sexual and emotional abuse may take place. Concerns may be increased further when we consider that children are the most impressionable social group and tend to be at greater risk of behavioural influence than adults (Davidson and Martellozzo 2004).

Therefore, it should be imperative, as Martin Calder (2004) rightly suggests, to encourage appropriate and safe use of the internet by assisting children and young people to feel comfortable navigating the information highway. In fact, 'the most important issue surrounding child abuse and the internet is child protection, not computer technology' (Jones 2003, in Gallagher *et al.* 2006: 105) because technology alone is always fallible and offers no guarantees of child protection. However, if technology were to be combined with education and awareness among children, parents and teachers and effective inter-agency partnership working, it would be easier to maximise the few available resources and move one step closer to making cyberspace a safe place for young and vulnerable internet users.

There have already been considerable efforts to increase online child protection internationally. The G8 countries have agreed a strategy to protect children from sexual abuse on the internet. Key aims include the development of an international database of offenders and victims to aid victim identification, offender monitoring and the targeting of those profiting from the sale of indecent images of children. Internet service providers and credit card companies, such as the UK's Association for Payment Clearing Services, have also joined the international movement against the production and distribution of sexually abusive images of children online. Their efforts have focused primarily on attempting to trace individuals who use credit cards to access illegal sites containing indecent images of children. There has also been an attempt to put mechanisms into place which would prevent online payment for illegal sites hosted outside the UK.

Organisations like the Virtual Global Taskforce (VGT) and the Internet Watch Foundation (IWF) are making some headway in attempting to protect children online. VGT is an organisation that comprises several international law enforcement agencies from Australia, Canada, the United States, the United Kingdom and Interpol. Through the provision of advice and support to children VGT aims to protect children online and has recently set up a bogus website to attract online groomers. A report to VGT by a child has recently led to the conviction of a sex offender for online grooming and the possession of indecent images (VGT 2006).

The Internet Watch Foundation (IWF) is one of the main government watchdogs in this area. Although based in the UK the IWF is a part of the EU's Safer Internet Plus Programme. As Robbins and Darlington (2003) have pointed out, this programme has four main aims:

- to fight illegal internet content;
- to tackle harmful internet content;
- to promote a safer internet environment;
- to raise awareness about internet dangers.

While the first three of these objectives have until now been largely the province of institutions and organisations, the fourth has immediate implications for the everyday use of the internet by the members of the public and, most significantly, children themselves. It is for this reason that this final objective – raising awareness about internet dangers – is discussed further here.

Teaching safety online

Measures to protect children include school-based programmes aiming to educate children, parents and teachers about the dangers posed by sex offenders in cyberspace. Such programmes are now routinely delivered to secondary school children in countries such as the USA, New Zealand and Canada as part of the school curriculum (Davidson and Martellozzo 2004).

In the USA, the ICAC (Internet Crime Against Children) Task Force has created a program to help both children and parents to understand the importance of the internet but also the danger that may be encountered while using it. The program has been developed by NetSmartz Workshop. NetSmartz is an interactive, educational safety resource from the National Center for Missing and Exploited Children (NCMEC) and Boys and Girls Clubs of America (BGCA) that uses age appropriate, 3-D activities to teach children and teens how to be safer when using the internet. NetSmartz has been implemented in more than 3,000 BGCA Clubs nationally, serving more than 3.3 million young people.

The program provides parents, children and teachers with an overview of online risks. It argues that in addition to the useful educational information available on the internet, internet content can include nudity or other sexually explicit material, hate or racist websites, promotional material about tobacco, alcohol or drugs, graphic violence, information about satanic or cult groups, or recipes for making bombs and explosives at home, as well as the dangers previously discussed. According to ICAC (2000) more than 30 million children in the USA alone use the internet. An ICAC report on the nation's youth (Wolak et al. 2004) suggests that: 1 in 4 children on the internet had had an unwanted exposure to inappropriate sexually explicit pictures; approximately 1 in 5 had received a sexual solicitation or approach; 1 in 17 had been threatened or harassed; and 1 in 33 had received an aggressive sexual solicitation (from someone who asked to meet them somewhere, called them on the telephone, sent them regular mail, money or gifts).

Sexual solicitation would normally take place in chat rooms (65 per cent) and on Instant Messenger (24 per cent) where the computer would be located at home (70 per cent), at someone else's home (22 per cent), at school (4 per cent) and at the library (3 per cent) (ICAC 2000). A similar program was designed and delivered by Safer Schools officers in the UK in 2002, in response to demand from local parents, for use with 12–13-year-old children. This age group has been identified as particularly active and independent users of the internet (O'Connell 2003). Such educational programs help children and parents to understand that some people use the internet as a tool for sexually abusing children.

David Finkelhor *et al.* (2000) found that females were targeted at twice the rate of males, but it is important to know that males can also be victims of sexual solicitation on the internet. We strongly support this view (see also Davidson and Martellozzo 2004) and argue that children should be informed that girls and boys are equally at risk. We found that the vast majority (140, 70 per cent) of the children that took part in their study thought that girls were much more at risk. The children seemed to use gender stereotypes to explain why girls are more at risk of sexual abuse (Martellozzo 2004). Girls were described as weaker and boys as stronger and more able to defend themselves. Several children also noted that most cases covered by the media involve the sexual abuse, abduction and killing of girls. This point raises a stimulating opportunity to reflect on how the media construct, in a straightforward and unambiguous manner, the perversity of adults who are sexually attracted to (predominantly female) children and adolescents (Greer and Jewkes 2005). However, 'the reality is almost certainly more complex and more uncomfortable than such representations tend to suggest' (Greer and Jewkes 2005: 19). While it is the case that males perpetrate most sexual abuse against female victims, it seems important to reinforce the point with children and parents that boys are also at risk (Davidson and Martellozzo 2004).

When examining online relationships, it is important to bear in mind that time does not equal trust or knowing the person. In the real world parents spontaneously ask their children questions like: 'where are you going?' 'who are you going with?' 'what time will you be home?' These three questions could be reformulated to form the basis of a parent–child discussion about internet use: 'what sites will you visit?' 'who will you talk to?' 'how long will you be online?' 'where will you be using the computer?'

This is one of the most important internet safety messages that can be delivered. Supervision by parents and guardians is an effective method of protecting children online. Often parents/guardians are more concerned with monitoring television viewing than with supervising access to the internet. It is also important for children to feel comfortable talking to their parents if they are involved in anything that makes them feel frightened, uncomfortable or confused. Often children are afraid to communicate bad experiences online for fear their internet use will be taken away (Davidson and Martellozzo 2004). Thus, trust should be created and maintained.

Conclusion

In this chapter we have explored the extent to which the internet can be seen as a dangerous place, particularly for children, by looking at how sex offenders behave online. Such analysis challenges traditional views of what constitutes child sexual abuse in the real world; it explores how abuse is perpetrated in cyberspace and the attempts made by law enforcement agencies to reduce this serious problem.

The first part of the chapter introduced the Sexual Offences Act 2003 and it is suggested that online child abuse comprises not only the production and distribution of indecent images of children but also 'online grooming' which involves a process of socialisation during which an offender interacts with a child in order to prepare her for sexual abuse (Sexual Offences Act 2003). In particular, section 15 of the Sexual Offences Act 2003 in England and Wales makes 'meeting a child following sexual grooming' a serious offence. This new offence, facilitated by the anonymous nature of cyberspace and its vague boundaries, has risen exponentially during the past two years and the police are taking steps to adopt new methodologies to detect and prevent such abuse.

In relation to the types of offences perpetrated in cyberspace, we have focused primarily on the production and distribution of indecent images of children and on grooming a child for the purpose of facilitating the sexual abuse of that child. There are a number of reasons why the use of indecent images of children is important to sex offenders. Christiane Sanderson (2007) suggests that such abusive material provides an underground supportive community where sex offenders validate and normalise their interest in children. Indecent images are also used in the grooming process whereby abusers may use child abuse images as tools to coerce, excite, seduce and corrupt a child. Indecent images of children are also a powerful control method. As argued by Burgess and Hatman (cited by Fedoroff 1997), indecent images are produced at the psychological expense of the

351

photographed child, because the use of those images binds the victim by normalising the acts and ultimately by acting as a source of blackmail for the child. Jo Sullivan and Anthony Beech (2004) believe that people who download child abuse images from the internet are more likely to groom a child and eventually offend against a child by acting out their fantasies.

Finally, in analysing the steps taken by law enforcement agencies to reduce the problem of online abuse, we have shown the different attempts that have been made to protect children from online and offline sexual abuse. However, despite moves on the part of law enforcement agencies, governments, the IT industry and organisations such as VGT and IWF to control online abuse, such efforts are largely failing. There is evidence to support the assertion that the number of children that are groomed, manipulated and eventually victimised every day online is increasing. Also the number of indecent images of children on the internet continues to increase and the images become ever more disturbing, involving a greater degree of violence and increasingly younger children worldwide in the most vulnerable of our societies. John Carr of the NCH in the UK suggests, in a recent report *Out of Sight, Out of Mind* (2006), that governments are failing to make the growing trade in indecent images of children a high enough political priority and that the hidden nature of the offending and lack of public awareness contribute to this failure.

Notes

1 This chapter has sought to avoid the term 'paedophile' and used, instead, the term (child) 'sex offender', 'abuser' or 'suspect' when discussing case studies. The authors felt that the term 'paedophile' is very misleading as to the nature and causes of child sexual abuse.

2 Throughout this chapter, we have sought, as much as possible, to avoid the use of the term 'child pornography' and have preferred to use terms like 'indecent images of children' or 'child abuse images'. The reason for this choice is mainly because it is felt that the term 'child pornography' has become a passive term and fails accurately to describe the reality which is 'the record of systematic rape, abuse and torture of children on film and photograph, and other electronic means' (Edwards 2002: 1–21).

References

Ashenden, S. (2004) *Governing Child Sexual Abuse. Negotiating the Boundaries of Public and Private, Law and Science.* London and New York: Routledge.

Beckett, C. (2007) *Child Protection. An Introduction* (2nd edn). London: Sage Publications.

Calder, M. (2004) *Child Sexual Abuse and the Internet: Tackling the New Frontier.* Lyme Regis: Russell House Publishing.

Carr, J. (2006) *Out of Sight, Out of Mind: Tackling Child Sexual Abuse Images on the Internet – A Global Challenge.* London: NCH Children's Charity.

Castells, M. (1996) *The Network Society.* Oxford: Blackwell.

Castells, M. (2004) *The Power of Identity* (second edition). Oxford: Blackwell.

Cobley, C. (2005) 'The legislative framework', in A. Matravers (ed.) *Sex Offenders in the Community: Managing and Reducing the Risks.* Cullompton: Willan.

Corby, B. (2006) *Child Abuse. Towards a Knowledge Base.* Buckingham: Open University Press.

Craig, L., Browne, K. and Beech, A (2004) *Identifying Sexual and Violent Re-offenders*, presented at the British Psychological Society Conference, Division of Forensic Psychology, 22 March, Leicester University.

Davidson, J. (2004) 'Child sexual abuse prevention programmes: the role of schools', in O. Giotakos, R. Eher and F. Pfafflin (eds) *Sex Offending Is Everybody's Business*, 8th International Conference of the International Association for the Treatment of Sexual Offenders, 6–9 October. Pabst: Lengerich.

Davidson, J. (2005) 'Victims speak: comparing child sexual abusers and their victims' account of offline offence circumstances', *Journal of Victims and Offenders*, 1: 159–74.

Davidson, J. (2006) 'Victims speak: comparing child sexual abusers and child victims accounts, perceptions and interpretations of sexual abuse', *Victims and Offenders*, 1 (2): 159–74.

Davidson, J. and Martellozzo, E. (2004) *Educating Children about Sexual Abuse and Evaluating the Metropolitan Police Safer Surfing Programme.* Available at http://www.saferschoolpartnerships.org/ssp-topics/evaluations/documents/ssfindingsreport.pdf

Davidson, J. and Martellozzo, E. (2005) *The Internet and Protecting Children from Sex Offenders Online: When Strangers Become 'Virtual Friends'.* Available at http://www.oii.ox.ac.uk/research/cybersafety/extensions/pdfs/papers.

Edwards, S. (2002) 'Prosecuting child pornography possession and taking indecent photographs of children', *Journal of Social Welfare and Family Law*, 22 (1): 1–21.

Feather, M. (1999), *Internet and Child Victimisation.* Paper presented at the *Children and Crime: Victims and Offenders Conference*, convened by the Australian Institute of Criminology, Brisbane, 17–18 June 1999, cited in

J. Stanley (2001) *Child Abuse Prevention Issues Number 15 Summer 2001, Child Abuse and the Internet.*

Fedoroff, J.P. (1997) 'Myths and misconceptions about sex offenders', *The Canadian Journal of Human Sexuality*, 6: 43–52.

Finkelhor, D. (1984) *Child Sexual Abuse: New Theory and Research.* New York: Free Press.

Finkelhor, D., Kimberly, J. and Wolak, J. (2000) *On Line Victimisation: A Report on the Nation's Youth.* Alexandria, VA: National Center for Missing and Exploited Children.

Gallagher, B., Fraser, C., Christmann, K. and Hodgson, B. (2006) *International and Internet Child Sexual Abuse and Exploitation.* Centre of Applied Childhood Studies. University of Huddersfield.

Gillan, A. (2003) 'Race to save new victims of child pornography', *The Guardian*, 4 November.

Goldson, B., Lavalette, M. and McKechnie, J. (eds) (2002) *Children, Welfare and the State.* London: Sage Publications.

Greer, C. and Y. Jewkes (2005) 'Extremes of otherness: media images of social exclusion', *Social Justice*, Special Edition on Emerging Imaginaries of Regulation, Control and Oppression, 32 (1): 20–31.

Home Office Task Force on Child Protection on the Internet (2003) *Good Practice Models and Guidance for the Internet Industry on: Chat Services; Instant Messages; Web Based Services.* London: Home Office.

Internet Crime Against Children (ICAC) (2000) http://www.icactraining.org/TF_contacts.htm

Internet Crime Against Children (ICAC) (2004). NetSmartz Presentation. University of New Hampshire.

Jewkes, Y. (ed.) (2003) *Dot.cons: Crime, Deviance and Identity on the Internet.* Cullompton: Willan.

Krone, T. (2004) *A Typology of Online Child Pornography Offending*, Trends and Issues in Crime and Criminal Justice No. 279. Canberra: Australian Institute of Criminology.

Krone, T. (2005) 'Combating online child pornography in Australia', in E. Quayle and M. Taylor (eds) *Viewing Child Pornography on the Internet. Understanding the Offence, Managing the Offender, Helping the Victims.* Lyme Regis: Russell House.

Livingstone, S. and Bober, M. (2004) *UK Children Go Online: Surveying the Experiences of Young People and Their Parents.* London: LSE Report.

Livingstone, S. and Bober, M. (2005) *Internet Literacy Among Children and Young People.* London: LSE Report.

Marshall, P. (1997) *The Prevalence of Convictions for Sexual Offending*, Research Findings No. 55. London: Home Office.

Martellozzo, E. (2004) 'Child pornography on the internet: police strategies', in O. Giotakos, R. Eher and F. Pfafflin (eds) *Sex Offending Is Everybody's Business*, 8th International Conference of the International Association for the Treatment of Sexual Offenders, 6–9 October Pabst: Lengerich.

Martellozzo, E. (forthcoming PhD thesis) *Metropolitan Police Practice: Protecting Children Online: Exploring the Work of the High Technological Crime Unit.* University of Westminster.

Morrison, T., Erooga, M. and Beckett, R. (1994) *Sexual Offending Against Children.* London: Routledge.

National Offender Management and the Scottish Executive (2006) *Consultation on the Possession of Extreme Pornographic Material.* www.homeoffice.gov.uk/documents/cons-extreme-porn-3008051/1?version=1

O'Connell, R. (2003) *A Typology of Child Cybersexploitation and Online Grooming Practices.* Preston: Cyberspace Research Unit.

Pritchard, C. (2004) *The Child Abusers. Research and Controversy.* Open University Press.

Quayle, E. and Taylor, M. (2001) 'Child seduction and self-representation on the Internet', *Cyberpsychology and Behaviour*, 4 (5): 597–607.

Quayle, E. and Taylor, M. (2002) 'Paedophiles, pornography and the internet: assessment issues', *British Journal of Social Work*, 32: 863–75.

Quayle, E. and Taylor, M. (2003) 'Model of problematic internet use in people with a sexual interest in children', *Cyberpsychology and Behaviour*, 6 (1): 93–106.

Robbins, P. and Darlington R. (2003) 'The role of the industry and the Internet Watch Foundation', in A. MacVean and P. Spindler (eds) *Policing Paedophiles on the Internet.* The New Police Bookshop. Bristol: Benson Publication.

Sanderson, C. (2007) *The Seduction of Children. Empowering Parents and Teachers to Protect Children from Child Sexual Abuse.* London: Jessica Kingsley Publishers.

Sullivan, J. and Beech, A. (2004) 'Are collectors of child abuse images a risk to children?' in A. MacVean, and P. Spindler (eds) *Policing Paedophiles on the Internet.* The John Grieve Centre for Policing and Community Safety.

Taylor, H., Holland, G. and Quayle, E. (2001) 'Typology of paedophile picture collections', *The Police Journal*, 74 (2): 97–107.

Thomas, T. (2000) *Sex Crime: Sex Offending and Society.* Cullompton: Willan.

Virtual Global Taskforce (VGT) (2006) in www.virtualglobaltaskforce.com/news/Dutch-study.html accessed on 04/06/2006.

Wartley, R. and Smallbone, S. (2006) *Child Pornography on the Internet.* Washington, DC: US Department of Justice.

Wolak, J., Finkelhor, D. and Mitchell K. (2004) 'Internet-initiated sex crimes against minors: implications for prevention based on findings from a national study', *Journal of Adolescent Health*, 35 (5): 424–33.

Wyre, R. (2003) 'No excuse for child porn', *Community Care*, 1489: 38–40.

Chapter 18

The 'paedophile-in-the-community' protests: press reporting and public responses[1]

Jenny Kitzinger

It is December 2006: a group of up to 300 people gather outside a bungalow in a small English village. Some pelt the property with eggs, a brick is thrown through a window. They chant 'paedophile out' and wave banners reading 'move the monster'. Such scenes have become familiar over recent years. This particular incident was triggered by a front-page story in the *News of the World*, revealing that this bungalow housed the notorious Robert Oliver. Oliver had been jailed in 1989 for the gang rape and manslaughter of the 14-year-old Jason Swift. He was released eight years later, and had been trailed by journalists ever since. 'WE UNCOVER KILLER PAEDOPHILE', the *News of the World* headline declared, 'BECAUSE OFFICIALS WON'T' (10 December 2006). 'Oliver, 52, has certainly made every effort to conceal his identity since moving into his council bungalow' commented the paper.

> But that didn't stop the *News of the World* tracking him down to his new lair [...]. Since we last snapped him Oliver has ditched his specs and grown out his crew cut. But there was no disguising his evil eyes. Neighbours were horrified when we revealed the truth about the pot-bellied pervert.

Within hours protestors had started to gather outside the address provided by the newspaper. By the end of the next day, 20 police officers, some wearing riot gear, moved in to take Oliver to a new secret location (*News of the World*, 10 December 2006).

Of all the crimes on the statute books in the UK, it is sex crimes against children by strangers which excite most expressions of outrage and collective disgust. They provoke front-page newspaper calls for policy changes and create community direct action. This chapter examines this phenomenon and asks: what makes people come out onto the streets, joining together to demand change – and what does this tell us about the role of the media? Some public responses to media stories are immediate, highly visible and dramatic. Such events would include momentous national disasters or terrorist attacks (e.g. 9/11) or the death of celebrities (e.g. Princess Diana). Detractors of public responses to some events dismiss them in terms such as copycat riots or media induced hysteria. However, such 'explanations' fail adequately to account for how journalists mediate our sense of ourselves, our communities, our world and our sense of anger, mourning or injustice. This chapter takes a closer look at these processes. It does so by looking at specific media campaigns and the waves of public protest and civil unrest in response to convicted sex offenders being released into the community.

The sexual abuse of children has a long history of attracting front-page attention (Kitzinger 2004). It often becomes subject to national spectacle. The whole country or even the whole 'world' is often said by journalists to 'hold its breath' during the search for missing children or be 'united in shock' at the discovery of the dead body (e.g. *The People*, 18 August 2002; *The Express*, 19 August 2002). Parents cling more tightly to their offspring, newspaper readers write in demanding the death penalty for the offender, the parents of the victims lead calls for policy change, petitions are organised and, sometimes, the public take to the streets in protest. This chapter explores how sexual abuse became a focus for unprecedented local action across many different UK cities from the mid-1990s onwards. These public protests were not confined to letter-writing campaigns or signing petitions set up by newspapers. They included demonstrations, civil disobedience and attacks on suspected paedophiles. For a while the professionals looked as if they were losing control of the policy-making agenda as citizens took the law into their own hands. The police had to be brought in to protect released sex offenders. Monitoring, supervision, treatment and housing of offenders were disrupted, and policy-makers had to reconsider legislation, policy and practice.

The rise of the paedophile problem

The origins of the problem that erupted in the 1990s and has sporadically continued to cause problems into the twenty-first century lay several decades earlier. Its history can be traced back to some of the famous serial child sex murderers who populated the 1960s, 1970s and 1980s. This included people such as Sydney Cooke and his co-conspirator Robert Oliver (subject of the protests described in the opening paragraph above). These high-profile serial offenders were, for many years, the public face of sexual violence. In the 1990s and early 2000s, these individuals, dubbed by the tabloids as 'the most hated' people in Britain, were now due for release or had begun living incognito across the country.

Under the law as it stood they could change their names and live anywhere they wanted and their neighbours would not know. This raised a problem for policy-makers, one that was not addressed by more recent legislation. There had been government efforts to find new ways of tracking such offenders after release. In December 1996 Michael Howard (then Home Secretary) introduced legislation to monitor sex offenders and this generated extensive media interest, for example 'Paedophile lists for police' (*The Times*, 19 December 1996); 'Crackdown on sex offenders unveiled' (*The Guardian*, 19 December 1996). The reporting of the problem in the mid-1990s initially followed routine media practice whereby media agendas are traditionally set by high-status official sources (such as government bodies) (Tuchman 1978). However, media coverage and public debate rapidly shifted as particular communities and parts of the media began to agitate for public access to the register and demand that communities be notified when dangerous individuals moved into their neighbourhood. Journalists (and pressure groups) picked up on community notification legislation in the USA. This legislation, known as Megan's Law, was introduced in 1996, named after a seven-year-old New Jersey girl, Megan Kanka, who was raped and murdered by a convicted sex offender who lived across the street. Such legislation should, it was argued, be introduced in the UK. Such calls were given added impetus in 1999 by the abduction and murder of Sarah Payne. The eight-year-old disappeared as she returned home after playing with her sister and brothers. Roy Whiting, a convicted paedophile, was later jailed for her murder. Her parents became tireless campaigners for legal changes and newspapers such as the *News of the World* and the *Sun* called for 'Sarah's Law' to be introduced into the UK to echo Megan's Law in the US. Even before this, however, the question of what happened when communities did discover known (or suspected) paedophiles in their midst was becoming an issue. Toward the end of 1996 and into 1997 the 'big story' for the media, and a major headache for policy-makers, became not government initiatives, but public fear and anger. Headlines in the national press included:

Parents in dark as paedophiles stalk schools (*The Guardian*, 24 November 1996)

Town not told of paedophiles' stay (*The Times*, 12 October 1997)

Stop hiding perverts say protest mums (*Daily Mail*, 3 February 1997)

Jeering mothers drive paedophile off council estate (*The Times*, 11 January 1997)

Paedophile out of prison 'fearful for life and limb' (*The Observer*, 15 December 1996)

Protest rapidly spread from one area to another. It was not only the national media (such as the *News of the World*) that were important here: local newspapers were also crucial. Although often ignored when thinking about the media, the local press can play a key role[2]. Indeed, many of the national stories about paedophiles started out on the front page of local papers and some neighbourhood protests were sparked by local press reports rather than vice versa. Headlines from local papers included:

Angus mums on alert over local sex offender (*Press and Journal*, (Aberdeen) 17 June 1998)

Parents besiege abuser's house (*Press and Journal*, 17 July 1997)

Residents pledge to continue campaign (*Leicester Mercury*, 4 July 1998)

Give us the right to know (*Torquay Herald Express*, 2 September 1997)

Parents' paedophile poster campaign (*Evening Gazette* (Teesside), 26 January 1998)

Panic hits town over perverts (*Belfast Telegraph News*, 22 March 1997)

Sex offender's home torched (*Belfast Telegraph News*, 6 October 1997)

Such articles often included quotes from the host of local residents' groups which formed in response to the supposed paedophile threat. Such reports were also often accompanied by photographs of local people marching with banners declaring 'Perverts out' (*Press and Journal*, 9 June 1997) or children carrying placards reading: 'Make me safe' (*Torquay Herald Express*, 2 September 1997). *The Manchester Evening News* published a front-page spread about a local sex offender alongside a photograph of him in his car behind a smashed windscreen after 'a vigilante mob had vented their anger' (cited in Thomas 1997: 68). The tone of some of this reporting was overtly provocative and was clearly intended both to reflect, and to endorse, public rage[3].

Many newspapers took a more proactive role than merely reporting local unrest (with whatever degree of approval). Some took on the role of guardians of public safety, especially in relation to particular dangerous individuals. When Robert Oliver was released, the *Sun* asked readers to phone an emergency number if he was spotted (*The Guardian*, 18 October 1997) and, when he moved to Brighton, the local paper, the *Evening Argus*, published his picture on their front page with the headline 'Beware this evil pervert' (*Evening Argus*, 14 October 1997).

In other cases, journalists alerted people to the presence of paedophiles, either through knocking on the doors of neighbours and asking how they felt about living near a sex offender or through outing them on the front page. *The Sunday Express* printed photographs and details of offenders with their last known address under the headline 'Could these evil men be living next door to you?' (cited in Thomas 1997). The Scottish *Daily Record* produced a similar campaign, devoting the bulk of one issue to asserting a 'Charter for our children' and demanding 'The legal right for communities to be told when a pervert moves into the area' (*Daily Record*, 25 February 1997). Alongside articles headed 'End the suffering', 'Pervert's playground' and 'Monster freed to kill', they published a double-page 'Gallery of shame' with 38 photographs and names of convicted offenders and details of their offences[4]. Some of these were described as 'people power' success stories: one was 'hounded out of Drumchapel housing scheme because of his sick background' and another 'forced into hiding' while 'PEOPLE power drove sick child molester, Christie, 50, out of Stirling' (*Daily Record*, 25 February 1997).

'Moral panics' and 'lynch mobs'?

Such media attention, and the public reactions it reflected, triggered and amplified, presented a major problem for those involved in monitoring and housing convicted sex offenders. The media were accused of whipping up 'hysteria', creating a moral panic and encouraging a lynch-mob mentality. Routine community notification and the automatic right of public access to the sex offenders register is opposed by many professionals working in this field, including chief constables, chief probation officers and the NSPCC (*The Guardian*, 19 February 1997).

The main reason for their opposition is the belief that it will not protect children. Instead it may result in vigilante action and drive offenders underground making it less possible to monitor or treat them. Indeed the Association of Chief Officers of Probation (ACOP) documented ten cases where the press had lent editorial authority to campaigns to identify and expel offenders, leading to disruption of supervision and, sometimes, to acts of violence (ACOP 1998). Convicted abusers were driven from their homes, leaving behind arrangements put in place to monitor them (such as electronic tagging and video surveillance) and often absenting themselves from any treatment programmes. Robert Oliver ended up moving from London to Swindon to Dublin to Brighton, eventually to Bristol and then the village in Somerset, before being exposed again and moving to an, as yet unrevealed, new location. One of the ironies was that police and probation services ended up spending huge amounts of time and money protecting sex offenders from the public rather than vice versa (Adams 1998).

In addition, other people are often caught up in the violence and harassment aimed at sex offenders. Hostels have been attacked (whether or not convicted sex offenders are in residence). The wife and child of one offender were named and driven from their home after it was set on fire. In an earlier case a young girl died after a house in which she was staying was burnt down (*The Guardian*,

10 June 1997). In Birmingham, the 81-year-old mother of a convicted sex offender was forced to move and her home wrecked when the *Birmingham Evening Mail* twice publicised the address of her and her son. In Manchester, a man was badly beaten by a gang who mistook him for a paedophile named by the *Manchester Evening News* (reported in *The Guardian*, 10 June 1997).

The panic about paedophiles has also been used to victimise individuals with no known official record of sex offences (and with no connection to convicted offenders). The *Sunday Times* documented '30 cases where men wrongly suspected of abusing children have been beaten and humiliated by gangs bent on driving them out of their homes' (*Sunday Times*, 2 November 1997). Sometimes it would seem a convenient way of harassing unpopular or minority members of the community. Reading between the lines of some reports it appears that gay men and those with mental disabilities are particularly likely to be victimised.

There seems no easy resolution to the problem of paedophiles in the community, and the policy debate continually throws up conflict and contradictions. In June 2006 there seemed to have been some 'progress' with the front page of the *News of the World* trumpeting: 'SARAH'S LAW VICTORY' (18 June 2006), other papers reported that the Home Secretary, John Reid, might adopt 'Megan's Law': 'I'll name sex offenders; U-turn will give parents the right to know where paedophiles live' (*Daily Mail*, 19 June 2006). However, this was quickly followed by criticism in the broadsheet press and with the government being accused of surrendering reason in favour of a populist agenda:

> Ministers accused of 'mob rule' agenda (*Daily Telegraph*, 21 June, 2006)

> Crime and punishment: a tawdry story involving Labour politicians and the press (*The Independent*, 23 June 2006)

> Child sex offenders: playing to the press gallery (*The Guardian*, 20 June 2006)

> Blair is a tabloid slave, and we all pay a heavy price (*Sunday Times*, 25 June 2006)

The Children's Commissioner and police chiefs were both reported as coming out against any attempt to adopt 'Megan's/Sarah's Law' in the UK.

Megan's Law won't work, Reid warned: children's commissioner speaks out (*The Guardian*, 22 June 2006)

Police chiefs condemn Reid for 'complying with tabloid wishes' (*The Guardian*, 20 June 2006)

At the same time the government clarified its resistance to any 'carbon copy' of the US legislation.

No 10 stays cool on rush to bring in Sarah's Law (*Daily Telegraph*, 20 June 2006)

UK Minister rejects 'carbon copy' of Megan's Law (*The Observer*, 23 July 2006)

The debate continues to rumble as this chapter is prepared for publication. A government task force examining whether a US-style 'Megan's Law' should be introduced in the UK suggests that parents and carers worried about suspected paedophiles maybe should get the right to ask police about the background of a cohabitee or close neighbour.

Women could check if a partner is a paedophile (*Daily Mail*, 17 November 2006)

Single mothers to be offered paedophile check on partners: report says people should also have right to know if sex offenders live in their area. (*The Guardian*, 17 November 2006)

Clearly the media have played a role at both a public and a community level. The media certainly contributed to the spiral of unrest across the country in the mid-1990s and certain papers, most notably the *News of the World*, have continued to fuel such action into the early years of the twenty-first century. Some coverage has been at the very least counterproductive if not blatantly irresponsible. However, the media did not create community protests out of thin air and it is fundamentally unhelpful to dismiss media and community reactions as a moral panic. This concept implies that the panic is totally unjustified and that it is state-sanctified – neither of which could be asserted in this case without qualification. More fundamentally moral panic theory fails to pay attention to the processes through which a panic is engendered and therefore offers a way of glossing over rather than truly investigating public reactions (Miller *et al.* 1998). To accuse the media of whipping up 'hysteria' and creating 'lynch mob' violence is equally inadequate and also ignores key sites through which community reactions evolve. (The very term 'lynch mob' is used to signal irrationality in ways which, in addition, obscure the history of lynching and its position in relation to *institutional racism*.)

Instead of dismissing public and media reactions as proof of their failure to match the rationality and objectivity of the policy-makers, it is crucial to give detailed attention to the questions raised by the protesters and their criticisms of public policy. This is essential if we are to understand the many complex levels on which the media can play a role in social policy issues.

Theorising community and media protest

The paedophile-in-the-community coverage was driven by factors operating on three levels. The first level concerns policy and practice initiatives. The second relates to local community responses and the role of local media. The third level involves the underlying construction of the paedophile which underpinned the whole debate. I shall deal with each of these in turn.

Policy and practice: new initiatives and unanswered questions

The initial decision to establish a register placed the issue of paedophiles-in-the-community on the public agenda. But it did so in ways which begged more questions than it answered. How will these offenders be monitored? Who should have access to this information? Policy and practice on this issue were clearly underdeveloped and often inconsistent. Legal rulings and professional disputes received extensive media attention. There were, for example, several cases exposing uncertainty about sex offenders' housing rights ('Town considers banning sex offenders from council houses' *The Guardian*, 9 January 1997; 'Eviction of paedophile justified, court rules', *The Guardian*, 20 February 1997). Confusion also surrounded probation officers' responsibilities to pass on information about their clients to prospective employers. The Home Office originally advised probation officers not to notify employers about sex crime convictions in case employees were sacked leading to court actions for damages. This advice was quickly withdrawn leading to headlines such as: 'Home Office confusion on paedophiles' (*The Guardian*, 5 December 1996).

Policy on notification to the general public seemed to develop in a similar ad hoc fashion. Particular high-profile cases raised questions such as: if a housing officer takes it upon him/herself to inform tenants about a released sex offender on their estate should he/she be disciplined? Should schools be told, but not pass on the information to parents, or does this place head teachers in an untenable position? Should police inform the public, but only under very special circumstances? One couple in North Wales, for example, were granted Legal Aid to sue police for publicising details about their sexual offences (*Manchester Evening News*, 9 June 1997). In some cases public warnings were released: 'Police warn of threat to young males: town on paedophile alert' (*The Guardian*, 15 October 1997). In other cases communities were not informed or only provided with information after media exposure. In a clear example of direct interaction between the media and policy decisions one London council decided to warn parents about a 'very dangerous' convicted abuser who had moved into their area, but only after learning that a television documentary was to name the man (*The Guardian*, 27 March 1997). It was not until September 1997 that guidelines came into force clarifying procedures. Police were given the power to warn head teachers, youth group and play-group leaders and local child protection agencies that a convicted sex offender had moved into their area – but not to broadcast the name generally unless a professional risk assessment indicated that this was necessary.

In the meantime, public fears and critical media interest were increased not only by the obvious confusion but also by the fact that the Sex Offenders Act left certain loopholes. These loopholes were graphically illustrated by cases such as that of Graham Seddon – a convicted abuser, detained by officers in June 1997 carrying a bag containing toys. He was, he said, looking for a child. Seddon was (briefly) detained in a Liverpool hospital but could not be kept against his will. The notorious Robert Oliver had also slipped through a loophole. Judged to be neither repentant nor rehabilitated this man was released without any compulsion to comply with supervision; legislation compelling such compliance could only be applied to those released after a certain date.

In the second half of the 1990s there was thus a confluence of events (such as the release of particular notorious individuals) and the development of policy and procedures which heightened public attention to this threat. The original highly newsworthy government initiatives set the news agenda, but that agenda was rapidly transformed through the questions it opened up, combined with obvious areas of uncertainty and the subsequent direct action from ordinary citizens.

Neighbourhood reactions: democracy, trust and local networking

The local media clearly fed into neighbourhood responses and helped to identify targets for popular anger (Bell 2002). However, concern about children's safety was certainly not a new phenomenon. The paedophile had already been established as public enemy number one and, long before 1996, fear of the predatory paedophile was etched into the bedrock of parents' anxieties. This came out clearly in the focus group discussions I conducted during the early 1990s: parents who participated in my research routinely talked about the heart-stopping moment when they looked round and realised their young child had disappeared from their side or described the daily pattern of worry every time a son or daughter was late home.[5]

This research also highlighted how some communities felt under siege. People spoke about predatory men coming onto the housing estates and, in almost every group, parents described incidents where 'shady' individuals had been seen behaving suspiciously around playgrounds or children had been approached by strangers. Such events inevitably become the topic of conversation, e.g. outside the school gate (Kitzinger 2004).

The press reporting of the protests that emerged from the mid-1990s onwards highlights how some working-class communities also often felt neglected by central government – a lack of public transport or decent shops, poorly resourced schools, an absence of employment opportunities, all left them feeling alienated and mistrustful. Housing inequalities further exacerbated the crisis. Released prisoners, including convicted sex offenders, tend to be placed in hostels or offered housing in working-class areas and often on council estates. Many protesters expressed anger and frustration at the fact that their fate was to be decided by faceless bureaucrats who rarely lived in such areas themselves. The question often asked in public meetings called to reassure people was: 'How would *you* feel if he was living next door to you and your kids?' Council tenants who were expected to put up with living next to an incinerator, playgrounds built on polluted sites, damp housing or a failing local school were now also expected to tolerate the country's most dangerous predators dumped on their doorsteps (people living on council estates are also, of course, less likely to have access to private transport, safe play areas and consistent childcare, all of which may mute concerns about children's safety).

Given this background it is hardly surprising that the idea that known sex offenders were to be secretly housed in their neighbourhoods added insult to injury. The child's placard 'Make me safe' perhaps carries more demands than community notification about paedophiles and the names of some of the protest groups express their desire for more agency in their lives (e.g. 'People's Power'). Some protest groups also chose names which encapsulated their disillusionment with official protection and monitoring procedures (e.g. 'The Unofficial Child Protection Unit'). This disillusionment (and some hope and expectations) was vividly articulated by the founder of the (anti-vigilante) group: 'Scottish People Against Child Abuse'.

> People must be able to sit back and be responsible. If they saw something constructive being done, maybe they would start having trust again in the authorities. The Government is there because we trusted them to look after us and protect our children, but they are not doing that yet. (*The Scotsman*, 16 October 1997)

Official incompetence was a recurring theme both in local discussion (as reported in the local press) and in national coverage. Internationally high-profile cases of multiple sex abusers (ranging from Marc Dutroux in Belgium to Fred and Rosemary West in the UK) suggested that the professionals could not be trusted to monitor and investigate properly. Dutroux was able to continue his activities even though police were notified that he was building dungeons to imprison abducted children (Kelly 1996). The police were regular visitors to Cromwell Street but the Wests were apparently able to continue to rape and murder their victims undetected. Both these cases served as a backdrop to public concern. In 1997 this concern was underlined with the murder of Scott Simpson in Aberdeen by a known sex offender. The bungling of the Scott Simpson case received extensive coverage. Social services (who were supervising the boy's murderer at the time) were blamed for not following guidelines and failing to convey relevant information to the police. The police were also criticised for 'serious corporate failure' in investigating the nine-year-old's disappearance. The name of Scott Simpson was evoked by those campaigning for community notification in future cases. His murder suggested that the experts and professionals could not provide sufficient protection on their own.

For some protesters it was clear that direct action (ranging from seeking media publicity to vigilante activities) represented the only way of having their voices heard. 'Look, how else do you get noticed?' commented the leader of Paulsgrove Residents Against Paedophiles; 'How else is anyone going to listen to a common person like me? At least we were listened to, and we got something done' (Katrina Kessell, quoted in *The Observer*, 4 February 2001).

The local media, for their part, were usually happy to cooperate. Local media have a special remit to address community priorities. Local newspaper editorials demanding (or in effect providing) community notification presented the papers as standing up for their constituents, asserting a strong neighbourhood identity and fulfilling their functions as representative of 'the people'. While local media have problems representing *some* local concerns (such as pollution from a factory which is key to providing local jobs), the sex offender presented an apparently clear-cut common enemy and outsider. As the *Daily Record* declared: 'The Record believes action must be taken NOW to confront the plague of abuse that wrecks young lives and disgusts all right-minded Scots' (*Daily Record*, 25 February 1997).

In understanding media and public reactions it is important not to be dismissive when the public come into conflict with the experts or when NIMBYism[6] seems to come into conflict with the wider public good. Community concern and the conditions under which people are forced to live should not be underestimated. As feminist journalist and author Bea Campbell points out, community notification may not be the best way of protecting children, however:

There is a piety around the notion of 'the mob' which doesn't take responsibility for what some communities endure. A liberal disposition can't cope with what these communities are facing. There are communities, there are children, who live in a permanent panic about when he's going to get out of prison. That's not the tone which infuses the debate. (Bea Campbell, interview with author)

The issue of former neighbours returning from prison to live near their victims is certainly one which has been pushed forward by media attention. A housing worker whom I interviewed expresses some ambivalence about the media's role. On the one hand, she commented, attention from journalists was unhelpful (resulting in a defensive reaction from parts of the housing authority and whipping up unnecessary fear on the estate). However:

The media were useful in that the tenants had tried telling their housing officer and had not succeeded in persuading her to listen. It is a shame that the council obviously felt inaccessible so that they had to go to the press. There are lessons to be learned from that. But the press made sure that the council reacted. (Housing officer, interview with author)

In this particular case, local and national media attention also led to further enquiries from tenants about other individuals on this estate. This, in turn, led to the exposure of another case in which children might be at risk and there had been a failure in inter-departmental communication. According to the housing officer I spoke with this led to 'significant policy shifts about the sharing of professional information and adoption of protocols and guidelines to support that'.

The media then cannot be seen as merely interfering in an area best left to the experts. Public debate and involvement in social policy issues is a democratic and practical imperative. Questions from the media and the public (as neighbours, tenants and citizens) can disrupt important policy initiatives: however, they can also be vital in pushing issues onto the policy agenda and refining procedures.

Nonetheless, there were far more fundamental problems with the whole way in which the debate about paedophiles was framed in public discourse (including community responses, media coverage and policy-making). These problems have roots that go much deeper than the immediate concerns raised by the public outcry in the second half of the 1990s. With this in mind I would like to finish this chapter by problematising the whole way in which the paedophile was constructed as an object of social concern at that time and highlighting some of the problems which were obscured by focusing on convicted offenders.

Framing paedophiles: public, media and policy gaps in addressing risk

The paedophile has become the dominant way through which sexual threats to children are conceptualised and articulated; however, the term paedophile is laden with ideas and assumptions which confine thinking about this issue to a very narrow focus. The paedophile as a concept is enmeshed in a series of stereotypes which place the child sexual abuser outside society (Silverman and Wilson 2002; Jenkins 1992; Kelly 1996). Such conceptualisations were amply illustrated in the press reporting about paedophiles-in-the-community. The *Daily*

Record's 'Gallery of shame', for example, perpetuated all the old stereotypes, highlighting particular words in bold block capitals. Struggling for a variety of negative epithets to describe their gallery of 38 sex offenders the paper ran through the usual list warning readers of 'TWISTED Dickons [who] got eight years for raping two young sisters', 'WEIRDO Sean Regan, who 'was dubbed "The Beast"' and 'DEPRAVED paedophile Harley' who 'preyed on terrified children as young as six'. Other convicted offenders were variously described as: 'EVIL Herriot', 'PERVERT teacher', 'SEXUAL predator' and 'SEX BEAST'. In among these highlighted adjectives one man was simply described as 'BACHELOR Paritt' (with its gay implications) and three of the descriptions highlighted a disability (e.g. 'DEAF Duff posed as a priest as he prowled the street' and 'DEAF MUTE Eaglesham, 66, carried out a series of sex attacks on a 10-year-old girl') (*Daily Record*, 25 February 1997).

Portraits of paedophiles do more than simply stereotype (and reinforce prejudice against particular minority groups). The term singles out the sexual abuse of children, as if there were no connection between the acts of sexual abuse and exploitation perpetrated against boys and girls and those perpetrated against adult women. Marc Dutroux raped and abused both children and adult women (his oldest known victim was 50). He also engaged in trafficking, yet he was continually dubbed a 'paedophile' – a term which obscures the fact that this is not just a 'sexual preference' but a way of exercising power and exploiting women and children for financial gain (Kelly 1996).

Having a special term such as 'paedophile' also supports the view that they are a separate species, subhuman or 'a breed apart' (Hebenton and Thomas 1996). One piece of information released by the Home Office during the height of the paedophile crisis was the fact that, by the time they are 40, one man in 90 has been convicted of a serious sex offence, such as rape (of adults), incest or gross indecency with a child (Marshall 1997). This fact, combined with evidence that most perpetrators of sexual assault are never convicted, suggests that every community is likely to have its share of sex offenders. The release of the Home Office statistic received some media attention, particularly focusing on offences against children. Headlines included:

One man in 60 is a 'sex offender' (*Daily Mail*, 19 June 1997)[7]

Paedophile figures alarm Ministers (*The Times*, 19 June 1997)

Thousands of child sex offenders 'at large' (*The Guardian*, 19 June 1997)

However, this report was quickly forgotten and such statistics are rarely integrated into the narrative of stories about paedophiles-in-the-community. The fact that most paedophiles-in-the-community are undetected and probably well integrated into their neighbourhood was rarely raised. The fact that most people would already know a sex offender was ignored.

To acknowledge that sexual violence (in all forms and along diverse continua) is quite so endemic would have undermined the narrative thrust of most paedophile-in-the community stories. By confining their attention to a minority of convicted offenders and defining those who sexually abuse children as a certain type of person, 'a paedophile', the media were able to focus not on society but on a few dangerous individuals within it. The problem of sexual violence is represented by the newspaper image of a man with staring eyes or an evil smirk. He looks different from ordinary folk – and his evil or deviance is written on his face. He is certainly not an ordinary member of the community and sex offenders are often labelled as 'beasts, devils, queers or sissies' (Kitzinger 2004: 125). There is, of course, a tension here between, on the one hand, the implication that paedophiles are easy to spot, and on the other hand the idea that they might appear ordinary and be able to merge into the background to manipulate and deceive. In spite of the *News of the World*'s claim that there was no way to hide Oliver's 'evil eyes', what actually came across in some vox pops with neighbours was how ordinary he seemed. One neighbour 'had spoken to him over the garden fence nearly every day since he moved in […] He says hello almost every morning and we have spoken about gardening' (*The Express*, 12 December 2006). Another 'used to go to bingo with him on a weekly basis, oblivious to his true identity' (*Somerset County Gazette*, 14 December 2006), while a third commented: 'He was at the Christmas fair last week chatting and talking to people, of course nobody knew who he was then. When we found out he was a paedophile we were just horrified' (*Western Morning News*, 12 December 2006)

Most of the time, however, newspapers prefer to frame paedophiles as 'beasts' and 'fiends' (however cunningly disguised) who could be singled out, electronically tagged, exposed and expelled. If paedophiles are literally 'evil personified', then such evil can be exorcised by excluding these individuals from society. This individualised approach fits with certain strands in criminological discourse (see

371

Hebenton and Thomas 1996). It also fits with the whole media shift toward 'dumbed down' personalised stories whereby, for example, journalists focus on the noisy and anti-social 'neighbour from hell' rather than examining the problem of sink estates through analysis of employment, recreation facilities and housing condition (Franklin 1997).

The concept of the paedophile is flawed. It locates the threat of abuse within the individual (rather than in social, cultural or bureaucratic institutions). In the context of abuse in children's homes, for example, attention can be focused on the cunning infiltrator while ignoring the nature of the care system, funding and resourcing. In the case of other sites of abuse attention is confined to the outsider and the loner leaving the role of fathers and the institution of the family unquestioned. The paedophile is a creature that embodies stranger-danger. He reflects and sustains a focus on abusers as outcast from society rather than part of it. As feminist activist and academic Liz Kelly argues, the concept of the paedophile helps to shift attention away:

> ... from the centrality of power and control to notions of sexual deviance, obsession and 'addiction'. Paedophilia returns us to [...] medical and individualised explanations [...]. Rather than sexual abuse demanding that we look critically at the social construction of masculinity, male sexuality and the family, the safer terrain of 'abnormalities' beckons. (Kelly 1996: 45)

If we adopt the word paedophile and see it as synonymous with child sexual abuse then we narrow the policy agenda. The fact that most children are assaulted by someone that they know virtually disappears from the debate and policies which would be deemed unacceptable if applied to 'ordinary men' become allowable (Kelly 1996: 46).

The fundamental critique here is that the notion of the paedophile restricts definitions of the problem and thus limits how we can envisage solutions. The term helps to obscure important aspects of sexual violence and shifts attention 'away from political solutions addressing male power and the construction of masculinity toward a range of "problem-management" solutions' (Kelly 1996: 46). The latter include long-term incarceration, risk assessment tribunals for dangerous men and individual therapy.

Conclusion

This chapter has explored the role of the media, particularly the local media, in engaging with audiences not only as 'receivers' of information but as activists and message creators. I have highlighted the positive as well as problematic impact of coverage during the crisis over paedophiles-in-the-community and identified factors that shaped and maintained the momentum both of media attention and of public anger.

In presenting this study I have tried to demonstrate the intertwined levels of analysis which can contribute towards theorising the relationship between the media, social policy and 'the public'. It is not enough solely to focus on the media as a cause of people's beliefs, we need also to consider what motivates those who seek out media publicity and engage in direct action. It is also often unhelpful to dismiss the media as interfering or to blame the press for 'hype'. Instead, it is necessary to recognise the media's role as an avenue for networking between those with common concerns and as a forum for public debate. At the same time, however, it is vital never to accept the terms of that debate as cast in stone and always to question what is left off the agenda as well as what is addressed. There are fundamental gaps in the framing of the 'paedophiles-in-the-community' scandal by the media, not least that it failed to address the problem of most paedophiles in the community. However, this does not make the protests illegitimate. Respecting the concerns people raise and their responses and engagement with media campaigns in this way means that one can combine detailed analysis of protest and crisis coverage with critical reflection on the underlying assumptions which frame public discourse and shape visions for social policy. Such approaches can, I hope, allow us to develop more grounded theories both about so-called 'moral panics' and about the power of the media more generally.

Notes

1 An earlier version of the main part of this chapter appeared in Kitzinger (2004).
2 Although it is sometimes neglected as a research object, the local and regional media influence many national and international policy-making processes from road building to the disposal of nuclear waste (Franklin 2006).

3 Other reports urged caution and restraint. The Aberdeen *Press and Journal*, for example, reported efforts to reassure the public and condemn vigilante action: 'Crowd (self) control' (*Press and Journal*, 6 August 1997); 'Police and community condemn vigilantes' (*Press and Journal*, 10 June 1997). Similar reports and editorials appeared in other papers, e.g. 'Sex crime vigilantes not answer' (*Yorkshire Evening Post*, 6 February 1997); 'Have faith in the police to shield our children' (*Express on Sunday*, 10 August 1997).

4 The *Bournemouth Evening Echo*'s 'Protect Our Children' campaign involved setting up a register of convicted sex offenders, compiled from newspaper reports. This was, however, available only to workers with children. Other papers, such as *The Guardian*, adopted a policy of only 'outing' offenders if there was evidence that supervision had broken down and children were at risk.

5 I conducted 49 focus groups about child sexual abuse, and a further 30 groups about a specific campaign to challenge sexual violence. For a full account of the method and findings see Kitzinger (2004).

6 NIMBYism: 'not in my back yard' approach to social problems.

7 This 1 in 60 figure focused on a particular part of the data.

References

ACOP (Association of Chief Officers of Probation) (1998) *Recent Cases of Public Disorder Around Sex Offenders Which Have Impeded Surveillance and Supervision.* London: ACOP.

Adams, D. (1998) 'The "at risk" business', *Police Review*, 30 January, pp. 16–17.

Ashenden, S. (2002) 'Policing perversion: the contemporary governance of paedophilia', *Cultural Values*, 6 (1–2): 197–222.

Bell, V. (2002) 'The vigilant(e) parent and the paedophile: the *News of the World* campaign 2000 and the contemporary governmentality of child sex abuse', *Feminist Theory*, 3 (1): 83–102.

Critcher, C. (2002) 'Media, government and moral panic: the politics of paedophilia in Britain 2000–1', *Journalism Studies*, 3 (4): 521–35.

Franklin, B. (ed.) (1999) *Social Policy, the Media and Misrepresentation.* London: Routledge.

Franklin, B. (2006) *Local Journalism and Local Media: Making the Local News.* London: Routledge.

Greer, C. (2003) *Sex Crime and the Media.* Cullompton: Willan.

Hebenton, B. and Thomas, T. (1996) 'Sex offenders in the community: reflections on the problem of law, community and risk management in USA, England and Wales', *International Journal of the Sociology of Law*, 24: 427–43.

Jenkins, P. (1992) *Intimate Enemies: Moral Panics in Contemporary Great Britain.* New York: Aldine de Gruyter.

Kelly, L. (1996) 'Weasel words: paedophiles and the cycle of abuse', *Trouble and Strife*, 33: 44–9.

Kitzinger, J. (2004) *Framing Abuse: Media Influence and Public Understanding of Sexual Violence Against Children.* London: Pluto Press.

Marshall, P. (1997) *The Prevalence of Convictions for Sexual Offending,* Research Findings No. 55. London: Home Office Research and Statistics Directorate.

Miller, D., Kitzinger, J., Williams, K. and Beharrell, P. (1998) *The Circuit of Mass Communication: Media Strategies, Representation and Audience Reception in the AIDS Crisis.* London: Sage.

Silverman, J. and Wilson, D. (2002) *Innocence Betrayed: Paedophilia, the Media and Society.* Cambridge: Polity Press.

Thomas, T. (1997) 'How could this man go free: privacy, the press and the paedophile,' in E. Lawson (ed.) *Child Exploitation and the Media Forum: Report and Recommendations.* Dover: Smallwood Publishing Group, pp. 67–9.

Tuchman, G. (1978) *Making News.* New York: Free Press.

Index